Economic Development in Early Modern France

Privilege has long been understood as the constitutional basis of Ancien Régime France, legalizing the provision of a variety of rights, powers, and exemptions to some, while denying them to others. In this fascinating new study, however, Jeff Horn reveals that Bourbon officials utilized privilege as an instrument of economic development, freeing some sectors of the economy from preexisting privileges and regulations, while protecting others. He explores both government policies and the innovations of entrepreneurs, workers, inventors, and customers to uncover the lived experience of economic development from the Fronde to the Restoration. He shows how, influenced by Enlightenment thought, the regime increasingly resorted to concepts of liberty to defend privilege as a policy tool. The book offers important new insights into debates about the impact of privilege on early industrialization, comparative economic development, and the outbreak of the French Revolution.

JEFF HORN is Professor of History at Manhattan College.

Cambridge Studies in Economic History comprises stimulating and accessible economic history which actively builds bridges to other disciplines. Books in the series will illuminate why the issues they address are important and interesting, place their findings in a comparative context, and relate their research to wider debates and controversies. The series will combine innovative and exciting new research by younger researchers with new approaches to major issues by senior scholars. It will publish distinguished work regardless of chronological period or geographical location.

A complete list of titles in the series can be found at:
www.cambridge.org/economichistory

Economic Development in Early Modern France

The Privilege of Liberty, 1650–1820

Jeff Horn
Manhattan College

CAMBRIDGE
UNIVERSITY PRESS

CAMBRIDGE
UNIVERSITY PRESS

University Printing House, Cambridge CB2 8BS, United Kingdom

Cambridge University Press is part of the University of Cambridge.

It furthers the University's mission by disseminating knowledge in the pursuit of education, learning and research at the highest international levels of excellence.

www.cambridge.org
Information on this title: www.cambridge.org/9781107046283

First published 2015

Printed in the United Kingdom by Clays, St Ives plc

A catalog record for this publication is available from the British Library

Library of Congress Cataloging in Publication data
Horn, Jeff (Historian)
Economic development in early modern France : the privilege of liberty, 1650–1820 / Jeff Horn.
pages cm. – (Cambridge studies in economic history)
Includes bibliographical references and index.
ISBN 978-1-107-04628-3
1. Economic development – France – History. 2. France – Economic conditions – 17th century. 3. France – Economic conditions – 18th century.
I. Title.
HC275.H667 2015
330.944'03–dc23

2014049632

ISBN 978-1-107-04628-3 Hardback

Contents

Acknowledgments

This book stems from one of *those* conference experiences. At the 2004 Western Society for French History meeting in Lubbock, Texas, I presented a paper on privileged enclaves. The session had a good crowd and almost every single person in the room – led by Suzanne Desan, Dena Goodman, Daryl Hafter, Colin Jones, and Victoria Thompson – told me to write a book about the enclaves. I figured that many smart people couldn't be wrong, so I decided to take their advice. The Western has nurtured this project from the beginning, and I have benefited enormously from the conversations and critiques of my colleagues as I explored parts of my ever-growing subject in talks delivered in 2007–2010 and 2012–2013. Thanks everyone!

A spring 2008 sabbatical from Manhattan College allowed me to begin sustained research on privileged enclaves. As a Scholar-in-Residence in New York University's Faculty Resource Network, while happily ensconced in the bowels of Columbia University's Baker Library, I soon realized that concentrating solely on the enclaves would only scratch the surface of privilege's importance in the early modern economy. Thanks to John Shovlin for pushing me on this issue. Expanding the project's scale and scope was made possible by a summer stipend from the National Endowment for the Humanities in 2009 and a summer grant from Manhattan College in 2010. I could not have conducted the additional research in Marseille, Aix-en-Provence, Rouen, and Paris needed to supplement materials gathered for *The Path Not Taken: French Industrialization in the Age of Revolution, 1750–1830* (MIT Press, 2006) and collected while on sabbatical in 2008 without that support. I am particularly grateful to Anne Ward of NYU, Anne Perotin-Dumon at the Archives Nationales, and the entire staff at the Archives de la Chambre de Commerce et Industrie de Marseille-Provence for facilitating my research. Throughout the process, John Gormley, Manhattan College's ILL specialist, tracked down much-needed books.

Writing this book has been a labor of love lasting over three summers (2011–2013) and two winter breaks (2012–2013). Again, I am indebted to the Faculty Resource Network for my time as a University Associate at NYU in the summer of 2011 and to Manhattan College for a spring 2014 sabbatical, when this lengthy manuscript was thoroughly edited. Michael Watson at Cambridge University Press has been the soul of professionalism, and the Press' anonymous readers made many useful suggestions to improve the book. Cobbling together a presentation to Manhattan College's Dante seminar in April 2011 clarified what I wanted to say at a critical moment. My readers have been generous with their time and encouragement. Daryl Hafter read several chapters in her wise way. Gail Bossenga made thoughtful comments on two chapters that helped enormously. Michael Fitzsimmons allowed me to suborn him as a reader and consistently responded with valuable suggestions. David K. Smith and I have been friends for almost twenty-five years but I've never appreciated his deep learning and keen eye for the nuances of the early modern era more than when working on this book. Cyndy Bouton was indefatigable in reading chapters, suggesting ways to think more broadly about my findings, and providing much appreciated reassurance. Nicknamed my "Beta Readers," these colleagues and friends have improved this book immeasurably and made writing this book even more fun. Last but never least, Len Rosenband, my "Alpha Reader," saw some awfully rough drafts and helped me to make sense of the complex issues I wanted to explore. My arguments would be more limited and less precise without you, old friend. I look forward to repaying the favor for all my readers.

My wife Julie doesn't quite understand why I wanted to write another monograph, but she made it possible. Julie, this book is dedicated to you.

Abbreviations

ACCIMP	Archives de la Chambre de Commerce et Industrie de Marseille-Provence
AD	Archives Départementales de la or du
AM	Archives Municipales de
AN	Archives Nationales de France [CARAN]
BN	Bibliothèque Nationale de France

Unless otherwise noted, all books in French are published in Paris.

1 Introduction

Profits and economic development during the old régime

"How many people cannot buy new products, or need something just for a short time, or do not need the best quality goods and go to find what they need in the faubourg Saint-Antoine?" Beginning in the mid-seventeenth century, Parisian shoppers frequented this quasi-suburb on the city's eastern edge in search of bargains for their everyday needs. Not surprisingly, the city's guild masters sought to shut down this retail outlet for inexpensive products made on the cheap by thousands of workers "without quality" and "without experience or training," who enjoyed "the liberty of work," free from any inspection and without following the standards mandated by guild regulations. Paris' guilds claimed that even vigilant customers were constantly "tricked" into purchasing "fraudulently made goods," which undermined "public confidence" in their wares.[1]

These accusations were made around 1717, but conflict between guild masters and the faubourg Saint-Antoine's "false workers" characterized Paris' world of production from the 1640s to the Revolution. In legal terms, the struggle was between competing sets of privileges. Within city limits, guilds monopolized the manufacture and sale of most goods, the training of the industrial workforce, and the organization of the production process. Letters-patent granted in 1657 gave "poor workers" inhabiting the faubourg the "freedom" to exercise any trade.

[1] The quotes are from *Mémoire des Dames Abbesse et religieuses de l'Abbaye Saint Antoine des Champs les-Paris, des Proprietaires des Maisons du Faubourg Saint-Antoine, et des Pauvres Ouvriers qui y travaillent pour satisfaire à l'Arrêt du Conseil du 28 Novembre 1716 qui ordonne à ceux qui prétend avoir les Privileges, Franchises et autres Exemptions dans la Ville et Fauxbourgs de Paris, de représenter leurs Titres devant Messieurs les Commissaires du Conseil, nommé par le même Arrêt*, n.d. [1717] and *Requête au Roi et à Nosseigneurs les Commissaires députés par Sa Majesté en exécution de l'arrêt du 28 Novembre 1716*, n.d. [1717] both found in AN F12 781C. Unless otherwise noted, all translations are my own. The faubourg Saint-Antoine has attracted a great deal of scholarly attention. See Alain Thillay, *Le faubourg Saint-Antoine et ses "faux ouvriers": La liberté du travail à Paris aux XVII et XVIIIe siècles* (Champ Vallon, 2002) and Steven Kaplan, "Les corporations, les 'faux ouvriers' et le faubourg Saint-Antoine aux XVIIIe siècle," *Annales. Histoire, Science Sociales*, 43: 2 (1988), 353–78.

Paris' guild wardens (*jurés*) were expressly forbidden from "troubling or harassing them in any form or manner" under threat of stiff financial penalties. These letters-patent expressed royal charity more than industrial policy. Expressly linked to the founding of a general hospital, the letters-patent noted that this charitable institution was insufficient to provide poor veterans and workers excluded from guild structures a means of earning a livelihood.

The 1657 letters-patent did all that, and more. The "liberty of work" enjoyed by this privileged enclave attracted both entrepreneurs and workers. The faubourg Saint-Antoine's population exploded: the number of workers mushroomed from a few hundred in the 1650s to close to 10,000 during the Regency. The economic impact of this major exception to guild control grew in proportion, earning the faubourg an outsized position in the city's manufacturing sector.

At stake in the conflict between Paris' guilds and the denizens of the faubourg Saint-Antoine was control over the production and sale of manufactured goods in France's largest city. As Paris' and the realm's economy recovered from the devastating depression that accompanied the war of Spanish Succession (1702–1713), guild wardens stepped up their campaign to subordinate the faubourg. A royal commission was established in 1716 "to examine the titles of the masterships and liberties of the city of Paris," including the privileges of the faubourg Saint-Antoine. Bourbon administrators generally supported the pretensions of the masters: many officials were deeply concerned by the intermittent lawlessness of the faubourg's workers. The royal state, however, proved unwilling either to commit sufficient resources and political will to impose guild oversight or to allow the masters to do it themselves. Although the wardens sought to enforce their legal authority at several different reprises, often with the support of the lieutenant-general of police, political resolve to realize guild control was lacking at the highest levels of French government. Clearly, the royal council did not accept the marquis d'Argenson's characterization of the "disobedient inhabitants of the faubourg." This lieutenant-general of police claimed that "the majority of these workers … used their liberty to make things badly [*mal faire*]."[2]

Perhaps the council feared the workers' claim that they preferred to "renounce their liberties rather than suffer inspections" of their goods by their "irreconcilable enemies." Whatever the reason, repeated reprieves

[2] Arthur Michel de Boislisle and Pierre de Brotonne (eds.), *Correspondance des contrôleurs généraux des finances avec les intendants des provinces*, 3 vols. (Imprimerie Nationale, 1888, 1897), I: 392.

accorded to the abbess of Saint-Antoine as seigneur of the faubourg to produce documents justifying the workers' privileges indicates that the government suspected that abolishing the "liberty of work" would destroy the vibrancy of this major contributor to the French industrial economy. Officials' dedication to protecting this manufacturing powerhouse waxed after 1750 even as the enclave grew more fractious. In the conflict between privileges, this enclave's productive success appears to have trumped the monopolies of Paris' powerful guilds. As this vignette suggests and this book will demonstrate, the legal framework involving privilege, liberty, and their interaction undergirded the world of production and played a central role in state policymaking in the era between 1650 and 1820.[3]

For the French monarchy, the use of privilege as an instrument of economic development was "a beautiful madness."[4] Privilege was the constitutional basis of the early modern state, legalizing the provision of a variety of rights, powers, and exemptions to some, while denying them to others. Privileges were held by: individuals, both male and female; firms including the East Indies Company and the various royal manufactures; groups such as the nobility, the clergy, the guilds, and "Portuguese Jews"; and geographical entities including nearly every city and almost all provinces. But individuals, groups, cities, and provinces were not passive recipients of state initiatives; they articulated their own claims about their privileges and liberties that existed outside state structures. The bewilderingly complex puzzle of privilege, regulation, legal custom,

[3] The four previous paragraphs are based on the following documents. The primary sources are in AN F12 781C, especially the *Requête au Roy et à Nosseigneurs de son Conseil, Commissaires nommé pour l'examen des Titres des Maîtrises et Franchises de la Ville de Paris*, n.d. [1727]. On the purpose of the original privilege, see Thillay, *Le faubourg Saint-Antoine*, 74–77, 89–95; the quotations are cited on 82 and 94. Jean-Louis Bourgeon argues that Paris' *corporations* were limited in power and in the goods they produced in "Colbert et les Corporations," in Roland Mousnier (ed.), *Un Nouveau Colbert* (SEDES, 1983), 241–53. See also Arlette Farge, *Fragile Lives: Violence, Power and Solidarity in Eighteenth-Century Paris*, trans. Carol Shelton (Cambridge University Press, 1993 [1986]) and Arlette Farge and Jacques Revel, *The Vanishing Children of Paris: Rumor and Politics before the French Revolution*, trans. Claudia Miéville (Cambridge, MA: Harvard University Press, 1991 [1988]).

[4] The deputies of commerce referred to unlimited liberty of commerce, manufacturing, and shipping but, in many ways, the phrase sums up the state's paradoxical approach to economic development. *Avis des Députés du Commerce sur un Mémoire qui leur a été communiqué par Monseigneur le Directeur Général des finances, dans sa lettre du 8 mars 1778*, n.d. [1779], AN F12 719. I explore this vision of privilege in "'A Beautiful Madness': Privilege, the Machine Question and Industrial Development in Normandy in 1789," *Past & Present*, 217 (2012), 149–85. The approach outlined here is suggested by Gail Bossenga, "Estates, Orders and Corps," in William Doyle (ed.), *The Oxford Handbook of the Ancien Régime* (Oxford University Press, 2012), 141–66.

and historical precedent that characterized Bourbon France challenges any attempt to construct an understanding of state policy applicable to the entire realm. As anyone interested in this place and time knows all too well, exceptions were the rule. The impediments and opportunities arising from this exceptionalism must be evaluated to understand how such a composite, seemingly incoherent structure was able to function, particularly when it came to economic matters.

In a fit of "beautiful madness," Bourbon officials deployed privilege to foster commercial and industrial development. Economic innovators sought privileges that conferred greater freedom to operate. Entrepreneurs and inventors hoped to avoid guild rules on the number of workers they could hire or who those workers could be. They also wanted to be able to try out new techniques, new machines, and new designs, which guilds almost always refused to sanction. Substantial investment was required to make and sell products that transcended local monopolies. Most investors strove to minimize risk before committing resources: a privilege was the best available guarantee. Well-known competitive successes associated with state grants of privileges freeing the beneficiary from the rules that bound most others sustained this view of the market. Such exemptions will be termed the "privilege of liberty."

A paradox characterizing early modern French economic policy can now be glimpsed. The most effective tactic available to Bourbon administrators was to accord privileges that bypassed existing structures, thereby liberating innovators. Layering privileges was an enduring aspect of the *bricolage* (makeshift quality) inherent in French state-building, especially with regard to taxes. What was novel about how the Bourbon regime engaged in the enduring project of economic development was that new privileges granted by the central state focused specifically on exempting the bearer or bearers from *other* privileges whose unfettered ability to operate within the context of a state-granted monopoly will be referred to as the "liberty of privilege."[5] The practice of using one privilege to undermine or sidestep another began to be applied systematically in the third quarter of the seventeenth century. This approach to policymaking grew organically out of earlier means and methods, in large part through trial and error. Once in place and recognized as an effective strategy, state use of the privilege of liberty accelerated over the course of the eighteenth century, often taking new forms in different places or when applied to fresh trades. Yet the royal administration continued to grant individuals, groups,

[5] Privilege should not be confused with the economic term "rent" developed by David Ricardo (as opposed to the temporary use of a good or property.) As we shall see, privilege disappeared from France in 1795, but "rent" continued.

chartered companies, and places liberties of privilege. Both major aspects of privilege were applied frequently during the era from 1650 to 1789. Economic privileges survived the initial cataclysm of the French Revolution, disappearing much more slowly than has been recognized. Elements of privilege were revived in the first two decades of the nineteenth century before withering away.[6]

In the mid-eighteenth century, the social and political resonance of these policies shifted dramatically in reaction to Enlightened critiques of privilege in the name of liberty. Bourbon policymakers, ever more influenced by "improvers" such as the Physiocrats and affiliated factions of intellectuals, increasingly deployed the language of liberty to justify the long-standing practice of granting privileges intended to promote economic growth.[7] Administrative recourse to liberty to defend privilege as a policy tool marked a major shift in French political economy and French political culture. The privilege of liberty was seen as a stepping stone to greater things.

The depth of the shift in attitudes about privilege can be glimpsed in abbé Emmanuel-Joseph Sieyès' influential "Essay on Privileges" of 1788. He asserted that systematic use of exemptions undermined the legitimacy of France's economy, government, and society.[8] Condemnations of privilege that emphasized the increasingly rickety structure of the society of orders ignored its effectiveness and the dynamism of state-sponsored

[6] The two previous paragraphs consider issues raised by Pierre Deyon and Philippe Guignet, "The Royal Manufactures and Economic and Technological Progress in France before the Industrial Revolution," *Journal of European Economic History*, 9 (1980), 611–32 who argue that possession of privilege(s) frequently did not translate into a viable much less a profitable enterprise. On the political issues associated with tax privileges, see Gary B. McCollim, *Louis XIV's Assault on Privilege: Nicolas Desmaretz and the Tax on Wealth* (University of Rochester Press, 2012), Rafe Blaufarb, *The Politics of Fiscal Privilege in Provence, 1530s–1830s* (Washington, DC: Catholic University of America Press, 2012), and Michael Kwass, *Privilege and the Politics of Taxation in Eighteenth-Century France: Liberté, Égalité, Fiscalité* (Cambridge University Press, 2000).

[7] "Physiocrats" is a shorthand referring to diverse groups of improvers and/or economists active in eighteenth-century France. See John Shovlin, *The Political Economy of Virtue: Luxury, Patriotism, and the Origins of the French Revolution* (Ithaca, NY: Cornell University Press, 2006). In the eighteenth century, the language of liberty justified the existence of privileges. The Physiocrats, other improvers, and writers such as Montesquieu used that language to oppose the claims of an "absolute" monarchy. But just as privileges came to be layered over one another, so too did liberties. The monopolistic elements of liberty and the freedoms made possible by privilege are essential aspects of the paradox at the heart of this book. For general outlines of the evolution of the concepts of liberty and privilege, see Nannerl Keohane, *Philosophy and the State in France: The Renaissance to the Enlightenment* (Princeton University Press, 1980) and the essays collected in Philip T. Hoffman and Kathryn Norberg (eds.), *Fiscal Crises, Liberty and Representative Government 1450–1789* (Stanford University Press, 1994).

[8] Michael Sonenscher (ed.), *Emmanuel Joseph Sieyès: Political Writings including the Debate between Sieyès and Tom Paine in 1791* (Indianapolis: Hackett, 2003), 68–91.

economic reform. This study explores how a combination of the privilege of liberty and the liberty of privilege enabled the old régime economy to grow enough to compete with France's international rivals. For contemporaries, Bourbon France's increasing reliance on the privilege of liberty after 1750 to stimulate economic growth heightened the impact of the paradox inherent in this administrative practice. Resolution of the paradox of the privilege of liberty came only after the outbreak of the French Revolution offered new means of curing France of its "beautiful madness."

This book melds the commercial and industrial experiences of multiple regions with a national perspective and evaluates French political economy in light of the broad sweep of economic history along with certain conceptual issues of economic development. Although a provocative interpretation of the process of early modern economic change is advanced, this study is not informed by contemporary political or economic debates but rather has emerged organically from sustained scrutiny of the archival record.[9] Thus, the arguments are not framed combatively, although issues of historiographical significance are not ignored. This study centers on the Bourbon state, but the complex interplay of privilege and liberty in old régime France also occurred in other parts of Europe. The institutional dimensions of Europe's exploitation of Atlantic, East Indian, and Mediterranean trade networks also demonstrate the global impact of the privilege of liberty.

International challenges and the emergence of a liberal consensus

Acclaimed for its exploitation of Atlantic trade networks, the old régime's economy is blamed for perpetuating inequality, generating insufficient tax revenue to permit the Bourbons to defeat their archenemy across the channel, and failing to initiate an industrial revolution.[10] Such understandings rely too heavily on Enlightenment-era polemics and

9 Adherents of the economic approach pioneered by Douglass C. North may reject the term "privilege of liberty" as an inherent contradiction. Although I engage many of the same issues, my approach to political economy should not be understood as part of the ongoing debate touched off by the publication of *Institutions, Institutional Change and Economic Performance* (Cambridge University Press, 1990).

10 This is especially true of historians working in English. See Carl Wennerlind and Philip J. Stern (eds.), *Mercantilism Reimagined: Political Economy in Early Modern Britain and Its Empire* (Oxford University Press, 2013) and Leandro Prados de la Escosura (ed.), *Exceptionalism and Industrialisation: Britain and its European Rivals, 1688–1815* (Cambridge University Press, 2004). For an alternative view, see James C. Riley, *The Seven Years War and the Old Regime in France: The Economic and Financial Toll* (Princeton University Press, 1986).

look backward from the perspective of the French and industrial revolutions. To recover the possibilities intrinsic to the period, this account of France's approach to economic development focuses on the epoch from Louis XIV's assumption of personal rule in 1661 to the outbreak of the Revolution. The final chapter delineates the contours of the French Revolution's engagement with economic privilege before considering the complex legacy of the old régime's deployment of privilege in the thirty years after 1789.

When Louis XIV personally took up the reins of power, France's economy was in disarray. The domestic turmoil of the Fronde compounded the effects of decades of war. Open hostilities with the Habsburgs from 1635 to 1659 distorted or destroyed markets and trade relations. Despite these dislocations, France's economy had notable strengths, even exporting 80 million *livres* (£6 million) worth of manufactured goods to England and the Netherlands. At first, Louis XIV concentrated on restoring order and reviving the authority of the central state, re-appropriating control over revenue appropriated by the nobility during the Fronde. In addition to recovering lost revenue, Louis XIV needed to generate new income to fund his ambitions, both military and architectural. To fulfill these aims, Louis XIV chose Jean-Baptiste Colbert to oversee the French economy.

As controller-general of finance from 1665 to 1683, to which control of the navy and colonies was added in 1669 and oversight of the royal household in 1671, Colbert improved the efficiency of royal administration while using patronage effectively. Under his leadership, France made great headway in meeting its rivals head-on, both on the waves and in the competition for customers. Precise economic data do not exist, but royal finances represent a measure of this hardworking official's success. In 1661, the budget deficit was about 22 million *livres*. By 1683, the surplus had climbed to 29 million *livres*. Ninety years after Colbert's death, Jacques Necker wrote that:

> Colbert believed that taxes have no goal but the wellbeing and defense of society: he refused to enrich the royal treasury at the expense of public wealth . . . He examined existing taxes, modified them, and lowered them substantially, but with so much justice and wisdom that in releasing industry, commerce, and agriculture from the immense weights that had prevented their movement, the king's receipts grew.[11]

In Chapter 2, we will examine how systematic use of privilege to encourage economic development began under Colbert's prudent stewardship.

[11] Jacques Necker, *Eloge de Jean-Baptiste Colbert: discours qui a remporté le prix de l'Académie françoise, en 1773* (Dresden: Frères Walther, 1773), 23.

Colbert's approach to reinvigorating French commerce and industry long survived him. His immediate ministerial successors – the marquis de Seignelay (his eldest son) and Louis de Phélypeaux, count de Pontchartrain who was succeeded by his own son, the marquis – continued Colbert's policies. Strategies inaugurated early in Louis XIV's personal reign persisted thanks to dynastic politics, continuity of patron–client networks, chronic shortage of state funds available for economic development, and the mounting difficulty of effecting fundamental changes during the turbulent, war-torn era encompassing the Sun King's later years, the Regency, and the first decades after Louis XV came of age. As a result, the Colbertian paradigm of fostering economic development by using privilege to nurture liberty survived basically unchallenged much longer than it might have otherwise, until 1750.[12]

Influential improvers grouped around Jean-Claude-Marie Vincent de Gournay and François Quesnay rose to prominence around mid-century. Although the two circles had distinct views on many issues, they are often referred to collectively as the Physiocrats. However one describes them, these "economists" sought to change French practice by shifting economic policy in favor of liberty at the expense of privilege. In 1754, de Gournay informed a potential entrepreneur from Lyon who wanted to establish a cotton mill to make muslins that "You cannot count on an exclusive privilege. The council [of commerce] has resolved not to accord any." Two months later, he concluded, "I would like to leave the manufacture of these fabrics completely free [*en toute liberté*]."[13] Physiocratic endorsement of aspects of what became known as liberalism responded to French military defeats and Great Britain's burgeoning wealth and power so evident after 1750. International competitiveness, both economic and military, intertwined with the improvers' hopes to create a more equitable domestic polity, supported a new, liberal approach to economic policymaking.

To effect change, these intellectuals escalated their critiques of privilege's role in the society of orders. The publicity accorded to their attacks on privilege within French public opinion has displaced actual Bourbon policy, which frequently used some privileges to circumvent

12 The four previous paragraphs rely on Pierre Clément (ed.), *Lettres, instructions et mémoires de Colbert publiés d'après les ordres de l'empereur*, 10 vols. (Imprimerie impériale/nationale, 1861–1882), II (1): cxxv and Florian Schui, *Early Debates about Industry: Voltaire and His Contemporaries* (Houndsmills: Palgrave, 2005), 80. On the continuation of Colbert's networks and policies, see Sara Chapman, *Private Ambition and Political Alliances: The Phélypeaux de Pontchartrain Family and Louis XIV's Government, 1650–1715* (University of Rochester Press, 2004).

13 Takumi Tsuda (ed.), *Mémoires et lettres de Vincent de Gournay* (Tokyo: Kinokuniya Co., 1993), 174, 189.

others. Historians' acceptance of these criticisms at face value has also introduced a static, almost structuralist, quality to our understandings of the principles and practices of French economic policies. Such analyses do not reflect the dynamism of government action in eighteenth-century France. The Bourbon state was no enemy of capitalism. State-sponsored economic reform in the eighteenth century exhibited a vibrancy, a creativity that has been downplayed in favor of the ossifying effects of measures like the Ségur Ordinance of 1781 requiring military officers to have four generations of nobility. The role of privilege in France's society of orders was never that linear or simplistic.

From the late 1720s, many privileges were limited or eliminated, and the administration grew increasingly hesitant to grant new ones. Yet, the state continued to rely on privilege, especially the privilege of liberty, as a tool of economic development. In many places and cases, the privilege of liberty assumed a mounting role in state practice, in large measure because of the lack of feasible alternatives. Only in the late 1780s did the Bourbon state restrict its use of the privilege of liberty to foster economic growth. This divergence of rhetoric from reality is absent from nearly all accounts of French political economy during the age of Enlightenment.[14]

Bourbon officials' deep-seated commitment to "improvement" for the purpose of economic development challenges interpretations based on the work of Jürgen Habermas. He emphasizes the distinction between "insiders" and "outsiders" to explain "the structural transformation of the public sphere." Systematic introduction of "capitalistic" policies by state officials dedicated to improvement suggests that this distinction has been both overdrawn and overemphasized. Throughout the eighteenth century, adherents of privilege and liberty worked together, switched positions, and collaborated to find and implement the most effective means of promoting economic development. Peter Jones noticed these practices, but this study explicitly demonstrates the fullness of state officials' dedication to reform over the long term. In economics,

[14] For the three previous paragraphs, consult the following sources. On French views of England, see François Crouzet, "The Sources of England's Wealth: Some French Views in the Eighteenth Century," in *Britain Ascendant: Comparative Studies in Franco-British Economic History*, trans. Martin Thom (Cambridge University Press, 1990 [1985]), 127–48. On the Physiocrats' "patriotism," see Shovlin, *The Political Economy of Virtue*, 118–50. The limitation of privilege is discussed in Jeff Horn, *The Path Not Taken: French Industrialization in the Age of Revolution, 1750–1830* (Cambridge, MA: MIT Press, 2006), 17–21. For the dynamism of state action in the decades before 1789, see Steven L. Kaplan, *La fin des corporations* (Fayard, 2001). Overemphasis on the "reactionary" aspects of the state began with Alfred Cobban, *The Social Interpretation of the French Revolution* (Cambridge University Press, 1965) and has many current adherents.

structural transformation of the public sphere had to wait until 1789–1791 (see Chapter 8).[15]

The art of the possible and the limitations of the absolutist state

Absolutism and mercantilism shaped the deployment of privilege. From an economic perspective, these terms, like the old régime itself, conjure impressions of hide-bound, top-down state insistence on unproductive policies including hoarding currency, high tariffs, overemphasis on exports and import substitution, while preventing competition through the establishment of monopolies. But neither mercantilism nor absolutism quite earns its negative reputation in the English-speaking world. Viewing French economic policy through the prism of privilege reveals the possibilities and constraints faced by Bourbon policymakers and their heirs after 1789.

Mercantilism was not only a set of economic goals but also the articulation of early modern capitalism. To increase national wealth, the Bourbon government implemented a cluster of policies that later became known as mercantilism to manage and oversee the marketplace while stimulating trade, industry, and communication. In Chapters 3, 5, and 7, we shall explore the royal state's determination to protect consumers and the "reputation" of French manufactures as essential aspects of mercantilism. Attention to the balance of trade and currency stocks accompanied a profound reliance on regulating individual economic activity to stimulate and/or maintain foreign and domestic competitiveness.

In France, mercantilism was not fundamentally a response to weakness. As the demographic colossus of western Europe, the Bourbon monarchy's size and economic potential meant that, within certain important constraints, French policymakers could choose their economic pathway to a greater degree than nearly all of their competitors. The diversity and lack of interaction between many parts of the realm led decision makers to emphasize the development and expansion of their contiguous territories rather than the exploitation of their overseas empire.

The critiques of Physiocrats like publicist Pierre Roubaud strongly influenced the state's choices. He criticized colonies as economic distractions: "the spirit of monopoly and conquest" encouraged the

[15] Jürgen Habermas, *The Structural Transformation of the Public Sphere: An Inquiry into a Category of Bourgeois Society*, trans. Thomas Burger with the assistance of Frederick Lawrence (Cambridge, MA: MIT Press, 1989) and Peter M. Jones, *Reform and Revolution in France: The Politics of Transition* (Cambridge University Press, 1995).

practice of despotic government at home and abroad as "the French adopted the savage life *en masse*."[16] Like their British, Dutch, and Spanish rivals, empire and foreign trade were essential to French economic growth, but, for policymakers, the importance of colonies and overseas commerce stemmed primarily from how well they stimulated metropolitan economic development.

As in the case of Austria, "internal colonization" responded to the war-making needs of the absolutist state and English and Dutch seafaring dominance. French mercantilism admitted to some areas of competitive inadequacy, but it also reflected a set of deliberate choices. For domestic political reasons, despite the multiplicity of threats facing the realm and numerous military reverses, Bourbon France never resolved to mobilize for war as thoroughly as its smaller, maritime rivals during the long seventeenth century. Unlike either the English or the Dutch, the fundamental purpose of French mercantilist policies was never survival through the waging of economic warfare; rather, state action melded political and economic concerns. Bourbon mercantilism can best be understood as a statist approach to economic development in a time of ongoing warfare punctuated by periodic internal crises.[17]

At the same time, mercantilism was the economic expression of a system of patronage linking the central state to diverse localities.[18] Colbert and his successors used such networks to organize power and production while sustaining political stability. Inventors, manufacturers, artisans, and merchants were among the most important clients of high-ranking officials. These economic actors supplemented, complemented, broadened, and deepened the political ties connecting decision makers in Paris and Versailles to the provinces. In exchange for privileges, industrial and commercial entrepreneurs provided information, support, and resources for Bourbon officials. Yet, as we shall see, these relationships were heavily weighted in favor of the economic welfare of the kingdom as a whole.

16 Pierre-Joseph-Antoine Roubaud, *Histoire générale de l'Asie, de l'Afrique et de l'Amérique*, 5 vols. (Des ventes de la Doué, 1770–1775), III: 345 and V: 68 cited in Paul Cheney, *Revolutionary Commerce: Globalization and the French Monarchy* (Cambridge, MA: Harvard University Press, 2010), 157, 159.

17 On this view of mercantilism, see Jeff Horn, "Marseille et la question du mercantilisme: privilège, liberté et l'économie politique en France, 1650–1750," *Histoire, économie & société*, (2011/2), 95–112. In the two previous paragraphs, for similar views of the strategic aspect of economic and political administration in the provinces, see William Beik, *Absolutism and Society: State Power and Provincial Aristocracy in Languedoc* (Cambridge University Press, 1985) and Philippe Minard, *La fortune du colbertisme: État et industrie dans la France des Lumières* (Fayard, 1998). See also Jean-Paul Bertaud, *Guerre et société en France: de Louis XIV à Napoléon Ier* (Armand Colin, 1998).

18 I owe this point to David K. Smith.

Chapters 2–7 demonstrate that reliance on privilege made the practice of mercantilism both capitalist and absolutist. During the old régime, the economic and political aspects of French government activity were thoroughly intertwined, making it impossible to consider one without the other. Separating the political from the economic or vice versa distorts the realities faced by early modern French decision makers. In Chapter 8, the same nexus helps to understand the era after 1789, though not always in expected ways.

Even though it created a potentially hegemonic fiscal–military state, the Bourbon monarchy was never "absolute." As we shall see in Chapter 7, an inability to impose its will marked government efforts to reform the world of work in the aftermath of the temporary, partial abolition of the guilds executed by controller-general of finance Anne-Robert-Jacques de Turgot in 1776. His successor, Jacques Necker, a former Swiss banker who became director-general of finance, restored the guilds and permitted textile producers to choose the degree of inspection that their goods would undergo. Necker asserted that "Good faith is the first rule of all legitimate commerce. The royal council has prescribed general rules for the new guilds which, without hindering talent and industry, seem capable of sustaining reciprocal confidence between buyer and seller."[19] However, the results did not meet the council's expectations.

François-Marie Bruno, count d'Agay and intendant of Picardy, reported in 1778 that "The government's successive choice of opposing systems ranging from submitting all textiles to regulation to an indefinite liberty ... has created an obstacle to the proliferation of industry and facilitates fraud." "Loss of confidence" lowered sales and had a ripple effect:

> Picardy's small producers sell their unfinished fabric to merchants in Amiens who prepare them for sale in other cities or abroad. Producers do not know who will buy their goods ... Each reduction of the price paid for their fabric leads them to lower the quality and quantity of the raw materials used to avoid selling at a loss.[20]

Across France, masters refused to join the restored guilds or to follow their rules. They systematically avoided government inspection and rules assuring quality standards. Nor did wardens control the guilds as closely as they had before 1776. The "absolutist" state could issue regulations and impose reforms, but it could not enforce compliance.[21]

[19] *Édit du Roi, concernant les communautés d'Arts et Métiers dans la Ville de Rouen*, February 8, 1778, AN F12 786.

[20] Comte d'Agay, *Lettre à M. Necker*, April 21, 1778, AD Somme C350.

[21] James B. Collins goes so far as to reject the entire notion of absolutism in favor of "monarchial state." See his *The State in Early Modern France*, 2nd ed. (Cambridge

Geography was an intractable impediment to administrative action. The sheer size and difficulty of traversing the terrain between north and south and from east to west hampered the expansion of the transportation system and precluded the emergence of a unified domestic market until after 1850. France was simply too large and too diverse to be administered as a coherent whole with existing technology, unlike rather flat and compact entities such as England or the Netherlands. Local, provincial, and regional approaches to development were eminently rational; they should not be condemned as reflections of a political system that its critics described as archaic, outdated, or insufficiently dedicated to efficiency.

Other limitations have received less scholarly attention, but were at least as significant. In human terms, Bourbon policymaking was circumscribed by numerous cleavages within the elite, a largely uneducated workforce lacking several vital technical skills, and a lingering deficit of talented administrators to staff the far-flung bureaucracy. Most importantly, however, France suffered a chronic shortfall of political will. Mercantilist policies responded to the state's limited power of command and its relative lack of control over many key provinces and groups, as witnessed by its inability to eliminate internal tolls and tariffs to create a true national market. Bourbon officials recognized that effective governance of this fractured, fractious realm was an exercise in the art of the possible. As an approach to economic development, the old régime's reliance on the privilege of liberty was a sensible method of achieving necessary goals with limited means.

Production, trade, and profit

As economic policy, French mercantilism was the absolutist state's response to certain attitudes about profits, production, and entrepreneurialism. From the fifteenth century, royal officials recognized the constraints inherent in the society of orders. Nobles faced losing their privileged status if they engaged in trade or manufacturing. Urban guilds enjoyed monopolies of production and sale that drastically curtailed output, discouraged technical change, and restricted profits. Most merchants and manufacturers aspired to join the nobility. To speed the process, they preferred quick windfall profits to developing long-term commercial relationships that were potentially more lucrative. Having made their fortune, entrepreneurs shed their businesses as soon as practicable in favor of "living nobly."

University Press, 2009). On the guild reforms, see Kaplan, *La fin des corporations*, 138–362 or, in English, Horn, *The Path Not Taken*, 17–50.

All early modern European states shared these problems to some degree. Until 1789, however, France's agricultural bounty, manufacturing productivity, and trade position, both in Europe and globally, enabled the economy to thrive. The Bourbons contended for the mastery of Europe, but the French economy was not as efficient as it could have been. Nor did it maximize either profits or output.[22] In 1787, the inspector of manufacturing for the generality of Guyenne, François-Paul Latapie, was "really embarrassed to report on the state incentives given to Sieur Merget['s glassworks] ... The director seems to know his art ... but the length of time he left the crystal to bake led to its total ruin and signaled mixing problems that unfavorably prejudice the success of an establishment founded on economy and precision."[23] Such problems were evident to contemporaries from the Renaissance to the Revolution, and beyond. French political economy sought to overcome long-standing attitudes toward profit, production, and entrepreneurialism by regulating individual activity, awarding various kinds of monopolies, and granting the privilege of liberty.

From 1295, derogation laws restricted nobles' economic activities. Violators could lose their noble status if they engaged in professions ranging from trade and manufacturing to farming and clerical work. Landownership, particularly when associated with a seigneur's duties and a noble lifestyle, was considered the ideal in the wake of the publication of jurist Charles Loyseau's *A Treatise on Orders and Simple Dignities* in 1610. Beginning with Colbert in 1669, the royal administration steadily increased the number of professions that nobles were permitted to practice until, by 1767, only retail trade was forbidden.

In practice, all restrictions had sizeable loopholes. A number of professions such as glass-making, iron-founding, and mining had always been exempt. Some cities, including Lyon, Marseille, and Troyes, enjoyed privileges that liberated noble residents from derogation. The provinces of Brittany and Artois even allowed younger sons of strapped noble families to suspend their status temporarily to engage in trade, manufacturing, or some other prohibited activity. Among others, Guy Richard demonstrated the impressive quality and quantity of direct noble involvement in trade and industry. Some nobles openly invested in

22 For France's economic position within Europe and how well it held up across the divide of 1789, see Paul Bairoch, "L'économie française dans le contexte européen à la fin du XVIIIe siècle," *Revue économique*, 40: 6 (1989), 939–64. See also my review of the evidence in Jeff Horn, "Avoiding Revolution: The French Path to Industrialization," in Jeff Horn, Leonard N. Rosenband, and Merritt Roe Smith (eds.), *Reconceptualizing the Industrial Revolution* (Cambridge, MA: MIT Press, 2010), 87–106.

23 François-Paul Latapie, *Rapport*, n.d. [1787], AD Gironde C4465.

commercial or industrial projects, while others hid their speculations behind middlemen or by using assumed names. Noble participation in trade, manufacturing, and finance waxed in the seventeenth and eighteenth centuries, especially after 1770.

Most nobles, however, hesitated to take up the gauntlet cast down by the abbé Gabriel-François Coyer, who exhorted them to have the "spiritual courage" to escape their "lack of utility." Inspired by Montesquieu's *The Spirit of the Laws*, Coyer urged French nobles to imitate the English aristocracy by engaging in trade. It would help both "the fatherland" and themselves.[24] Yet, for the majority of nobles, the capitalistic ethos of maximizing production and minimizing costs to enhance profits was incompatible with a noble lifestyle. Such practices seemed too "bourgeois." As a result, few searched resolutely for profits, though nearly all nobles struggled to develop additional sources of revenue to support the growing expense of "living nobly." Noble prejudice against certain kinds of economic activities proved a far more difficult cultural barrier to surmount than legal restrictions. Among nobles, Loyseau had far more adherents than Coyer, even on the eve of the Revolution. The economic activities surveyed by Richard were undertaken by a distinct though clearly growing minority of nobles.

France's "bourgeoisie" also had practical constraints and cultural attitudes about economic productivity to overcome. As Jean-Pierre Hirsch and Philippe Minard have argued, entrepreneurs (both nobles and commoners) wanted the state to protect them from competition *and* to allow them to manage their workforces and make their goods without interference. It is impossible to read French government documents from the period without being stunned by entrepreneurs' incessant demands for exemptions from the rules, regulations, taxes, and tolls that bound others. Yet such demands were overshadowed by merchants, manufacturers, and artisans' insistence that their own privileges and/or monopolies be enforced against any and all encroachment: they clearly did not want to face competition. Hirsch and Minard demonstrated that, for entrepreneurs in early modern France, such attitudes were complementary, not contradictory.[25]

[24] Gabriel-François Coyer, *La noblesse commerçante*, 2nd ed. (1756), 214–15.

[25] The five previous paragraphs are based on Michael L. Bush, *Rich Noble, Poor Noble* (Manchester University Press, 1988), 86–87, 106–07, Guy Richard, *La noblesse d'affaires au XVIIIe siècle* (Armand Colin, 1974), Guy Chaussinand-Nogaret, *The French Nobility in the Eighteenth Century: From Feudalism to Enlightenment*, trans. William Doyle (Cambridge University Press, 1985 [1976]), 84–116, and the chapters by Roger Mettam and Julian Swann in Hamish M. Scott (ed.), *The European Nobilities in the Seventeenth and Eighteenth Centuries*, vol. 1 *Western Europe* (New York: Longman, 1995), 114–73. See especially Jean-Pierre Hirsch and Philippe Minard, "'Laissez-faire

These views reveal entrepreneurs' high degree of dependence on the state. They also remind us that a great deal of entrepreneurial activity focused on attracting state support if only as a means to an end. French entrepreneurs were "industrious" in the manner outlined by Jan de Vries, but the economic context, both domestic and international, pushed their actions in different directions than their British and Dutch counterparts. The evidence presented in this book suggests that France should not be excluded from discussion of the role of industriousness in the early modern economy.[26]

Valuable exemptions and powerful administrative protection did not ensure behavior conducive to long-term economic development. As will be explored in Chapter 5, Marseille was granted free port status in 1669. The city and its chamber of commerce enjoyed numerous privileges that amounted to a French trade monopoly with the Levant.[27] In 1699, the director-general of commerce, Jean-Baptiste de Lagny, complained bitterly about Marseillais' use of their privileges: "They cry for more liberty because they do not know their true interests and because they do not restrain themselves ... they ruin their own commerce and endlessly distort the realm's manufactures. They waste gold and silver to introduce merchandise whose distribution and sale is ruinous to the public."[28] Sometimes it seemed as if the French state was caught between the Scylla of privilege and the Charybdis of protection, with no safe channel to pass between them.

The prevalence of the social goal of amassing sufficient capital to withdraw from trade or manufacturing, purchase a state office, and become noble was a major concern. Jacques Savary des Bruslons' *Dictionnaire universel de commerce* grumbled that "wholesalers so easily quit the trade that made them rich."[29] This aspiration contravened royal

nous et protégez-nous beaucoup' pour une histoire des pratiques institutionnelles dans l'industrie française (XVIIIe-XIXe siècle)" in Louis Bergeron and Patrice Bourdelais (eds.), *La France n'est-elle pas douée pour l'industrie?* (Belin, 1998), 135–58.

26 Jan de Vries, *The Industrious Revolution: Consumer Behavior and the Household Economy, 1650 to the present* (Cambridge University Press, 2008).

27 The Levant refers to Ottoman Turkey's domains along the Mediterranean from Dalmatia to Egypt including the islands, notably Crete and Cyprus. North Africa, nominally under Turkish control, usually was treated separately by the French government. Some statistics lump them together.

28 Louis Bergasse and Gaston Rambert, *De 1599 à 1789*, vol. 4 of Gaston Rambert (ed.), *Histoire du commerce de Marseille*, 7 vols. (Plon, 1954), 217–18.

29 Jacques Savary des Bruslons with Philemon-Louis Savary, *Dictionnaire universel de commerce, d'histoire naturelle et des arts et metiers*, rev. ed., 5 vols. (Copenhagen: Cl. Et Ant. Philibert, 1762), IV: 356. Robert Forster, *Merchants, Landlords, Magistrates: The Depont Family in Eighteenth-Century France* (Baltimore: Johns Hopkins University Press, 1980) illustrates how one family made the transition from merchant to noble.

policy and put France at a disadvantage compared to other nations, he reported. Such cultural practices impeded sustained economic development especially in times of war or domestic unrest.

Across France, entrepreneurs dissatisfied with limited but safe profits or who were unable to earn a sufficient income frequently resorted to smuggling. In 1770, the intendant at Metz reported that "large numbers of foreign textiles were entering France illegally" through the province of Lorraine, which was outside the customs frontier. Customs officials could not stop the influx. Merchants and manufacturers who undertook this trade "find no obstacles. They counterfeit the inspector of manufacturing's lead certification marks. The trademark of the [East] Indies company is forged clandestinely in Switzerland and serves as a passport for a multitude of European-made muslins."[30] In Chapters 2, 4, 6, and 8, aspects of the vast underground economy will be delineated. Even for those who did not engage in the practice, smuggling shaped attitudes about profit, production, and entrepreneurialism.[31]

The manufacturing sector had further problems. Nearly every guild master depended on the monopolies held by urban trades. Guilds tended to limit output to the needs of local consumers and set prices accordingly. Other producers (including some masters) attempted to maximize profits, with mixed success, by making products for exchange. Certain French wares, usually luxury goods, had markets across Europe and around the globe. But within the realm, French manufactures circulated less than they might have: poor communications compounded the effects of high internal tariffs and tolls. Privileges held by guilds, seigneurs, road builders, municipalities, provinces, and the Roman Catholic Church compounded the effects of geography and terrain to further fragment France's domestic market by slowing down and increasing the cost of long-distance trade.

Yet, in another facet of the paradox of privilege, fragmented markets created niches that additional privileges could exploit, spurring development. A profoundly segmented market encouraged flouting industrial regulations and the fraudulent sale of inferior goods. Such behavior infuriated customers, lowered manufacturing profits, and shed light on the supply side of the consumer revolution.[32] These constraints

30 Delaville, *Observation sur l'introduction des étoffes étrangers par la Lorraine et les Trois Evêchés*, September 1770, AN, F12 675.

31 Michael Kwass has begun to publish on this subject. See his "The Global Underground: Smuggling, Rebellion, and the Origins of the French Revolution," in Suzanne Desan, Lynn Hunt, and William Max Nelson (eds.), *The French Revolution in Global Perspective* (Ithaca, NY: Cornell University Press, 2013), 15–31.

32 State consumer protection should be included in histories of consumption. A starting point to this voluminous subject is John Brewer and Roy Porter (eds.), *Consumption and the World of Goods* (London: Routledge, 1993).

and opportunities illustrate essential structural differences between France and its English and Dutch competitors.

Efforts to stimulate France's industrial economy frequently ran afoul of producers' propensity to boost profits by avoiding state regulation. The royal council responded to customer complaints of cheating and/ or fraud by reasserting the state's responsibility to protect consumers. In 1753, Charles-Jean-Baptiste des Galois de la Tour, intendant of Provence, avowed that "for some years, the poor quality of the leather on sale at the Beaucaire fair must be attributed to the tanners' bad faith and greed." These artisans "do not clean the skins and dry them only one-third of the mandated time" before storing them in humid places in order to increase their weight. Tanners sell "four rolls of leather packed together and tied so as to make inspection very difficult." As a bundle could weigh up to 220 pounds, "buyers usually make their decisions based on the top piece." "Infidelities" mounted up: "Shoemakers find that 40–50 percent of the leather is wasted." De la Tour ordered that "all merchandise for sale at a fair must follow the regulations exactly and in good faith."[33] The state, however, could not enforce these regulations because of the lack of honest, competent inspectors. Consequently, such ordinances had little practical effect on the products sold to customers.

These examples do not tell the whole story – far from it – but they reveal the challenges faced by old régime political economy. Windfall profits stemming from risky trade ventures, smuggling, or fraud enticed many entrepreneurs away from more productive pursuits while hindering the law-abiding. Most guild masters preferred the reliability of small, steady profits to the uncertain perils of unfettered competition. For those entrepreneurs who succeeded in earning their fortunes, the siren song of noble status drained the will to compete. Preference for an aristocratic lifestyle informed most nobles and clergy who controlled an impressive proportion of the country's wealth. During the age of Enlightenment, France elaborated new economic mindsets focused on competition, but for most people and in most places, those mindsets were a work in progress, not an accomplished fact.

To inculcate a more competitive approach to entrepreneurialism, French policymakers and officials needed to surmount existing attitudes about profits, production, and entrepreneurialism. This was no easy task. Ongoing budget shortfalls compounded by shortages of administrative talent and political will were accentuated by devastating world wars

[33] *Ordonnance de l'intendant de la Tour*, April 18, 1753, AD Bouches-du-Rhône 1F12.

that buffeted Bourbon France in 1688–1697, 1702–1713, 1740–1748, 1756–1763, and 1777–1783. The French state could not impose a capitalist system any more than it could force entrepreneurs to exhibit a capitalistic spirit. That does not mean that royal administrators did not try. Ironically, privilege was an "improving" state's most effective means of encouraging more capitalistic entrepreneurial practice.

From the mid-seventeenth century, royal officials regularly provided privileges whose chief attribute was exemption from the strictures of the society of orders. This paradoxical approach to economic development is an underappreciated aspect of both mercantilism and the emergence of French capitalism. Three central conclusions emerge concerning the nature of economy and society in early modern France. First, privileges of liberty were vital to the economy's ability to compete. It is worth emphasizing that the economy did not merely survive. From a long-term perspective, despite ups and downs at the beginning and end of the period, France's economy flourished between 1661 and 1789. A corollary of this argument is that state use of privileges of liberty was a short-term fix to enduring structural problems that were not resolved until the mid-nineteenth century. The privilege of liberty's effectiveness allowed the government to avoid enacting reforms that might have fostered more broadly based economic growth. Finally, by exposing the paradox whereby exemptions to the old régime's rules and regulations were the state's most effective tool of economic development, the privilege of liberty played a dynamic role in undermining the society of orders, thereby helping to bring about the French Revolution. Chapter 8 reveals that privilege outlived the upheaval of 1789, before disappearing completely by 1795. Revived tentatively under the Consulate, privilege assumed a significant position in economic policymaking under the Empire before dwindling under the Restoration. Privilege, "a beautiful madness," played a central role in state-sponsored economic development from Louis XIV to Louis XVIII.

Adam Smith saw no beauty in this madness. He critiqued guilds as a form of cartel, which "ends in a conspiracy against the public, or in some contrivance to raise prices" often by restricting production or price fixing. Such limits constrained wages and consumption. This appraisal formed part of Smith's general condemnation of monopolies. He shunned chartered companies or domestic monopolies as inefficient. Smith, of course, leavened his theoretical principles with realistic judgments. For example, although he noted that "Monopoly, besides, is a great enemy to good management which can never be universally established but in consequence of that free and universal competition," Smith admitted that "To expect, indeed, that the freedom of trade should ever be restored in Great Britain, is as absurd as to expect that an Oceana or Utopia should ever be established in it."[34]

Recognizing the absurdity of expecting the reign of "free and universal competition" in Britain, much less France, helps to underscore privilege's importance as a tool of Bourbon economic policy. Compared to Britain, France had an inadequate network of riverine and road transport, limited access to the sea, far greater size, and difficult geographical barriers. "Free and universal competition" was impossible both physically and in terms of access to information or market function. Smith's theories were based on assumptions that explain why no contemporary European state, including Britain, followed his precepts on monopoly and free trade. Privilege was a practical tactic deployed by states focused on the art of the possible.

France was never the sole European polity in which privilege structured government action. Indeed, for centuries, privilege was the essential aspect of European property rights and a crucial feature of state-building. The degree to which privilege, and property rights more generally, would be respected required delicate negotiation. Striking a stable equilibrium was difficult, but maintaining it was harder, especially in wartime. The relationship of privilege to the wider polity generated persistent conflict in medieval and early modern Europe. To wage war successfully, states, whether "absolutist" or not, needed to be able to infringe on or usurp privileges from provinces, cities, groups, and individuals. The comparative literature on state-building and the process of centralization focuses on the differing processes of getting elites to consent to that infringement. In most European polities, the rulers of fiscal–military states accepted certain limits on how money was raised and spent, while recognizing the right of elites to participate in governance. This compromise was the foundation of "absolutism."[35]

Such perspectives on the political economy of privilege miss both the specificities and significance of the French case. This book argues that privilege was not (or not just) a barrier to be overcome. Nor was unqualified protection of property rights required to achieve high levels of economic growth. These otherwise rich literatures overlook the fact

[34] Adam Smith, *The Wealth of Nations*, ed. Edwin Cannan (New York: the Modern Library, 2000),136–65 (Bk. I, Ch. X, Pt. 1) and the quotes are from 148, 170 (Bk. I, Ch. XI, Pt. 1), 501 (Bk. IV, Ch. II). See also Robert M. Larsen, "Adam Smith's Theory of Market Prices," in John Cunningham Wood (eds.), *Adam Smith: Critical Assessments*, 7 vols. (London: Routledge, 1996 [1984]), III: 479–90, esp. 484.

[35] John Brewer and Eckhart Hellmuth (eds.), *Rethinking Leviathan: The Eighteenth-Century State in Britain and Germany* (Oxford University Press, 1999), 1–21.

that state creation of overlapping or competing privileges was a deliberate and effective means of fostering industrial and commercial expansion. Bourbon France borrowed heavily from abroad, but it ran the country on its own terms and in its own way. The exercise of governmental authority developed unique forms, some of which lasted well into the nineteenth century. This book emphasizes the interaction of state use of power and the process of economic development without assuming that those forms were either fixed or unlimited. The lived experience of economic actors demonstrates that the instruments of state power were contingent and diverse. That contingency and the distinctiveness of France's response are left out of accounts of "absolutism," centralization, and the formation of the fiscal–military state. Both individually and collectively, French mercantilists deserve recognition for their creative approach to problem solving, farsightedness, and clarity of purpose.[36]

The Bourbon state's exceptional use of privilege also helps to explain why it became the object of increasing opprobrium in the second half of the eighteenth century. Too great a focus on politics obscures the economic and material bases of public perceptions of privilege. For example, although Stephan Epstein's account of Tuscany's stagnation vis-à-vis England and Holland after the Black Death emphasizes the importance of "institutional flexibility," his stress on the greater authority and control of local privilege-holders in Tuscany does not consider why the power of privilege was so much greater in one place than in another. Regina Grafe and Alejandra Irigoin's analysis of Spain

36 The two previous paragraphs respond to important analyses of absolutism and the roles of the protection of property and representative institutions in early modern economic growth. On "absolutism," in addition to the works cited above on tax privileges, see Beik, *Absolutism and Society*, Sharon Kettering, *Patrons, Brokers and Clients in Seventeenth-Century France* (Oxford University Press, 1986), Roger Mettam, *Power and Faction in Louis XIV's France* (Oxford University Press, 1988), Collins, *The State*, Jean-Laurent Rosenthal, "The Political Economy of Absolutism Reconsidered," in Robert H. Bates *et al.* (eds.), *Analytic Narratives* (Princeton University Press, 1988), 64–108, Hilton L. Root, *The Fountain of Privilege: Political Foundations of Markets in Old Regime France and England* (Berkeley: University of California Press, 1994), Jean Egret, *La Pre-Révolution Française (1787–1788)* (Presses Universitaires de France, 1978), John Brewer, *The Sinews of Power: War, Money and the English State, 1688–1783* (Cambridge, MA: Cambridge University Press, 1990) and Peter R. Campbell, "Absolute Monarchy" in William Doyle (ed.), *The Oxford Handbook of the Ancien Régime* (Oxford University Press, 2012), 11–38. For a brief but cogent description of the property protection and representative institutions literature, see Stephan R. Epstein, *Freedom and Growth: The Rise of States and Markets in Europe, 1300–1750* (London: Routledge, 2000), Chapter 2. See also Mark Dincecco, "Fiscal Centralization, Limited Government, and Public Revenues in Europe, 1650–1913," *Journal of Economic History*, 69: 1 (2009), 48–103 and the fine essays in Hoffman and Norberg (eds.), *Fiscal Crises, Liberty and Representative Government 1450–1789*.

and its empire underscores the trade-off of privilege for security in the context of emergent "instruments of legality" that cemented the crown's constitutional position. In the French case, however, the quid pro quo demanded by the state in exchange for the granting of privilege was *development*! Political support, financial contributions, and acceptance of state mandates were necessary parts of the equation, but, it should be emphasized, minor parts. As we shall see again and again, political consequences factored into state policies that favored some over others, but what made France distinctive is that with reference to liberties of privilege and privileges of liberty, economic issues took pride of place. Without recognizing that commitment, it is impossible to place state-sponsored reforms in their proper context.

While Bourbon administrators sometimes resorted to drastic short-term measures to meet extreme circumstances (especially in 1709–1711, 1745–1747 and 1756–1761), they generally took a long view of how to improve the realm's taxation inequities and financial shortfalls. The Bourbon approach to governance provides a better model for understanding continental Europe than either Britain or Prussia as France was both inward focused and deeply interested in a broader world. French mercantilism emphasized economic growth and increasing employment. "Mercantilists" were just as interested in "improving" the economy as Physiocrats and their fellow travelers. In Chapters 4 and 7, we shall see that the chief difference was in the mix of policies the various groups of reformers sought to implement and the institutional mechanisms they believed could achieve their goals most effectively.[37]

Bourbon administrators' focus on economic development illuminates their astonishing administrative creativity and impressive understanding of the commercial and industrial foundations of power. Beginning under Louis XIV, French officials recognized that economic development was essential to the struggle for the mastery of Europe and acted accordingly, using privilege as both a weapon and a tool. By examining the emergence of the state's use of privilege as a coherent strategy of economic development and tracing the effects of that approach on

[37] Regina Grafe and Alejandra Irigoin, "A Stakeholder Empire: The Political Economy of Spanish Imperial Rule in America," *Economic History Review*, 65: 2 (2012), 609–51, esp. 633. See also Regina Grafe, *Distant Tyranny: Markets, Power, and Backwardness in Spain, 1650–1800* (Princeton University Press, 2011). Epstein, *Freedom and Growth*, Chapter 3. Although the essays gathered in Brewer and Hellmuth (eds.), *Rethinking Leviathan*, expressly avoid consideration of France, their analysis is deeply complementary to mine. This understanding of institutions owes much to the many contributions of Sheilagh Ogilvie, especially her *Institutions and European Trade: Merchant Guilds, 1000–1800* (Cambridge University Press, 2011).

French economy and society, this book seeks to tell a different, sometimes inconvenient, set of stories about the period. As a framework of analysis, privilege sheds light on the contradictions, complexities, and opportunities inherent in the society of orders, the coming of 1789, and the economic legacies of both the Revolution and the old régime in the first decades of the nineteenth century.

2 Privileged enclaves and the guilds

Liberty and regulation

> Immunities, privileges and exemptions must be regarded as abuses which cannot be abolished too soon. Clergymen, nobles or commoners [*roturiers*], we are all equally the subjects of the same King; it is against the essence of being a subject to claim to be distinguished from the rest by the privilege of not paying tribute to the Prince. What I am stating about comparisons between subjects applies equally to the relationship between provinces; in particular the clergy and nobility, as the two premier orders of the Kingdom, must seek to distinguish themselves by their eagerness to contribute to the expenses of the State rather than by immunities and exemptions. Nothing is more important for the good order of a kingdom than uniformity and it is to be wished that it may reign in the law and in taxation.[1]

This provocative rejection of privilege in favor of equality was not a product of the age of Revolution. John Law wrote this passage in *Memoir on Royal Taxes* in 1719, less than a year before he was appointed controller-general of finance. Yet, even as "immunities, privileges and exemptions" increasingly came to be "regarded as abuses" by royal administrators and reformist commentators alike, they were deployed regularly as essential means of jump-starting economic development. This practice began in earnest after 1650 and continued until the 1780s. To understand this seeming paradox, it must be recognized that as a tool of Bourbon political economy, privilege was linked to both status and space.

This chapter explores the economic importance of privileged enclaves. By this term, I mean a distinct territorial entity with the right to create and apply a legal framework different from a greater whole. Such legal authority represented *the* vital aspect of property rights in the early modern era. Almost thirty-five years ago, William H. Sewell, Jr. observed that "privileges everywhere stood in a relationship of superiority to other forms of property" and that "there was a marked tendency at all levels of

[1] Cited by James H. Shennan, *Philippe, Duke of Orléans: Regent of France 1715–1723* (London: Thames and Hudson, 1979), 109–10.

society for material property to be converted into privilege – or into forms of property that gave access to privilege." Unfortunately, Sewell's understanding of privilege has been largely ignored, especially with regard to territorial enclaves.[2]

These numerous entities ranged in size from a feudal holding smaller than a city block to an entire city, or even a whole province. Within French borders, legally separate enclaves like the Comtat Venaissin, centered on Avignon and held by the Pope, and the duchy of Lorraine were the largest territories held by foreign princes, but numerous smaller territories such as the principality of Orange also dotted the economic landscape. These sovereign spaces functioned as privileged enclaves. Nobles, clergy, and certain commoners recognized the profits to be made from using their rights and powers as feudal lords. Thanks to privileges of liberty, innovators could circumvent the limitations on production and exchange imposed by diverse liberties of privilege such as those of the guilds.

Seigneurs' efforts to develop the industrial, commercial, or agricultural potential of either their own properties or those places where they enjoyed judicial rights were almost always carried out in conjunction with agents of the royal state. This partnership was essential to Bourbon state-building and French economic development. After exploring this relationship, I will examine how cities and provinces utilized privilege, not always successfully, as a means of generating commercial and industrial growth.

French administrators and entrepreneurs used privilege to take advantage of the possibilities inherent in the *bricolage* of the Bourbon state. The fits and starts of French state formation left a legacy of loopholes available for imaginative entrepreneurs and resourceful officials to exploit. Economists and economic historians often denigrate privilege for encouraging rent-seeking behavior. Rent-seeking behavior is characterized by the attempt to obtain a greater share of existing wealth through manipulation of the sociopolitical environment rather than by

2 Renauld Bueb, "La théorie de l'enclave dans le droit féodale de l'Ancien Régime," in Paul Delasalle and André Ferrer (eds.), *Les enclaves territoriales aux Temps Modernes (XVIe-XVIIIe siècles: Actes du Colloque de Besançon)* (Besançon: Presses Universitaires Franc-Comtoises, 2000), 9–22, esp. 10–11. Many Anglo-Saxon explanations of superior British economic success focus on property rights. For a stimulating discussion, see Alessandro Stanziani, *Rules of Exchange: French Capitalism in Comparative Perspective, Eighteenth to Early Twentieth Centuries* (Cambridge University Press, 2012), 38–57. See also Robert C. Allen, *The British Industrial Revolution in Global Perspective* (Cambridge University Press, 2009), 5, 125, 129. On the notion of property, see William H. Sewell, Jr., *Work & Revolution in France: The Language of Labor from the Old Regime to 1848* (Cambridge University Press, 1980), 115–33, 119. I owe this observation to David K. Smith.

creating new wealth. I argue that this scholarly criticism, although accurate as far as it goes, focuses only on one facet of the situation. Spatially delineated legal rights stemming from privilege offered a host of opportunities for entrepreneurialism – some legal, some not. These rights functioned as institutions in the sense pioneered by Douglass C. North. Hemmed in by tax-collecting inequities, limited resources, frequent wars, and recurrent domestic political crises, Bourbon administrators polished this diamond in the rough as the most effective tool of economic development available to them. The remarkable success of their approach to fostering industrial and commercial growth testified to their resourcefulness and fortitude. At the same time, the scale and scope of economic growth based on privilege reveals the vast potential of France's old régime.[3]

Seigneurs and the guild system: loopholes and economic opportunities

Seigneurialism framed the opportunities and constraints faced by many French entrepreneurs. Feudalism is blamed because France's agricultural productivity lagged behind its Dutch and English neighbors. This criticism emphasizes heavy-handed use of feudal rights by seigneurs as the critical limiting factor. Robert Forster, however, demonstrated noble landlords' entrepreneurial dynamism, while Philip T. Hoffman concluded that the behavior of privileged landowners did not "block economic growth."[4] Feudal rights and dues were vital parts of their analyses. These important accounts demonstrate profound variations in noble attitudes toward profit and its maximization, as discussed in Chapter 1. Nobles used diverse methods to manage their various types of landed property and wide range of potentially profitable feudal rights. Although commoners could purchase these legal rights and not all high-ranking clergy were nobles, the vast majority of seigneurs were noble. In their exploitation of their rights and duties, seigneurs' social origins signified little difference.

3 Gail Bossenga, "Estates, Orders and Corps," in William Doyle (ed.), *The Oxford Handbook of the Ancien Régime* (Oxford University Press, 2012), 141–66, esp. 141–42, Robert D. Tollison and Robert Ekelund, *Mercantilism as a Rent Seeking Society* (College Station: Texas A&M University Press, 1982), Hilton L. Root, *The Fountain of Privilege: Political Foundations of Markets in Old Regime France and England* (Berkeley: University of California Press, 1994), and Douglass C. North, *Institutions, Institutional Change and Economic Performance* (Cambridge University Press, 1990).

4 Robert Forster, "The Noble as Landlord in the Region of Toulouse at the End of the Old Regime," *Journal of Economic History*, 17: 2 (1957), 224–44 and *The Nobility of Toulouse in the Eighteenth Century: A Social and Economic Study* (Baltimore: Johns Hopkins University Press, 1960). See also Philip T. Hoffman, *Growth in a Traditional Society: The French Countryside 1450–1815* (Princeton University Press, 1996), 7.

What concerns us here is the economic potential of the legal authority available to seigneurs, especially those exercising *haute justice* (high justice) in criminal and civil affairs. High justice has typically been examined within a judicial framework or in political terms. Economically, the most important legal authority conveyed by high justice was the power of *police*. Here too scholars have emphasized the judicial and political impact of *police* power in maintaining the social order. Since almost all old régime economic regulation was based on *police* power, *hauts justiciers* (seigneurs with this right) governed many and perhaps most markets and workplaces.[5] In agriculture, beyond helping to spread advanced techniques, this authority had limited effectiveness. In commercial exchange, and especially in industry, seigneurial authority allowed privileged enclaves to assume a major role in the French economy. Seigneurs had the right to create spaces – conceived of both physically and conceptually – that encouraged innovation. Liberty was no absolute. A relative absence of regulation conveyed liberty in economic matters. As a policy tool, *hauts justiciers*' *police* powers could be applied to a wide array of goals. In some places and times, this authority preserved a stagnant set of economic relations, but many seigneurs deployed their rights to promote commercial and industrial development.

Seigneurs with *police* powers regulated markets and the world of work in both rural and urban spaces. Michael Sonenscher believes that every significant urban area in France had at least one enclave. Large cities frequently had multiple enclaves either inside their walls or close by in the *faubourgs* or *banlieue* (suburbs or outskirts). Paris had twelve major enclaves and Rouen had fourteen. The total number of privileged enclaves is unknown. Unsurprisingly, the economic importance of these enclaves, within regionally fragmented markets, much less for the realm as a whole, has been undervalued by contemporaries and later scholars.[6]

Seigneurs' *police* powers could authorize many privileges of liberty. Producers could be exempted from many regulations and allowed to avoid oversight from guilds or tax collectors. New or different

[5] Verdicts involving capital punishment or penalties of more than 1,000 *livres* could be appealed either to a *parlement* or to the crown. Only crimes against the king and counterfeiting were exempt from the jurisdiction of high justice. Marcel Marion, *Dictionnaire des institutions de la France aux XVIIe et XVIIIe siècles* (New York: Burt Franklin, 1968 [1923]), 320.

[6] The two previous paragraphs are based on Guy Lemarchand, *La fin du féodalisme dans le pays de Caux: Conjoncture économique et démographique et structure sociale dans une région de grande culture de la crise du XVIIe siècle à la stabilisation de la Révolution (1640–1795)* (Lille: ANRT, 1989), 267–91, Jeff Horn, "'A Beautiful Madness': Privilege, the Machine Question and Industrial Development in Normandy in 1789," *Past & Present*, 217 (2012), 149–85, and Michael Sonenscher, *Work & Wages: Natural Law, Politics and the Eighteenth-Century French Trades* (Cambridge University Press, 1989), 64.

manufacturing techniques and technologies could be explored and novel products could be designed and then modified according to entrepreneurs' perceptions of market demand. Production could be organized more efficiently or into larger enterprises. Seigneurs could permit anyone to enter most trades, including, in numerous *hautes justices*, women and religious minorities, thereby multiplying the pool of potential entrepreneurs. Seigneurs could provide these privileges of liberty at almost no cost, either to themselves or to the central state. Even elites or institutions that dabbled only episodically in economic improvement could benefit from this strategy. Once established, France's strong emphasis on legal precedent enabled privileges of liberty to be overseen by royal administrators working with seigneurial officials. Such opportunities existed throughout the early modern era, but they were taken advantage of far more systematically after 1750.

Not all seigneurs with the right of high justice carved out economically significant privileged enclaves. This failure stemmed from lack of interest, the encroachment of other institutions, or the absence of markets, resources, or labor reserves. Turning a privileged enclave into productive space required a convergence of legal, material, and personnel assets, which were more common in northern France and along the coasts and major rivers. The abilities and energy of individual entrepreneurs and groups of workers mattered, but not as much as the legal and physical environment and access to markets and raw materials.

As shown in Chapter 1, a dearth of support from the royal government doomed the efforts of the guilds of Paris to assert control over the faubourg Saint-Antoine. However, this pattern did not apply to the city's other enclaves. In legal terms, the Temple, Saint-Jean-de-Lateran, Saint-Martin-des-Champs, Saint-Germain-des-Prés, the Hospital of the Trinité, Saint-Denis de la Chartre, la rue de Lourcine in the faubourg Saint-Marcel, the Gobelins royal tapestry manufacture, the Prévôt de l'Hôtel, the Hospital of the Quinze-Vingts, and the Cour Saint-Benoît, along with certain educational institutions and the mansions of royal princes, were controlled by seigneurs with the right of high justice (unlike the faubourg Saint-Antoine). Before 1675, a number of seigneurs created and managed their own *corporate* regimes. Other territories were designated as "free" of guild control. That year, the state downgraded seigneurial authorities in Paris in favor of the judicial power of the Châtelet, cutting the number of *hauts justices* from forty-four to twelve. Extending the authority of Paris' guilds into the suburbs curtailed the possibilities of developing new privileged sites. Seigneurial power shrank even further in 1746. In most Parisian enclaves, artisans required guild certification and were subject to guild rules. Goods and workshops were liable to guild inspection. Only the clerical seigneurs of Saint-Germain-des Prés, Saint-Jean-de-Lateran, Saint-Martin-des-Champs, and Saint-Denis-de-la-Charge successfully maintained the "liberty of work."[7]

Paris' guild wardens attempted to extend their authority over the privileged enclaves in 1704–1705, 1716–1727, 1734, 1739, 1749, 1759, 1761–1769, 1776–1780, and 1783. Many seigneurs failed to maintain their enclave's freedom. The effectiveness of guild inspections waxed and waned, especially at the boundary between trades. But the nearly universal legal rights of inspection held by Parisian guilds after 1727 do not seem to have undermined either the carnivalesque atmosphere or the liberty to work in what Balzac described in *Cousin Bette* as "the sovereign faubourg . . . the faubourg Saint-Antoine."[8]

Official unwillingness or inability to exert control over the faubourg Saint-Antoine was mirrored in Bordeaux. In this bustling port and booming metropolis, the regulatory privileges of ecclesiastical seigneurs clashed with the guilds' "exclusive privileges" over artisanal production and the sale of manufactured goods.[9] Bordeaux's masters successfully restricted the economic impact of seigneurial rights in law, though not in practice. Geography, demographic factors, and the legal environment shaped the creation and maintenance of Bordeaux's privileged enclaves.

[7] The primary sources regarding the privileges of Paris' enclaves are found in AN F12 781B-E. See Alain Thillay, *Le faubourg Saint Antoine et ses "faux ouvriers": La liberté du travail à Paris aux XVIIe et XVIIIe siècles* (Champ Vallon, 2002), 108–13, Sonenscher, *Work & Wages*, 64–66, Alan Williams, *The Police of Paris 1718–1789* (Baton Rouge: Louisiana State University Press, 1979), 166–67, and Steven L. Kaplan, "Les corporations, les 'faux ouvriers' et le faubourg Saint-Antoine au XVIIIe siècle," *Annales. Histoire, sciences sociales*, 43: 2 (1988), 353–78. On the seigneurs of Paris, see Bernard Quilliet, "Les fiefs parisiens et leurs seigneurs laïcs au XVIIIème siècle," *Histoire, économie et société*, 1: 4 (1982), 565–80.

[8] On the ups and downs of guild authority, contrast the protections for the faubourg Saint-Antoine in the *Avis des Députés du Commerce sur la Requete des Officiers Aulneurs et visiteurs de Toiles de la ville et faubourg de Paris*, n.d. [1739], AN F12 703, with the more expansive authority granted in the *Arrêts du Conseil d'État* of February 21 and May 19, 1764, cited by Thillay, *Le Faubourg Saint-Antoine*, 109, n. 2. On the atmosphere of the faubourg, see Steven Laurence Kaplan, "Social Classification and Representation in the Corporate World of Eighteenth-Century France: Turgot's 'Carnival,'" in Steven Laurence Kaplan and Cynthia J. Koepp (eds.), *Work in France: Representations, Meaning, Organization, and Practice* (Ithaca, NY: Cornell University Press, 1986), 176–228. The quote from Balzac is cited by Kaplan, "Les corporations," 361, and comes from *La Comédie humaine de Honoré de Balzac*, trans. Katherine Prescott Wormeley, vol. 25 (Boston: Roberts Brothers, 1896), 544.

[9] An early version of the material on Bordeaux appeared in Jeff Horn, "Privileged Enclaves: Entrepreneurial Opportunities in Eighteenth-Century France," in Kathryn A. Edwards and Carol E. Harrison (eds.), *Proceedings of the Western Society for French History: Selected Papers of the 2004 Annual Meeting*, 32 (Ann Arbor: Scholarly Publishing Office of the University of Michigan University Library, 2006), 29–45.

Compared to other major French cities, the regulation of production in Bordeaux was incomplete and slipshod. Of the city's eighty-five organized trades, only thirty-nine had statutes issued by the crown and registered by the *parlement* (a law court with certain legislative attributes) of the province of Guyenne. Ten other trades, such as the butchers, ropemakers, and stockings-makers, had informal regulations without official status. An astonishing thirty-six trades, such as the clockmakers, wool merchants, barrel-makers and furriers, were recognized as "free trades" open to anyone. To give a sense of the relative importance of these groupings, in 1762, 40 percent of the city's artisans labored in recognized trades, 6 percent were in regulated trades, and 54 percent labored in unregulated trades. These figures do not include the vast numbers of false or illicit workers who thronged the city.

The city's rapidly expanding population and trade provided opportunities for Bordeaux's guilds, but their lack of legal protections constituted a threat to their monopolies. Fueled by a twentyfold increase in the value of the goods coming into and out of its port, Bordeaux grew from 45,000 inhabitants in 1700 to 110,000 in 1790, thanks to immigration. By the 1780s, artisans made up 45 percent of the city's population. In this context, two of France's most economically important privileged enclaves emerged: the *sauvetats* (clerical reserves) of Saint-Seurin and Saint-André.[10]

Beginning in the thirteenth century, the canons of the collegial chapter of the basilica of Saint-Seurin and the cathedral chapter of Saint-André collectively exercised high justice as seigneurs of their parishes. Identified by crosses on the streets, Saint-André was enclosed within the city walls, while Saint-Seurin was located in the suburbs. Both enclaves were thoroughly integrated into the city's economy. With approximately 400 registered artisanal workshops in 1777, along with thousands of false and illicit workers, the two *sauvetats* housed a considerable percentage of the industrial and commercial population of the urban agglomeration. Although entrepreneurs from Saint-Seurin and Saint-André were officially prohibited from selling their wares within city limits, even the most painstaking guild-run inspections could not keep goods made in the

[10] The two previous paragraphs are based on Paul Butel and Jean-Pierre Poussou, *La Vie quotidienne à Bordeaux au XVIIIe siècle* (Hachette, 1980), 27–28, 140, Daniel Heimmermann, "The Guilds of Bordeaux, *les métiers libres* and the *sauvetats* of Saint-Seurin and Saint-André," in Barry Rothaus (ed.), *Proceedings of the Western Society for French History: Selected Papers of the Annual Meeting* (Boulder: University Press of Colorado, 1998), 25, Bernard Gallinato, *Les corporations à Bordeaux à la fin de l'ancien régime: Vie et mort d'un mode d'organisation du travail* (Lille: ANRT, 1988), 19, 286, 290–95, and François-Georges Pariset (ed.), *Bordeaux au XVIIIe siècle* (Bordeaux: Fédération historique du Sud-Ouest, 1968), 196.

sauvetats from flooding into Bordeaux. By 1790, more than half the population of the metropolitan area lived outside the city proper, shifting the dynamics of the urban market. Saint-Seurin alone had nearly 19,000 inhabitants, making it more populous than all but thirty French cities. To preserve their increasingly contested monopoly, the wardens of Bordeaux's guilds attempted a variety of tactics.

Under the protection, and rather lax oversight, of their ecclesiastical seigneurs, leather-, wood-, and metal-working as well as the production of cotton textiles and luxury goods for export increasingly clustered in Saint-Seurin and Saint-André. The rapidly expanding building trades were also headquartered there. Bordeaux's first factories – making starch and porcelain – were built in Saint-Seurin. Other innovations both in the organization of labor and in the use of new technologies, including the forging of crucible steel and the use of coke in iron-making, were found exclusively in the privileged enclaves. Unimpeded by guild regulations enforcing traditional methods, entrepreneurs in the *sauvetats* developed new products and executed fresh designs. In a 1782 petition to the *parlement* of Guyenne, the joiners' guild of Bordeaux attempted to denigrate the *sauvetats*' entrepreneurs, referring to them as "*novateurs*" (innovators).[11] This insult would have been taken as a compliment in Saint-Seurin and Saint-André. By the end of the old régime, attitudes toward innovation increasingly divided the guild masters of Bordeaux from entrepreneurs in Saint-Seurin and Saint-André.

The canons of Saint-Seurin and Saint-André permitted liberty to reign. Their policies strengthened the competitiveness of Bordeaux's industrial sector by allowing any qualified worker to become a master in their jurisdictions. In Saint-Seurin, a worker did not have to serve an apprenticeship or spend time as a journeyman. To become a master locksmith, a worker had only to present a masterpiece and pay a fee of 80 *livres*. By explicitly refusing to allow guild regulation to prescribe techniques or to exclude potential entrepreneurs, the seigneurs of Saint-Seurin and Saint-André turned a negative into a positive. They rebuffed the guild system and minimized industrial regulation to create territorial and legal spaces where entrepreneurs, workers, and consumers were comparatively free to try new things.

"Innovators" located in the *sauvetats* enabled the metropolis of southwestern France to imitate technological progress occurring in other places and to produce goods that satisfied the demands of the fickle whims of fashion. Since much of the *sauvetats*' production was exported, these competitive activities aided the French economy as a

[11] *Adresse à Nosseigneurs de Parlement*, n.d. [1782], AD Gironde 3J E703.

whole. They also remind us of the importance of location: market access allowed these privileged enclaves to be successful. Without the tolerant attitudes toward technical innovation that prevailed in these clerical reserves, this bustling hub of the Atlantic economy would have had fewer products to export, thereby limiting growth.

In the eighteenth century, guild masters and the *sauvetats*' entrepreneurs squabbled over raw materials and skilled labor. Geography played a major role in the guilds' ability to manage access to raw materials. Bordeaux's relative isolation from supplies of most raw materials and the region's rudimentary road network increased reliance on water transport. Goods generally arrived either down the Garonne River or up the Gironde estuary. Control of the docks was essential to the guilds' position. For example, anyone selling hides had to offer Bordeaux's master glove-makers first choice. The stock was then picked over by the city's other leather-working *corporations* before a producer in one of the enclaves even had a crack at it. Coal arriving at the city docks was also monopolized by the guilds, impinging on iron forging in the *sauvetats*. In theory, these rules existed to ensure the quality of guild output, but the masters' domination of vital raw materials arriving via water compounded the lack of alternative supplies to restrain some industries in the privileged enclaves. Guild controls also encouraged rent-seeking as well as profit-taking through smuggling and fraud.[12]

Supplies of skilled labor were as constrained as stocks of raw materials. Bordeaux's *corporations* deployed a "right of first refusal" to prevent journeymen from working in the privileged enclaves. This authority was particularly important because the city's guilds trained relatively few apprentices. The local economy relied on the regular arrival of experienced laborers. Journeymen were supposed to register with their guild in order to be placed. In 1782, the *parlement* of Guyenne ruled that "Masters as well as non-masters in the *sauvetats* may not accept

[12] The four previous paragraphs are based on *Adresse au Contrôleur Général*, July 31, 1777, AN F12 757A, *Almanach de commerce, d'arts et métiers pour la ville de Bordeaux et de la province pour l'année commune 1779* (Bordeaux: Bergeret, 1779), AM Bordeaux 9Ca 1, *Mémoire pour les maîtres cloûtiers de la Ville de Bordeaux*, n.d. [March 1762], AN F12 757A, *Mémoire pour les maitres serruriers sans jurandes habitants la ville et fauxbourgs de Bordeaux responsif à celui des maitres jurandés dans la même ville*, n.d. [1780], AN F12 757A, Marguerite Castel, "La formation topographique du quartier Saint-Seurin," *Revue historique de Bordeaux et du département de la Gironde*, 14: 3 (1921), 165, Ariste Ducaunnès-Duval, *Inventaire sommaire des registres de la Jurade: 1520 à 1783*, vol. 3 (Bordeaux: Nouvelle F. Pech, 1905), 196, Alan Forrest, *Society and Politics in Revolutionary Bordeaux* (Oxford University Press, 1975), 13, Daniel Heimmermann, "Work and Corporate Life in Old Regime France: The Leather Artisans of Bordeaux (1740–1791)" (PhD dissertation, Marquette University, 1994), 12, Heimmermann, "The Guilds of Bordeaux," 29, and Gallinato, *Les corporations à Bordeaux*, 47–48.

workers who have not first registered with the community." Journeymen were also required to inform the guild when they left a job to request a new placement. Skilled workers were prohibited from finding their own positions or from accepting the blandishments of other masters.[13]

The joiners' guild grudgingly admitted Bordeaux's competitive disadvantage vis-à-vis the privileged enclaves. Its wardens acknowledged that skilled laborers frequently left their employ when they tried to discipline them, forcing masters to poach workers from one another to make up for their inability to attract workers from outside the city or to match the working conditions found in the *sauvetats*. The wardens responded by claiming that control over labor was intrinsic to their privileges. Their petition asserted that guild masters should monopolize "the best and the most skilled workers because they have more right to public trust because of their authentic proofs of [superior] capacity. It is only just that the masters have the most capable workers to help them."[14] This vision of *corporate* privilege had powerful support in legal precedent and from both municipal and royal officials. In practice, however, journeymen generally avoided formal placement in favor of the liberties of the privileged enclaves where their associations or brotherhoods, known as *compagnonnages*, held sway.[15]

The liberties afforded by the privileged canons of Saint-Seurin and Saint-André protected journeymen who resisted the domination of Bordeaux's masters. When a journeyman in trades with brotherhoods such as the carpenters, locksmiths, blacksmiths, saddlers, stonemasons, tailors, cabinetmakers, and shoemakers arrived in Bordeaux, he immediately contacted his "brothers" at the inn or cabaret that served as their headquarters, which was located in one of the *sauvetats*. For a payment of one *livre* upon arrival and three more upon departure, a placement officer (*rôleur*) found the new arrival not only a job but a place to live and eat. By submitting to the discipline of the "head journeyman," arrivals accepted the brotherhood's placement and attended its ceremonies and festivals as well as masses for its patron saint.

Compagnonnages strenuously enforced their control over placement as well as the rights and privileges of journeymen. Groups of journeymen frequently banded together to visit shops where masters employed skilled

13 *Arrêt de la cour de parlement de Bordeaux*, January 26, 1785, reproduced in the *Journal de Guienne*, 162 (February 9, 1785).

14 *Adresse à Nosseigneurs de Parlement*, n.d. [1782].

15 The two previous paragraphs are based on Gallinato, *Les corporations à Bordeaux*, 47–51, Butel and Poussou, *La Vie quotidienne à Bordeaux au XVIIIe siècle*, 145, and *Lettre des Jurats de Bordeaux à M. Joly de Fleury, Ministre des Finances*, September 23, 1783, AM Bordeaux BB179 registre, 152–54.

workers who were not journeymen or who had not joined the brotherhood. Those workers were forced to leave the shop and beaten. In December 1778, a master tailor who refused to pay a journeyman before the completion of the job was bullied by twelve journeymen who forced him to turn over the money on the spot. As these incidents suggest, Bordeaux's brotherhoods were aggressive and prone to violence. The journeymen's most devastating tactic, "damnation" or boycott, relied on group solidarity.

By "damning" a specific workshop, a guild, or even a whole city, groups of journeymen could impose their will regarding wages, hiring, and working conditions on individual masters, an entire trade, or on the city itself. Boycotts repeatedly struck the saddlers (1760–1766, 1773), locksmiths (1766, 1781), bakers (1768), cabinetmakers (1781, 1787), and turners (1771–1776). In 1766, journeymen locksmiths damned Bordeaux's guild for a year. Every journeyman in the city left their job, but to "better manage their plan" some journeymen remained at work in Saint-Seurin and Saint-André to ensure that no newly arriving locksmith took a position in the city of Bordeaux. Fifteen years later, the master cabinetmakers griped that their journeymen threatened damnation if they did not "receive an increase in their salary . . . and for work to start an hour later and finish an hour earlier . . . They also wanted masters to pay each of them fifteen *sols* every year on their patron's feast day in place of the meal they used to receive."[16] Journeymen's brotherhoods frequently protected themselves by disputing the city watch's control of the streets. In conjunction with the guilds' dependence on skilled labor from elsewhere and the safe havens afforded by the privileged enclaves, Bordeaux emerged as a major stop on the *tour de France* that journeymen took before seeking to become a master.[17]

Bordeaux's masters defended their liberties of privilege by increasing their efforts to inspect all goods entering the city and by limiting guild memberships to family members. The inadequate benefits and considerable expense of becoming a master encouraged journeymen to establish shops in Saint-Seurin or Saint-André rather than invest the time and effort to join a guild. In trades such as shoemaking, tailoring, cabinetmaking, button-making, pin-making, and construction

16 Cited by Jean Cavaignac, "Le compagnonnage dans les luttes ouvrières au XVIIIe siècle: L'exemple de Bordeaux," *Bibliothèque de l'École des chartes*, 126: 2 (1969 [1968]), 397.

17 The three previous paragraphs are based on Heimmerman, "Work and Corporate Life," 532–35, 548–50, Butel and Poussou, *La Vie quotidienne à Bordeaux*, 135–38, Cynthia M. Truant, *The Rites of Labor: Brotherhoods of Compagnonnage in Old and New Regime France* (Ithaca, NY: Cornell University Press, 1988), 138–47, and Cavaignac, "Le compagnonnage," 391–98.

(*charpentiers* and *architects*), there were more shops in the privileged enclaves than in the city itself. From the 1760s, the masters' fragile position led them to insist evermore urgently on the priority of *corporate* privileges over seigneurial privileges.[18]

Neither the military exigencies of the Seven Years' War nor express commands from high-ranking Bourbon administrators deterred Bordeaux's guilds from pressing their claims. In 1761–1762, Pierre Babaud de la Chaussade received a contract to supply metalwork for four warships under construction. This influential noble held royal writ to eight seigneuries and also ran four large-scale forges along the Loire River. De la Chaussade was an innovative producer who transplanted forging techniques from western Germany and the Netherlands to his "industrial-seigneurial labor force," to borrow historian Paul Bamford's useful phrase. He brought master metalworkers and journeymen in a variety of trades from La Rochelle and from the arsenal at Rochefort to provide nails, hardware, and anchors for the navy. As part of his royal commission, de la Chaussade was permitted to set up retail outlets in ports where he engaged in military supply.

Conflict in Bordeaux arose for three reasons. First, the guilds feared to compete with de la Chaussade. Not only were his goods technically superior, but they were produced by workers who earned less, since wages were lower along the Loire than in Bordeaux. Nor did he have to pay guild membership costs. The wardens worried that de la Chaussade would undercut their prices and destroy their monopoly. Second, wardens from the metal-working guilds refused to allow de la Chaussade to recruit journeymen in Bordeaux for military work outside the city because of the difficulty of replacing them. Third, the guilds objected to de la Chaussade's plan to have two large forges located in Saint-Seurin complete some unfinished goods before shipboard installation.

To defeat de la Chaussade, the guilds relied on the municipality. A mayor and six aldermen (*jurats*) governed the city. Collectively, they wielded both executive authority and *police* power. As seigneurs of twenty suburban parishes, they were also fervent defenders of the liberty of privilege. On behalf of the locksmiths, nailsmiths, and blacksmiths, the

[18] René Passet, *L'Industrie dans la généralité de Bordeaux sous l'intendant Tourny* (Bordeaux: Éditions Bière, 1954), 98, Gallinato, *Les corporations à Bordeaux*, 286, *État des Corps et Communautés libres ou faisette leurs ouvrages dans de lieux privilegiés*, 1776, and *État des Corps et communautés d'Arts et Métiers de la ville de Bordeaux qui ont des statuts*, 1776, both in AD Gironde C1005.

municipal attorney petitioned the royal government "to maintain these trades' exclusive privilege of working without alteration against de la Chaussade's fatal infringements." The petition claimed that this noble wished to "destroy statutes authorized by the king that would introduce a prejudice against the well-being of the military and the particular interests of the inhabitants of Bordeaux." The municipality also threatened de la Chaussade's local agent, physically prevented his metalworkers from leaving the city, and seized his goods before they reached safe haven in Saint-Seurin. In the countersuit, de la Chaussade complained that guild wardens had contracted several merchants to provide semifinished iron brought from abroad to be sold at a loss to undermine his enterprise. In wartime, such misuse of their *police* and inspection privileges, de la Chaussade asserted, was "contrary to the good of the state and of the public."

In vain, the council of commerce ordered the Bordelais to cease and desist. De la Chaussade believed that the intendant could overcome the guilds' "cabal" against him. He was wrong. Guild intransigence outlasted the war and de la Chaussade's willingness to invest time, energy, money, and political capital in opening up Bordeaux's metal-working market. Guild success in rebuffing de la Chaussade emboldened them to renew their campaign to enforce their monopoly against privileged enclaves and disobedient journeymen alike.[19]

Supported by a succession of intendants, the municipality acting as seigneur successfully imposed some guild privileges on the *sauvetats*. All overlapping legal rights were resolved in favor of city interests. In 1759, Bordeaux's newly created police were authorized to enter the *sauvetats*, and in 1773 they could patrol. Limited guild inspection was imposed in 1769 and a few guilds received more extensive regulatory powers in 1783. The municipality issued ordinances aimed at cracking down on journeymen's violence and insubordination. But repeated edicts handed down to artisans and workers in these two enclaves

[19] The four previous paragraphs rely on the *Almanach historique de la province de Guienne pour l'année bissextile 1760*, 338, AM Bordeaux 4Ca 1, Anonymous, *Mémoire*, 1761, Charles-Robert Boutin, *Lettre à Trudaine*, April 16, 1762, Maire, Lieutenant de Maire, Jurats, Gouverneurs de Bordeaux, *Lettre à Trudaine*, September 2, 1762, Pierre Babaud de la Chaussade, *Lettre au Contrôleur-Général*, September 17, 1762, and letters from de la Chaussade to Trudaine dated March 19, October 20, and November 9, 1762. The quote is found in all three addresses, dated March 21, 1762. The final quotes are from de la Chaussade's letter of October 20, 1762. All these documents are found in AN F12 757A. On de la Chaussade's family and enterprises, see Paul W. Bamford, *Privilege and Profit: A Business Family in Eighteenth-Century France* (Philadelphia: University of Pennsylvania Press, 1988), 184–88. He emphasizes de la Chaussade's conflict with Bordeaux's merchants rather than with the city's guilds.

were no more effective than royal commands to the city's guild masters had been.

In the decade before the outbreak of the Revolution, the wardens of several guilds repeatedly complained that, protected by the lax oversight of their seigneurs, the journeymen of Saint-Seurin and Saint-André completely ignored their orders. Cabinetmakers protested in 1781 that "forever animated by a spirit of independence, journeymen live only to subject their masters to a horrible despotism."[20] In practice, the liberty provided by the privileges of the *sauvetats* of Saint-Seurin and Saint-André remained in effect until the Revolution of 1789.

Wages rose after 1740 as enhanced administrative attention to "workers' interests" sought to curb the independence of entrepreneurs and journeymen in Bordeaux's privileged enclaves.[21] Liberties granted by ecclesiastical seigneurs survived decades of concerted attack by the municipality, the city's guild wardens, and the intendant, in large measure because an agitated work environment fueled the threat from below. By making use of their privileges, the canons of Saint-Seurin and Saint-André boosted Bordeaux's hot-house growth in the second half of the eighteenth century.[22]

In Paris and Bordeaux, metropolitan economic growth was linked closely to the creation of privileged enclaves established by clerical seigneurs. They permitted chaotic, fractious work environments to bloom, which helped larger enclaves like the faubourg Saint-Antoine and the *sauvetat* Saint-Seurin to endure the interference of guild wardens, municipal authorities, and royal administrators. In these two instances, privilege was used negatively. Liberty stemmed from a relative absence of regulation. Although the patterns occurring in Paris and Bordeaux could be multiplied, these examples should not overshadow official concern about the license that went with the liberty found in these enclaves. Seigneurial enclaves like those that emerged in Paris and Bordeaux did not represent the most common use of privilege related to industrial matters. In many French cities, royal administrators and their local deputies deployed privilege positively and prescriptively to encourage industrial growth and provide goods for exchange.

20 Cited by Cavaignac, "Le compagnonnage," 401–02.

21 The quote is from a note by the secretary of the intendant in 1787 cited by Pariset (ed.), *Bordeaux au XVIIIe siècle*, 361.

22 *Avis des Députés du Commerce sur la demande des Maitres de la communauté des Menuisiers de Bordeaux*, March 7, 1769, AN F12 715, AM Bordeaux, *Livre des privilèges* (Bordeaux: G. Gounouilou, 1878), 581–85, 654–59, and Heimmerman, "Work and Corporate Life," 573.

Cities and provinces: the conflict of guild and territorial privileges

Territorial privilege often clashed with *corporate* privilege. Guild monopolies concentrated production, but privileged producers generally preferred maintaining their position to either innovation or expansion. Royal administrators' confidence in urban guilds' ability to improve the realm's industrial position so marked under Louis XIV faded under his successors, especially after 1750. But privilege remained at the heart of French industrial policy until the outbreak of the Revolution. French officials increasingly made use of territorial rights to create privileged enclaves where the strictures of the *corporate* system either did not apply or were much reduced.

Cities occupied a paradoxical position in French political economy. In feudal society, towns were always more "free," that is, more privileged, than the countryside. With urban privileges of liberty came obligations: to belong to some sort of *corporate* body and to help care for the poor, among others. Cities possessed the most common, the most widespread, and the most economically important territorial privileges. Urban privileges of liberty functioned as both a pole of attraction and a pole of repulsion on the compass of the Bourbon monarchy's approach to economic policy. Merchandise made by privileged producers in French cities filled market niches and propelled both domestic and foreign trade. Quality goods of guild manufacture satisfied consumers from Pondicherry to Port-au-Prince. At the same time, restrictions stemming from privilege, especially guild privilege, drove innovative producers and a great deal of low-wage handwork out of urban spaces and into the countryside. The dynamic tension between the poles diversified the spaces available for entrepreneurialism and generated energy that powered economic growth.[23]

All too frequently, historians focus attention on either the solely positive or the solely negative role of privilege. We must recognize that both aspects were embedded in the early modern economy. The complementary results of overlapping and competing privileges must also be understood to reconstruct and evaluate industry and commerce between the age of Louis XIV and 1789. Used positively, privilege protected

[23] Pierre Goubert, *The Ancien Régime: French Society, 1600–1750*, trans. Steve Cox (New York: Harper & Row, 1973 [1969]), 205–08. For a view of guilds as "regressive," see Paul Butel, *L'Économie française au XVIIIe siècle* (SEDES, 1993), 205–06. On the reurbanization of work, see Pierre Dardel, *Commerce, Industrie et Navigation à Rouen et au Havre au XVIIIème siècle: Rivalité croissante entre ces deux ports*, vol. 1, *La Conjoncture* (Rouen: Société libre d'émulation de la Seine-Maritime, 1966), 126–31.

producers. Used negatively, privilege shunted industrial development into new areas. Cities were at the heart of French industrial policy in the early modern era, forming the primary locus of both positive and negative outcomes.

Jean-Baptiste Colbert pursued a two-pronged strategy in deploying privilege to encourage urban industrial production. Once it became clear that the drastic increase in tariff rates imposed in 1667 was insufficient to stimulate French manufacturing, Colbert became a partisan of monopolies based on privilege. He granted exclusive privileges to numerous royal manufactures, both publicly and privately run; to chartered companies tasked with developing French overseas trade; to inventors, innovators, or entrepreneurs who expanded vital industries; and most importantly to guilds. No other figure in French history extended privileged monopolies so wide or so far. Although we will encounter clear limits to Colbert's reliance on monopoly and his adoption of the privilege of liberty (see Chapters 4, 5, and 7), the essential point is that the use of privilege and monopoly was inextricably linked to Bourbon state-building.

For Colbert, guild oversight was the most effective means of regulating the production process. As part of a comprehensive effort to create hierarchies in commercial and industrial matters, guilds supervised individual producers, disciplined workers, and ensured the training of apprentices. Generally speaking, guilds concentrated production, facilitated state oversight, and encouraged entrepreneurs to think about satisfying demand over the long term. Beginning in 1669, aldermen exercised the *police* of manufactures in cities without seigneurs. A consultative royal council of commerce advised Colbert from 1664 to 1676, but he remained the linchpin of royal policymaking. As secretary of state of the king's household as well as controller-general, he received reports concerning the *police* of manufacturing from municipal aldermen, seigneurial judges, and royal intendants alike. Between 1664 and 1683, Colbert presided basically unchallenged over the French economy.

Colbert had high hopes for the new administrative structure with its clear lines of authority. He intended to both break down local customs and knit together fragmented markets. Colbert did not immediately seek to tap the financial opportunities afforded by guild, urban, and provincial privileges. That soon changed. Gail Bossenga argues that Colbert's efforts to rationalize markets and improve the quality of French manufactures were tied more to the concrete problem of raising money than to an abstract, long-term problem like fixing the economy.

Increasing tax revenue was vital, especially to attract tax farmers and investors. That privilege could support both goals does not lessen its significance as a tool of economic policy. In extending the guilds' sway, Colbert's positive economic goals included fostering international competitiveness, establishing uniformity and order, and rationalizing the productive and commercial environment, all while building up the monarchy's bureaucratic capacity.[24]

The expansion of guild power under Colbert should not, however, be overestimated or assumed. Although the number of *corporations* in Paris grew by twenty-five in 1673–1674 to reach 114, this extension was the result of the state's slow assumption of greater authority over the suburbs and privileged enclaves dating from 1657, when there were only sixty guilds. Some cities experienced drastic *corporate* expansion: Dijon received twelve new guilds; Châlons-sur-Marne eleven; Rennes nine; and Lyon, Poitiers, and Tours each got eight. In essential sectors like woolens, where France was at a competitive disadvantage in international markets, Colbert insisted on spreading guilds in hopes of achieving import substitution. In the province of Poitou alone, he imposed drapers or dyers guilds on 157 cities or large villages.

In many other places, expanding *corporate* organization of artisanal production was far less significant. Bordeaux got only one new guild; Amiens and Carcassonne two; Montpellier, Orléans, and Reims three; while Nîmes and Rouen each obtained four. It should not be forgotten that the *corporate* regime encompassed many occupations unrelated to production that were undergoing professionalization. These occupations included liberal arts like scribes, along with legal professions like bailiffs

[24] Offices could be created and sold. Frequently, local institutions could borrow money at better rates of interest than the central state. In many cases, these institutions also paid fees or facilitated tax collection more efficiently than other methods available to the royal government. Generally speaking, such exactions began during the Nine Years War (1688–1697) and picked up speed over the next century. See Nora Temple, "The Control and Exploitation of French Towns during the Ancien Régime," in Raymond F. Kierstead (ed.), *State and Society in Seventeenth-Century France* (New York: New Viewpoints, 1975), 67–93, Gail Bossenga, *The Politics of Privilege: Old Regime and Revolution in Lille* (Cambridge University Press, 1991), William Beik, *Absolutism and Society in Seventeenth-century France: State Power and Provincial Aristocracy in Languedoc* (Cambridge University Press, 1985), and Michael Kwass, *Privilege and the Politics of Taxation in Eighteenth-Century France* (Cambridge University Press, 2000). Colbert emphasized the importance of industrial work to increase direct tax payments. For the previous three paragraphs, see Bossenga, "Estates, Orders and Corps," 141–66, Jean-Louis Bourgeon, "Colbert et les Corporations," in Roland Mousnier (ed.), *Un Nouveau Colbert* (SEDES, 1983), 241–54, Jean-Louis Journet and Daniel Dessert, "Le lobby Colbert: un royaume ou une affaire de famille?" *Annales, societies, civilisations*, 30: 6 (1975), 1303–36, and Jean-Yves Grenier, "Une économie d'indentification: Juste prix et ordres des marchandises dans l'Ancien Régime," in Alessandro Stanziani (ed.), *La qualité des produits en France (XVIIIe-XXe siècles)* (Belin, 2003), 25–53.

and notaries; so in a number of places, guild expansion was not necessarily related directly to economic matters. Expansion of *corporate* regimes seems to have been related to the depth of the existing system and the political economy of local production. Despite such uneven distribution, Colbert's extension of the guild system was significant, particularly in the context of Bourbon state-building.[25]

Colbert's enlargement of the reach of privilege as part of the consolidation of absolutism is the positive side of the story. On the other hand, granting *corporations* to a host of new occupations and imposing guilds on numerous urban or semi-urban areas curbed free labor and free enterprise. Colbert extended regulation because he distrusted the work ethic of the common laborer. He wrote the intendant of Poitiers that they "are well off from their labors and therefore must be constrained to work [longer hours] to pay taxes to the king." Free enterprise was distrusted because, without the anxiety caused by oversight, French producers made inconsistent, low-quality goods fit only for local consumption. In 1671, Colbert told the intendant in Toulouse that "merchants in Paris and Lyon complain that defaults in the length and width of fabrics made in Languedoc have destroyed the market for these goods." That same year Colbert wrote the mayor and aldermen of Paris that "The king believes that to pressure the manufactures of the realm to work in conformity with the statutes and regulations that have been issued, it is important to induce fear in those who make defective fabric or those who accept it [for sale]." Colbert hoped that taxes and regulation would encourage greater labor productivity, while enabling entrepreneurs to produce quality goods suitable for export.[26]

Guilds comprised only one aspect of state strategy. Empowering guilds was complemented by a spate of industrial regulations. After years of consulting manufacturing and marketing experts from all over the country, Colbert issued the first "national" industrial regulation to govern woolens production in 1669. The stated intent was to compel both workers and wardens to follow rules that would improve manufacturing quality. The measure established minimum sizes, thread counts, and qualities for raw materials in various types of woolen fabrics. A new set of officials were tasked with gathering information and verifying industrial

[25] The previous four paragraphs rely on Prosper Boissonnade, *Colbert: le triomphe de l'étatisme, la fondation de la suprématie industrielle de la France, la dictature du travail: 1661–1683* (Marcel Rivière, 1932), esp. 4–5, 14–16, 245–47.

[26] The first quote is cited by Boissonnade, *Colbert*, 5, and the other two are from Pierre Clément (ed.), *Lettres, instructions et mémoires de Colbert publiés d'après les ordres de l'empereur*, vol. II, part 1: *Industrie, Commerce* (Imprimerie impériale, 1861–1873), 607, 615.

practice: these officials evolved into the inspectors of manufacturing who played an increasingly critical role in economic policymaking. Between 1665 and 1681, Colbert elaborated on the general regulation on woolens by issuing at least twenty-six specific guidelines governing fabrics made only in certain places. These rules applied not only to large-scale woolens centers like Amiens, Carcassonne, Reims, and Sedan but also to sites where Colbert hoped to encourage the industry, such as Elbeuf, Lisieux, Louviers, and Romorantin. These regulations could be extensive: Amiens' ran to 248 articles, though most were much shorter. In 1669, a "general instruction" mandated rules for dyeing woolens and two years later another for silk stockings appeared, confirming the precedent. From this impressive, but sector-specific beginning, the mania for regulation only intensified.

Prosper Boissonnade estimates that between Colbert's death in 1683 and the domination of the council of commerce by "improvers" in 1753, approximately 1,000 industrial guidelines, either general or local, were issued by the Bourbon state. Subsequent excess should not, however, obscure the original intent. Colbert's resort to regulation stemmed from a deep-seated belief that only quality merchandise could win and retain export markets and that consumers were most satisfied when they consistently got the quality of goods they paid for. Quality was to be demonstrated and displayed through the use of a distinctive border, marking, sign, or symbol that showed where the item had been made, by whom, and with what attributes. This "trademark" was to be verified by guild wardens or state officials (see Chapters 7 and 8).

Colbert used privilege to favor consumer protection over product innovation or the lowest possible sale price. His market-sensitive approach diverges profoundly from the unwillingness of many English magistrates to allow the market mechanism alone to set prices until the early nineteenth century. This early modern divergence reverses a number of commonplace assumptions about how the rulers of England and France understood the state's regulatory role and the depth of the potential threat from below if food prices rose too much.

Just as Colbert underestimated the work ethic of French laborers, he overestimated the ability of royal administrators to fashion more productive workers who would follow orders from above. He also misjudged the depth of local resistance to such "industrial absolutism." Uniformity was as much a chimera in industrial practice as it was in politics. Colbert's misplaced confidence in the power wielded by state officials in the face of decades of determined resistance from producers and laborers is shared by far too many economists and economic historians. Despite these missteps, Colbert's inauguration of an economic policy based on the privileges of urban institutions dominated the political economy of industrial development from the mid-1660s until 1750.[27]

At the provincial level, privilege divided the *pays d'état* (provinces with representative estates that collected taxes) from the *pays d'élections* where the royal state directly controlled tax collection. *Pays d'état* fringed the realm. Generally, these spaces enjoyed far more autonomy, in part because they negotiated tax payments with the crown and in part because other institutions like the estates or the parlements existed to contest the will of the central administration. During the reign of Louis XIV, with only a few exceptions like Languedoc (see Chapter 5), provincial economic privileges were under assault. In the eighteenth century, the vestiges of provincial rights represented only a slight impediment to development, but considered more positively, they also furnished means of overcoming limitations of economic activity stemming from other privileged institutions.[28]

Lille in Flanders was an urban environment where the economy was dominated by conflicting municipal, seigneurial, and provincial privileges. This French-speaking (Walloon) city was conquered by Louis XIV in 1667. With the cities of Douai and Orchies and their

[27] For the four previous paragraphs see the following sources. On the inspectors of manufacturing and for the most influential recent analysis of Colbert's actions and their consequences, see Philippe Minard, *La fortune du colbertisme: Ètat et industrie dans la France des Lumières* (Fayard, 1998), see also Paul Mantoux, *The Industrial Revolution in the Eighteenth Century: An Outline of the Beginnings of the Modern Factory System in England*, rev. ed. (New York: Harper & Row, 1961), 83–88, Martin J. Daunton, *Progress and Poverty: An Economic and Social History of Britain 1700–1850* (Oxford University Press, 1995), 274, Clément (ed.), *Lettres, instructions et mémoires de Colbert*, II (1): 459–60, 832–41, and Boissonnade, *Colbert*, 210–11, 214.

[28] From 1663 to 1715, Louis XIV restricted the powers of the provincial estates by eliminating their right to oppose registration of royal edicts, declarations, or letters-patent. He stopped convoking the estates of Quercy (1673), Rouergue (1673), Alsace (1683), and the Franche-Comté (1704). The remaining estates were found in Artois, Cambrésis, Tournai, the Four Valleys, Wallonian Flanders, Maritime Flanders, Hainault, the Pays Messin, Béarn, Foix, Nébouzan, Bigorre, Labourd, Soule, Navarre, Brittany, Burgundy, Languedoc, and later Corsica. Less formal versions existed for the Mâconnais and Charolais, as well as Bresse and Bugey. Provence had a variation on the institution under a different name. Of the 60 "provinces" composing eighteenth-century France, 24 were *pays d'états* in one form or another. See Roland E. Mousnier, *The Institutions of France under the Absolute Monarchy 1598–1789: Society and the State*, trans. Brian Pearce (University of Chicago Press, 1979 [1974]), 607, 610–11. On elite politics under Louis XIV, see Roger Mettam, "Power, Status and Precedence: Rivalries among the Provincial Elites in Louis XIV's France," *Transactions of the Royal Historical Society*, 5th series, vol. 38 (1988), 43–62, and more generally, James B. Collins, *The State in Early Modern France*, 2nd ed. (Cambridge University Press, 2009).

feudal dependencies (*châtellenies*), Lille formed the new province of Walloon Flanders. The capitulation agreement gave the city and province "all the privileges, customs, usages, immunities, rights, liberties, freedoms, jurisdiction, justice, police and administration accorded previously by the kings of France or other sovereign princes in this region." Inhabitants of Flanders did not pay taxes in lieu of feudal dues (*franc-fief*) or the salt tax (*gabelle*), and its payments in place of military service (*taille*) were nominal. No resident performed unpaid labor on the roads (*corvée*). The province also retained a separate currency based on the *florin*, keeping the mint alive.

Flanders remained outside the kingdom's customs barriers. Most goods were taxed at 12–15 percent *ad valorem* when entering France. As compensation for being disconnected from the dense network of canals and roads tying Lille to the southern Netherlands, merchants and manufacturers in Flanders were granted an important privilege. Through (newly purchased) Dunkerque, they could import raw materials from abroad and export manufactured goods without paying duties. This arrangement encouraged the province to continue to manufacture internationally competitive goods. These import–export rights were the province's most zealously guarded privileges.

The capitulation agreement added privileges designed to stoke the region's economic engine. Because "the city is and has always been founded on commerce and the work of artisans" and the quartering of troops is "incompatible with commerce and the exercise of trades and manufactures," the garrison was housed in barracks. Lille's guild structures and *police des manufactures* was preserved, and "no tools, serfs or inhabitants may be moved to another city as a colony or through abduction of these artisans, male or female workers, or mechanics either by the authorities or by secret prompting." These measures were particularly important in Flanders because in the fifteenth century, villagers in the feudal dependencies had begun providing and preparing raw materials for Lille's guilds to turn into cloth. To circumvent guild privileges that enforced small-scale production, especially the stricture limiting wool weavers to operating six looms, Lille's merchants outsourced and later subcontracted work to cheaper rural or semi-urban laborers in the increasingly industrialized villages of Roubaix, Tourcoing, and Lannoy. At first, this merchant-driven operation remained under guild control. They monopolized key manufacturing processes including dyeing and "finishing" the cloth, while guild inspectors monitored the importation of raw materials either for mixing into the weave or for dyeing, which determined which goods were made in what styles. Lille was also the sole legal point of sale. The city and its guilds also controlled rural production through inspection, a monopoly on storing goods before or after sale, and an exclusive right to train apprentices.[29]

Franklin Mendels described this production process, which occurred throughout Flanders, as "proto-industrialization." Although there are significant problems with this term in the fashion he used it, Mendels' model helps to understand Flanders' evolving symbiosis of urban and semi-urban producers in Flanders. Lille's guilds faced increasing competition from lower-cost producers outside the city. By operating in the high justices of the feudal dependencies, merchants avoided the *corporate* system. "Liberty" in the enclaves wrestled with urban "privilege" to determine the fate of Lille's monopolies. This long-running conflict illuminates privilege's shortcomings as a tool of economic development. Privilege provided the legal justification for both the dominant position of Lille and its guilds in textile manufacture and the "liberties" that permitted seigneurs to protect nascent enterprises funded by urban merchants. As Gail Bossenga points out, the merchants won the battle, but this success should be understood as the triumph of certain privileges over others rather than the victory of liberty over *corporate* monopoly.[30]

When Louis XIV's army seized Lille, Roubaix's privilege to make certain types of woolens was already two centuries old. In 1469, Charles the Bold, duke of Burgundy, authorized the seigneur to establish *corporations* to regulate, inspect, and develop the village's growing output. Lille's efforts to ban manufacture in the *châtellenies* in 1534 and again in 1547 led Emperor Charles V to confirm Roubaix's *corporate* structure in 1553. Producers in the *châtellenies* were, however, limited to making the coarsest grades of cloth, and Lille's guilds received inspection rights. In 1609, a general regulation for manufacturing textiles outside the city was issued by the Habsburgs. It funneled semifinished production to Lille for weaving, dyeing, and finishing. Lille was also confirmed as the sole site where finished fabrics from the feudal dependencies could

[29] The reprint of the *capitulation* agreement is in *Recueil des Edits, déclarations, arrests et réglemens: qui sont propres et particuliers aux provinces du Ressort du parlement de Flandres* (Douai: J. Fr. Willerval, 1730), 12–24. For the three previous paragraphs, see Bossenga, *The Politics of Privilege*, 16–17, 19–20, 24–25, and Gail Bossenga, "Protecting Merchants: Guilds and Commercial Capitalism in Eighteenth-Century France," *French Historical Studies*, 15: 4 (1988), 695. On the interaction of guilds and merchants in Lille, see Jean-Pierre Hirsch, *Les deux rêves du commerce: Enterprise et institution dans la region lilloise (1780–1860)* (Éditions de l'EHESS, 1991).

[30] Franklin F. Mendels, "Proto-industrialization: The First Phase of the Industrialization Process," *Journal of Economic History*, 32 (1972), 241–61. See also the essays by Pierre Deyon and Christiaan Vandenbroeke in Sheilagh C. Ogilvie and Markus Cerman (eds.), *European proto-industrialization* (Cambridge University Press, 1996), 38–48, 102–17 and Bossenga, "Protecting Merchants," 693–703.

be sold. Under this system, each village came to specialize in a different low-quality fabric. Repeated administrative ordinances and legal rulings from Lille's guilds and municipality, the *parlement* of Douai, and the provincial estates confirmed the city's monopolies. But lower wages, lesser costs, greater opportunity of business entry and in the production process prompted workers and entrepreneurs to abandon Lille. From a peak of 2,000 looms making the city's signature fabric, a variety of woolen velour, by 1732 only 100 looms remained inside city walls.

Beginning in the late seventeenth century, Lillois tried to damn the flood, but it was too late. Rural production far surpassed Lille's. In 1693, the intendant reported that there were 20,000 spinners in Lille and 44,000 in the *châtellenies*. Lille's municipality issued a regulation in 1697, approved by the royal council two years later, that imposed an additional tax on incoming fabrics not listed in the 1609 measure. Ostensibly, this tax paid for a second inspection certifying quality before sale, but the intent was clearly to equalize costs and restore urban competitiveness. Conflict about whether Lille's privileges allowed imposition of a surcharge on goods made in the *châtellenies* raged for the next three decades. To resolve the dispute, in 1728, the seigneurs' high bailiffs along with the prince of Rohan-Soubise petitioned the royal council to eliminate the supplemental tax on fabrics entering Lille. After four years of appeals, the council of commerce issued a policy statement that summarized the central government's long-standing support for *corporate* control of production.

The council of commerce upheld guild and urban privileges. The deputies recognized but did not encourage the cost advantages of Roubaix, Tourcoing, and other textile-producing villages. Because seigneurs in the *châtellenies* set lower guild fees and inspection charges and there were few if any municipal taxes, Lille's costs were too high to compete. The council rejected the "pretentions" of Roubaix's manufacturers who claimed that:

> exclusive privileges are contrary to the freedom of commerce and the industry of particulars ... The deputies agree that exclusive privileges exist that are contrary to the freedom of commerce, but having examined this issue, it does not appear that the privileges of the city of Lille are of that type. On the contrary, we think that they [Lille's privileges] are advantageous to commerce and manufacturing, necessary to the state and to the king's service ... in a city as important as Lille ... For the good of commerce and of manufacturing, it is an absolute necessity that the regulations be observed exactly.

Sloppy manufacture, skimping on raw materials, and taking advantage of lower taxes to pinch Lille's workers did not find favor with the deputies of commerce. They worried that the province would lose customers in traditional export markets: "The length and width of bolts of cloth are prescribed by the regulations. Foreigners buy them because of their confidence in those regulations. If that confidence is lost and foreigners find themselves deceived, this quite considerable commerce will be lost."[31] For the deputies, Lille's privileges were both legitimate and necessary because only guild inspection reliably ensured that producers followed the rules and made quality goods.

The council also worried about the flight of workers from Lille. With fewer taxpayers, the city would be "impoverished" and less money would be available to purchase or confirm venal offices. At the same time, the deputies of commerce emphasized the fidelity and trustworthiness of privileged producers and their workers as far less likely to flee a frontier province in time of war or to emigrate abroad. The Lillois also deserved support because urban textile workers had no alternative source of income. In the *châtellenies*, farm work supplemented industrial wages. The deputies "found no help or advantage from the establishment of manufacturing in the countryside." They recognized that manufacturers in the high justices of Roubaix, Tourcoing, and Lannoy had the "liberty" to make many types of rough woolens, but they upheld Lille's guild monopolies to manufacture more complicated and more lucrative fabrics.[32]

Producers in the *châtellenies* continued to push the boundaries. The council of commerce's ruling simply drove the *châtellenies*' growing output underground and encouraged the expansion of guild masters' economic roles. In addition to manufacturing goods, they became independent merchants responsible for the (licit and illicit) merchandising of their wares. For the purposes of inspection and sale, Lille's masters who were either unwilling or unable to compete were reduced to claiming that goods

31 *Avis des Deputés du Commerce sur les contestations portées au conflit entre les sayeteurs et bourgeteurs de Lille et les fabricants du bourg de Roubaix*, August 1, 1732, AN F12 699.

32 The four previous paragraphs are based on Théodore Leuridan, *Histoire de la fabrique de Roubaix* (Roubaix: V. Beghin, 1863), 15–32, 60–72, Maurice Braure, *Lille et la flandre wallonne au XVIIIe siècle* (Lille: Émile Raoust, 1932), 376, Roger Chartier, Guy Chaussinand-Nogaret, Hubert Neveux, and Emmanuel Le Roy Ladurie, *La ville des temps modernes de la Renaissance aux Révolutions* (Seuil, 1998 [1980]), 86, and Bossenga, *The Politics of Privilege*, 16–17. In 1722, confirmation taxes for Louis XV's crowning came to one million *livres*. Fifteen years later the city paid 770,000 *livres* to repurchase municipal offices. Victor Derode, *Histoire de Lille et de la Flandre Wallonne*, 4 vols. (Lille: Librairie de Vanackere, 1977 [1848–1877]), II: 309. For a good description of the kind of production taking place in the *châtellenies*, see the examination of linen weaving in the nearby Cambrésis by Liana Vardi, *The Land and the Loom: Peasants and Profit in Northern France, 1680–1800* (Durham, NC: Duke University Press, 1993), 125–202.

made by manufacturers in Roubaix, Tourcoing, and Lannoy were their own. "Naturalizing" woolens made in the *châtellenies* for the purposes of inspection generated some profits for masters but left urban workers underemployed or starving. Smuggling and fraud reached new heights, allowing profit-taking, but did not employ textile workers or encourage innovations in production.

Despite its ineffectiveness, Lillois continuously sought administrative action to defend their monopolies. A 1759 ordinance by Lille's municipal authorities prohibited producers in the *châtellenies* from selling their wares to merchants or manufacturers from other provinces "to safeguard the reputation of French textiles." Intendant Antoine-Louis-François Lefèvre de Caumartin issued an ordinance in 1760 that banned Tourcoing from making a type of fabric made there for decades. This measure seems to have been the straw that broke the camel's back. After Lille's inspectors seized several bolts of cloth, Roubaix's producers demanded "complete liberty either in the countryside or in the city for anyone to make any kind of woolen cloth" for "the good of commerce." Official reactions from Paris and Versailles to both measures demonstrated that attitudes had changed.[33]

Caumartin's edict attracted the attention of the intendants of commerce, led, in this matter, by Daniel-Charles de Trudaine. These influential improvers overturned the injunction against Tourcoing's manufacturers. With the support of controller-general of finance Henri Bertin, they initiated one of the old régime's most important industrial reforms. In September 1762, the royal council decreed that most woolen and linen fabrics (*étoffes*) could be woven and finished (*apprêté*) in the countryside or in unincorporated towns or cities "without being disturbed by guild manufacturers." Producers were required to adhere to national regulations and their goods received a different trademark than guild-made merchandise. Intended to stimulate "innovation and emulation," this edict broke the monopolies of cities and guilds across the realm, not just in Flanders. The royal council acted because "it is essential to eliminate the obstacles that harm the progress of industry." The inhabitants of the *châtellenies* around Lille celebrated their "liberation." They thought they could weave and dye all sorts of cloth openly and legally.[34]

33 The two previous paragraphs are based on Yves-Marie Hilaire (ed.), *Histoire de Roubaix* (Dunkerque: Les Editions des Beffrois, 1984), 86–87 and Braure, *Lille et la flandre wallonne au XVIIIe siècle*, 383. The quotes are cited by Hilaire.

34 Hilaire (ed.), *Histoire de Roubaix*, 87–90 and Braure, *Lille et la flandre wallonne au XVIIIe siècle*, 383–85. The quotes are from the edict reprinted in Maurice Vanhaeck, *Histoire de la sayetterie à Lille*, 2 vols. (Lille: Lefebvre-Ducrocq, 1910), II: 349–50.

They were wrong. Lille's chamber of commerce convinced the intendant that the national regulations differed so greatly from local practice that implementation was impossible. Caumartin stalled publishing the decree until September 1764 by claiming that many workers were emigrating and that popular fears of unemployment had necessitated mobilizing troops. Lillois hoped for an official province-wide delay: they got their wish in July 1765. Despite official reports that Lille "abused its privileges," this exemption remained in place until April 1776 when another, better-known reformer, Anne-Robert-Jacques de Turgot, voided it. Again, local officials in Flanders refused to implement the decree. Finally, in November 1777, the province of Flanders and the city of Lille were ordered to follow new textile regulations that permitted rural manufacture and broke guilds' legal monopolies for good (see Chapter 7).[35]

In the late 1770s, the expansion of rural industry and Flanders' declining reputation in vital export markets led manufacturers from Roubaix and Tourcoing to join Lillois in demanding the application of the new regulations. Roubaix's high bailiff declared that "the manufacturers all tell me that following regulations assures the solidity and size necessary for fabrics to be usefully employed by the consumer . . . and [that] it is an incontestable truth that the best-regulated manufactures have always expanded."[36] By favoring one set of privileged producers over another, royal administrators advanced policy goals, but where geography, resources, market access, and entrepreneurialism did not come together, results were uneven at best. On their own, privileges did not guarantee sales or profits. In the case of Lille's guilds, shifting local attitudes toward regulation meant that, in practice, their privileges resembled Shakespeare's "sound and fury signifying nothing."

What effect did these privileges have on Lille and Flanders? Under French rule, the city's textile industry declined precipitously. Between 1673 and 1708, Lille's guild wardens inspected an average of almost 165,000 bolts of cloth annually. From 1708 to 1730, that figure fell to about 85,000 bolts a year, and then to 48,000 in 1740 and 35,000 bolts in 1775. Lille's merchants and richest guild manufacturers may have found privilege worth defending, but the same cannot be said for the bulk of the

35 Hilaire (ed.), *Histoire de Roubaix*, 90–93. The quote is cited by Braure, *Lille et la flandre wallonne au XVIIIe siècle*, 386–87.

36 *Procès-verbal de la réunion du lieutenant bailli et echevins avec des gardes jurés et marchands-fabriquants de ce bourg [Tourcoing]*, June 3, 1780, AN F12 676A and *Précis pour le Magistrat et gardes de la manufacture de Roubaix contre le Magistrat, Marchands et fabricants de la ville de Lille*, 1780, AN F12 657. The quote is from *Mémoire pour les magistrat de Roubaix, les gards jurés des manufactures et tous les bons fabricans de ce bourg, Reclamans contre les dispositions des Lettres Patentes du Roi concernant les Manufactures, données à Marly le 5 May 1779 registrées au Parlement de Flandres le 12 Janvier 1780*, 1780, AN F12 676.

urban population. Widespread fraud and smuggling kept commerce alive, but created few jobs. Although the city's economy diversified and ultimately innovated once the masters were allowed to mechanize in 1777, Lille's workers were impoverished, illiterate, and underemployed. Bouts of machine-breaking in 1789 indicate the depth of their desperation.[37]

Production blossomed in the *châtellenies* but did not compensate for Lille's collapse. Roubaix grew swiftly to become a city in its own right. In 1703, Roubaix produced 6,900 bolts of cloth, in 1723, 13,600, and in 1762, 32,000. With the end of Lille's tutelage, Roubaix's output climbed to 52,400 bolts in 1787 but fell to 30,000 the following year due to the Anglo-French commercial treaty. In a petition, manufacturers in Roubaix, Tourcoing, and Wattrelos identified the chief cause of Lille's lack of competitiveness: "Lille's guild manufacturers cling to privilege. They are put to sleep by it because they are confident that no rural resident has the liberty to make the same fabrics." As a result, they have "fallen insensibly into indifference regarding the perfection of their work." Flanders' textile industry was damaged by privilege; clearly, this institution was no universal remedy. Seigneurial privileges shielded producers outside Lille, but by the time that industry in the *châtellenies* burst the bonds imposed by the guilds, other factors impinged on the region's competitiveness.[38]

Beyond privilege, woolens manufacture in Flanders suffered certain impediments. In the early modern era, woolens were the largest branch of the textile industry in Flanders, in France as a whole, and across Europe. French woolens output increased more than 76 percent in square ells (*aunes*) between 1716 and 1789, with 57 percent of that increase coming from Normandy, Picardy, Flanders, and Champagne. With raw wool prices on the rise because of insufficient domestic supplies, French producers increasingly had to import expensive quality wool from abroad, which squeezed profit margins. Changing tastes and improved quality by France's competitors in key product categories limited Flanders' exports both at the top and bottom of the market. The Spanish crown's 1779 decision to restrict imports of French goods into its colonies palpably shrank the sale of Flanders' woolens. Preference for lighter fabrics and the shift in women's fashions to a color palette that differed from Lille's dyeing specialties also contributed to the decline, as did "*anglomanie*," the emerging preference for English goods. Unlike

[37] William M. Reddy, *The Rise of Market Culture: The Textile Trade & French Society, 1750–1900* (Cambridge University Press, 1984), 60, Vanhaeck, *Histoire de la sayetterie à Lille*, II: 355, and Derode, *Histoire de Lille et de la Flandre Wallonne*, II: 334–35.

[38] Hilaire (ed.), *Histoire de Roubaix*, 83, 90, 95, 110–11. The quote is cited on 90.

their Norman competitors who improved their dyeing processes, naturalized English spinning techniques, and invented new fabrics, woolens manufacturers in Flanders failed to develop new products or new specialties fast enough to maintain sales.

The *corporate* system itself was not the chief barrier to innovation. Other guilds in Lille's textile industry, most notably those producing and marketing linen thread, were among the most dynamic and inventive in the city. This guild retained control over rural production. In woolens, however, long-term conflict between privileged producers encouraged wrangling over market share and regional division of labor instead of finding new customers or engaging in technical and/or product innovation. In economic terms, privilege was a double-edged sword whose utility depended on the wielder's skill and fortitude.[39]

Enclaves and sovereignty: competition in a new key

Within French borders, numerous territories possessed by foreign princes, either as seigneurs or exercising sovereign rights, constituted a notable example of the spatial and legal limits of absolutism. These enclaves included Provençal *seigneuries* held by the prince of Monaco and the holdings of German princes in Alsace, but the early modern era's most economically significant sovereign enclaves were the duchy of Lorraine, the Comtat Venaissin, and the principality of Orange. Although these enclaves adopted many elements of France's regulatory structures governing economic activity, each sovereign (or their representatives) took advantage of different aspects of privilege to exploit loopholes in the realm's tax, trade, toll, and guild rules to encourage economic development.

France became deeply involved in Lorraine's affairs during the Protestant Reformation. In 1648, the treaty of Westphalia established Bourbon dominion over the bishoprics of Metz, Toul, and Verdun. French forces occupied the duchy from 1670 to 1697 and again from 1702 to 1713. The territory was accorded to the former king of Poland, Stanislaw Leszczyński, Louis XV's father-in-law, in 1737, with the understanding that it would fall to France upon his death. This populous duchy of 800,000 inhabitants was annexed to France in 1766 after almost three decades of administrative assimilation.

39 Butel, *L'Economie française au XVIIIe siècle*, 220–07, esp. 221, Hilaire (ed.), *Histoire de Roubaix*, 87, 90, 110–11 as well as the *Mémoire des négociants de Lyon*, September 11, 1780, and *Mémoire des négociants de Morlaix*, January 13, 1780, both in AN F12 676B, and Louis Villard, *Mémoire de Tournée dans le Département de l'Inspection de Picardie en Juin et Juillet 1785*, AD Somme C372. On the linen thread guild, see Bossenga, *The Politics of Privilege*, 152–59.

When the papacy acquired the seigneurie of Avignon in 1348, it had already controlled the surrounding territory, the Comtat Venaissin, for a century. From the sixteenth century, an archbishop, acting as papal legate, governed the territory of 90,000 (in the mid-eighteenth century), of whom about one-third lived in Avignon. After 1663 when France seized the Comtat, an archbishop served as vice-legate. Under French rule, Comtadins retained "many rights, privileges, liberties, powers, freedoms, and exemptions that have been granted them" by various popes or previous monarchs.[40] When the territory was occupied in 1768–1774, the French crown whittled away at its privileges. Yet, papal sovereignty and some vestiges of privilege remained through the end of the old régime. Only in 1791 did France finally annex the Comtat Venaissin.

The principality of Orange, located twenty-five kilometers north of Avignon in the Rhône valley, dated from the twelfth century. Completely encircled by the Comtat Venaissin, Orange was doubly enclaved. This territory of 10,000 inhabitants was occupied by Louis XIV in 1660–1665 and 1685–1697. Under the House of Bourbon-Conti, Orange became French in 1703. It retained its tax and transit privileges. These princes held the enclave until 1731, when Louis XV purchased it for the royal domain. The privileges of these sovereign territories – especially their exemption from entry or exit taxes on nearly all goods – afforded numerous opportunities for entrepreneurialism and undermined privileged monopolies in France.[41]

The privileges of Avignon and the Comtat Venaissin frustrated French entrepreneurs. Harboring Catholic, Protestant, and Jewish peddlers and merchants, the Comtat's "right of transit" lowered costs on commercial exchange throughout the Midi and facilitated large-scale smuggling of printed materials, paper, silks, printed linen, and muslins as well as tobacco products past French customs. Many French taxes like the *capitation* (head tax) or municipal levies simply did not exist, lowering overheads. In the Comtat, silk manufacturing, as well as the production of leather goods, woolens, books, paper, jewelry, and other merchandise enjoyed comparative advantage. A privilege explicitly exempting the enclave from France's guild system allowed local officials to ban *corporations*. Many French textile manufacturers made use of the enclave's low costs to have unfinished goods bleached or dyed there.

[40] *Arrêt du Conseil d'État en faveur des Habitans de la Ville d'Avignon et du Comtat Vénaissin*, March 16, 1734, AD Bouches-du-Rhône A51.

[41] The previous three paragraphs are based on Lucien Bély (ed.), *Dictionnaire de l'Ancien Régime: Royaume de France XVIe-XVIIIe siècle* (Quadrige/PUF, 2002 [1996]), 116–17, 759–61, 930–31. See also Collins, *The State*, 40–41, 212–13, 310–11.

The deputies of commerce observed that "as there are no guilds or any inspection in the Comtat, they make silk fabrics that are lighter and smaller than the same goods made in Lyon, Tours, or Nîmes according to the regulations. These fabrics can be sold for a lower price, the infallible method of being preferred to French goods." Furthermore, the deputies testified that "apprenticeships are not required in the Comtat and fees are unnecessary to become a master." No one had to "contribute to the expenses of their communities, to the cost of inspections ... or to fund court-cases against masters and workers who contravene the regulations." The deputies concluded that "these advantages lead silk workers to leave [Lyon, Tours, and Nîmes] to populate Avignon and the Comtat Venaissin."[42] Privileges of liberty capitalized on the region's high-quality raw silk. The industry boomed, beginning in the seventeenth century. Privileged producers in other places responded by asserting their monopolies to undermine the enclave's competiveness.[43]

From the late sixteenth century, guilds in Lyon, Tours, and Nîmes held privileges to manufacture silk. Even before Louis XIV occupied Avignon, Lyon's silk manufacturers tried to nullify the Comtat's privileges. In 1652, the Lyonnais successfully lobbied the royal council to levy a heavy new tax on silks and other goods from the Comtat. In conjunction with tightening customs enforcement around the enclave, this measure put 12,000 Comtadin silk-workers out of work and caused riots. Pope Innocent X complained and the tax was soon removed, but the Comtat's status as a bone of contention between France and the Holy See helps to explain the enclave's occupation eleven years later. Although the Comtat's privileges were confirmed by Louis XIV, they were infringed upon repeatedly to favor French silk-working.[44]

Taxes were increased on Comtadin and other "foreign-made" silks in 1687, 1717, and 1722. A turning point came in the 1730s. Struggling silk manufacturers argued once again that the Comtat's silk industry infringed on their privileges. They pushed the royal council to ban the entry of "silk fabrics or other goods made or exchanged by the city of

[42] *Reflexions des Députés du Commerce sur le Memoire des habitans d'Avignon et Comtat Venaissin qui leur a été communiqué*, May 30, 1733, AN F12 700.

[43] *Avis des Deputés du Commerce sur les plaintes portées par MM les fermiers generaux au sujet des commerces reciproques qui se font de la Provence avec le Comtat*, September 3, 1731, AN F12 699, Louis Loubet, *Carpentras et le Comtat-Venaissin avant et après l'annexation: Etude historique* (Carpentras: Tourrette, 1891), 129–32, and *Arrêt du Conseil du Roi concernant l'imprimerie et la librarie d'Avignon et du Comtat Vénaissin*, August 10, 1769 (Gallica).

[44] Denis Woronoff, *Histoire de l'industrie en France du XVIe siècle à nos jours* (Seuil, 1994), 42, Pierre Charpenne, *Histoire des réunions temporaires d'Avignon et du comtat Venaissin à la France*, 2 vols. (Calmann Lévy, 1886), I: 21–24, and *Arrêt du Conseil d'État en faveur des Habitans de la Ville d'Avignon et du Comtat Vénaissin*, March 16, 1734.

Avignon and the Comtat Venaissin under penalty of confiscation and a 1,000 *livre* fine." To combat smuggling, the general tax farmers also convinced the council to decree that textiles dyed or bleached in the Comtat could not return to France even if a duty was paid. Three years of inquiry by the deputies of commerce decided the enclave's fate. As noted earlier, the deputies did not defend the silk producers' *corporate* or municipal privileges. They recognized that the Comtat's privileges encroached on venerable silk monopolies but refused to intervene on their behalf. Instead, the deputies made a strategic choice between privileges: they reinstated the enclave's transit and manufacturing rights to strengthen the competitiveness of the French silk industry as a whole.

The deputies hoped that restoring the privilege of liberty would encourage Comtadins to "perfect" silk manufacture. Comtois competition was also supposed to encourage emulation by other producers. The royal council reversed its earlier decision in March 1734, "judging it apropos not only to lift the prohibition that had been imposed, but also to provide new facilities and to favor [Comtadins] even more by reducing taxes on the exchange of goods between the king's subjects and the inhabitants of Avignon and the Comtat." New customs rates almost completely restored the *status quo ante*. The deputies of commerce and the royal council clearly recognized the ripple effect of competition. The privilege of liberty was supposed to stimulate innovation among monopolistic producers in France's traditional production centers.[45]

The deputies' shifting views are important, in part, because of the timing. Negating guild privileges and urban monopolies to support freer trade and liberty of manufacture are positions usually associated with "liberalism" or the ideas of the Physiocrats. The fate of the Comtat Venaissin, therefore, has broader implications. At least a generation before the dawn of the Physiocratic moment around 1750, state reformers increasingly preferred privileged liberties to privileged monopolies. This preference should be understood as a transitional approach, but the essential point about timing is that the movement against privilege in favor of liberating trade and manufacture from the yoke of regulation was

[45] The two previous paragraphs are based on *Avis des Deputés du Commerce sur la lettre de M. De Fontamieu, par laquelle il donne avis qu'il est informé que les marchands de la ville et principauté d'Orange, sont chargé d'une grande quantité d'indiennes, de mousselines et de tabac, surquoi il demande des ordres relatif à celui est porté pour la lettre que son subdelegué à Orange lui a écrit à ce sujet*, August 20, 1731, AN F12 699, *Reflexions des Députés du Commerce sur le Memoire des habitans d'Avignon et Comtat Venaissin qui leur a été communiqué*, May 30, 1733, and *Arrêt du Conseil d'État en faveur des Habitans de la Ville d'Avignon et du Comtat Vénaissin*, March 16, 1734.

based on lessons of administrative practice. They did not stem from developments in economic theory.

As we shall see in Chapters 4–8, "liberal" policymaking remained tentative and incomplete. The 1734 edict maintained one absolute prohibition. Manufacturing printed linen cloth (*toiles peintes*) remained illegal, safeguarding the East Indies Company's monopoly on printed fabrics.[46] An additional ban was negotiated with the papacy: tobacco could no longer be grown in the Comtat to protect the royal monopoly by eliminating smuggling. Clearly, Bourbon officials believed that some monopolies were worth upholding. The deputies of commerce had no sympathy when the manufacturers of Orange – completely enclaved within the Comtat Venaissin – complained that Comtadins were stealing their customers. With industry in Orange subject to French regulation and inspection after the king took possession in 1731, the Comtat could now sell woolens for less. The deputies responded that goods from Orange were better made and that if manufacturers in Dauphiné could compete successfully with the Comtat, so could they. Regulating the Comtat was "neither possible nor practical. Each sovereign has the right to govern as they judge suitable for the well-being and interest of their subjects."[47]

Political considerations shaped the enjoyment of privilege and liberty. With ready supplies of paper at hand, little censorship, innumerable opportunities for smuggling, and taking advantage of Jewish and Protestant entrepreneurs, the Comtat housed a booming printing industry dominated by seditious or scandalous books and broadsheets distributed clandestinely. In August 1769, during the enclave's occupation, the royal administration finally closed this loophole. The council imposed a regulation created for Paris' printers and booksellers in 1723 and applied in provincial France in 1744. The new rule forced more than half the Comtat's printers (nine of sixteen) to close shop and compelled the rest to submit to rigorous inspection. Privilege and liberty faced obvious constraints even in a supposedly "sovereign" enclave.[48]

[46] French printed textiles were not yet made of cotton. Even the more primitive linen versions were considered to be too competitive by the East Indies Company.

[47] *Avis des Deputés du Commerce sur les représentations qui sont faites par les fabricants de la Principauté d'Orange sur l'inégalité qui se trouve entre leur commerce et celui des Avignonais sur la fabrication des étoffes appellés serges d'Orange*, July 5, 1734, AN F12 700.

[48] The two previous paragraphs are based on *Arrêt du Conseil d'État en faveur des Habitans de la Ville d'Avignon et du Comtat Vénaissin*, March 16, 1734, *Avis des Deputés du Commerce . . .*, July 5, 1734, *Arrêt du Conseil du Roi concernant l'imprimerie et la librarie d'Avignon et du Comtat Vénaissin*, August 10, 1769, Loubet, *Carpentras et le Comtat-Venaissin avant et après l'annexation*, 103, and Madeleine Ventre, *L'imprimerie et la librairie en Languedoc au dernier siècle de l'Ancien régime 1700–1789* (Mouton, 1958).

Territorial privileges heightened competition and facilitated entrepreneurialism in early modern France. Privileged enclaves ranging in size from tiny clerical preserves in Paris to the substantial duchy of Lorraine were important exceptions to administrative attempts to create or impose uniformity, a policy often associated with Bourbon absolutism. Seigneurs and sovereigns granted or maintained privileges that conflicted with those held by guilds, cities, and provinces and then shielded their subjects or vassals from the consequences. Events in Paris, Bordeaux, Lille, and the Comtat Venaissin indicate the scale and scope of privilege as a Northian institution. The experiences of these privileged spaces also demonstrate an important evolution in the attitudes of French officials toward privilege and liberty that predates the current emphasis on the role of the Physiocrats. By supporting some privileges against others, the deputies of commerce and the royal council clearly recognized the utility of special exceptions to regulatory uniformity as a spur to entrepreneurialism. These examples also reveal the ad hoc, fragmented nature of French state reliance on the privilege of liberty at the expense of rent-seeking guild and urban monopolies. The next chapter presents the other side of the coin. Framed more positively, it explores the impressive potential of this approach to development in Normandy, where the privilege of liberty conceived of spatially was applied most extensively.

3 The privilege of liberty put to the test
Industrial development in Normandy

The Norman is naturally active and works hard when it is a question of his interest. He makes profits from all the resources of work and economy ... Of all the provinces of the French realm, Normandy contains the most industry.

Jacques Savary des Bruslons with Philemon-Louis Savary (1759)[1]

By his [Jean-Baptiste Colbert's] efforts, Europe became tributary to our manufactures ... And how did our commerce grow so quickly to such a degree of splendor? Because of the privileges that this minister recognized as necessary to the progress of industry.

Remonstrance of the *parlement* of Paris (1776)[2]

The province of Normandy made use of all its resources. As inspector general of manufactures and noted author Jacques Savary des Bruslons remarked, its inhabitants had a reputation for both industriousness and industrial production. At the same time, Normans demonstrated a thoroughgoing devotion to taking advantage of every sort of privilege they could acquire, claim, or invent. This combination of attributes enabled Normandy to become and to remain early modern France's most industrialized province, a veritable Lancashire on the Seine.

No province was better integrated into Bourbon state structures than Normandy. Organized into three generalities – Rouen, Caen, and Alençon – overseen by intendants who deployed a flock of subdelegates, Normandy was administered both more thoroughly and more effectively than any other province. With two regiments quartered in Rouen, and additional detachments garrisoning Normandy's long and vulnerable

[1] Jacques Savary des Bruslons with Philibert-Louis Savary, *Dictionnaire universel de commerce, d'histoire naturelle et des arts et métiers*, new ed., 5 vols. (Copenhagen: Claude and Antoine Philibert, 1759), V: 175–76.

[2] *Remonstrances du Parlement de Paris contre les Èdits portant l'abolition des corvées pour la confection des chemins, la suppression des Jurandes, la suppression des Offices sur les ports, quais, balles et chantiers de Paris & des droits attribués à ces offices, la suppression des Droits sur les grains aux entrées de Paris, etc. présentées en mars 1776* (Amsterdam: Marc-Michel Rey, 1776), 63–64.

coastline, the governor and the intendants had ample troops at their disposal. As the provincial capital, Rouen housed a wealth of institutions, royal, provincial, and local. They included the *parlement*, a chamber of commerce, the municipality, the intendant and a subdelegate, an inspector of manufacturing and his deputy, the guilds, tax collectors for various state levies and for the city's municipal duties (*octrois*), and inspectors at the two cloth halls (*Halle aux Toiles*) for local and "foreign" merchants, among a host of others. Given this extraordinary degree of oversight, it should not surprise that the province of Normandy contributed disproportionately to French finances. In the seventeenth century, Normandy contributed 15 percent of royal tax revenues. As the realm grew with the acquisition of Lorraine and as Atlantic trade reached new heights, that figure declined to a still impressive 10–11 percent at the end of the old régime. This depth of state authority encouraged royal officials to use Normandy to experiment with a political economy centered on the privilege of liberty.[3]

As demonstrated in Chapter 2, beginning with Jean-Baptiste Colbert in the 1660s, the French state implemented the privilege of liberty across the length and breadth of the realm. Tactical use of the privilege of liberty was, however, limited: in part by geography; in part by institutional, local, and municipal rivalries; and in part by the necessities of wartime political economy. By its very nature, privilege was an ad hoc policy instrument, but the entrenchment of state power in Normandy permitted a more systematic and sustained deployment of the privilege of liberty. Louis XIV's wars sapped the province's wealth and made Normandy more dependent on the state than ever before. Alexis de Tocqueville, that famous son of the province, noted, "It never occurred to anyone that any large-scale enterprise could be put through successfully without the intervention of the State."[4] The archival record makes plain that in Normandy the Bourbon administration, although far from "absolute,"

[3] Zoë Schneider, *The King's Bench: Bailiwick Magistrates and Local Governance in Normandy, 1670–1740* (University of Rochester Press, 2008), 22, Christine Le Bozec, *La Normandie au XVIIIe siècle: Croissance, Lumières et Révolution* (Rennes: Éditions de l'Ouest-France, 2002), 9–10, and Comité régional d'histoire de la Révolution française (Haute-Normandie), *La Révolution en Haute-Normandie 1789–1802* (Rouen: Editions du P'tit Normand, 1988), 12. I disagree heartily with the depiction of administrative ineptitude in William M. Reddy, "The Textile Trade and the Language of the Crowd at Rouen 1752–1871," *Past & Present*, 74 (1977), 62–89, esp. 62–74.

[4] Alexis de Tocqueville, *The Old Régime and the French Revolution*, trans. Stuart Gilbert (Garden City, NY: Anchor Books, 1955), 69. Some of the ideas and evidence in this chapter appeared in Jeff Horn, "'A Beautiful Madness': Privilege, the Machine Question and Industrial Development in Normandy in 1789," *Past & Present*, 217 (2012), 149–85.

granted and coordinated privileges of liberty relatively harmoniously though hardly without dispute.

Normandy's remarkable place in French political economy seems to have emerged during the reform of the *police des manufactures* at the dawn of the eighteenth century. In cities across France, Louis XIV's administration created the office of the lieutenant-general of police (chief police magistrate) in 1699 with impressive powers of economic supervision. Intended at least partly to raise revenue to pay off war debt, municipal administrations and judicial bodies throughout France hastened to purchase the office to cement their local authority.[5]

The municipality bought the office of lieutenant-general of police of "the city, suburbs and outskirts of Rouen" in 1700. Conflict between the powers of this magistrate and four local seigneurs possessing the right of high justice arose almost immediately. Nor was the position of this office vis-à-vis royal prerogative clearly delineated, as the king was also viscount of Rouen. As in Bordeaux, Lille, and Paris, the welter of overlapping rights provided an opportunity to apply the privilege of liberty by favoring some privileges over others.

To the four existing high justices in and around the provincial capital, ten new privileged enclaves were added in 1702 through the "dismemberment of the viscounty of Rouen and its alienation by the king." Therefore, Rouen, its suburbs, and outskirts came to have fourteen *hautes justices* with *police* power beyond the sway of either the chief police magistrate or the city's guilds. Supervision of these seigneurs' territories was exercised by royal officials, usually the intendant or his chief deputy, Rouen's subdelegate. The new seigneurs included high-ranking nobles such as the duke of Montmorency and powerful clerical institutions like the archbishopric of Rouen and the abbeys of Fécamp and Bonne-Nouvelle, along with the chapters of churches such as Rouen's La Chartreuse de Saint-Julien and Saint-Ouen. Almost all of these seigneurs named bailiffs to protect their financial interests and implement their commands, but the economic policies at work in these enclaves came from the intendant and his subdelegate.[6]

This partnership between the central state and high-ranking nobles or eminent clerical institutions furthered the pattern established by Colbert in the 1660s. He created royal manufactures and granted privileges of liberty to Louviers held by Rouen's archbishop and the duke d'Elbeuf. As we shall see, these privileges were administered by crown agents serving

[5] See Jean Ricommard, *La lieutenance générale de police à Troyes au XVIIIe siècle* (Hachette, 1934).

[6] The previous two paragraphs are based on Louis-Thiroux de Crosne, *Lettre à M. de Tolozan*, August 27, 1779, AN F12 786.

simultaneously as seigneurial bailiff. Thus encouraged, high-quality woolens manufactures prospered in both towns. With the formation of new privileged enclaves in and around Rouen to supplement the large number of preexisting Norman territories with the right of high justice, the royal government now had sufficient spaces, willing seigneurial partners, and an industrious population habituated to manufacturing available to deploy the privilege of liberty more broadly. Over the course of the eighteenth century, the state's strategic use of the privilege of liberty speeded the province's industrial growth and supported France's international competitiveness. Normandy's experiences demonstrate both the successes and limitations of Bourbon political economy based on the privilege of liberty.

Privilege and the development of networks of production

Economic development in Normandy relied on privilege to establish and maintain networks of production. Like Lille, Rouen was at the heart of a vast system of textile manufacture that stretched dozens of miles in every direction. From the seventeenth to the mid-nineteenth century, domestic industry dominated large parts of the countryside. Like their English and Dutch competitors, Norman industriousness stemmed from a desire to consume. But for the Normans, high food prices and a growing population ensured that consumption would remain focused on subsistence rather than on manufactured goods, though some undoubtedly purchased items that were ostensibly beyond their means.[7] With sixty-five to seventy inhabitants per square kilometer in 1713, this province of 1.8 million (in the 1780s) was nearly one-third more densely populated than the generality of Paris. Extensive noble and clerical landholding limited direct exploitation of the soil, but tenant farmers achieved a threefold increase in the production of cereals. A system of royal roads traversing the province linking Paris to the booming ports of Rouen, Le Havre, Dieppe, and Cherbourg was well begun but unfinished when the old régime collapsed. Water transport remained essential. The Seine River was the province's chief axis of exchange with the interior and to foreign markets and supply sources. Ports buttressed the province's commercial and industrial development after 1715. By tonnage, Rouen's port traffic more than doubled in the eighteenth century, with the value quintupling as the increase in relatively

[7] On consumption, see Jan de Vries, *The Industrious Revolution: Consumer Behavior and the Household Economy, 1650 to the present* (Cambridge University Press, 2008).

cheap bulk goods was far surpassed by growth in more expensive merchandise. The provincial capital handled 16 percent of French seaborne commerce in 1789. Fueled by Atlantic trade, Le Havre grew even faster, tripling in port volume. Dieppe and smaller ports like Honfleur and Saint-Valéry-en-Caux also saw impressive gains. These gains were both cause and effect of the eighteenth-century development of networks of industrial production and commercial exchange based on privilege.[8]

As in Flanders, merchants and manufacturers based in Rouen began "putting out" wool to be carded and/or spun in rural households in the thirteenth century. Normandy's production pattern, however, differed significantly from that of Flanders. The guilds of the provincial capital exercised authority not just in the city proper but also over the suburbs and outskirts, which mitigated some of the conflicts that plagued Lille, Bordeaux, and Paris. Rouen had plenty of low-rent and low-wage space available to expand production. The volume of exchange in Normandy represented the greatest difference: Lille's privileged monopoly of the textile market (until the 1760s) was impossible for a commercial hub like Rouen.

Most Norman woolens were made and dyed according to the general regulations of 1669. On Rouen's eastern fringe, Darnetal had an entrenched guild system with its own thriving market for thread made in the countryside. Eleven miles to the south sat Elbeuf and a further eleven miles southward was Louviers. These privileged enclaves provided competition from the cradle for Rouen, pushing *corporate* entrepreneurs to improve business practices and marketing techniques while cutting costs and accepting limited profits. In this context, state deployment of the privilege of liberty encouraged flexibility and promoted technological improvement, while providing options and outlets that minimized the bitter legal and political conflicts that sapped Flanders' competitive position.

Normandy boasted production networks in five different categories of textiles in a multitude of local styles at a full range of price points. Output ran the gamut from "superfine" cloth suitable for clerical vestments to coarse linen burlap used to wrap metal goods for shipping. Initially, wool and linen dominated the province's textile industry. In the late seventeenth century, they were joined first by "mixed" or blended fabrics in which the warp and weft were made of different threads, then by cotton, and finally after 1758, by printed cotton or *indiennes*. To

[8] Comité régional d'histoire de la Révolution française (Haute-Normandie), *La Révolution en Haute-Normandie 1789–1802*, 12–15 and Le Bozec, *La Normandie au XVIIIe siècle*, 13, 18.

delineate all these networks is beyond the scope of this book, but recognizing the role of privilege in the development of these webs is essential to understanding early modern economic development.

Privilege shaped Normandy's textile networks in three fundamental ways. First, commercial privileges governing the sale, transport, and export of finished goods and raw materials enabled the province's textiles to sell in markets from Paris to Pondicherry. Second, the right of guilds, selected places, and some individuals to make use of certain technologies or chemical processes whether new or in common use constituted a privilege that powerfully influenced which goods were made, where, and at what cost. These privileges shaped French international competitiveness. Finally, privileges relating to skilled labor and markets structured access to experienced and competent workers, the training of apprentices, and the makeup of the pool of potential entrepreneurs. The unique characteristics of each type of privilege and their interplay can be glimpsed in the emergence of a network producing mixed-fiber textiles radiating from the city of Rouen. In fact, the very existence of mixed-fiber textiles demonstrates the flexibility of production in Normandy and the ability of that province's entrepreneurs to imitate styles pioneered elsewhere.

Guild regulations dating from the fifteenth century permitted Rouen's masters to work with only one type of fiber, whether wool, linen, silk, hemp, or cotton. Even guilds that initially were allowed to blend fibers, usually for decorative or ornamental purposes, were soon forbidden to do so. In 1531, the city's silk trimming and cloth guild (*passementiers*) was forbidden to use "any threads of linen, wool, or other yarn" to prevent "abuses" in following the rules governing the length and/or weight of their goods. In practice, this prohibition was flouted as the silk trimming and cloth guild used gold and silver thread in their designs. Throughout the seventeenth century, the cloth-makers' guild (*toiliers*) adulterated many fabrics with threads of cheaper fibers. In 1676, the royal council of commerce headed by Colbert expressly banned the practice, establishing a 50-*livre* penalty for violators. A 1693 regulation for the generalities of Caen and Alençon stated that "all cloth . . . will be composed of the same type of thread without alternation or mixing." The first article of a new regulation for the generality of Rouen promulgated in 1701 banned mixing fibers. Enforcement was delegated to guild wardens and inspectors of manufacturing. This ban was reiterated in 1731. How then could mixed-fiber textiles be made?[9]

[9] The silk trimmings and cloth guild statutes are reprinted in Charles Ouin-Lacroix, *Histoire des anciennes Corporations d'Arts et Métiers et des Confréries Religieuses de la capital de la Normandie* (Rouen: Lecointe Frères, 1850), 646, 707–11. Conseil Royale de Commerce, *Reglements pour les longeurs, largeurs et qualities des Toiles qui se fabriquent en Normandie*,

Although formally outlawed by guild regulations, entrepreneurs innovated to satisfy fashion's craving and to avoid losing markets to English competition. According to two different inspectors of manufacturing, the fad began with the arrival of the king of Siam's first ambassador in 1684. Enthusiasm for his colorful clothes, made of a patterned silk-cotton blend, swept the court. Such blends were made in England, so to keep the court's custom, French manufacturers tried their hand at making this expensive fabric, known as *siamoise* after the ambassador.

The turning point came during the Nine Years War (1688–1697) when a Rouennais merchant firm, Delarue Brothers, acquired forty bales of cotton. Ėtienne Delarue decided to see if *siamoises* might be made in Normandy. First, he needed to recruit a guild master to weave the fabric. After several silk trimming and cloth masters refused, a cloth-maker named Pigny made the province's first *siamoise* with silk warps and cotton wefts in 1694. Rouen's cloth-makers almost immediately figured out how to replace silk with a stronger fiber, namely linen, to create a relatively inexpensive cotton–linen blend that was simple to make and easy to dye. In concert with two wealthy cloth-makers, Bigot and Jacques Cousin, who had extensive putting-out operations near Yvetot, Delarue diffused the method of making this innovative fabric. They hoped to develop a new industry and substitute for costly British wartime imports.[10]

The market for *siamoises* expanded rapidly. Fabrics made with warps of linen, silk, hemp, or wool and cotton wefts were generally known as *rouenneries*, though, from 1703, that name also applied to cloth made solely from poor grades of cotton. Used at first for women's skirts and petticoats, these fabrics made excellent slip covers, bed hangings, and other home furnishings as well as women's clothes. By 1732, the region around Rouen produced 107,000 bolts of *rouenneries*, rising to 181,000 bolts in 1736 and reaching a height of 310,000 bolts in 1749. Normandy exported textiles chiefly to Spain and Portugal for transshipment to the colonies, but also to England and the Low Countries. The province's textiles also found markets all over the country, especially in Paris, Lyon, and the neighboring provinces of Picardy and the Orléanais. Tens of thousands of Normans earned their livelihoods spinning, weaving, dyeing, transporting, and selling cotton-blend fabrics. Cotton

August 14, 1676, the 1693 measure is appended, and *Arrêt du Conseil d'Ėtat du Roi portant reglement pour toutes les Toiles qui se fabriqueront dans l'étendue de la Generalité de Rouen*, December 24, 1701 (both on Googlebooks).

10 There is some dispute over these pioneers' names. *Pigny* is sometimes spelled *Pinel* and *Bigot* is *Bigault* while *Cousin* is sometimes *Thierry*. I have used the eighteenth-century names.

blends led naturally to all-cotton fabrics: mixed-fiber cloth sparked the takeoff of Normandy's cotton industry, the largest in France. Referring to Ėtienne Delarue, intendant of commerce Daniel-Charles de Trudaine told the Rouennais, "You ought to erect a golden statue on your walls."[11]

Making blended fabric was specifically forbidden by national and province-specific guidelines alike, both for guild and for non-guild producers. How then was this new product category, indeed, this new industry, able to survive and thrive? Protections afforded by seigneurial privilege illustrate how mixed-fiber cloth could be made and sold, while showing how networks of production spread their tentacles across the province. As demonstrated below, seigneurs provided liberty from control by guild producers. Unjustly reputed by some historians for resisting innovation, Norman entrepreneurs introduced and diffused blended fabrics throughout the province. Beginning in the late seventeenth century, seigneurial authority combined with state regulatory support to circumvent the restrictions imposed by guild privileges to develop a popular product category. Local privileges of liberty so successfully encouraged industrial development in this model province that the tactic emerged as a centerpiece of Bourbon political economy in the second half of the eighteenth century.

The introduction of mixed-fiber fabrics in Normandy also reminds us of the possibility of alternative means of developing large-scale flexible production in the manner delineated by Charles Sabel and Jonathan Zeitlin. An institutional approach based on political economy helps to explain why rule violations were accepted after the fact. Flexible production was not simply or even primarily a technological matter before the onset of the industrial revolution. When a product found markets, entrepreneurs found ways to ramp up production.[12]

[11] The three previous paragraphs are based on Pierre Dardel, *Commerce, Industrie et Navigation à Rouen et au Havre au XVIIIème siècle: Rivalité croissante entre ces deux ports*, vol. 1, *La Conjoncture* (Rouen: Société libre d'émulation de la Seine-Maritime, 1966), 117, Serge Chassagne, *Le coton est ses patrons: France, 1760–1840* (Ėditions de l'EHESS, 1991), 26–27, Ouin-Lacroix, *Histoire des anciennes Corporations d'Arts et Métiers*,109–13, Savary des Bruslons with Philibert-Louis Savary, *Dictionnaire universel de commerce*, IV: 731. Trudaine's quote is cited by André Rémond, *John Holker: Manufacturier et grand fonctionnaire en France au XVIIIième siècle 1719–1786* (Marcel Rivière, 1946), 42. The production figures apply only to goods that were officially inspected. Actual output was at least one-third greater. Gay Gullickson provides higher figures based on a different, older work by Dardel in *Spinners and Weavers of Auffay: Rural Industry and the Sexual Division of Labor in a French Village, 1750–1850* (Cambridge University Press, 1986), 63, n. 113.

[12] Charles F. Sabel and Jonathan Zeitlin, *World of Possibilities: Flexibility and Mass Production in Western Industrialization* (Cambridge University Press, 2002), 1–36. See also Daryl M. Hafter, *Women at Work in Preindustrial France* (University Park: Pennsylvania State University Press, 2007), 149–63, Reddy, "The Textile Trade," 66–71, and Louis Bergeron, *France Under Napoleon*, trans. R. R. Palmer (Princeton University Press,

Privileged enclaves played a vital role in the emergence of this fledgling industry. Although Rouen housed the main cloth halls where domestic and foreign merchants could purchase large lots, the village of Saint-Georges-du-Vièvre, twenty-six miles southwest of Rouen, had a busy weekly cloth market. Paul Voisin de Saint-Paul, the baron of Bourgtherould who bought the fief in 1691, managed the market, but inspection was conducted by cloth-makers from the distant provincial capital. This situation was disturbed when the regulations of 1693 for the generalities of Caen and Alençon permitted local, that is, seigneurial, judges to inspect and mark cloth brought to privileged markets. As a result, when the first blended fabrics were made, a major market outlet for cloth that was also exempt from state inspection existed outside the *corporate* system. Based on the later locations of the pioneering masters' workshops, I strongly suspect but cannot conclusively demonstrate that Rouen cloth-makers' trial efforts were conducted in one of the city's privileged enclaves, most likely Saint-Gervais. Thus shielded, mixed-fiber fabrics gained a foothold in enclaves where flexible production was feasible and entrepreneurs empowered to take risks. Normandy's first trials with all-cotton cloth took place in the privileged enclave of Bolbec, then part of the duchy of Longueville.[13]

Rapid expansion of trade in *rouenerries* forced both *corporations* and the state to play catchup. The laxity of guild inspection noted in every regulation of the era encouraged master cloth-makers to jump on the bandwagon. Merchants and manufacturers from Rouen immediately began putting out cotton for domestic spinning across the northern parts of the province. Blended cloth was woven in the privileged enclaves of Bolbec, Darnetal, Elbeuf, Louviers, and Yvetot. Both rural outworking and urban finishing occurred under seigneurial protection. This system posed as grave a threat to Rouen's domination of the province's textile industry as it did to Lille's. From 1700, the actions of Rouen's guild masters indicate their realization that if production in areas beyond their control was not reined in, the city would be excluded from a booming product category.

1981 [1972]), 177–80. For alternative views focusing on quality production, see Alessandro Stanziani (ed.), *La qualité des produits en France, XVIIIème-XXème siècles* (Belin, 2003).

13 *Arrêt du Conseil du Roi portant Reglement pour les Manufactures de Toiles des Generalités de Caen et d'Alençon*, April 7, 1693 (Gallica), Chassagne, *Le coton*, 26, Armand Montier, *Recherches sur le commerce et la fabrication dans le lieuvin aux XVIIe et XVIII siècles dites Rouens-Fleurets-Blancards d'après des documents inédits* (Pont Audamer: Ernest Dugas, 1874), 13–15, Ouin-Lacroix, *Histoire des anciennes Corporations d'Arts et Métiers*, 110–11, and a local history site: http://hombeline.e-monsite.com/pages/la-creation-du-village-les-premiers-siecles/le-roux-voisin-le-cordier.html (accessed July 11, 2012).

After initially turning a blind eye to the manufacture of *rouenneries*, guild wardens exerted their privileges. Lobbying by the city's silk trimmings and cloth masters led the *parlement* of Rouen to issue an ordinance in 1709 recognizing this guild's right to make the new blended fabric, thereby legitimizing *corporate* production. In 1718, the cloth-makers demanded and received state recognition of their rights. As production spread, fraudulent sale of blended fabric as all-cotton along with skimping on size, thread count, and the quality of raw materials became commonplace. Bourbon administrators attempted to police the new industry, though with limited success. The royal council issued general regulations in 1718, 1719, 1720, and 1723 that mandated sizes, thread counts, and qualities for different fabrics and various aspects of the production process. Only in 1731 was an effective standard devised: it governed both all-cotton and blended fabrics. The difficulties of enforcing the royal council's orders reveal what was at stake in the competition between privileged interests and how everyone involved in the dispute could claim to represent the "good of commerce."[14]

At mid-century, blended fabrics were woven all over Normandy. *Siamoises* of linen and cotton were woven in the privileged enclaves of Darnetal, Elbeuf, Louviers, and Yvetot, as well as in Rouen. Silk-wool blends were made in Rouen by the silk trimming and cloth guild, while the upholsterers' guild created cotton-wool blends for furniture coverings and wall hangings. Silk-cotton and cotton-linen blends were manufactured by guild masters in a number of small cities around the province as well as in several privileged enclaves in Rouen's suburbs. Domestic spinning of linen thread was done mostly in the *pays de caux* (northwest of Rouen) from flax grown or purchased in market towns like Bolbec or Pont Audamer. In poorer villages, merchants or their factors delivered the bulky raw flax on consignment. Cotton was spun in homes and workshops in a thirty-mile-wide circle around Rouen, especially in the suburbs and outskirts of the provincial capital. Cotton was almost always furnished by Rouennais merchants or their factors. These entrepreneurs also collected the finished thread and took it to Rouen. To cut out the middlemen, thousands of domestic workers sold their own thread or cloth at markets in high justices like Saint-Georges-du-Vièvre or Bernay in the suburbs of Pont Audamer. For other than local sale, finished cloth always ended up in Rouen. The near-exclusive location of

[14] Chassagne, *Le coton*, 26–27, Montier, *Recherches sur le commerce et la fabrication*, 20–22, and Ouin-Lacroix, *Histoire des anciennes Corporations d'Arts et Métiers*, 112–13. More generally, see David Kammerling Smith, "'Au bien du commerce': Economic Discourse and Visions of Society in France" (PhD dissertation, University of Pennsylvania, 1995).

blended fabric's markets and weaving centers in Normandy's privileged enclaves is striking.

Privilege facilitated specialized production and division of labor. Each privileged enclave exploited different market niches. Darnetal was one of the first Norman textile-producing enclaves to experiment with cotton and cotton blends. However, after a 1723 state edict forced many Norman manufacturers to suspend operations for three months, Darnetal's entrepreneurs dedicated themselves to perfecting their dyeing and finishing techniques for the manufacture of woolens. Cotton production dwindled. Saint-Gervais went the other direction: its entrepreneurs abandoned blends to focus on all-cotton fabrics. Like Darnetal, Elbeuf initially produced cotton blends in blue and white stripes, but dropped out to focus on wool. In both places, the cotton sector revived a generation later. Based on the high-quality work of its bleachers' guild, Louviers initially made white *siamoises* but switched to stripes in a wide variety of colors. The city, suburbs, and outskirts of Rouen made a little bit of everything but focused on striped and windowpane patterns. Rouen also produced the finest grades of *siamoise*. Yvetot had a similar trajectory to Louviers, though at a lower price point. From simple bleached *siamoises*, the Yvetotois developed expertise in blue and white patterned fabrics for upholstery. They too made windowpane patterns and stripes of both common and fine quality. Normandy's manufacturers developed diverse products to satisfy varied customers in widely scattered markets. Privilege was the key to economic development through the emergence of flexible production.

In Rouen, finished textiles were sold either to French and foreign merchants or to the city's large contingent of wholesalers. As a major mercantile and industrial center, Rouen's merchants brought in raw materials and sent ships and cargos of manufactured goods around the world. Although merchants in smaller cities and towns participated in the putting-out process for blended fabrics, Rouen monopolized the wholesale market because of the energy and wealth of its entrepreneurs, its position as a regional transport center linked to a major port, and because of its commercial and industrial privileges.[15]

[15] The previous three paragraphs are based on Gullickson, *Spinners and Weavers of Auffay*, 22, 62–63, Savary des Bruslons with Philibert-Louis Savary, *Dictionnaire universel de commerce*, IV: 1031, V: 177–79, Jean-Baptiste Goy, *Mémoire sur les Bureaux de toilerie établie dans la ville et généralité de Rouen et sur le Commerce de ses fabriques en conséquence de la tournée générale que l'inspecteur des manufactures vient d'y faire*, November 12, 1782, AN F12 650, *Arrêt du Conseil d'État*, June 28, 1723, AN AE BIII 284, Ouin-Lacroix, *Histoire des anciennes Corporations d'Arts et Métiers*, 111–12.

Rouen's economic vibrancy represents a competitive success of Bourbon mercantilism. Although neither French industrial growth nor its commercial expansion measured up to that of England or the Netherlands on a per capita basis, fuzzy national statistics must not obscure Normandy's achievements. This large and populous region whose industrial output rivaled that of far larger countries *did* compete effectively with its North Sea neighbors. Until the emergence of a true national market in the second half of the nineteenth century, France was composed of regional economies that were more or less integrated into broader networks of exchange. Many regions grew only slowly during the early modern era, but a number of others competed successfully. Privilege played a major role in helping certain regions to develop, but as discussed in Chapter 2, it was not always equally effective, in large measure due to the institutional nexus.[16]

As many commentators have noted, both in the eighteenth century and today, *corporate* organization of production raised costs. The regulation of 1718 governing the manufacture of blended cloth in and around Rouen mandated multiple steps that usually involved the cooperation of four different guilds. Wholesale merchants were involved at the beginning and end of the procedure. They acquired cotton, wool, linen, hemp, and silk for distribution to households, workers, or masters either through their factors or by direct sale. They also purchased the bulk of the finished fabrics. Spinning took place outside guild control, but the thread was combed and combined into bundles of similar lengths and strengths either by a master comber or by a worker whose comb had been guild inspected and certified.

Depending on the kind of cloth to be made, thread was usually bleached or dyed – by different guilds, naturally – before being woven, although occasionally it was done afterward. Dyeing "in the city, suburbs, or outskirts of Rouen or in the countryside" had to be undertaken by someone registered with the guild. Each dyer had to mark their work with a "particular brand." The same was true for bleachers. Bleached and dyed clothes were inspected and certified.

The thread then went to a weaver who put the different fiber threads on the loom as warp and weft. This weaver was a subcontractor working at home or a journeyman or some other worker directly employed either by a master cloth-maker or by a silk trimmings and cloth master. For most

[16] Here I reject the view of Tim C. W. Blanning, *The French Revolution: Aristocrats versus Bourgeois?* (Houndsmills: Macmillan, 1987), who revives an argument made by Edward W. Fox, *History in Geographic Perspective: The Other France* (New York: W.W. Norton, 1971).

large-scale weavers of blended cloth who operated under Rouen's *corporate* umbrella, in Saint-Gervais or in Darnetal, guild experts conducted two separate inspections. First the cloth was inspected on the loom and again upon completion. Other producers had to bring their goods to the city's cloth hall to be inspected and branded. With so many steps and so many inspections, managing production profitably was a complex process that required understanding the regulatory system as well as considerable managerial skill.

Heavy transport charges and many delays plagued guild production. Was this the cheapest, easiest, or fastest way to make blended fabrics? No. However, division of labor, individual responsibility for quality, and multiple inspections encouraged the manufacture of relatively uniform, well-made goods. The system frequently did not function as intended, but it protected customers from fraud far better than would be the case once manufacturers and traders received greater liberty in the second half of the eighteenth century. For wholesale merchants and French policymakers, protecting consumers through the manufacture of consistent, quality goods was essential to an industry dependent on long-distance trade and repeat business. For them, the added costs stemming from the *corporate* system were worth it, a market-based reality that critics who dismiss the guilds as inefficient or rent-seeking frequently overlook.

There was one major exception to the doubly privileged weaving of blended fabrics undertaken by guilds in Rouen and in the high justices. Due to the efforts of Rouen's merchants, cottage industry in the *pays de caux* developed prodigiously over the course of the eighteenth century. Rural and village households made blended fabrics with stripes or windowpane designs along with linen and cotton cloths from threads they spun themselves, purchased from their neighbors, or received from a merchant's factor. According to Savary des Bruslons, these blends did not have to be branded and frequently deviated from the sizes mandated by the regulations. Officials tolerated them because the fabrics were put to different uses than fabrics made in privileged enclaves. Both from a competitive standpoint and from the perspective of political economy, the liberty of the *pays de caux* complemented the privileges of the high justices to maximize employment while keeping costs low, and furnishing a wide variety of products of different qualities and prices.[17]

[17] The four previous paragraphs are based on Chassagne, *Le coton*, 25–27, Gullickson, *Spinners and Weavers of Auffay*, 62–63, Savary des Bruslons with Philibert-Louis Savary, *Dictionnaire universel de commerce*, IV: 1031, V: 177–79, *Arrêt du Conseil d'État*, December 24, 1701, Goy, *Mémoire*, November 12, 1782, *Suite du nouveau recueil des Édits,*

The Norman pattern of local specialization can be seen as a means of avoiding competition. But in a developing industrial sector characterized by seemingly unlimited demand, such specialization should also be understood as a profoundly rational entrepreneurial strategy. By allowing producers to seek out markets with little competition, specialized production helped to ensure the steady profits needed for expansion and avoided dips in employment, which was essential to retaining scarce skilled labor. That the localities' specialties evolved over time demonstrates the market sensitivity of Normandy's merchants and textile manufacturers. Based on geographically distinct privileged enclaves, specialized production also curtailed (but did not eliminate) costly legal battles or commercial struggles over market access or share. This approach enabled the province's entrepreneurs to expand simultaneously into many different areas and product categories. Encouraging specialized production in privileged enclaves was rational political economy in early modern France.

Royal officials played a vital role in developing Normandy's textile production networks. Regulating the size and quality of various categories of textiles "branded" French goods in the emerging global marketplace. Intervention by inspectors of manufacturing, intendants, and their subdelegates ensured a measure of compliance with the regulations and minimized bottlenecks that throttled production. As we shall see in Chapter 7, the Bourbon administration granted some new privileges and gave financial assistance to a few innovative entrepreneurs or inventors, but managing liberties of privilege and privileges of liberty were the state's most important contributions to the formation of these webs of production.

State regulations did more than establish standards. They also determined the placement of markets, their duration, and the role of Rouen in overseeing them. The 1701 cloth-making regulation restored the provincial capital's supervision of subsidiary markets like Saint-Georges-du-Vièvre and Bernay, thus maintaining the privileges of Rouen and these high justices. The government also protected Rouen's pivotal role in the developing networks of textile production by keeping inspection centered there. This was particularly true in mixed-fiber

Déclarations, Lettres Patentes, Arrêts et Réglemens de Sa Majesté lesquels ont été enregistré au Parlement; ensemble des Arrêts et Réglemens et autres de ladite Cour le tout depuis l'année 1717 jusqu'en mil sept cens vingt-six (Rouen: Jean-Baptiste Besongne, 1741), 166–69, and the 1731 regulation reprinted in Ouin-Lacroix, *Histoire des anciennes Corporations d'Arts et Métiers*, 646–55.

fabrics. Only after 1760 were inspection offices created in Bolbec, Elbeuf, Louviers, and Yvetot.[18]

Bourbon administrators reigned in the liberty of privilege when the *corporations* tried to dominate their workforces or to limit domestic industry. On behalf of the *parlement*, the provincial capital's cloth inspectors proposed in 1722 that "for the general good of this industry, [*siamoise*] looms should be restricted to the city and suburbs of Rouen and to the cities and market towns of the generality where there are guilds and masters." However, other inspectors, like Augustin Lerougé de Laval, rejected the measure: "it would stop the progress of this industry, so large and so useful to the families it helps feed." The deputies of commerce defended the role of the market. One deputy wrote that "it does not serve the good of the state or that of the province of Normandy to prevent workers from making goods of linen and cotton nor to restrict this industry to the city." The deputies questioned whether "reducing spinning and weaving to the city and suburbs of Rouen would not destroy the natural liberty that everyone ought to have at home to choose what work pleases them," before recommending that "nothing change in the state of manufactures in Normandy." As a sop to the *parlement* and Rouen's guilds, the royal council mandated a three-month moratorium (July to September 1723) on production outside the provincial capital and its suburbs, but no general ban was issued.[19]

The creation of networks of production in blended fabrics in Normandy is a complicated story. Market demand permitted rules to be broken and rationalized retroactively. Limits stemming from the state of existing technologies from the end of the seventeenth century through the 1730s meant that the only effective way to expand production was to add workers. Such conditions shaped the creation of seemingly inefficient but nonetheless quite rational networks. Import substitution and the employment of an expanding population justified state intervention, both to protect existing privileged manufactures in urban areas and to maintain productive liberties in the countryside. Together, privilege and liberty created a major manufacturing sector that midwifed one of France's signature industries.

[18] The three previous paragraphs are based on *Arrêt du Conseil d'État*, December 24, 1701, Goy, *Mémoire*, November 12, 1782, Ouin-Lacroix, *Histoire des anciennes Corporations d'Arts et Métiers*, 646–55 and 111–12.

[19] The quotes in this paragraph are from Chassagne, *Le coton*, 26–29. See also *Arrêt du Conseil d'État*, June 28, 1723.

The limits of seigneurial oversight: specialization, collective opportunities, and the role of the state

Strategic deployment of the privilege of liberty in Normandy began with Colbert. From the 1660s, he worked with or co-opted high-ranking nobles and clergy to expand the industrial potential of territories enjoying high justice. What distinguishes the situation in Normandy from the examples explored in the previous chapter is the systematic, sustained nature of state involvement in the project of development. Administrators' engagement with Normandy's high justices demonstrates both the workings of the privilege of liberty and how these spaces fit into the provincial and national economies.

Even when they exercised their *police* and market privileges energetically, Normandy's seigneurs left most of the hard work of encouraging industry while regulating entrepreneurs and workers to agents of the central state. Seigneurs lobbied for the creation of inspection bureaus, protected inventors and entrepreneurs who had gained the favor of the royal administration, and used their judicial authority to support state initiatives. Princes, dukes, and archbishops along with lower-ranking nobles and clergy cooperated with the Bourbon state by naming the local subdelegate their bailiff or by allowing their bailiff to add the post of subdelegate. More importantly, seigneurs used *police* privileges to enact state developmental strategy, which did not necessarily maximize their own or their clients' immediate interests.

Rouen's archbishop was Normandy's greatest feudal lord. In addition to overseeing 1,388 parishes, 131 priories, and 31 monasteries and abbeys, with 6,500 clergy and religious (in 1698), this powerful cleric possessed the right of high justice in all his lands. The archbishop was master of the port of Dieppe (population of 25,000 in 1789), as well as the large seigneuries of Fresnes-l'Archevêque, Cliponville, d'Envronville, les Andelys, Bouteilles, Aliermont, and Gaillon, all of which stretched over several parishes. From the standpoint of industrial policy, however, the archbishop's two most important territories were the viscounty of Déville, which included a string of villages northwest and west of Rouen along the Cailly River, and the county of Louviers (14,000 inhabitants in 1789, half living in the city). Feudal rights from these territories generated a colossal 173,000 *livres* annually.

Some archbishops, like Dominique de la Rochefoucauld, wielded even greater economic power. Appointed archbishop in 1759, he soon became a cardinal. He remained in office until the promulgation of the civil constitution of the clergy in 1790. This son, brother, uncle, and cousin to dukes was also named abbot of Fécamp (among other positions). A wealthy abbey with revenues of 85,000 *livres*, Fécamp enjoyed rights of high justice in six parishes in Rouen's western suburbs, of which Saint-Gervais and Oissel were the most important, along with the barony of Villefleur with fifteen parishes in Le Havre's suburbs, and another four parishes near Caudebec. Multiple benefices magnified the impact of the cardinal-archbishop's cooperation with royal authorities on Norman industrial policy.[20]

Louviers began producing woolens in the thirteenth century. A "general ordinance" for the manufacture of woolens dates from 1325. For a small city, Louviers had a considerable number of guilds mostly related to the production and distribution of textiles (twenty in 1696 and twenty-three in 1728). The archbishops of Rouen, however, kept the guild system weak and under close control. As a matter of policy, Louviers' guilds were not allowed to collect sufficient fees to employ experts – either outsiders or locals – to perform inspections. Instead, the archbishop's bailiff had sole responsibility to enforce industrial and commercial regulations and to inspect machines, workshops, and goods.

Although woolens were already flourishing in Louviers (sixty looms and 1,900 workers) and the putting-out system was widespread in the county, Colbert sought to expand output and improve quality. In 1681, Louviers received an additional privilege. Uniquely, the measure naming the city's manufacturers a collective "royal manufacture" gave the archbishop's bailiff special regulatory powers. He became responsible for assuring the use of the highest-quality wool, suitable for making clerical vestments, and guaranteeing the production of standard-sized bolts of cloth. With this measure, for the woolens industry, Louis XIV effectively delegated the archbishop's *police* power to the bailiff. The bailiff presided over a "bureau des manufactures de Louviers" whose paid staff oversaw production and conducted inspections. In exchange, Rouen's intendant obtained the right to approve the bailiff's appointment. The practice of having the subdelegate and bailiff either be the same person or be closely related soon began.

Louviers' "superfine" woolens were expensive. A bolt cost 450–550 *livres*, a far cry from the 40-*livre* selling price of a bolt of Lille's common

[20] The two previous paragraphs are based on Maurice Veyrat, *La haute justice des archevêques de Rouen, comtes de Louviers 1197–1790*, thèse de doctorat en droit (Rouen: Éditions Maugard, 1948), 31–33, 55–57, Robert Langlois (vicomte d'Estaintot), *Recherches sur les hautes justices féodales existant en 1789 dans les limites du département de la Seine-Inférieure* (Rouen: A Lestringant, 1892), 17, 35, 46, 51, Julien Loth, *Histoire du Cardinal de la Rochefoucauld et du diocese de Rouen pendant la Révolution* (Évreux: Imprimerie de l'Eure, 1893), 23–24, 50, and Guy Lemarchand, "Le temporal et les revenues de l'abbaye de Fécamp pendant le XVIIe et le XVIIIe siècle," *Annales de Normandie*, 15: 2 (1965), 528.

woolen twill. Raw wool comprised 60–70 percent of that cost, with dyestuffs costing another 10–15 percent. At best, two weavers working a loom made two bolts a month; sixteen or seventeen days each was more common. Preparing the wool, spinning the thread, dyeing, and finishing of cloth all required careful attention to maintain Louviers' "reputation," which sustained high profits per unit sold.

From Colbert's day to 1750, the French state generally delegated the maintenance of quality production to guilds overseen by inspectors of manufacturing and other officials (see Chapter 2). With the formation of the royal manufacture, Louviers' guilds lost the authority to supervise the production process, but they could still limit access to their collective privileges, ostensibly to maintain high-quality production. Generations of bailiffs and guild masters conspired to keep firms "in the family" and to exclude even qualified "outsiders." Officials nurtured the formation of an entrepreneurial oligarchy by suspending the creation of new masters in key woolens centers between 1717 and 1758. Despite the deputies of commerce's clear disapproval, for over forty years, only relatives, either by blood or marriage, could become a master, but only of an existing firm. A ruling by the bailiff, endorsed by the royal council, thanks to lobbying by the archbishop, barred new firms. Even after the ban was lifted, Louviers' masters maintained their oligarchy by charging exorbitant fees for apprentices from outside their families and by requiring new masters to pay 1,000 *livres* to join the community versus 50 *livres* for the son of a master.[21]

When Louis Frontin, a large-scale woolens master in Elbeuf, requested authorization to set up a mill in 1766, Louviers' masters pressured the bailiff to reject his petition. They successfully mobilized their administrative patrons to ratify the decision with an ordinance from the intendant. In 1774, another Elbeuvian guild master, Louis-Mathieu Racine, sought to establish a mill in Louviers. Lovériens claimed that Racine was acting as a front for Frontin and other Elbeuvians who wanted to sell their inferior wares under Louviers' trademark. With one of their own established in Louviers, fraud would run rampant and "the reputation of the city's woolens would

[21] The four previous paragraphs are based on Jean-Michel Chaplain, *La Chambre des tisseurs–Louviers: cité drapière 1680–1840* (Champ Vallon, 1984), 27, 37, 41, 70, 72, Veyrat, *La haute justice des archevêques de Rouen*, 167–73, Dominique de la Rochefoucauld, *Lettre à M. de Trudaine*, September 26, 1774, AN F12 760, Jean-Baptiste Goy, *Mémoire général sur les bureaux de visite et de marque établis dans la ville et généralité de Rouen*, December 15, 1787, AN F12 1365, *Sentiment des députés au Conseil de Commerce*, March 3, 1717, AN F12 694, *Arrêt du Conseil d'État du Roi*, September 27, 1740, AN AE BIII284, and *Avis des Députés au Conseil de Commerce sur la requette des maitres fabricants de draps de la ville de Louviers*, July 26, 1746, AN F12 705.

suffer considerable damage." If their reputation suffered, masters would have to lay off workers, which would threaten public order. In sum, were Racine to become a master, "all their hard work and sacrifice perfecting their art would be destroyed."

The archbishop and the intendant were drawn into the fray, as was Anne-Robert-Jacques de Turgot, the controller-general of finance. Turgot commanded intendant Louis-Thiroux de Crosne to issue an ordinance making Racine a master. When the wardens delayed, the subdelegate convened the community on February 9, 1775 and gave them direct orders, but resistance persisted. In May, Turgot required them "to receive Racine as a master in their community." The Lovériens held out through July. That Louviers' masters could flout the orders of the intendant and the controller-general displays once again the limitations of French administrative authority. More importantly, however, state persistence on behalf of an innovative, qualified entrepreneur confirms the royal government's growing commitment to at least some measure of liberty even if it was only by ensuring access to privilege in a monopolistic productive environment. According to Lovériens, the state's intervention ended the profitability of the old way of doing things and played a major role in the mechanization of the city's industry in the 1780s.[22]

It might seem counterintuitive to combine widespread use of privilege with a reliance on markets to set prices. In practice, however, these very different beasts were often yoked together to facilitate economic development. Markup was the key to profitability for high-end producers like Louviers. To maintain profits, the Lovériens limited competition by restricting the number of firms and reined in costs by maintaining firm control over labor.

Privilege enabled masters to dominate skilled workers. Throughout the seventeenth century, woolens production in Louviers involved both rural and urban labor. The city's masters provided raw wool to the interestingly

[22] The quotes in the two previous paragraphs are from *Mémoire pour les entrepreneurs des manufactures des draps fins de Louviers contre le sieur Racine se disant maitre de la communauté des fabricants d'Elbeuf et aspirant à la maitrise de celle de Louviers*, n.d. [1774], AN F12 760. See Louis-Thiroux de Crosne, *Lettre à M. De Trudaine*, n.d. [February 1775], Anne-Robert-Jacques de Turgot, *Lettre du Contrôleur-Général aux fabricants de draps de Louviers*, May 19, 1775, and Anne-Robert-Jacques de Turgot, *Lettre du Contrôleur-Général aux fabricants de draps de Louviers*, May 19, 1775. In two letters, Jean Holker fils, *Lettre à M. De Trudaine*, March 30 and April 30, 1775 supported Racine while Dominique, Archvêque de Rouen, *Lettre à M. De Trudaine*, September 26, 1774 did not. All these documents are found in AN F12 760. See also Anne-Robert-Jacques de Turgot, *Lettre à de Crosne*, February 3, 1775, AD Seine-Maritime C135.

named "masters from Avignon" located in surrounding villages (see Chapter 4). By long tradition, these informal subcontractors carded the wool and then gave it to women who spun it, either in a workshop or, more frequently, at home. Every two weeks, the "master" collected the skeins and returned them to a guild producer for dyeing, weaving, and finishing. This situation was increasingly unacceptable to Louviers' entrepreneurs. Their profits required producing more thread, of better quality, furnished more reliably and on a schedule, and all for less cost. Since piece workers were excluded from this closed system, theft of high quality wool was also a major problem.

To rectify the situation and to end "frequent mutinies" by Normandy's woolens workers over wages, the deputies of commerce recognized that official mandates were insufficient. As in Bordeaux, when a 1723 regulation attempted to prevent workers from changing employers unless fired, "nearly all the woolens workers of Louviers left their masters demanding twelve *sols* for each pound of thread not ten." Six masters gave into the demand, "fomenting the spirit of mutiny among the workers" who refused to return to work, even when the bailiff imposed a 30-*livre* fine for leaving a job unfinished.[23] In 1729, the deputies threatened workers with prison if they did not return to their "duty" and work for 10 *sols* a pound. The deputies also imposed a new requirement, a "certificate of discharge" (*billet de congé*), on Louviers' recalcitrant workers. Workers now had to give two weeks' notice if they planned to leave. Nor could workers depart without finishing whatever job they had committed to undertake and had paid off all debts. Workers could not start a new job without a certificate of discharge from their previous employer.

Masters' solidarity enabled certificates of discharge to subordinate Louviers' workers. Ignoring the intendant's ruling that workers should be rehired according to seniority, the entrepreneurs of Louviers fired the leaders of the "mutiny." Masters also rejected a recommendation from the deputies of commerce to increase the piece rate one *sol* per pound. In 1735, masters convinced the bailiff to impose certificates of discharge on domestic workers, not only in the city of Louviers, but also for subcontractors throughout the county. Mediocre remuneration, exacting work standards, and tight regulation meant that Louviers' masters had difficulty finding and retaining skilled labor. Masters complained that workers were lazy. "If four days [of labor] earns them enough to survive for the rest of the week, they will work no more,

[23] *Avis des Députés au Conseil de Commerce sur une lettre du Sieur Chréstien inspecteur des manufactures de draperie de la généralité de Rouen*, August 29, 1729, AN F12 698.

preferring to be idle." When entrepreneurs offered them more money: "the poorer quality of the work is clear." They asserted that "spinners would improve their dexterity and perfect their tasks if they worked without interruption throughout the week."[24]

The royal council adopted Louviers' model. On January 2, 1749, certificates of discharge were required for all French workers in the guild system. In the name of masters' "domestic authority," workers were turned into the legal equivalent of minor children. This ordinance can best be understood as the liberty of privilege taken to its furthest extent.

Protected by their privileges, masters constrained their labor force. Throughout the 1750s, Louviers' entrepreneurs refused to release skilled workers even after they had fulfilled their obligations. Numerous complaints from workers, confirmed by a succession of inspectors of manufacturing, made clear the extent of masters' power. The deputies of commerce described the situation as "tyranny," which "by depriving workers of their natural liberty turned them into slaves." The intendant was ordered to intervene by allowing inspectors of manufacturing to liberate specific workers from their masters' hegemony.

Despite the intrusion of agents of the central state, masters refused to give certificates of discharge into the 1760s, though less systematically. This refusal led to repeated strikes, a high incidence of theft, and frequent shortages of skilled labor. After the assault on the guild system and its reorganization in the mid-to-late 1770s (see Chapter 7), the restiveness of Louviers' workforce intensified. Facing growing competition both at home and abroad, labor recalcitrance convinced the city's entrepreneurs to invest in mechanization. The central state aided this process by granting additional privileges to entrepreneurs who naturalized Arkwright's water frame and imported steam engines to use in spinning. Louviers' privileged entrepreneurs also received the privilege of operating multiple mills in different textile sectors to make the best possible use of their capital and business skills. The high quality and limited volume of Louviers' woolens (4,400 bolts in 1786) heightened the ability of privilege to trump liberty in French industrial policy. In sum, Louviers benefited from a productive environment in which privileged manufacturers made high-quality goods by oppressing a vulnerable labor force. Louviers' masters maintained this system

[24] *Avis des Députés au Conseil de Commerce sur une lettre de M. l'Intendant de Rouen et un procès-verbal du Subdélegué de l'Intendance à Louviers*, January 7, 1737, AN F12 702.

thanks to the royal manufacture's liberty from the shackles of the guild system and national regulations.[25]

In Elbeuf, the workings of the privilege of liberty echoed Louviers', but here, state officials played an even more active role in fostering economic development. Where Louviers made luxury goods with an international reputation that sold for exorbitant prices, Elbeuf took a different route. Elbeuf made good-quality woolens at a reasonable price point that competed in export markets with English and Dutch goods. Consistently squeezed from below by competition from other Norman producers "in the Elbeuf style" and constrained by the need to stay well below prices for "superfine" woolens of luxury producers, Elbeuf's masters innovated continuously, manipulating their privileges and liberties to earn profits.

Elbeuf's woolens industry and *corporate* system also dated from the thirteenth century. Like a number of Norman textile centers including Bolbec, Darnetal, Rouen, and Yvetot, in the seventeenth century Protestants pioneered improving quality to expand production. From his family in the Netherlands, Nicolas Lemonnier learned to make "Holland-style" fine woolens. To transfer the technique to Elbeuf, he employed Dutch artisans on long-term contracts around 1610. By the time Colbert created Elbeuf's "royal manufacture" in 1667, its masters annually produced 2,000 bolts of fine woolens.

Elbeuf's woolens guild collectively received impressive privileges. In exchange, they agreed to follow regulations and make the goods mandated therein. Every member of the guild automatically enjoyed the rights given to the royal manufacture as a whole. Outsiders could become masters if they paid modest fees, but only if "there are masters in place who wish to quit their operation." This rule legalized oligarchy by limiting the number of firms. (This initial restriction was lifted quickly when sales skyrocketed.) A noteworthy element of the regulation was

[25] The eight previous paragraphs are based on Chaplain, *La Chambre des tisseurs*, 37–41, Veyrat, *La haute justice des archevêques de Rouen*, 279, Jeff Horn, *The Path Not Taken: French Industrialization in the Age of Revolution* (Cambridge, MA: MIT Press, 2006), 22–23, *Avis des Députés au Conseil de Commerce sur le procès-verbal de l'assemblée des maitres et des ouvriers de la manufacture de Louviers de 23 mars 1730 au sujet du salaire des ouvriers*, April 4, 1730, AN F12 698, *Avis des Députés du Commerce sur le mémoire du Sieur de Boisroger, inspecteur à Elbeuf et Louviers à l'occasion d'un refus des maitres des manufactures à donner des billets de congé à leurs ouvriers*, December 7, 1756, AN F12 710, *Lettre des entrepreneurs des manufactures de Louviers à M. De Tolozan*, August 24, 1777, AN F12 1365, Goy, *Mémoire*, December 15, 1787, and *Procès-Verbal des séances de l'Assemblée provinciale de la généralité de Rouen tenue aux Cordeliers de cette Ville, aux mois de Novembre et Décembre 1787*, AD Seine-Maritime C2112*.

that widows had the same privileges as their husbands. Not only could widows keep a firm open for a set amount of time, as was typical in most guilds, but they also could operate indefinitely and even train apprentices. While I have no conclusive evidence to explain the unusual position enjoyed by widows in Elbeuf and in Normandy more generally, I suspect that it is a legacy of the province's *coutume*, its legal traditions.[26]

In the 1667 regulation, masters escaped guild constraints on the number and training of their employees. Although they were not supposed to filch workers from one another, masters could hire *anyone* they wanted in any position: this included foreigners, Protestants, and non-Christians, as well as women. Elbeuf's masters could also employ as many workers as they wanted. These opportunities were quite unusual for guild masters, but other aspects of labor relations reflected standard *corporate* practice. Workers could be fired with a mere twenty-four hours' notice, but they had to inform their masters of their intent to leave "when the bolt was being raised" on the loom. They could not depart "until the bolt that had been mounted was completed." The regulation empowered masters to recover wool, thread, tools, and machines from domestic workers or subcontractors outside the city. Inappropriate use of a masters' property was "to be treated as household theft and punished corporally." Masters also received priority-purchase rights for high-quality wool in Elbeuf's market. Finally, no tax collector or judicial clerk could seize a master's materials, tools, or machines in a thirty-mile radius around Elbeuf.[27]

Regulations specified the quality of wool and dyestuffs, the number of threads composing various fabrics, and the length and width of the bolt. Weekly inspections by guild wardens were to confirm a master's observance. Masters were also obliged to have their accounts publicly verified by guild wardens. Each quarter looms and tools were to be examined closely by specialists. Before fulling, woven cloth had to be brought to the cloth hall for review by experts to find defaults in the weaving. After a final inspection, bolts of woven cloth were marked with both the name of the manufacturer and the seal of the royal manufacture. Only then could the cloth be sold, generally in Rouen. In practice, many "mandatory" guild inspections were disregarded. Wardens undertook some inspection and the inspectors of manufacturing stationed in Elbeuf appear to have fulfilled their responsibilities consistently and

26 Hafter, *Women at Work*, 68–69, 239–42.

27 The quotes in the two previous paragraphs are cited by Alain Becchia, *La draperie d'Elbeuf (des origines à 1870)* (Publications de l'Université de Rouen, 2000), 24, 26.

assiduously. Although defective work was seized and either destroyed or sold as scrap for the benefit of the poor, inspection did not always fulfill state objectives. Clearly, the central state believed that the best way to ensure the manufacture of fine woolens over the long term was to foster the establishment of large, stable family firms. These firms benefited from *corporate* organization, most notably a monopoly of production and the ability to control membership. But as a royal manufacture, the masters of Elbeuf escaped most limits on labor, size, and innovation imposed by the guild system. In short, the privilege of liberty enabled Elbeuf's entrepreneurs to make the specified goods with whom and however they wished.[28]

Self-regulation by masters proved problematic. Elbeuf had no oversight that resembled the independent regulation, inspection, and adjudication provided by Louviers' bailiff. According to historian Jeffry Kaplow, under the House of Lorraine, the duke d'Elbeuf's bailiffs delegated regulation of the woolens trade to guild wardens. Protected from Rouen's *corporations*, Elbeuf's masters could do essentially what they wished. Elbeuvians became known for dominating their labor force by limiting wages and worker movement as well as fraud. More positively, Elbeuf also developed a reputation for product and technical innovation.

Elbeuf's masters imitated many of the tactics and strategies practiced by Louviers' entrepreneurs. But as their woolens were not as good as those of Louviers, so too the Elbeuvians were less successful in maintaining their monopoly, dominating their workforce, or partnering effectively with the royal administration. Paradoxically, Elbeuf's aggregate output grew far more rapidly, although individual firms were much less profitable than in Louviers. Despite a high barrier to guild entrance with an apprentice fee of 300 *livres* and a further 300 *livres* to be paid upon acceptance, the number of manufacturers in Elbeuf rose from eleven in 1667, to thirty in 1684, to thirty-seven in 1700, and to eighty-six in 1750 before falling to seventy-six in 1787. This impressive increase overcame determined resistance to accepting new masters who literally were not part of the family.

When wardens rejected the admission of Jean-Baptiste Cavé in 1783, intendant de Crosne commented that "this is not the first time that Elbeuf's manufacturers have tried to control work and industry by closing entry into the community to everyone but their

28 The four previous paragraphs are based on Becchia, *La draperie d'Elbeuf*, 14–31, 155–68 and Jeffry Kaplow, *Elbeuf during the Revolutionary Period: History and Social Structure* (Baltimore: Johns Hopkins University Press, 1964), 23–24.

children." Royal officials rejected the Elbeuvians' attempt "to reserve membership to the sons of masters by excluding every aspirant without that quality" and repeatedly forced them to accept new masters from "outside."[29] By clinging so zealously to their privileges, Elbeuf's masters roused state intervention to break up their monopoly. The growing number of firms suggests that the masters' actions represented a rearguard effort rather than the more effective controls exercised by Lovériens.

In Elbeuf, curbing worker theft while retaining and maximizing the output of skilled labor were related problems compounded by the increasing number of masters. Concerns over maintaining production quality and minimizing costs led Elbeuf's masters to seek controls over their workers similar to Louviers'. Certificates of discharge established by the regulation of 1749 provided Elbeuvians with the authority to limit wages, monopolize skilled labor, and prevent collective action. Jacques-François Vallon de Boisroger, inspector of manufacturing, soon charged Elbeuvians with a systematic attempt to "constrain the liberty of their workers" by refusing to give certificates of discharge to employees who wished to depart. In 1763, masters defended their use of the regulation of 1749, claiming that the "subordination" of workers was necessary: "experience has shown that the more workers are paid, the less they work." Getting laborers to "perfect" their tasks helped to keep prices "moderate," which was "essential" to competing with the English and Dutch. Masters asserted that in "all professions and mechanical arts ... the goal of the laws that form the basis of civil society is to remove harmful possibilities and to force [workers] to contribute to the general and common good."[30]

Elbeuvian justification of guild domination was echoed throughout France. In 1766, the royal council responded by curbing masters' power: rural workers were liberated from certificates of discharge. The spread of liberty through limitations of *corporate* privileges has generally been understood in Smithian terms. Within Bourbon political economy, such restraints complemented and extended the impact of the privilege of liberty. Economic policymaking had not yet become as theory driven as it has since become. Nor were government decisions yet understood primarily as deploying one approach or another. Rather the state's activities existed along a continuum of possible actions that often melded different conceptual approaches.

29 Louis-Thiroux de Crosne, *Lettre à Tolozan*, August 19, 1784, AD Seine-Maritime C129.
30 *Adresse au Monseigneur le Contrôleur Général des Finances par le commun des habitants d'Elbeuf*, 1763, AN F12 674.

Thoroughgoing state support and seigneurial protection along with the domination of the workforce did not guarantee high profits. Based on reports from an inspector of manufacturing, Jeffry Kaplow calculated the profit per unit sold for Elbeuf's woolens. For a bolt of 30 *aunes* (35.55 meters), costs ran to 449 *livres*, 10 *sols*. Raw wool was the biggest expense at 294 *livres*, 16 *sols* (66 percent). Spinning and dyeing were the next largest expenses at 47 *livres*, 16 *sols* (11 percent), and 24 *livres* (5 percent), respectively. As each bolt sold for about 500 *livres*, that left a nominal gross profit of 51 *livres*, 10 *sols*. After depreciation and losses of materials during processing, Kaplow concluded that net profit per bolt was about 30 *livres* or about 6 percent of the purchase price. He cites a venerable study of Louviers that reported similar figures. A bolt of 25.25 *aunes* that sold for 391 *livres*, 8 *sols*, cost 358 *livres*, 16 *sols* to make, leaving a nominal gross profit of about 8 percent. I have serious doubts about these figures, especially those of Louviers, as the purchase prices usually reported for their goods were between 450 and 550 *livres*. The Elbeuf figures included all the bolts that received inspection stamps, but as the inspector noted, many bolts of lesser quality cloth were sold illegally as of the requisite quality. Manufacturers also reported higher costs for labor, raw materials, and semifinished goods like spun thread to state officials than they necessarily paid.

Contemporary reports suggest that Kaplow's figures reflect administrative views of the time but noted opportunities for windfall profit. In 1778, Boisroger reported that "they [Elbeuf's manufacturers] seek incessantly to make a quick fortune. It does not matter to them at what price. Manufacturers, I have been assured, can make up to 200-*livre* profit on a bolt of woolens . . . although ordinarily, a well-made cloth, provides a legitimate profit of 30–40 *livres* at most." Given these low margins even with the domination of the workforce, it does not surprise that so many Elbeuvians resorted to fraud by skimping on the size of their cloths and on the quality of raw materials. The push to enter the trade suggests that stable profits along with the prestige and protection of the guild were sufficient incentives for many entrepreneurs.[31]

[31] The seven previous paragraphs are based on Kaplow, *Elbeuf*, 27–39, who cites Lucien Barbe, "Histoire de l'Industrie du Drap à Louviers," *Bulletin de la Société d'Études diverses de l'Arrondissement de Louviers*, 2 (1894), 55–56, and Becchia, *La draperie*, 27, 52–55, 266–70. The quote from Boisroger is cited by Becchia, *La draperie d'Elbeuf*, 267. See also Jean-Baptiste Goy, *État d'appréciation des matières premières et de main d'oeuvre des toiles et toileries de Rouen pour l'année 1779*, March 24, 1780, AN F12 658A and Goy, *Mémoire*, December 15, 1787.

In the face of growing competition and the limits on their privileges, Elbeuf's masters innovated. Their improvements took three chief forms. First, in the 1780s, they began to mechanize the spinning process, but long before then, the masters had improved thread quality through worker training and close oversight. Elbeuvians also created new designs, although many of their most successful ideas closely mimicked their competitors' products. Second, effective use of *police* authority allowed masters to extend the work-day and the work-year without raising daily wages or piece rates. Although these initiatives often ran afoul of royal regulators, enough succeeded that the city earned a reputation both for sharp practice and for being a progressive industry leader. Third, Elbeuf's masters cheated. The royal manufacture was notorious for exporting woolens "of very bad quality," using cheap wool and inferior dyeing techniques. Masters skimped on the thread count and sold poorer grades of cloth as more expensive goods. From their perspective, low profit margins made such tactics and strategies necessary. Maintaining the "reputation" of Elbeuf's royal manufacture was difficult, especially when the cost of raw materials was high. When masters had to cut costs to maintain their price point, cheating ensued.

The central state supervised production thoroughly. As in Louviers, the duke's bailiff had to be approved by the intendant. For most of the eighteenth century, either he or a close relative served as subdelegate. Guild inspection remained the chief administrative control over the royal manufacture. In this case, however, initially it was Rouen's guilds that exercised this check because Elbeuf's woolens had to be brought to the provincial capital and inspected before they could be sold. Only in 1731 was a woolens inspection office established in Elbeuf staffed by officials appointed by the subdelegate and overseen by the inspector of manufacturing. On-the-ground agents of the central state were more effective in supervising masters and preventing "abuses" in manufacture. In combination with the 1762 measure permitting rural industry, the 1766 ordinance that freed domestic workers outside Elbeuf from certificates of discharge curbed masters' control over rural labor.

From 1758, the intendant forced the guild to accept masters from outside "to restore the liberty that they [Normandy's woolens manufacturers] ought to enjoy according to their statutes and regulations." In 1725, three new masterships were created to honor Louis XV's marriage and an additional four were instituted in 1767. The intendant moderated the hefty entry fee for apprentices to facilitate an influx of new blood. In addition, officials kept close watch on the use of raw materials, adding a mandate in 1710 requiring that only Spanish wool be used in Elbeuf's best fabrics with lesser qualities for lesser fabrics set forth in 1719. Even after most French textiles were permitted to avoid inspection in 1781, the state scrutinized Elbeuf.

Effective state supervision, docile workers, and energetic entrepreneurs combined to make the royal manufacture of Elbeuf Normandy's leading woolens center. Its seventy-six masters employed about 15,300 men, women, and children, of whom less than one-third lived in Elbeuf (out of a population of about 5,800). In the 1780s, official figures assert that Elbeuf annually produced an average of 18,700 bolts of woolen cloth worth 9.35 million *livres*. (These figures suggest a price of 500 *livres* per bolt, casting further doubt on the profit calculation discussed above.) The absence of the seigneur or his bailiff as a regulatory presence shifted responsibility for the royal manufacture to agents of the central state and to masters themselves. Elbeuf showed what the privilege of liberty could accomplish in early modern France.[32]

From the 1660s, the French state used privilege to co-opt and then shape the woolens industries of production located in Norman high justices such as Elbeuf and Louviers. Recognizing the threat of what would today be termed rent-seeking behavior when additional privileges were added to guild rights, royal administrators created overlapping or competing institutional frameworks to keep that predilection in check.[33] Bourbon officials limited the impact of guild privileges and of *corporate* rules more generally by enforcing national regulations and by protecting or extending liberty, especially with regard to rural domestic workers. Different structures emerged in different places depending on the authority and diligence of the seigneur's agents. The mix seems to have worked. Internationally competitive textile manufactures developed in privileged enclaves across the province. Elbeuf and Louviers led the way, but Bolbec, Darnetal, Orival, Saint-Sever, and Yvetot also expanded. Within the broader outlines of French economic policy, deployment of the privilege of liberty in the high justices of Normandy represented a major triumph.

32 The three previous paragraphs are based on Kaplow, *Elbeuf*, 27–39, Louis-Thiroux de Crosne, *Lettre à Tolozan*, August 19, 1784, AD Seine-Maritime C129, *Avis des Députés*, January 7, 1737, *Avis des Députés*, September 7, 1756, Goy, *Mémoire*, December 15, 1787, Jean-Baptiste Goy, *Lettre à Tolozan*, October 1, 1785, AN F12 760, Jean Holker fils, *Lettre à Monseigneur Trudaine*, April 10, 1769, AN F12 657, *Procès-verbal de l'assemblée général des fabricants drapiers d'Elbeuf*, August 28, 1767, AD Seine-Maritime C129, Pierre de Copré, *Lettre*, November 12, 1785, AN F12 760, Daniel-Charles de Trudaine, *Lettre à John Holker fils*, March 11, 1769, AN, F12 675, and *Arrêt du Conseil d'État portant règlement pour le choix, la visite et la marque des laines qui doivent entrer dans la fabrique des draps d'Elbeuf*, September 9, 1719 (Gallica).

33 See *Arrêt du Conseil d'État du Roi concernant la police d'observer dans les manufactures de Drap d'Elbeuf et de Louviers*, February 14, 1780, AN F12 786.

The successes and failures of the privilege of liberty: early modern enterprise zones

Bourbon administrators deployed privilege, liberty, and that distinctive amalgam, the privilege of liberty, to foster long-term economic growth. Over the course of more than a century, the French state turned Normandy's extensive network of privileged enclaves into early modern versions of present-day "enterprise zones." Then as now, enterprise zones are geographically defined spaces where a government offers special conditions or incentives to encourage economic activity.[34] In Normandy, an impressive number of enterprise zones fashioned through the privilege of liberty emerged as internationally competitive and technologically innovative industrial centers. But not all privileged enclaves were equally productive or profitable. Particular institutional circumstances in Normandy's high justices strongly influenced the productive success or economic failure of an enterprise zone.

Enterprise zones revolved around "emulation." As a policy goal, emulation was directed at diverse objectives. In Normandy, French administrators hoped to "excite emulation" of painstaking manufacturing methods, the business practices of innovative entrepreneurs, industrious and skilled workers, and the use of English-style spinning jennies. Officials approached these objectives pragmatically, testing different approaches making use of privilege, liberty, or the privilege of liberty as needed to accomplish its goals. State policies should be evaluated not simply for their direct benefit but also with reference to the ripple effect of emulation.[35]

Upper Normandy's industrial development radiated from Rouen. Thus far, I have emphasized how the privilege of liberty co-opted *corporate* structures and minimized the impact of guild monopolies and restrictions. In the faubourg Saint-Sever, across the Seine River from the provincial capital, the privilege of liberty supported technological innovation and spurred emulation by Rouen's guilds. State policy and seigneurial cooperation enabled Rouen, far more than Paris, Lille, or Bordeaux, to turn privileged enclaves into productive assets that

[34] Historians have increasingly adopted the concept as a framework of analysis. See, for example, Roger Goddard, "Small Boroughs and the Manorial Economy: Enterprise Zones or Urban Failures?" *Past and Present*, 210 (2011), 3–31.

[35] Goy, *Mémoire general*, December 15, 1787, *Édit du Roi concernant les Communautés d'Arts et Métiers dans la Ville de Rouen*, February 8, 1778, AD Seine-Maritime C122, *Lettre de la Bureau d'Encouragement de Rouen à M. Boyetet*, August 7, 1788, AN, F12 658A, *Mémoire pour les fabriquants d'Elbeuf*, May 27, 1783, AN F12 760, and Pierre Godinot, *Toileries, Toiles fortes et autres et blancards et étoffes de passementeries: Mémoire sur l'État actuel de ces fabriques*, December 6, 1777, AN F12 658A.

complemented and stimulated existing producers. This complementarity enhanced Rouen's, Normandy's, and France's competitiveness. In Paris, Lille, and Bordeaux, local authorities effectively challenged the collaboration of seigneurs and the royal government. Normandy's deep integration into Bourbon state structures made administrative intervention on behalf of seigneurial privilege-holders decisive, reminding us of the need for a local or at most regional approach to evaluating French economic development. Thanks to the confluence of access to markets and raw materials, geography, legal environment, and available entrepreneurs, Saint-Sever became a vital part of an industrial complex that encompassed the city, suburbs, and outskirts of Rouen along with nearby privileged enclaves like Darnetal and Saint-Gervais.

Saint-Sever's industrial potential had long been clear to French policymakers. Henri IV granted the first privileges to technological innovators who set up shop in Saint-Sever, but use of the privilege of liberty intensified after 1750. By the end of the old régime, at least seven royal manufactures were chartered there. Although three different seigneurs shared control, for *police* purposes, the territory was part of a high justice controlled by the abbey of Bonne-Nouvelle. Bonne-Nouvelle allowed Rouen's subdelegate to nominate their bailiff and to supervise the enclave closely. This complaisant attitude enabled Saint-Sever to become an integral part of state industrial policy. Certainly, no territory in Normandy more clearly fulfilled the functions of an enterprise zone.

In the 1780s, Saint-Sever vied with Paris' faubourg Saint-Antoine as France's liveliest center of technological innovation. This suburb housed at least twenty large-scale proto-factories devoted to cotton spinning along with more than fifty mills involved in the manufacture, dyeing, or finishing of various types of cotton cloth. It also had twenty-three ceramics workshops, dozens of bottle- and glassmakers, and France's largest lead laminate works. Manufactures of nitric acid, sulfuric acid, and copper sulfate as well as a chlorine bleaching plant made Saint-Sever a major producer and user of industrial chemicals. All these enterprises were either the first or among the first of their kind in France. In 1773, James Hargreave's spinning jenny was naturalized there. Fifteen years later, many of France's English-model spinning jennies operated in this privileged enclave. But Saint-Sever did more than naturalize the innovations of others: its entrepreneurs developed a new method of making copper sulfate and a more economical process of chlorine bleaching. Across the Seine River from Rouen, an intimate community that shared market access, sources of capital, and an entrepreneurial spirit developed a demand-driven approach to technical innovation.

Immigrants and foreign nationals, particularly English and Irish, contributed greatly to Saint-Sever's long-term success as a center for innovation (see Chapter 6). The enclave's English colony dated from the Regency, but Jacobite John Holker, a Manchester manufacturer, provided a significant boost in the mid-1750s. An offer from local entrepreneurs to fund an English-style mill led Holker to entice cotton workers from Lancashire. Royal financial subsidies and the grant of various privileges of liberty enabled Saint-Sever to attract not only refugees, but also British entrepreneurs and skilled workers seeking opportunity. In 1789, Saint-Sever had a manufacture of calicos, two machine shops, two dyeworks, and an earthenware-maker imitating Staffordshire, all run by Englishmen, largely with English or Irish labor. British workers naturalized new technologies and different approaches to organizing production that were imitated not only throughout Normandy but also in other French industrial centers. These foreign residents also taught desperately needed craft knowledge. Better spinning techniques and effective use of coal as fuel were the most important, but hardly the only hard-won methods developed abroad that spread to France via Saint-Sever.

An example demonstrates the workings of the privilege of liberty in Saint-Sever. To persuade English dyers James Morris and James Hope to set up a mill for blue cotton cloth, at the request of the prior of Bonne-Nouvelle, the royal council issued a privilege in 1762. Morris and Hope were authorized to "dye in public, and all are forbidden to disturb them." Morris and Hope determined what dyestuffs to use along with the appropriate methods, machinery, and even the length of time each different type of fabric should be dyed. Nor did these émigrés have to endure the seven-year process (at the very least!) of becoming guild masters. *Corporate* limitations on the quantity, religion, and gender of journeymen and apprentices did not apply: English Protestants and some women worked in their shop. Among its many attractions, Saint-Sever avoided steep taxes (between 4 and 15 percent) imposed on manufactured goods entering the city of Rouen. In addition, Morris and Hope were exempted from lodging soldiers, the royal head tax (200–300 *livres* in Upper Normandy for a manufacturer), and the (at that time) 15 percent income tax (*vingtièmes*). Despite the ongoing war with Britain, Morris, Hope, and their children became naturalized French subjects. Thanks largely to the privilege of liberty, the mill prospered for almost three decades, although it did not diffuse English techniques as widely as its boosters had hoped (see also Chapter 6).[36]

[36] The quotes are cited by Claude Berthollet, *Rapport sur un mémoire de M. Hope rélativement aux teintures de coton en bleu*, September 5, 1788, AN F12 1341A.

As patron of cotton manufacturing and the English colony in Saint-Sever, Holker obtained the most wide-ranging privileges of liberty. In 1752, he received a privilege to establish a "royal manufacture of cotton velours and fabrics" in association with three local manufacturers and a Parisian merchant. The enterprise enjoyed a fifteen-year exemption from duties on imported raw materials. None of its employees was liable for civic responsibilities such as militia service. Holker collected an impressive 90,000 *livres* in subsidies in exchange for keeping four copper presses in constant production and allowing other entrepreneurs to see the mill in operation. To encourage the transfer of craft-based mechanical knowledge that made these technologies effective, the royal government offered pensions to Holker's workers. They also earned a bonus for every French worker trained to make cotton velours "*à l'anglaise*."

State investment and seigneurial protection paid significant dividends. Thirty years later, Holker's mill remained "the largest of its type" in France. Two hundred looms produced almost 3,000 bolts of cotton cloth annually worth more than 550,000 *livres*. Holker installed a set of purpose-built machines including feeding cloths known as roving billies and simple spinning reels to spin finer thread and weave larger fabrics. His use of machinery improved quality while saving labor and raw materials. The mill directly employed about 350 men and women. Holker also "put out" raw cotton to thousands of female spinners in Saint-Sever and in villages to the south. Mills started by local entrepreneurs located in the privileged enclaves of Bolbec, Elbeuf, les Andelys, Vernon, and Yvetot imitated his methods.

Holker's entrepreneurial success story was duplicated by succeeding generations. His son and namesake served as French consul general to the United States during the American Revolution, but first he established a manufacture of sulfuric acid and other chemicals prized by Normandy's textile industries for dyeing and printing. Founded in 1768, the manufacture pioneered the use of lead chambers and, eight years later, steam injection. Although it spawned several imitators and competitors, the family maintained this model enterprise for nearly 100 years. Beyond the privileges of liberty enjoyed by all entrepreneurs in Saint-Sever, the acid manufacture received a small export subsidy capped at 3,000 *livres*. Import substitution was clearly the chief goal of industrial policy in Saint-Sever. Father and son also collaborated to build a cotton mill in the privileged enclave of Oissel with horse-powered jennies and a carding machine that began operation in 1776. This establishment supplied fine thread to weavers across the region, but especially to the burgeoning mills of Saint-Sever, Saint-Gervais, and Rouen.[37]

Saint-Sever teamed domestic and foreign workers with entrepreneurs in an institutional environment that made it possible to pioneer several techniques and processes. Its mills and proto-factories drew on the labor of tens of thousands of domestic workers and provided thread and chemicals that sustained the region's industries. As the chemical industry developed and improved methods of using coal as fuel spread, this privileged enclave emerged as a major dyeing and bleaching center for Rouen's enormous complex of mills and manufactures. Entrepreneurs and workers trained in Saint-Sever took advantage of the host of handy high justices to found new mills. Parallel institutional frameworks in other high justices helped ease the difficulty of transplanting innovation. Other enclaves provided competition and greatly expanded the opportunities for entrepreneurship. Saint-Sever was early modern France's most effective enterprise zone.

Privilege, even the privilege of liberty, could not cure all ills. Although privilege was a relatively effective policy tool, we must also attend to instances where new technologies did not spread or additional opportunities were ignored. Such setbacks underscore the importance of the institutional context as well as the limits of this approach to development. Pont-de-l'Arche, eleven miles south of Rouen and three miles east of Elbeuf, was a royal fief ripe for privileges of liberty. In 1690, the government established a royal manufacture in Pont-de-l'Arche on the model of Josse Van Robais' mill outside Abbeville (see Chapter 6) to complement the woolens industries of Elbeuf and Louviers. The mill failed during the War of Spanish Succession because of labor unrest and poor direction. It was revived in 1715 on the condition that it be

[37] The eight previous paragraphs are based on Jeff Horn, "Privileged Enclaves: Entrepreneurial Opportunities in Eighteenth-Century France," in Kathryn A. Edwards and Carol E. Harrison (eds.), *Proceedings of the Western Society for French History: Selected Papers of the 2004 Annual Meeting* 32 (Scholarly Publishing Office of the University of Michigan University Library, 2006), 29–45, Chassagne, *Le coton*, 54, *Arrêt du Conseil d'État*, July 10, 1721, AN, F12 784, Goy, *Mémoire*, November 12, 1782, Goy, *Mémoire*, December 15, 1787, Dardel, *La Conjoncture*, 64, 124, 126–31, Jean Vidalenc, "Quelques remarques sur le rôle des Anglais dans la Révolution Industrielle en France particulièrement en Normandie, de 1750 à 1850," *Annales de Normandie*, 8: 2 (1958), 273–90, Jean-Pierre Bardet, *Rouen aux XVIIe et XVIIIe siècles: Les mutations d'un espace social*, 2 vols. (Société d'édition de l'enseignement supérieur, 1983), I: 206, Rémond, *John Holker*, 54–55, John R. Harris, *Industrial Espionage and Technology Transfer: Britain and France in the Eighteenth Century* (Aldershot: Ashgate, 1998), and *Bicententaire de la fondation de la Chambre de Commerce de Rouen 1703–1903: Aperçu Historique* (Rouen: Lecerf fils, 1908), 30.

moved to les Andelys (a high justice controlled by the archbishop of Rouen), leaving Pont-de-l'Arche without any appreciable industry.

Two generations later, the city fathers recognized that Pont-de-l'Arche was falling behind, particularly as industrial development spread rapidly across the region. In 1767, Pont's "principal inhabitants" endorsed the request of Louis and Charles Berrenger for an exclusive privilege to establish a woolens mill. The Berrengers sought privileges of liberty to exempt the enterprise from a variety of royal, provincial, municipal, guild, and seigneurial regulations, various commercial restrictions, and a number of taxes. The Pontois asserted that "This privilege, far from being an obstacle to the liberty of commerce, on the contrary, becomes a key without which they cannot find a way to open up the city['s trade], which, up to this point, does not exist." The city fathers appreciated the desolation of the industrial terrain. To find and retain skilled laborers while introducing new techniques and technologies would be a difficult task, especially in competition with Elbeuf and Louviers. These civic boosters likened state support for the Berrengers to the twenty-year "privileges and exemptions" offered to landowners or tenants who turned swamp into arable land. The Berrengers received the privilege of liberty, but their enterprise muddled along until the early 1790s without expanding or stimulating "emulation." In this case, the privilege of liberty did not fail, but neither did it fulfill its promise. The institutional context of this "uncultivated land," rather than the inadequacy of the policy tools, foiled the state's efforts.[38]

Normandy demonstrates that some privileges, like some institutions, and some industries are more likely to achieve the practical goals of a policy. For most of the early modern era, the high justice of Darnetal on Rouen's eastern flank benefited greatly from its various privileges. Darnetal's guild system dated to 1587. Its woolens guild embraced the town and all the villages in the valley to the northeast. At the end of the seventeenth century, membership in Darnetal's woolens guild ossified. To prevent the exclusion of journeymen and masters from Rouen, a 1688 royal edict ensured that "foreigners" could work and set up businesses in Darnetal. The guild was suspended by the seigneur, the duke de Montmorency, in 1697 but restored in 1700. The relationship between Darnetal and Rouen was decided definitively only in 1721, but by this point the state had

[38] The two previous paragraphs are based on Becchia, *La draperie*, 20, *Mémoire pour les Habitans de la Ville de Pont-de-l'Arche*, 1767, AD Seine-Maritime C136 and *Arrêt du conseil d'état rendu en interpretation de la declaration du 13 août 1766, concernant les privileges et exemptions accordés à ceux qui entreprendront de défricher les Landes et terres incultes*, October 2, 1766 (Gallica).

already curbed woolens masterships. Despite, or perhaps because of, the limited number of entrepreneurs, Darnetal flourished even though its guild masters exhibited a strong predilection for avoiding inspection to hide a profound lack of regulatory compliance. Although Darnetal's woolens were considered to be inferior to Rouen's, their low cost earned them markets throughout France. Darnetal also specialized in the production of woolen blankets. According to Savary des Bruslons, these blankets "covered half the realm."[39] Darnetal's rise contributed to Rouen's decline in woolens.

Entrepreneurial prospects in Darnetal bloomed in the 1750s. About eighty of Holker's English emigrants, including several Protestants, ended up in Darnetal, where they improved the technique of local workers and invigorated the woolens sector much as Saint-Sever did for cotton. A number of these emigrants were expert dyers, printers, or mechanics who knew how to harness the valley's fast-running streams to build better fulling mills. Small woolens producers throughout Upper Normandy sent their woolens to Darnetal for dyeing and/or fulling. In 1755 and again in 1764, royal officials imposed privileges of liberty on Darnetal by exempting first François Lambert, the best dyer in Darnetal, and then Bernard and Hyacinthe Jouin from many guild regulations, enabling them to build large dyeworks. The cotton industry also returned to Darnetal in this decade, offering many new possibilities for entrepreneurialism. Lifting the limitation on the number of woolens masters in 1758 enabled a number of foreign workers to establish fresh enterprises, either on their own or more frequently with local partners.

The guild reforms of 1776–1781 opened up opportunities for women who had previously been excluded from mastership in Darnetal (see Chapter 7). Royal administrators expended considerable energy enforcing the rules allowing "qualified" women to join guilds. According to the reforms of 1777–1778, the central state considered a woman to be qualified if she was the widow or daughter of a master, paid a fee to become "affiliated" to a guild, and "exercised their profession." Such women were in a far more favorable position than women who joined guilds independently. In 1778, 1782, and 1787, royal officials forced Darnetal's cloth-makers and woolens manufacturers to accept the widows and the daughters of masters, as they could easily demonstrate their competence. By the eve of the French Revolution, government actions combined with the high justice's privileges to widen

[39] Savary des Bruslons with Philibert-Louis Savary, *Dictionnaire universel de commerce*, V: 180.

access to industrial employment and increase the possibilities for small producers to become part of the guild system.

Despite increased opportunities, Darnetal's woolens industry stagnated. Masters' unwillingness to follow regulations led to widespread skimping on thread counts and fraudulent manufacture, especially in dyeing. Using their *corporate* authority and privileged access to the judicial system, Darnetal's guilds hobbled all attempts at inspection. Extensive cheating imperiled sales not only for Darnetal's textiles but also for producers like Aumale, which sent 9,000 bolts of cloth annually to Darnetal for dyeing. The town's producers were constrained by the relatively high wages paid to their urbanized, guild labor force and comparatively elevated guild charges. In 1763, inspector of manufacturing Jean-Baptiste Goy, however, blamed Darnetal's waning competitiveness on "the workers, who are accustomed to their old methods and do not wish to change them despite all the advantages that such changes might bring."[40] He found similar resistance to innovation a generation later in 1787. The city's masters feared to mechanize, recognizing that their embattled labor force might respond to any threat to employment with violence. Once producers were permitted to avoid following the regulations in 1781, the quality of Darnetal's signature woolens plummeted.

In the eighteenth century, Darnetal's wealth was based on woolens. Cotton never competed successfully with specialized producers in Saint-Sever, Rouen, and Saint-Gervais. Although wool was France's biggest industry, it was clearly a sector in relative decline, especially after mid-century. By focusing on cheaper woolens and systematically defrauding their customers, Darnetal's entrepreneurs made themselves vulnerable to shifting tastes and growing competition, both domestically and in foreign markets. In 1787, Darnetal sold 8,200 bolts of woolen cloth worth 3 million *livres,* but the Anglo-French commercial treaty devastated this privileged producer. On July 14, 1789, amid burgeoning joblessness and rising food prices, woolens workers from Darnetal initiated a major wave of machine-breaking in Saint-Sever, Oissel, and Rouen.

For most of the eighteenth century, privilege successfully enabled Darnetal's specialization in wool. Paradoxically, increased liberty of access for entrepreneurs and growing liberty in the manufacturing process placed Darnetal at a competitive disadvantage. Privilege allowed profits to be made, but the threat from below delayed innovation until after the Revolution. Policies that worked in other

[40] Jean-Baptiste Goy, *Mémoire sur les manufactures des draperies de Rouen, de Darnetal et de Bolbec,* December 16, 1763, AN F12 1365.

places did not succeed in Darnetal because of the institutional context shaping local attitudes toward the use of both privilege and liberty. As an enterprise zone, Darnetal never realized its potential.[41]

French industrial policy in Normandy should be understood as a piece. Although there were strategic advances and tactical retreats, the basic outlines of the state's guiding principles remained quite constant from Colbert to the outbreak of the Revolution of 1789. The central government fostered industrial development in enterprise zones situated in Upper Normandy's dense tangle of high justices. The experiences of places like Pont-de-l'Arche and Darnetal encourage a more nuanced assessment of administrative use of the privilege of liberty. But as a whole, Bourbon political economy achieved its aims in this model province.

By the end of the old régime, Normandy had a large and diverse manufacturing economy. Nor was this bustling region solely the preserve of declining or hide-bound industries: mechanized textile production on the English model, advanced metallurgical techniques, and efficient chemical manufacture were solidly implanted in Normandy. The province's economic and population growth was based on the mutual dependence of privileged urban manufacture and relatively free cottage industry. In rural high justices, Enlightened efforts to improve agricultural techniques also bore abundant fruit. State policy sustained broadly based economic development.

Royal administrators focused on Upper Normandy because of its heavy concentration of high justices and urban guilds. In 1789, Upper Normandy's privileged enclaves had an urban or semi-urban population of at least 120,000 (approximately 16 percent of the generality's

[41] The six previous paragraphs are based on *Arrêt du Conseil d'État*, July 10, 1721, AN F12 784, Goy, *Mémoire*, November 12, 1782, Goy, *Mémoire*, December 15, 1787, *Adresse au Roi et à Nosseigneurs de Son Conseil par des Gardes Inspecteurs des Draperies au contrôle de Rouen*, n.d. [December 1773], AD Seine-Maritime C126, Vidalenc, "Quelques remarques," 275, Jean-François de Tolozan, *Lettre à de Maussion*, September 7, 1787, AD Seine-Maritime C126, *Procès-verbal d'une délibération des gardes de la manufacture de draperie de Darnetal*, March 17, 1732, AN F12 674, Jean-François de Tolozan, *Lettre à de Crosne*, January 21, 1783, AN F12 786, *Rapport à M. Tolozan*, n.d. [1782], AN F12 786, *Arrêt du Conseil d'État du Roi*, December 3, 1782, AN F12 786, *Arrêt du Conseil d'État du Roi*, February 4, 1755, AN F12 1334B, *Adresse au Roi et à Nosseigneurs de Son Conseil par des Gardes Inspecteurs des Draperies au contrôle de Rouen*, n.d. [December 1773], AD Seine-Maritime C126, *Arrêt du Conseil d'État*, June 5, 1764, AN F12 1334B, *Avis des députés du commerce sur la requete de François Lambert, teinturier à Darnetal*, November 29, 1754, AN F12 709, and *Avis des Députés au Conseil de Commerce sur la requette présentée par les maitres drapiers de la ville de Rouen pour faire supprimer la jurande de leurs ouvriers et la réponse de ces ouvriers*, March 17, 1724, AN F12 695. See Hafter, *Women at Work*, 89–123, 149–63 for a discussion of the position of female masters in Rouen's *corporate* system.

population). These enclaves housed almost 90 percent of the generality's cotton manufacturing, the entire woolens and stocking trades, as well as the metallurgical, paper, glass, chemical, and ceramics industries. Inhabited by 2–3 percent of the realm's population, Upper Normandy generated 7–9 percent of French industrial output. As a whole, the province of Normandy produced one-quarter of French cottons along with much of its woolens and linen. In addition to textiles, it had significant metallurgical, glass, ceramics, sugar, paper, chemical, and leather industries. The experiment with establishing a network of enterprise zones in the high justices of Normandy deserves recognition as one of the major accomplishments of Bourbon industrial policy.[42]

The state's reliance on the privilege of liberty had unintended consequences. In the 1780s, the state's unfolding financial collapse combined with the Anglo-French commercial treaty, trade uncertainty in other French export markets, and agricultural shortages to undermine Norman faith in the royal administration and its policies. With more than 100,000 unemployed in Rouen's generality alone, the economic crisis struck Normandy more deeply than any other French province. Hungry Normans demanded bread, lower grain prices, or money to buy provisions in at least twenty-three separate incidents between February 13 and July 12, 1789. Foodstuffs were pillaged and farmers and the mounted police were assaulted when they refused to open up public granaries or to divert grain headed for Paris. From July to October, crowds resorted to widespread machine-breaking. Popular action destroyed 700 spinning jennies (44 percent of the French national total) located either in Rouen or in the surrounding high justices. The laboring classes' destruction of so many advanced textile machines damaged French exports and doused the competitive fires of many entrepreneurs.[43]

[42] Guy Lemarchand, *La fin du féodalisme dans le pays de Caux: Conjoncture économique et démographique et structure sociale dans une région de grande culture de la crise du XVIIe siècle à la stabilisation de la Révolution (1640–1795)* (Éditions du CTHS, 1989), 267–91, Comité régional d'histoire de la Révolution française (Haute-Normandie), *La Révolution en Haute-Normandie 1789–1802*, 12–13, Léopold Soublin, *Le premier vote des Normands (1789)* (Fécamp: EMTN, 1981), 51, Langlois, *Recherches sur les hautes justices féodales*, in Marc Bouloiseau (ed.), *Cahiers de doléances du tiers État du bailliage de Rouen pour les États généraux de 1789*, 2 vols. (Presses Universitaires de France, 1957, 1960), I: xlvi–ii, Alexandre Moreau de Jonnès, *Statistique de l'industrie de la France* (Guillaumin,1856), 322, and Goy, *Mémoire sur les Bureaux de toilerie*, November 12, 1782. The percentages attached to some figures differ from those reported in Horn, "'A Beautiful Madness,'" because I have discovered that additional territories were high justices.

[43] Comité régional d'histoire de la Révolution française (Haute-Normandie), *La Révolution en Haute-Normandie*, 21–22, 25, Jean-Pierre Allinne, "À propos des bris de machines textiles à Rouen pendant l'été 1789: Émeutes anciennes ou émeutes nouvelles?" *Annales*

The French government either provoked or could not contain the escalating economic pressures of the 1780s. Economic distress triggered and shaped the events of 1789. The economic origins of the French Revolution, however, should not taint early modern economic achievements. Royal administrators founded an industrial powerhouse in Normandy overcoming considerable constraints stemming from the administrative, political, and technological environments. Historians should appreciate the old régime's successes in Normandy rather than focus solely on the Bourbon state's inability to avert the French Revolution.

de Normandie, 31: 1 (1981), 37, 42, André Dubuc (ed.), *Textile en Normandie: Études diverses* (Rouen: Société libre d'Émulation de la Seine-Maritime, 1975), 145, Serge Chassagne, *Oberkampf: Un entrepreneur capitaliste au Siècle des Lumières* (Aubier, 1980), 153, and *Rapport des Travaux de la Commission intermédiaire de Haute-Normandie depuis le 20 Décembre 1787 jusqu'au 27 Juillet 1790* (Rouen: 1790), AD Seine-Maritime C2114*.

4 Companies, colonies, and contraband

Commercial privileges under the old régime

> [C]ommercial liberty does not consist of doing whatever one wishes. The goal of the state is to have useful commerce. To have useful commerce, restrictions and prohibitions are necessary ... It is commonly said that commerce needs both liberty and protection, but between them, liberty is more useful.
>
> Jacques-Claude-Marie Vincent de Gournay (1755)[1]

As the lifeblood of Bourbon political economy, commerce was perhaps the most closely scrutinized aspect of French economic relations. From the age of Colbert until 1795, commercial privileges were an essential element of state-sponsored economic development as part of a broadly based system usually referred to as mercantilism. Privilege's utility was challenged in the early 1750s by the rise of various groups of Enlightened improvers to positions of authority; their political economy emphasized liberty's effectiveness in fostering economic growth. In the arena of policy, improvers sought to eliminate internal tolls and tariffs, while drastically reducing customs rates. These goals underlay both the "single duty project," which aimed to create a unified domestic toll system, and the diverse set of commercial treaties signed in the 1780s.[2] Although improvers dominated economic policymaking after 1750, privilege remained vital to French commerce. How did privilege survive the improvers' commitment to promoting liberty? Vincent de Gournay points to the answer – commercial privileges endured because they were an effective means of making commerce useful to the state.

After 1775, the improvers' focus on commercial liberty had some notorious failures in the realm of public opinion. Anne-Robert-Jacques de Turgot's liberation of the grain trade and the Anglo-French commercial

[1] Jacques-Claude-Marie Vincent de Gournay, *Examen des avantages et des desavantages de la prohibition des toiles peintes*, 1755 (Gallica), 125–27.

[2] John F. Bosher, *The Single Duty Project: A Study of the Movement for a French Customs Union in the Eighteenth Century* (London: Athlone Press, 1964) and Jeff Horn, *The Path Not Taken: French Industrialization in the Age of Revolution* (Cambridge, MA: MIT Press, 2006), 51–88.

treaty take pride of place. Yet the spread of liberty at the expense of mercantilism dominates English-language historical considerations of early modern French economic decision making. Such an understanding of Bourbon political economy fails to capture the complexities of privilege's role in French commerce. Under Louis XVI, regulation was in retreat and liberty on the march in industrial matters. In commercial relations, privilege's significant position endured. Trade agreements lowering tariffs came just as privileges were granted to Bayonne and Lorient in 1784, turning them into free ports. The East Indies Company was revived the following year. The privilege of liberty's efficacy and liberty's shortcomings ensured that commercial privileges persisted as an indispensable tool of French policymaking.

The role of commercial privileges highlights the essential link between production and exchange. Physiocratic theory sometimes distorted that relationship by minimizing the importance of industry in favor of the primary sector.[3] In practice, however, Bourbon officials of all political and ideological stripes recognized the economy's dependence on the output and productivity of industry. Commerce, the development of French colonies, and extensive contraband relied on manufactured goods, not just on the production of commodities. Customers at home and abroad demanded industrial products. Without those products to sell, both for consumption and to exchange for raw materials and other manufactured goods, France would not have achieved the same degree of economic development. The primary sector alone could not satisfy demand either domestically or in key foreign markets. Industry was necessary for commerce to flourish. In Chapters 2 and 3, we saw how state use of privilege stimulated industrial output and provided high quality or novel goods. This chapter explores a parallel evolution in Bourbon political economy: privilege allowed French commerce to make the best possible use of its opportunities.

For French policymakers, the deployment of privilege to support commercial expansion was a considered and practical decision. Free ports, chartered companies, and entrepôts structured international commerce in the age of mercantilism; their creation reflected how central privilege was to Bourbon policymaking and early modern French economic development. On the other hand, enduring tax privileges combined with transportational shortcomings to constrain

[3] See the nuanced account in John Shovlin, *The Political Economy of Virtue: Luxury, Patriotism, and the Origins of the French Revolution* (Ithaca, NY: Cornell University Press, 2006), 102–13.

domestic commercial growth. Privilege sustained the regionalization of the French economy and provided myriad opportunities, both licit and illicit, for profit-taking. Bourbon administrators, like their contemporaries in other mercantilist states, used privilege as a tool in their quest to encourage economic development.

The interaction of commercial privilege and commercial liberty is a central theme of early modern European economic history. For France, this theme still awaits its historian. While recognizing that this interaction merits more thorough consideration, here my approach must be selective. This chapter explores the role of privilege in fostering trade-related competition and competitiveness. First, we shall briefly explore mercantilism as practiced by the Bourbon state, emphasizing its successes, methods, and loopholes, especially in France's commercial interactions with the rest of Europe. This discussion of mercantilism grounds the following section, which considers how privilege, especially trading monopolies, facilitated the rapid expansion of French foreign trade with the colonies and with areas outside Europe. The chapter concludes with a brief consideration of the impact of market fragmentation stemming from geographic and transportational limitations on French commercial policy. To ensure the utility of commerce, even those Bourbon administrators most committed to spreading liberty relied on privilege to accomplish their goals.

Myths of mercantilism: exports, smuggling, and free ports

That politics shaped commercial exchange was recognized widely on both flanks of the Channel. Rivalries between European states played out in economics. Political competition encouraged economic thinkers and policymakers alike to emphasize the need to make commerce useful. Philippe Minard argues that scholars have distorted our understanding of the period by emphasizing a dichotomy between mercantilism characterized as anachronistic or outdated and Physiocracy described as "modern."[4] In fact, the divisions between "mercantilists" or Colbertists and Physiocrats or "improvers" concerned methods and timing far more than the goals of political economy. In policy, theory, and government action, trade based solely on the profit motive was subordinated to

4 Philippe Minard, "'France colbertiste' versus 'Angleterre libérale'? Un myth du XVIIIe siècle," in Jean-Philippe Genet and François-Joseph Ruggiu (eds.), *Les idées passent-ils la Manche? Savoirs, representations, pratiques (France-Angleterre, Xe-XXe siècles)* (Presses de l'Université Paris-Sorbonne, 2007), 197–209.

commerce that benefited the state. Developing useful commerce was the chief goal of Bourbon trade policies.

In 1753, François Véron Duverger de Forbonnais' article "Commerce" in the *Encyclopédie* distinguished the trading profits of individuals from commerce's utility to the state. For Forbonnais, "foreign trade is concerned with procuring relative wealth" rather than exchange to gain wealth for its own sake. He identified nine objectives "proposed by the English in their books to judge the utility or disadvantages of the activities of commerce." These objectives highlighted "the export of surplus" agricultural or industrial goods, import substitution, and increasing exchange through reexports. Forbonnais stressed that "in a state, the objective of commerce is to support the work of the greatest possible number of men." In succeeding years, improvers like Ėtienne Bonnet de Condillac, Turgot, and Guillaume-François Le Trosne developed similar views on the purpose and place of commerce in political economy.[5]

A generation after Forbonnais, Adam Smith surveyed useful commerce as it related to a state's ability to prosecute foreign wars. "The real revenue and wealth of society" increased when foreign trade "carries out that surplus part of the produce of their land and labour and brings back in return for it something else for which there is a demand. It gives a value to their superfluities." He too wished to accentuate "the productive powers of labour" through import substitution. Smith's discussion of trade built on his analysis of value, which "has two different meanings, and sometimes expresses the utility of some particular object, and sometimes the power of purchasing other goods which the possession of that object conveys. The one may be called 'value in use'; the other, 'value in exchange.'" David Hume and Jeremy Bentham articulated related views on the political economy of commerce.[6]

5 "Commerce" in Denis Diderot and Jean Le Rond d'Alembert (eds.), *Encyclopédie ou Dictionnaire raisonné des sciences, des arts et des métiers, par une Société de Gens de lettres*, 28 vols. (1751–1772), III: 690–700 (ARTFL). Forbonnais is accounted a Neo-Mercantilist or Neo-Colbertist by some historians, but he too embraced reform. See also Ėtienne Bonnot de Condillac, *Le commerce et le gouvernement, considérés relativement l'un à l'autre* (Amsterdam: Jambert & Cellot, 1776), Anne-Robert Jacques de Turgot, *Réflexions sur la formation et la distribution des richesses* (1776), reprinted in Eugène Daire and Hyppolite Dussard (eds.), *Oeuvres de Turgot* (Guillemin, 1844), I: 7–66, and Guillaume-François Le Trosne, *De l'ordre social, ouvrage suivi d'un traité élémentaire sur la valeur, l'argent, la circulation, l'industrie & le commmerce intérieur & extérieur* (Frères Debure, 1777), all on Googlebooks.

6 Adam Smith, *An Inquiry into the Nature and Causes of the Wealth of Nations* (1776), Book IV, chapter 1 and Book I, chapter 4. On import substitution, see Chapter 2. See also Werner Stark (ed.), *Jeremy Bentham's Economic Writings*, 3 vols. (New York: Burt Franklin, 1952–1954), I: 371–74, III: 217–46, 381–418 and David Hume, *Writings on Economics*, ed. and intro. Eugene Rotwein, new intro. Margaret Schabas (Piscataway, NJ:

Emphasis on commerce's utility characterized these influential eighteenth-century political economists. That recognition suggests an argument critical of contemporary English-language approaches to mercantilism. All the thinkers mentioned above disparaged mercantilism's practices and criticized it as system and as policy. Yet, as we shall see below, the complementary economic analyses (with regard to the utility of commerce) articulated by Forbonnais and Smith were inspired by and reflected the economic practices of Jean-Baptiste Colbert, that notorious architect of French mercantilism, based fundamentally on privilege. My central point does not concern the genealogy of canonical economic ideas or the links between theory and practice. Instead, the echo of Colbert's "modernity" in the views of Enlightened reformers provides a glimpse of why privilege remained fundamental to French policymaking in a period committed to spreading economic liberty.

Perceptions of mercantilism as a system, either in theory or in practice, should not obscure its considerable successes. In foreign trade, eighteenth-century France was certainly doing something right. After the peace of Paris in 1783, Bourbon state involvement in trade, both to grant new privileges and to eliminate others, generated widespread complaints from the commercial classes. Despite their objections, it must be recognized that French commerce performed admirably, both from a long-term perspective and compared to other economic sectors and its competitors.

Eighteenth-century statistics must be used with great caution, but from what French policymakers knew about the balance of trade, long-term trends seemed both clear and encouraging. According to Ambroise-Marie Arnould's calculations, French exports increased fourfold in value between 1716 and 1787. Imports increased by a factor of 5 for the same period, while the positive balance of trade grew from 36 million to almost 57 million *livres*. These figures exclude the Levant: if trade with the Ottoman Empire is included, then the trade advantage falls to 38 million *livres*. The value of French commerce with the rest of Europe increased 400 percent. Trade with the East Indies expanded by a factor of 9 and Levantine trade grew by a factor of almost 9.5. Commerce with France's African and American colonies increased sixteenfold. Exports

Transaction, 2007 [1955]), 3–18, 60–82. In considering the role of trade assessment as a measure of reality, see Anthony Howe, *Free Trade and Liberal England 1846–1946* (Clarendon Press, 1997), and for this era, "Restoring free trade: the British Experience, 1776–1873," in Donald Winch and Patrick K. O'Brien (eds.), *The Political Economy of British Historical Experience, 1688–1914* (Oxford University Press, 2002), 193–214.

of agricultural products expanded 300 percent, manufactured goods nearly 375 percent, Asian and African exchange (other than to French colonies) including the slave trade more than 55 percent, and reexported West Indian colonial goods swelled almost 1,000 percent to become nearly half of all French exports.

These figures blur how impressive the expansion of French trade actually was. The year 1787 was a horrible one for French overseas trade in manufactured goods because of unrest in the Near East, the Dutch Republic, and the German lands along with the Anglo-French commercial treaty. If the figures had been based on 1785, the long-term improvements in France's commercial position would have been even more statistically striking.

More important than raw numbers is how the details highlight French commercial competitiveness. France's (as opposed to the colonies') primary sector registered spectacular gains with wool, wax, wood, ores, animals, grain, olive oil, dried cod, tobacco, and drinks, with wine and spirits leading the way. Primary-sector trade increased most rapidly with Africa (forty-threefold!) and the Antilles (940 percent). Despite these increases, by 1787, this sector represented only 22 percent of total exports, down from 33 percent in 1716. Manufactured goods, led by textiles, especially cotton, silk, woolen, linen, and blended-fiber fabrics, along with hats, stockings, handkerchiefs, blankets, ribbons, and fashion items, made solid gains (280 percent), but other manufactured goods such as paper, hardware, leather goods, and glassware grew even faster (525 percent). French manufactures went mostly to other European countries. The Levant absorbed 72 percent and the West Indies 23 percent of manufactured goods exported outside Europe. As with the primary sector, manufacturing did not keep pace with overall expansion, declining from 42 percent of all exports in 1716 to 34 percent in 1787. The West Indies drove eighteenth-century French trade performance. In 1787, the Antilles absorbed 14 percent of French exports, and reexported colonial products furnished 28 percent of total exports.

England was France's only trade deficit in 1716, representing more than 4 percent of all commerce. By 1787, France also had a negative trade balance with Portugal, Piedmont, Switzerland, and the United States. The total deficit with these countries comprised about 6 percent of all French trade. In 1716, France had favorable trade balances with Spain and its empire, Portugal, Piedmont, Savoy, Switzerland, the Netherlands, the Austrian Netherlands, the German lands, and the countries around the Baltic, especially Denmark and the Hanseatic cities. Those exchanges comprised 25 percent of total trade. That list narrowed somewhat in 1787 to Spain and its empire, the Netherlands, the Austrian Netherlands, the German lands, and the Baltic countries. The advantage represented 14 percent of French commerce. France was a major commercial power, with particular strengths in the Antilles, the Levant, and continental Europe, both for domestic goods and for colonial reexports.[7]

Economic historians rightly stress the need to deflate Arnould's figures by using constant prices. Even after this adjustment, French foreign trade tripled between 1716 and 1787 to reach parity with England's. France's rate of increase handily surpassed that of England and Wales, which grew about 240 percent. Export value provides an even better indication of France's eighteenth-century achievements. The war of Spanish Succession depressed French trade to less than half of English trade, but over the next four decades, the total value of French trade first rivaled and then surpassed Britain's. By the eve of the Revolution, French overseas commerce was worth one-third more than England's, despite the downturn of the late 1780s. Of course, per capita, English foreign trade far exceeded France's, but the gap was narrowing rapidly.

The bulk of France's commercial expansion preceded the start of the Seven Years' War in 1756 when Colbert's policies generally still held sway. The era of the improvers, the thirty years before 1789, witnessed uneven commercial performance and decline in some areas and sectors. In the first half of the eighteenth century, French mercantilism worked. France competed successfully with the English and Dutch. Uneven commercial performance after 1756 also suggests concrete reasons why privilege remained so important a part of French state action.[8]

These statistics are approximations at best. Merchants, manufacturers, and consumers all had a clear interest in understating exchange, production, and sales to escape taxes. At the same time, fraudulent manufacture and contraband were both exceptionally widespread and largely uncounted by the state. I believe all these trade figures to be significantly below actual levels, perhaps by as much as a third during

[7] The figures in the four previous paragraphs are derived from Ambroise-Marie Arnould, *De La balance du commerce et des relations commerciales extérieures de la France dans toutes les parties du globe particulièrement à la fin du règne de Louis XIV, et au moment de la Révolution*, 3 vols. 2nd ed. (Buisson, Year III [1795]), vol. 3, Tables 1–13. The problems of data collection, especially for the early eighteenth century, and the political use of the information submitted (usually to ask for privileges!) are surveyed clearly in Christiane Demeulenaere-Douyère and David J. Sturdy (eds.), *L'Enquête du regent 1716–1718: Sciences, techniques et politique dans la France pré-industrielle* (Turnhout, Belgium: Brepols, 2008), 29–59, esp. 34, 44–45.

[8] The two previous paragraphs are based on Paul Butel, *L'Èconomie française au XVIIIe siècle* (Sedes, 1993), 79–87. On Arnould's figures, see also François Crouzet, *Britain Ascendant: Comparative Studies in Franco-British Economic History*, trans Martin Thom (Cambridge University Press, 1990 [1985]), 17–20 and Guillaume Daudin, *Commerce et prosperité: La France au XVIIIe siècle* (Presses de l'Université Paris-Sorbonne, 2005), 229–40.

wartime. I provide what statistics exist for illustrative purposes, but the precise numbers should be taken with a brick of salt. The utility of early modern economic statistics is primarily to elucidate trends. Using them as absolutes is to give far too much credit to state bureaucrats and too little appreciation of the creativity of Europeans determined to avoid regulation and the payment of taxes. Inspector of manufacturing Jean-Baptiste Goy remarked that "It is not possible to know how many machines each manufacturer has in operation. One never has correct declarations on this subject. Manufacturers hide as much of their commerce from the state as they can for fear of an increase in their *capitation* [head tax] or that some new tax would be imposed."[9] Nothing demonstrates the limitations of economic statistics more than a consideration of smuggling.

Smuggling plagued French society. High tolls separated "provinces reputed foreign" from the bulk of France encompassed within the five large tax farms. Significant export and import taxes at the frontier fragmented French markets, limited exchange, and created artificial and sometimes absurd commercial niches for smugglers to fill. Smuggling depressed badly needed customs revenue and legitimate markets for certain manufactured goods. Fraudulent trade in salt and tobacco was particularly widespread. Raw wool, tobacco, books, cotton and woolen textiles, pottery, and hardware entered France clandestinely in exchange for paper, woolens, silks, sugar, tea, and spirits, especially brandy. Widespread avoidance of customs and the flouting of legal prohibitions made policing more dangerous and facilitated the spread of other forms of lawlessness. According to Vincent de Gournay, "Cheap goods surmount all prohibitions and all barriers. To stop a country's contraband, it is necessary to ensure that no profits come from the attempt."[10] Smuggling was the opposite of useful commerce.

Smuggling is, almost by definition, difficult to measure. The goods involved shifted over time. For example, tea replaced silk and linen textiles as the focus of smuggling into Britain. Around 1740, 3 million pounds of tea arrived clandestinely along the Kentish coast (versus 1 million imported legally), furnishing three-quarters of national consumption. After three decades of decline, tea smuggling blossomed once again during the war of American Independence when between

[9] Jean-Baptiste Goy, *Mémoire sur les Bureaux de Toilerie établis dans la ville et Généralité de Rouen, et sur le commerce de ses fabriques en conséquence de la tournée générale que l'inspecteur des manufactures vient d'y faire*, November 12, 1782, AN, F12 650.

[10] Takumi Tusda (ed.), *Mémoires et Lettres de Vincent de Gournay* (Tokyo: Hitotsubashi University, 1993), 27.

4 and 6 million pounds were smuggled into Britain each year, though not solely from French sources. But the English smuggled more than tea. Anticipating the eruption of hostilities, in the single month of January 1778, English smugglers brought almost 2.3 million *livres* of prohibited French textiles from Dunkerque. In 1768, intendant of commerce André-Timothée-Isaac Bacalan reported that "contraband from France into England provides fifteen percent [profit] for needle-point lace made of silk [*blondes*], 25–30 percent for merchandise of greater dimension."[11] Lace, table service, cambrics, silk stockings, and calf-skin gloves as well as bolts of fine linen and silk were much sought after. William Pitt the younger claimed that while 600,000 gallons of French spirits entered Great Britain legally in 1787, 3–4 million gallons arrived as contraband. Although certainly exaggerated, more reliable estimates put the amount of prohibited alcohol smuggled from Dunkerque into Britain at 500,000 gallons in 1787–1788. For the eighteenth century as a whole, France's licit commerce with England was overshadowed by the value of the smuggling trade, which grew from 4 to 5 million *livres* around 1730 to reach 9 million between 1750 and 1770. By 1783, the English government approximated the value of illegal trade (from all sources) at 50–70 million *livres* annually. Given the massive increase in illicit traffic into Great Britain, it is hard not to agree with historian François Crouzet that smuggling was "big business."

Dunkerque, Bayonne, Boulougne, Calais, Lorient, and Marseille dominated French maritime smuggling. However, most goods smuggled into France arrived by land even when Britain was the point of origin. France's land frontiers were porous. Undersecretary of foreign affairs Joseph-Matthais-Gérard de Rayneval complained that English goods sent to North Sea ports were commonly smuggled across French land borders. During the 1780s, he estimated that 8 million *livres* of British hardware entered France that way. Land routes through Flanders, Lorraine, the Three Bishoprics, Alsace, the Franche-Comté, the Jura, Dauphiné, and the Pyrénées witnessed significant influxes of illegal foreign goods in the eighteenth century. British hardware, cotton and woolen textiles, Swiss watches and weapons, Dutch books, American and Rhenish tobacco, and Italian raw silk flooded into the realm. Around 1750, smuggled tobacco furnished one-third of domestic consumption. For 1784, Arnould estimated that 10–11 million *livres* worth of British goods were smuggled into France, against 13 million *livres* of legal imports. Three years later Arthur Young guessed that the value of all

[11] André-Timothée-Isaac Bacalan, *Observations faites par M. de Bacalan Intendant du commerce dans son voyage en Picardie, Artois, Haynaut et flandre en l'an 1768*, AN F12 650.

goods brought illegally into France came to nearly 15 million *livres*, making Britain the preponderant, but far from the sole, source of contraband. Adam Smith surely exaggerated when he remarked that "smugglers are now the principal importers, either of British goods into France, or of French goods into Great Britain." But not by much.[12]

Whatever the precise numbers involved, smuggling's extent and location responded to the welter of overlapping privileged markets that composed early modern France. Privileges created opportunities for both licit and illicit trade that attracted entrepreneurs up and down the social scale. As economic policy, the privilege of liberty featured state exemption of some producers, some goods, and some spaces from the rules that constrained others. For Bourbon officials, deployment of the privilege of liberty constituted tacit acceptance of the institutional wellsprings that supported smuggling and fraud as well as a major attempt to co-opt it in the name of economic development.

Smuggling produced problems of public order. In 1729, controller-general of finance Michel Le Peletier des Forts complained that "Considerable groups of armed smugglers leading loaded horses cross the better part of the realm to the gates of Paris, not only without meeting the least opposition, but, most times, the intendants do not even make the effort to inform me."[13] Customs officials reported that armed bands of up to 100 men smuggled tobacco from privileged provinces and from abroad past the tax barriers. During the 1730s, a band led by Mandrin even entered cities in the Auvergne with impunity to free imprisoned smugglers. While inspecting Channel ports in 1768, de Bacalan observed that "smugglers wait for nighttime and storms as other sailors hope for good weather." When chased, English smugglers "attach light anchors to small barrels of brandy. They warehouse them by

[12] The three previous paragraphs are based on Renaud Morieux, *Une mer pour deux royaumes: La Manche, frontier franco-anglaise (XVIIe-XVIIIe siècles)* (Presses Universitaires de Rennes, 2008), 241–73, François Crouzet, "La contrebande entre la France et les îles britanniques au XVIIIe siècle," in Gérard Béaur, Hubert Bonin, and Claire Lemercier (eds.), *Fraude, contrefaçon et contrebande de l'Antiquité à nos jours* (Geneva: Droz, 2006), 35–59, Marie Donaghay, "The Exchange of Products of the Soil and Industrial Goods in the Anglo-French Commercial Treaty of 1786," *The Journal of European Economic History*, 19: 2 (1990), 384, Arnould, *De La balance du commerce*, I: 173, and Arthur Young, *Travels in France during the Years 1787, 1788 and 1789*, ed. and intro. Jeffry Kaplow (Garden City, NY: Archor Books, 1969), 390. The quote is from Smith, *Wealth of Nations*, Book IV, Chapter 3. Although piracy was certainly an important issue in commerce and international affairs, the repression of smuggling was central to the English seizure of Dunkerque in 1754, a factor completely overlooked by Anoush Fraser Terjanian, *Commerce and Its Discontents in Eighteenth-Century French Political Thought* (Cambridge University Press, 2013), 93ff.

[13] Cited by Albert Babeau, *La Province sous l'Ancien Régime*, 2 vols. (Firmin Didot, 1894), II: 214–15.

plunging them in the sea. They recover them later and leave them on the shore."[14] Contraband was the major economic activity of a significant number of villages, not just on the coasts or on the frontier, but also on the edge of internal customs or tax barriers.

Lorraine, with the Three Bishoprics of Metz, Toul, and Verdun enclaved within, was a locus for smuggling. The end of French occupation of Lorraine in 1713 heightened clandestine commerce. The restored duke refused to clamp down on illicit trade. When Stanislaw Leszczyński took over, his administration attempted to interdict contraband, but smugglers used the rugged terrain and uncertain boundary with France to escape his officials. Even granting the right of "hot pursuit" into French territory to Lorraine's customs officers did little to slow the flood of contraband into Champagne, Alsace, and the Franche-Comté.[15]

Open display of illegal foreign goods undermined the government's authority. As Pierre-Samuel Dupont de Nemours observed in 1788,

> Prohibitions are not respected because of the nation's customs, because important people have not been dishonored for favoring contraband, and because . . . poorly paid customs agents earn money from seizures. They have no incentive to impose large penalties or seize too many goods which would thoroughly discourage contraband.[16]

In the last decades of the old régime, the passion for English fashions, *anglomanie*, popularized law-breaking for profit. Amiens' intendant, François-Marie de Bruno, count d'Agay, sought to prevent guild manufacturers from diverting their efforts from industry to illicit commerce as was taking place in nearby Lille. Repeatedly, he imposed severe punishments on Amienois manufacturers who put their seals on contraband goods to allow them to reach Paris more easily. His efforts were unsuccessful. Inspector of manufacturing Louis Villard noted that

[14] André-Timothée-Isaac Bacalan, *Observations faites par M. de Bacalan* and *Lettre de Belterre subdélégué à Boulogne à l'Intendant de Picardie*, March 28, 1777, AD Somme C1377.

[15] The two previous paragraphs are based on Crouzet, "La contrebande," 35–59, Philippe Minard, "Markets, Norms and Conventions in the Eighteenth Century," in Perry Gauci (ed.), *Regulating the British Economy, 166–1850* (Surrey: Ashgate, 2011), 177–94, Arthur Michel de Boislisle and Pierre de Brotonne (eds.), *Correspondance des contrôleurs généraux des finances avec les intendants des provinces*, 3 vols. (Imprimerie Nationale, 1888, 1897), III: 455, and *Arrêt du conseil d'Etat qui permet aux commis des fermes de Lorraine et de Bar de poursuivre les contrebandiers, faux-sauniers et autres fraudeurs sur les terres de l'obéissance du roi, lorsqu'ils s'y réfugieront*, 1738 (Gallica).

[16] Pierre-Samuel Dupont de Nemours, *Lettre à la chambre du commerce de Normandie; sur le Mémoire qu'elle a publié relativement au Traité de Commerce avec l'Angleterre* (Rouen: Moutard, 1788), 48–51.

"Montreuil has few commercial or industrial resources other than some stockings looms. They make little but they serve as a pretext for fraud from Artois by exchanging inspection seals ... They also put their seal on foreign stockings which is how these goods spread throughout the realm." The following year, he despaired that Picardy's cotton manufacturers "do not take the slightest interest in the public good ... If they deprived [the public] of English cotton goods, they would be able to perfect their manufacture and rival the English."[17] He concluded that smuggling impaired the industrial competitiveness of both Amiens and Abbeville.

For more than a century, French officials cracked down unsuccessfully on smuggling. As Forbonnais pointed out in the *Encyclopédie*, "In all states of a certain size it is almost impossible to uproot contraband if it offers a considerable profit." Amid "general corruption," he worried that "Any slackening of *police* supervision has the consequence that it often becomes impossible for the legislator to repair the fatal effects."[18] That realization did not stop the Bourbon state from trying. Officials positioned brigades of mounted police to catch or deter smuggling. On rare occasions, the army was deployed to interdict smugglers. Savary des Bruslons wrote that in 1687 Louis XIV imposed stiff penalties on both "fraudulent merchants" and "clerks, guards, and others who are complicit with them or who facilitate their fraud."[19] In 1701, nine-year sentences to the galleys and losing the ability to conduct commerce or have a shop were added to the list of penalties. For the rest of the century, smuggling was potentially a "capital" crime because it impinged on privilege. Smuggling was so widespread in Normandy that a special commission was created in 1769 and renewed in 1775 to try "smugglers, fraudulent salt dealers, and ... their accomplices and adherents in the generalities of Rouen, Caen, and Alençon."[20] The letters-patent establishing the commission make clear that local judges could not be entrusted with the task.

Early modern France's regulatory mania for inspection, trademarks, and prohibitions stemmed largely from a desire to identify and punish smuggling, contraband, and fraud. Administrative correspondence

17 Louis Villard, *Mémoire sur les fabriques et la commerce de la Généralité de Picardie dressé après la tournée Générale du département faite en Juin et Juillet 1784* and *Mémoire de Tournée dans le Département de l'Inspection de Picardie en Juin et Juillet 1785*, both in AD Somme C372.

18 "Contrebande" in *Encyclopédie*, IV: 429–30.

19 Jacques Savary des Bruslons with Philibert-Louis Savary, *Dictionnaire universel de commerce, d'histoire naturelle et des arts et métiers*, new ed., 5 vols. (Copenhagen: Claude and Antoine Philibert, 1759), II: 762.

20 *Lettres patentes du Roi, portant réablissement de la Commission établie à Caen par Lettres patentes du 9 Octobre 1768, pour juger les Contrebandiers*, December 26, 1775, BN F-23629 (150).

among high-ranking officials in Paris and Versailles, intendants, and inspectors of manufacturing demonstrates that linkage beyond a doubt. The damage done by illicit commerce motivated two of the era's major attempts to spread liberty at the expense of privilege. Jacques Necker's "intermediate" system regulating textile production of 1777–1781 and the Anglo-French commercial treaty were both intended to limit the profits of smuggling and fraud, usually estimated at 15–20 percent, two to three times the legitimate profits of Elbeuf's woolens manufacturers (see Chapter 3). State action providing liberty was also meant to push French entrepreneurs away from smuggling toward industrial competition and useful commerce.[21]

Smuggling evokes a myth of mercantilism. No European state could stop illegal trade. With long, mountainous land frontiers and extensive coastlines, France, perhaps more than any other European state, was threatened by contraband. Illegal commerce cost the treasury dearly, undermined public order, and heightened disobedience to state mandates. Its very success damaged useful commerce by shifting profit-taking and trade competition into illicit channels and siphoning off entrepreneurs from more productive ventures. Tax and commercial privileges facilitated and enabled smuggling. Contraband's vast extent reminds us that early modern economic statistics are approximations at best. As French mercantilist policies relied on useful commerce to support development, minimizing smuggling emerged as an important objective of Bourbon political economy. Several administrative experiments associated with mercantilism can best be understood as efforts to utilize privilege to redirect the French taste for smuggling and contraband into useful channels.

Free ports exemplified a political economy reliant on the privilege of liberty. Free ports funneled smuggling, heightened French international competitiveness, and facilitated naval construction. Dunkerque, situated on the North Sea, between Artois and the Spanish Netherlands, was France's first free port. Louis XIV bought this city of 6,000 inhabitants from England in October 1662 for 5 million *livres*. He confirmed that "The port and its surroundings can remain a place where all sorts of

[21] The three previous paragraphs are based on François-Marie de Bruno, *Arrêté*, March 19, 1774, AD Somme C325, Louis Villard, *Mémoire sur les fabrications d'Abbeville*, September 19, 1783, AN F12 563, *Arrêt du Conseil d'État du Roi*, May 3, 1722, ACCIMP J1558, Delaville, *Observation sur l'introduction des étoffes étrangers par la Loraine et les Trois Evêchés*, September 1770, AN F12 675, *Avis des députés du commerce*, May 21, 1754, AN F12 709, *Mémoire pour la chambre de commerce de Picardie*, February 22, 1782, AN F12 677, and Marie Donaghay, "Calonne and the Anglo-French Commercial Treaty of 1786," *Journal of Modern History*, 50: 3 (1978), 1162.

merchandise can be brought, manipulated, and transformed without any interference from customs on the condition that the goods are re-exported." To "make its commerce more abundant and more flourishing than ever," Louis XIV resolved "to accord all the freedoms, exemptions, and immunities enjoyed by the most prosperous cities."[22] Dunkerque kept its free port. Foreign merchants and shippers who set up shop there could become naturalized subjects. In Dunkerque, sailors were exempted from many obligations and duties, which greatly assisted in recruiting for the navy and merchant marine. As we saw in Chapter 2, the Sun King intended to win over Flanders' inhabitants by confirming their privileges. In like manner, almost by accident, Dunkerque became France's first free port.

Louis XIV's policies intended to make Dunkerque the chief outlet for the provinces of Artois and Flanders, a major North Sea commercial port, and a naval threat to England and the Netherlands. These objectives met with considerable success. Dunkerque benefited from Flanders' extensive network of rivers and canals as well as from favorable customs regulations that minimized duties on imported raw materials and exported manufactures. Over time, Dunkerque became the principal conduit for agricultural products and manufactured goods from Flanders, as well as Artois, Hainault, and Cambrèsis. The port attracted a growing number of ships. By 1789, up to 1,400 ships, two-fifths French, called at Dunkerque. A flourishing carrying trade brought wine from Bordeaux, Nantes, and La Rochelle to the Netherlands. During the eighteenth century, colonial trade also grew swiftly. The upper city, which had the privilege of liberty to manipulate goods for reexport, focused on tobacco products and dried fish.

In wartime, Dunkerque's strategic position encouraged outfitting corsairs. The National Assembly's agriculture and commerce committee estimated in 1790 that the city's corsairs had taken 110 million *livres* worth of prizes. Dunkerque's corsairs, including the infamous Jean Bart, were such a threat that the treaty of Utrecht concluding the war of Spanish Succession (1702–1713) required destroying the port's fortifications. However, Dunkerque's greatest economic contribution came as France's most important smuggling center. By the 1720s, approximately 500 small ships regularly engaged in illicit trade, mostly with England through the Channel Islands. In the 1770s and 1780s, Dunkerque boasted about 1000 people engaged in smuggling. In the mid-1770s, Dunkerque's mayor estimated

[22] Quoted by Pierre-Antoine Herwyn, *Rapport fait à l'Assemblée Nationale, au comité d'agriculture et de commerce sur la franchise de Dunkerque* (Imprimerie nationale, 1790), 4–9.

annual illegal commerce to be around 15 million *livres*. Louis XIV's purchase paid off.

Dunkerque's takeoff began only after two decades of French rule. The free port's success was far from assured when Louis XIV granted Marseille the privilege of a free port in 1669. This subject will be explored at length in the next chapter, but a few observations are needed here. The impetus for Marseille's privilege was commercial competition with other free ports around the Mediterranean Sea. The goal was to recover market share in the Levant, not to confirm existing conditions. Like Dunkerque, Marseille's free port only began to prosper in the 1680s. The unceasing search for revenue during Louis XIV's later wars led royal administrators to impose burdensome taxes on both "free" ports. All limitations on the freedoms accorded by the ports' privileges were eliminated in 1700–1703, as part of the economic reorganization that accompanied the formation of the royal council of commerce and local chambers of commerce. Paradoxically, in exchange for confirmation of their status as free ports, Dunkerque and Marseille were excluded from colonial commerce. This prohibition lasted until 1719 for Marseille and 1721 for Dunkerque. Once the ban was lifted, both ports profited enormously from trade with the Antilles. From Dunkerque, colonial products were generally smuggled into England while Marseille exchanged theirs for Levantine raw materials. The privilege of liberty was tied intimately to the development of important networks of exchange. By the 1720s, it was clear that France's two free ports were major commercial successes.[23]

Throughout this book, I emphasize the rationality and creativity of Bourbon economic administration. The obvious material benefits to Dunkerque and Marseille and their hinterlands suggest a question: why did the state wait until 1784 to extend the privilege of liberty by creating more? Bayonne and Saint-Malo's repeated attempts to become free ports shed light on the political economy of granting commercial privileges of liberty.

[23] The four previous paragraphs are based on Christian Pfister-Langanay, *Ports, navires et négociants à Dunkerque (1662–1792)* (Société Dunkerquoise, 1985), 137–45, 209–14, 236, 255–56, 296–97, 327–28, Morieux, *Une mer pour deux royaumes*, 253, Alexandre de Saint-Léger, *La Flandre maritime et Dunkerque sous la domination française (1659–1789)* (Ch. Taillandier, 1900), 364, 369–70, 373, *Declaration du Roy, portant exemption de tous droits d'entrée et de sortie pour les marchandises, entrant et sortant par Mer de la Ville, Port et Havre de Dunquerque*, February 16, 1700, AN F12 1646, and *Arrêt du Consil d'État du Roi qui interdit le Commerce des Isles Françaises aux Négociants et Habitans de la ville de Dunkerque et les maintient dans la Franchise de leur Ville, Port et Havre, conformément aux Déclarations et Arrêts des mois de Novembre 1662, 30 Janvier et 16 Février 1700*, January 22, 1718 (Gallica).

Saint-Malo staged major attempts to gain free port privileges in 1688, 1713, 1733–1738, and 1759. After losing several overseas markets as a result of French wartime defeats, the city fathers sought the privilege of liberty to restore the port's fortunes. In 1733, municipal elites petitioned Louis XV claiming that "The only means of repairing these disgraces is by freeing the port which is closed, so to speak to other parts of the realm, but open to commerce with the North that nature has seemed to assign it. In little time, this freedom will restore the port's splendor." Malouins bemoaned their lack of a hinterland to provide goods and markets and "feared that if their commerce fell further, they would no longer be able to provide sailors for the French navy or resources for war." They requested "the same liberties which have enabled Marseille and Dunkerque to flourish" to make up for their "loss of privileges."[24]

Saint-Malo's efforts never met success. Rival ports forcefully countered their arguments. Printed memoirs distinguished between confirming preexisting commercial privileges as was done for Dunkerque and the establishment of a free port such as Marseille's. Nantes and La Rochelle demolished Saint-Malo's historical claims to additional commercial privileges, while Marseille pointed out that the lack of a hinterland and geographical isolation would undermine the utility of a free port. The Marseillais asserted that "Saint Malo's demand for liberty is contrary to state interests. The liberties of the various ports lower state revenues and are not useful if they provide only a slight benefit to those who enjoy them because, by being given to several commercial cities, they have become too common." According to rival ports, Malouin preference for easy profits would lead the city to become a center of smuggling just like Dunkerque. The Bordelais wondered "why Malouins think that they alone have suffered from misfortunes affecting all of France?" They believed that Malouins' "hyperbolic lamentation was worthy of the theater." The deputies of commerce and royal council repeatedly rejected Malouin requests despite powerful support from Brittany's influential estates.[25]

Saint-Malo's failures did not deter others. In a long printed memoir published in 1738, Bayonne's chamber of commerce echoed the

[24] *Mémoire au Roi des habitants de St. Malô*, 1733, ACCIMP D32.

[25] The quotes are from *Mémoire pour la ville de Nantes servant de reponse à celui de Saint Malo au sujet du port Franc*, 1737 and *Mémoire des Directeurs du Commerce de Guienne en réponse à celui de Saint Malo qui demande au Roi la franchise de son port*, 1737. See also *Observations de la Chambre de Commerce de la Ville de Marseille sur la requête presenté au Roi par les habitans de la ville de St. Malô*, October 7, 1733, *Mémoire pour la ville de La Rochelle servant de reponse à celui de Saint Malo au sujet de la Franchise de son port*, 1738, *Mémoire nouveau de Saint Malo en faveur de la franchise du port*, March 1759, and *Délibérations de la Chambre de Commerce de Marseille*, March 21, 1759. All documents found in ACCIMP D32.

Malouins' historical, practical, and situational claims. The chamber complained that "infringements" of their privileges kept them from enjoying the historical freedoms guaranteed them when the city became French. The difference, they asserted, was "that Bayonne has genuine privileges that distinguish it from all other French cities which ought to exempt it from every law, general or particular regulation, or other formalities already given and to come that apply within the general tax farm or in other provinces and cities."[26] Their arguments accomplished little. In 1779, the deputies of commerce ridiculed Bayonne for its dependence on privilege and flatly rejected the possibility of making the city a free port. Yet, only five years later, Louis XVI, at controller-general of finance Charles-Alexandre de Calonne's urging, created two additional free ports: Bayonne and Lorient.

Official reasoning for establishing new free ports in 1784 repeated arguments and assertions made earlier. For Bayonne, detailed letters-patent presented the city's historic privileges, position outside the general tax farm in a "foreign" province, and the goal of developing commerce and industry in the region. Despite the creation of a "free" port, those rights and privileges were limited drastically to "prevent fraudulent payments" from destroying the tobacco trade. Lorient's equivalent document is much shorter. It created a "free" zone "enclaved" within the larger port where colonial goods could be sold for transshipment to the north. Lorient was selected because of its access to the interior via the Loire River and deepwater harbor.[27]

So what changed between 1688 and 1784? Why did the French government suddenly double the number of free ports? The lack of any new justifications suggests that the shift had little to do with the merits of the case for freedom of trade. Historian John Bosher's explanation is the most convincing. Based on the *Secret Memoirs* of tax farmer Jacques-Mathieu Augéard, he argues that the impetus for new free ports came partly from the foreign ministry, which wanted them for diplomatic purposes as part of the count de Vergennes' campaign to convince England to sign a commercial treaty. More important to administrative decision making, however, wrote Bosher, was the belief that this particular privilege of liberty would advance the single duty project. The

26 *Mémoire de la Chambre de Commerce de Bayonne sur l'Ancien État de cette ville, et les revolutions arrives à son commerce, presenté, à l'occasion des discussions, qui lui ont été suscitées*, 1738 (Googlebooks).

27 This action refutes the distinction made by Tim Blanning on the distinction between maritime trade and domestic commerce. Bourbon policymakers recognized that France did not enjoy a truly national market, but their approach to both development and protectionism was based essentially on privilege. Tim C. W. Blanning, *The French Revolution: Aristocrats versus Bourgeois?* (Houndsmills: Macmillan, 1987), 10.

report by the National Assembly's committee of agriculture and commerce in 1790 explaining why the franchise of only Marseille and Dunkerque should be retained supports the view that the 1784 measure stemmed from reasons other than a belief in the efficacy of free trade (see Chapter 8). Even if personally committed to extending liberty, royal officials sought political reform more than liberal political economy in creating two new free ports in 1784.[28]

Encouraging useful commerce was a constant of early modern French economic policymaking. The seemingly disparate subjects discussed in this section represent an attempt to dispel certain myths in English-language understandings of French experience. First, eighteenth-century French foreign trade grew far more rapidly than its English rival, providing an important dose of economic optimism. Nor was this growth based solely on colonial products. France participated in various networks of exchange with the rest of Europe and across the Mediterranean in which colonial goods played an important but far from exclusive role. French commercial policy sparked import substitution and generated large surpluses that supported economic growth in diverse regions across the realm. France's troubled relationship with smuggling confirms arguments made in Chapters 2 and 3 about the very real limits of the power of the "absolutist" state as well as the opportunities and limitations inherent in the structure of the society of orders. At the same time, the vast extent of smuggling undermines faith in economic statistics and reminds us that the illicit economy cannot be excluded from comparative considerations of competitiveness, entrepreneurialism, and growth. Finally, France founded four free ports between 1662 and 1784. Louis XIV established Dunkerque and Marseille, while Louis XVI created Bayonne and Lorient. Both monarchs deployed the privilege of liberty to improve French commercial competitiveness and expand useful commerce but avoided saturating the system. In commerce, French mercantilism evolved considerably between

[28] The three previous paragraphs are based on Bosher, *The Single Duty Project*, 112–14, 156, *Avis des Députés du Commerce sur les demandes des Villes de Bayonne et de St. Jean de Luz, afin de l'affranchisement du Pays de Labourie, relativement à la Régie des droites de traites*, April 1, 1779, AN F12 1646, *Arrêt du Conseil d'État du Roi portant Règlement pour la franchise du Port de l'Orient*, June 26, 1784, *Lettres-patentes du Roi, portant confirmation et interprétation des Privilèges de la ville de Bayonne et de ceux du pays de Labourt; et Règlement relatif à la franchise accordée au Port de la ville*, July 4, 1784, Herwyn, *Rapport*, Étienne-David Meynier, *Rapport fait à l'Assemblée Nationale au nom du Comité d'Agriculture et de Commerce sur le régime à donner au port et au territoire de Marseille quant aux droits de douane*, n.d. [1791], and François-Pierre Lasnier de Vaussenay, *Rapport fait à l'Assemblée Nationale sur la franchise de Bayonne*, n.d. [1790]. Except as noted, all primary sources found on Googlebooks.

Louis XIV and Louis XVI, but its hallmarks remained flexibility, rationality, and reliance on the liberties that privilege could provide. For an historian of political economy, the hardest myth to dispel in the English-speaking world is the mistaken idea that French mercantilism did not work.

Opportunities abroad: empire and the chartered companies of the Levant, Africa, and the Indies

Bourbon France relied on privilege to take advantage of opportunities afforded by maritime trade both within Europe and across the seas. Although the precursor of the East Indies Company received a monopoly from Henri IV in 1604 and Cardinal Richelieu created a host of chartered companies, systematic state use of privilege to encourage commercial and industrial development began with Colbert.[29] To recover from the Fronde and almost twenty-five years of war with Spain while engaging in commercial competition with the Netherlands and England was a daunting task. Privilege was essential to French mercantilism: it encouraged entrepreneurs to invest both their energy and their capital in new markets, facilitated import substitution, and increased the circulation of goods and specie, while expanding the tax base. At the same time, mercantilism was a means of waging economic war. Without privilege, the Bourbon monarchy could not take advantage of its opportunities abroad.

The checkered history of Colbert's chartered companies is well known. Pointed criticism by improvers such as Forbonnais and André Morellet later echoed by Adam Smith still colors English-language understandings of Colbert's strategy and tactics. The "colonial pact" or "exclusive system" that firmly subordinated the colonies to the metropolis and encouraged the spread of the exploitive institution of slavery also received severe criticism. My purpose is not to offer a full account of the foundation of either the chartered companies or the French empire. Rather I seek to undermine another myth of mercantilism by demonstrating how the Bourbon state sought to develop foreign trade through implementation of privileges of liberty. Through the prism of political economy, I emphasize the flexibility, openness to new

[29] For a brief discussion of Cardinal Richelieu's failed attempts to use privilege to support colonization, see Pierre Clément, *Histoire de Colbert et de son administration*, 2nd ed. (Didier et Cie., 1874), I: 495–97. On the origins of the French East Indies Company, see Philippe Haudrère, *La Compagnie française des Indes au XVIIIe siècle (1719–1795)*, thése pour le Doctorat d'État, 4 vols. (Librairie de l'Inde, 1989), I: 19–38.

opportunities, and relative effectiveness of the privilege of liberty as a tool of French mercantilism.[30]

Colbert preferred private initiative and commercial liberty to government intervention. Extending privileges to chartered companies was solely a means to an end. In a 1670 letter to Jean-Charles de Baas, West Indies governor-general, Colbert wrote, "commerce, being the result of men's pure will, must necessarily be left free unless there is a vital necessity of limiting trade to a company or to certain individuals." When he revived the West Indies Company, Colbert reported that "His Majesty knows that a company composed of a number of powerful interested parties, working for a common good ... can trade more advantageously than individuals." Nor did Colbert turn a blind eye once privileges had been granted. He repeatedly lowered duties for independent traders who competed with a chartered company and eliminated companies that did not perform. In February 1679, he warned the director of the Levant Company, "when I find a greater advantage or an equal advantage [from open competition], I do not hesitate to take away any privilege." For Colbert and his ministerial successors, only a chartered company backed by the state had the resources, organization, and prestige to raise sufficient capital to acquire and exploit new markets.[31]

Like most economic policymakers, Colbert was a copycat. Although chartered companies had existed in France since the sixteenth century, from Richelieu's ministry, state-granted privileges to exploit the "two Indies" mimicked institutions in France's European rivals. The Netherlands' commercial successes were a particular inspiration. Using the privilege of liberty, Colbert hoped to adapt Dutch methods to make France into an entrepôt for goods from around the world. In 1664, he wrote, "If the kings of the North and the princes of the [Holy Roman] Empire wish to think seriously about trade with the East and West Indies, Louis XIV can make them solid propositions, incomparably more

[30] François Véron Duverger de Forbonnais, "Compagnie de Commerce," *Encyclopédie*, III: 739–43, André Morellet, *Memoires relatifs a la discussion du privilége de la Nouvelle Compagnie des Indes* (Amsterdam: Demonville, 1787), and Smith, *Wealth of Nations*, Book IV. On the chartered companies in the Americas, see Philip P. Boucher, "French Proprietary Colonies in the Greater Caribbean," in Lou Roper and Bertrand Van Ruymbeke (eds.), *Constructing Early Modern Empires: Proprietary Ventures in the Atlantic World, 1500–1750* (Leiden: Brill, 2007), 163–88.

[31] The first quote is cited by Léon Deschamps, *Histoire de la question coloniale en France* (Plon, 1891), 145. The others are from Pierre Clément (ed.), *Lettres, instructions et mémoires de Colbert publiés d'après les ordres de l'empereur*, 10 vols. (Imprimerie impériale, 1861–73), III (2): 694 and VII: 250. See also Jeff Horn, "Marseille et la question du mercantilisme: privilège, liberté et l'économie politique en France, 1650–1750," *Histoire, économie & société*, (2011/2), 95–112.

advantageous than anyone else." Colbert also understood the military implications of trade. A 1670 *Memoir* explained that

> Since the king took over administration of French finances, he has undertaken a monetary war against all other European states. He has already vanquished Spain, Italy, Germany, England, and some others ... All that remains is Holland. Their trade with ... the East Indies, ... the Levant, ... the West Indies, ... Cadiz, [and] the coast of Guinea enable them to resist strongly ... Your Majesty has created companies which, like armies, attack them everywhere.

Louis XIV's chartered companies targeted Dutch commerce. The first trial was the West Indies Company in May 1664.[32] Companies followed for the East Indies (1664), Africa and/or Bastion de France (1666, 1678, 1690, 1693, 1706, 1712), the North or the Baltic Sea (1669), the Levant (1670, 1678), Senegal (1673, 1679, 1684, 1696), Acadia or the beaver trade (1683, 1706), Mississippi (1684), the Mediterranean (1685, 1698), Guinea [*Cap nègre*] (1685, 1701, 1712), the Southern Oceans (1698), China (1697, 1712, 1715), Saint-Domingue (1698), Asiento [slave trade with Spanish America] (1702), Canada/New France (1706), Hudson's Bay (1710), and the Antoine Crozat Company of Louisiana (1712). The failures of most of the thirty-nine privileged companies created during the reign of Louis XIV suggest neither a lack of vision nor deficient commitment on the part of French policymakers. Rather, the dogged replacement of chartered companies demonstrates that Bourbon officials viewed these institutions as indispensable instruments of war and commerce.[33]

Indispensable did not mean either effective or profitable. Although the crown granted expansive and exclusive privileges, large sums were also required to found these enterprises. Louis XIV and his officials expended considerable energy and prestige to pressure nobles to purchase shares. Of the East Indies Company's 15 million *livres* of capital, the king put up 4 million. According to one of its boosters, the court invested an

[32] Other companies were chartered earlier in Louis XIV's reign. They included: the North/Baltic Sea (1644); Saint-Jean-de-Luz (1648); South America (1651, 1653, 1663); China (1660); and Ogeron [for small Caribbean islands] (1662). See Ėmile Levasseur, *Histoire des classes ouvrières et de l'industrie en France avant 1789*, 2nd ed., 2 vols. (Arthur Rousseau, 1901), 280–81.

[33] The first quote is cited by Louis Cordier, *Les Compagnies à charte et la politique colonial sous le ministère de Colbert* (Arthur Rousseau, 1906), 101 and the second by Clément (ed.), *Lettres, instructions et mémoires de Colbert*, III (2): 477. According to Steve Pincus, British economists and policymakers shared this view about competitiveness and privileged trading companies. See his "Rethinking Mercantilism: Political Economy, the British Empire, and the Atlantic World in the Seventeenth and Eighteenth Centuries," *The William and Mary Quarterly*, 69: 1 (2012), 3–34, 19. On Colbert's ambitions vi-à-vis the Dutch, see Joseph de Mazan, *Les Doctrines économiques de Colbert* (Arthur Rousseau, 1900), 93–136. See also Levasseur, *Histoire des classes ouvrières. . .avant 1789*, II: 280–81.

additional 2 million *livres* with Anne, the queen mother, Maria-Theresa, the queen, and the dauphin leading the way with investments of 60,000 *livres* each. Chancellor Pierre Séguier put in 50,000 *livres* and Colbert himself invested 30,000. This capital had plenty of opportunities to exploit. The company was given a fifty-year exclusive monopoly to trade with territories from the Cape of Good Hope in the west to the Straits of Magellan in the east. The company was granted ownership of all the islands it could occupy and was given a somewhat counterintuitive bonus of 50 *livres* for each ton of merchandise that it exported and 75 *livres* for each ton imported.

The West Indies Company received similar, and in many ways, even more impressive privileges. Of the company's 5.5 million *livres* of capital, the crown put up more than half. Colbert again supplied 30,000 *livres* and the tax farmers put in 700,000. Pressured by royal administrators, thirty-five cities invested. Lyon put up 1 million *livres*, Paris 650,000, Rouen 500,000, Bordeaux 400,000, and Nantes 200,000. For forty years, the company received the exclusive right to sail to or trade with Canada, Acadia, Newfoundland, the Antilles, Cayenne, and the African coast between Senegal and the Cape of Good Hope. In addition to customs exemptions, the company received a bonus of 30 *livres* per ton of imports and 40 *livres* per ton of exported merchandise. Initially the company enjoyed the sole right to authorize shippers to trade with its possessions. The company could even grant lands in fief and make war or peace. Settlers who agreed to stay at least eighteen months earned free passage. Artisans who remained in the colonies for eight years were declared masters without having to serve as journeymen or create a masterwork. They could not set up shop in a French city, however.

Other companies received lesser privileges and were capitalized at smaller sums. The company of the North was to compete directly with the Netherlands in the heart of its power by way of the North Sea. Yet its capital was fixed at a paltry 600,000 *livres*. In 1671, Colbert attempted to attract investors by forcing the company to pay dividends beyond its means. Clearly, the Bourbon state prioritized jump-starting commerce with the two Indies.[34]

Nearly all these chartered companies miscarried, most of them quite quickly, with little to show for the state's effort. Insufficient capital, overly strict regulation, poor administration, and sheer ineptitude plagued

[34] The three previous paragraphs are based on Levasseur, *Histoire des classes ouvrières . . . avant 1789*, II: 276–78, Boucher, "French Proprietary Colonies," 177, Pierre Bonnassieux, *Les grandes compagnies de commerce: Étude pour server à l'histoire de la colonization* (Plon, 1892), 171–72, and Henry Weber, *La Compagnie des Indes (1604–1875)* (Arthur Rousseau, 1904), 123.

all the privileged companies, but war and cutthroat competition from the English and Dutch were greater problems. Colbert admitted that supporting the company of the North was a "useless subterfuge. The company of the North is not succeeding any more than the others. When war broke out a year later with the Netherlands, it collapsed, never to recover."[35] His observation reminds us that the privileges given to the chartered companies were weapons of war far more than they were development strategies.

Even favored endeavors like the West Indies Company lasted only a decade (1664–1674), losing nearly 3.5 million *livres*. A 1665 revolt against company rule in Martinique was defeated, but the company could not recover from ship losses at English hands in the brief 1666–1667 war, fulfill colonial demand, or cope with Dutch competition. Corruption depleted the company's coffers and investors refused to throw good money after bad when the directors asked for more funds. Limitations on its monopoly of the carrying trade foreclosed any possibility that the company could ever earn a profit. In 1669, Louis XIV abrogated the company's privilege. Royal administrators allowed numerous merchants based in Nantes and Saint-Malo to trade with the American colonies without paying entry or exit fees to the company. Ship losses during the Franco-Dutch War completed the company's collapse.

Among the thirty-nine chartered companies created during the reign of Louis XIV, only the East Indies Company long survived. Wartime losses and commercial uncertainty undermined the effectiveness of state privileges and made maritime commerce unprofitable at best and impossible at worst. These lessons were not lost on Colbert. He recognized that monopolies impeded peacetime development and were unenforceable in war. In 1677, he wrote that he was "well persuaded that only commercial liberty strengthens colonies and allows them to grow." Three years later, Colbert added that "the unique means of regulating everything and putting it all in a position to produce an advantage for the inhabitants of the islands is to increase their number and to leave merchants completely free to buy and sell their goods."[36] The Antilles' spectacular growth after 1674 appeared to confirm that liberty was more effective than privilege in encouraging colonial development amid frequent maritime wars.

In this context, the reappearance of privileged companies after Colbert's death is striking. After 1683, successful chartered companies developed existing commercial ties. Despite intermittent profitability,

[35] Cited by Bonnassieux, *Les grandes compagnies de commerce*, 172.
[36] Both quotes are cited by Levasseur, *Histoire des classes ouvrières...avant 1789*, II: 279.

the Levant Company played a vital role in capturing this vital market from the English and Dutch (see Chapter 5). After several false starts, the Royal Africa Company established in 1740 made money consistently until the outbreak of the Revolutionary wars. To forge new bonds or to found colonies, however, only privileges attracted entrepreneurial talent and sufficient investment from nobles and non-nobles alike. The profitability of some British and Dutch companies fortified French confidence in the potential effectiveness of this institution. Bourbon policymakers understood that chartered companies were necessary for certain tasks, but ill-suited to fostering long-term commercial growth.[37]

Such an understanding helps to clarify the next phase in the Bourbon state's management of colonial development as well as its effort to turn France into the commercial hub of Europe. Peace returned in 1713 and Louis XIV passed from the scene two years later. The Regency adopted a *laissez-faire* attitude toward the colonies while relying on the politics of privilege.[38] As is well known, John Law founded the company of the West as a joint-stock company in 1717 based on the wreckage of the Mississippi Company. Renamed the West Indies Company two years later, the new company based in Lorient received a trade monopoly for French America. In May–June 1719, the rechristened "perpetual company of the Indies" absorbed the East Indies, China, and various Africa companies, giving it a monopoly of French maritime commerce. Its privileges were to last until 1770.

The collapse of Law's system in 1720 did not destroy the Indies Company, but its monopolies were diminished during reorganization. In North America, the company retained Louisiana and enjoyed a commercial monopoly including the beaver trade. The company also monopolized trade with Saint-Domingue, though not with any other island colony or Guyana. Except for Egypt, the company held all French trading rights in Africa from the Barbary Coast to the Cape of Good Hope in addition to the islands of present-day Réunion (Bourbon) and Mauritius (France). In Asia, the company monopolized trade except for the Levant and western Russia. Louis XV confirmed all these privileges in 1725.

37 The four previous paragraphs are based on Paul Butel, *Histoire des Antilles françaises XVIIe-XXe siècle* (Perrin, 2007 [2002]), 94–109, James Pritchard, *In Search of Empire: The French in the Americas, 1670–1730* (Cambridge University Press, 2004), 193–208, Butel, *L'Ėconomie française*, 124, Boucher, "French Proprietary Colonies," 178, and Gaston Rambert (ed.), *Histoire du commerce de Marseille*, 6 vols (Plon, 1954), IV: 236–37.

38 On the Regency's colonial policy, see Philip P. Boucher, *Les Nouvelles Frances: France in America, 1500–1815 – An Imperial Perspective* (Providence, RI: the John Carter Brown Library, 1989), 69–70.

This vast domain slowly shriveled. Although it had seventy-five ships in 1724, it could not maintain existing trade links in Africa or the Americas, much less cope with exploding demand for colonial and Asian goods. The company renounced its slave-trading monopoly in 1725. The Barbary Coast became the territory of the Royal Africa Company in 1730 and, the following year, the Indies Company returned Louisiana to the crown. Dividends were 150 *livres* per action from 1725 to 1746, and 70–80 *livres* in 1746–1758 and 1765–1768. These figures mislead because of the source of company revenue. In 1751, Voltaire commented that the company "had never paid the least dividend to its investors from the profits of its trade. It is the only European commercial company in this situation. In fact, its investors and creditors have always been paid through the royal concession of part of the duty on tobacco, which is irrelevant to its trade." With profits from India declining from 50 to 5 million *livres* between 1725 and 1769 and the benefit of China trade falling from 22 to 2 million *livres* over the same period, contemporaries recognized that the Indies Company's privileges had not fostered development commensurate with the scope of the government's investments. Asian trade volume was also essentially flat in the 1750s and 1760s, paling in comparison to American commerce's 60 percent increase. Only the distractions of frequent wars and constant domestic upheaval along with the desire to avoid dependence on foreign traders for Asian goods explain how the company survived the concerted attack of critics like de Gournay until its collapse in 1769 on the eve of the expiration of its privilege.[39]

The failure of chartered companies monopolizing French colonial commerce cleared a path for a different system to develop based on the privilege of liberty. At the same time that Law's company of the West was founded, the state created entrepôts to facilitate commerce by increasing the circulation of colonial goods. Until 1765, ships sailed from one European port to one colonial port and back. Entrepôts warehoused certain goods from the colonies and reexported them abroad without having to pay customs, though a minimal 3 percent charge remained. Both French subjects and foreigners could make use of entrepôts. In 1717, colonial entrepôts were established in Bayonne, Bordeaux, Calais, Dieppe, Le Havre, Honfleur, La Rochelle, Rouen, and Sète. In addition to those ports, Brest, Morlaix, Nantes, and Saint-Malo received

[39] Paul Butel provides a far less negative appraisal of the Company's commercial activities, especially in Asia. See *L'Économie française*, 125–28. Compare to Haudrère, *La Compagnie française des Indes*, II: 387–485. See also Terjanian, *Commerce and Its Discontents*, 147–52.

the privilege of conducting colonial commerce. "Goods or merchandise grown or made in the realm" were exempted from all entry and exit fees, whether inside the general tax farm or in a "foreign" province. These efforts were intended to nurture ports that had suffered during the war of Spanish Succession and to bring different ports and their hinterlands into rapidly developing Atlantic trade networks.[40]

The free ports of Marseille and Dunkerque were initially excluded from colonial commerce. The Regency government soon recanted, pressed by the deputies of commerce, who believed that "an entrepôt is indispensible [*sic*] for Marseille" and concluded that "the privilege of entrepôt had nothing to do with the free port." Marseille was allowed to conduct colonial trade in 1719. It was "impossible to distinguish what goods were destined for the islands and what goods were not" in Marseille's bustling free port. "The large number of French ships from different ports that throng the islands produces very advantageous effects for the inhabitants who can find more things they need at lower prices and can more easily sell their surplus." For similar reasons, Dunkerque was accorded "the privilege and the liberty to trade with the islands" two years later.[41] Other than minor adjustments, only the establishment of inspectors to verify the weight and size of barrels of foodstuffs headed west or bulk sugar or cotton entering France in 1744 altered the system before the twilight of the old régime.

In conjunction with the free ports, privileged entrepôts heightened competition in colonial goods, both in the Empire and in France. In the 1720s, coffee imports into the general tax farm were so robust and

[40] The four previous paragraphs are based on Weber, *La compagnie française des Indes*, 330–36, Savary des Bruslons with Savary, *Dictionnaire universel de commerce*, II: 330, *Èdit du Roi portant confirmation des Privileges accordé, Concessions et Alienations faites à la Compagnie des Indes*, 1725 (Gallica), *Avis des Députés du Commerce sur un projet d'arrêt qui a été redigé dans l'objet de refformer les abus éxistans dans la concession des privilèges en matière de commerce*, February 29, 1761, AN F12 712, and André Morellet, *Mémoire sur la situation actuelle de la Compagnie des Indes* (Desaint, 1769), xiv, 162, Deschamps, *Histoire de la question coloniale*, 251–52, Voltaire, *Le Siècle de Louis XIV* (1751), chapter XXIX, Butel, *L'Èconomie française*, 125, and Paul Butel, "France, the Antilles, and Europe in the Seventeenth and Eighteenth Centuries: Renewals of Foreign Trade," in James D. Tracy (ed.), *The Rise of Merchant Empires: Long-distance Trade in the Early Modern World, 1350–1750* (Cambridge University Press, 1990), 170. Morellet's book published the treatise of Jacques-Claude-Marie Vincent de Gournay, *Observations sur le rapport fait à M. le contrôleur général par M. de S*** le 26 juin 1755, sur l'état de la Compagnie des Indes*, 1755, x–xxiv. The quote is from *Lettres-patentes du Roi portant Reglement pour le Commerce des Colonies Françaises*, 1717 (Gallica).

[41] The quotes are from *Sentiment des députés au Conseil de Commerce sur le Mémoire de la Chambre de Marseille au sujet des Lettres patentes du mois d'avril 1717 portant réglement pour le commerce des Isles françaises de l'Amérique*, April 25, 1718, AN F12 694 and *Lettres-patentes du Roi qui accordant à la ville de Dunkerque le Privilège et la Liberté de faire le commerce aux Isles d'Amérique aux conditions qui y sont exprimées*, 1721 (Gallica).

avoided paying customs so successfully that a royal ordinance was issued in 1729 to ensure that Dunkerque's entrepôt was not abused. After 1748, up to ten ships a year left Dunkerque, usually headed to Africa to trade manufactured goods for slaves. After selling the slaves in the Antilles, Dunkerque's merchants returned laden with colonial goods. Some of this trade was licit: French coffee, tea, cotton, indigo, and sugar were reexported to the Netherlands or to Hanseatic ports, but as we saw above, much of the traffic in colonial products was smuggled into England. Marseille's entrepôt played a major role in the port's development and to eighteenth-century France's domination of trade with the Levant.[42]

By the time Marseille recovered from the outbreak of plague in 1720–1721, the Indies Company possessed a monopoly to import coffee into France. Marseille, however, retained the privilege of bringing Arabian coffee or mocha from the Levant. As an entrepôt, Marseille could also import coffee from the Antilles as long as it was then exported. Marseillais merchants took full advantage of their opportunity: from twelve ships annually in 1712–1716, Marseille sent an average of 122 in 1784–1788 filled with manufactured goods and Provençal agricultural produce. From the 1720s, sugar was the primary colonial product sought by the Marseillais. Coffee became an important commodity once the Indies Company abandoned its privilege in stages between 1732 and 1736. Entrepôts imported coffee freely so long as they paid a moderate tax of four *sols* a pound. Soon afterward, the duty was increased to a *livre* per pound. In exchange, all coffee introduced into Marseille's entrepôt could be exported overland to places like Geneva without paying customs and Antilles coffee imported through Marseille could be sold in France. Although this liberty was only temporary, Marseille became France's coffee clearinghouse as Europeans sought the "surprising and nearly miraculous effects" of coffee in ever-increasing quantities and qualities.[43] Marseillais became so adept at passing mocha off as Antilles

[42] The two previous paragraphs are based on Pfister-Langanay, *Ports, navires et négociants à Dunkerque*, 214, 217, 296, 301–02, 317, Saint-Léger, *La Flandre maritime*, 374, *Lettres patentes du Roi portant Reglement pour le Commerce qui se fait de Marseille aux Isles Françaises de l'Amérique*, 1719, *Arrêt du conseil d'Etat qui fixe à un an le temps de l'entrepôt des marchandises venant des îles et colonies françaises dans les ports y dénommés, et de celles qui seront déclarées par entrepôt pour lesdites îles*, 1723, *Arrêt du conseil d'Etat qui ordonne l'exécution dans les port et ville de Dunkerque des édits, arrêts et réglements concernant le commerce de la Compagnie des Indes, et notamment le privilege exclusif de l'introduction et de la vente du café dans le royaume*, 1729, *Arrêt du conseil d'Etat concernant l'entrepôt tant des marchandises destinées pour les îles et colonies françaises que de celles qui en viennent*, 1738, and *Arrêt du conseil d'état portant réglement sur le commerce des colonies françaises de l'Amérique*, 1744. Unless otherwise noted, these documents are available on Gallica.

[43] Savary des Bruslons with Savary, *Dictionnaire universel de commerce* I: 720–28, 722.

coffee that the state had to intervene to stop widespread fraud. After 1746, mocha could still enter France through Marseille, but Antilles coffee had to be reexported. By the 1750s, Antilles coffee, largely from Martinique, had conquered a number of Levantine markets, most notably Egypt. Coffee figured prominently in Marseille's favorable balance of trade with the Levant: two-thirds of the port's coffee exports went there despite booming demand in Spain and Italy.

Once the Indies Company lost its Antilles privileges in 1769, Marseille's trade grew even faster. Marseille developed new commercial links with Asia and expanded its trade with the Americas, especially in coffee. By 1789, Marseille had surpassed Nantes and Le Havre to become France's second leading port for American colonial goods. In the depressed conditions of the late 1780s, coffee comprised 42 percent of Marseille's imports from the Antilles (vs. 46 percent for sugar) and colonial reexports represented 52 percent of the port's total exports. Marseille's coffee trade with the Antilles reflected the general rise in French exports. Saint-Domingue increased its production of coffee from 7 million pounds in 1755 to 77 million in 1789 when more than half of the world's coffee was grown on the Jewel of the Antilles. By 1789, the total value of French coffee imports reached 104 million *livres*, a mere 4 million less than sugar. In one sense despite and in another sense because of its geographic position, Marseille's entrepôt facilitated its burgeoning commerce with the Antilles. As an institution, the privilege of entrepôts played a major role in the impressive growth of eighteenth-century French trade. Marseille's entrepôt was especially effective because it linked thriving maritime commerce, a large hinterland, and a notable concentration of entrepreneurs.[44]

[44] The two previous paragraphs are based on Charles Carrière, *Négociants Marseillais au XVIIIe siècle: Contribution à l'étude des economies maritimes*, 2 vols. (Marseille: Institut historique de Provence, 1973), I: 359–79, Thomas M. Doerflinger, "The Antilles Trade of the Old Regime: A Statistical Overview," *Journal of Interdisciplinary History*, 6: 30 (1976), 397–415, 35, Robert Paris, *Le Levant*, vol. 5, Gaston Rambert (ed.), *Histoire du commerce de Marseille* (Plon, 1957), 559–61, Haudrère, *La Compagnie française des Indes*, I: 421, Boucher, *Les nouvelles Frances*, 90, Charles Carrière, *Richesse du Passé Marseillais: Le port mondiale au XVIIIe siècle* (Chambre de Commerce et d'Industrie de Marseille, 1979), 35, Deschamps, *Histoire de la question coloniale*, 250, *Arrêt du conseil d'Etat qui ordonne que tous les cafés venant des Echelles du Levant pourront entrer dans la ville de Marseille et en sortir librement par mer, ainsi qu'avant l'arrêt du 31 août 1723*, 1724, *Arrêt du Conseil d'État qui permet aux negocians de Marseille, d'introduire pour la consummation du Royaume, les caffés provenant du crû des îles françaises de l'Amérique, en payant dix livres du cent pesant et d'en envoyé à Geneve en* transit, *sans payer aucuns droits; let tout en observant les formalités préscrites*, April 2, 1737, and *Arrêt du conseil d'état qui révoque la permission accordée par celui du 2 avril 1737, aux négociants de Marseille, d'introduire pour la consommation du royaume, des cafés des iles françaises de l'Amérique*, 1746. The royal ordinances are all found on

French economic policymaking in the period after 1750 featured systematic attempts to increase commercial liberty at the expense of the high level of state control commonly associated with mercantilism. This approach to development was based on both theory and practice: the trade statistics discussed above clearly demonstrate the magnitude if not the precise contours of France's commercial achievements. This success is even more remarkable in light of the interruptions stemming from two maritime wars (1756–1763 and 1777–1783). Not only was there widespread resort to smuggling and neutral shipping, but France also lost its hard-won North American empire and most of its influence in India. The Spanish crown's 1779 decision to restrict the flow of French textiles into its American colonies also moderated the pace of commercial expansion. The relative slowdown that came with the ascendancy of the partisans of liberty helps to explain some seemingly contradictory state actions involving privilege and liberty that accompanied the return of peace.

In August 1784, the Bourbon administration eliminated French ships' exclusive monopoly to conduct colonial trade by establishing six entrepôts: one each for Martinique, Guadeloupe, and Tobago, and three for Saint-Domingue. By admitting North American, British, and Dutch traders among others, the measure increased competition. Official intent was to limit smuggling, increase customs revenue, and ensure the food supplies of France's burgeoning colonies. Foreign traders could bring only dyestuffs, coal, pitch, and certain foods. They were permitted to purchase only partly refined molasses or rum. Revenue from additional taxes on food was to encourage the French fishing industry to supply the Antilles. Locally appointed inspectors were to certify what goods entered and left each entrepôt.

Although this measure simply legalized the realities of French trade in the Americas, it was deeply criticized in the ports. Echoes found their way into a significant number of *cahiers de doléances* (lists of grievances) of 1789. Despite the fact that "it had been necessary at different times to modify the severity of the prohibitions," especially in wartime, France's mercantile elite uniformly opposed eliminating the "exclusive" principle elaborated by Colbert in 1670 and repeated in government ordinances of 1686, 1698, and 1727. This criticism built on the vehement opposition of the deputies of commerce and the controller-general to an ordinance

Gallica. See also Jeff Horn, "A Different Triangular Trade – from the Antilles to the Levant via Marseille," in Joelle Neulander and Robin Walz (eds.), *Proceedings of the Western Society for French History: Selected Papers of the 2012 Annual Meeting*, 40 (2014), 37–44. This argument about the entrepôt mirrors Paul Butel's for Bordeaux. *Les négociants bordelaise: L'Europe et les Iles au XVIIIe siècle* (Aubier, 1974), 125.

issued in July 1767 admitting that colonies "were only valuable when [foreign] commerce and shipping is prohibited."[45] Belying those words, however, the ordinance established two entrepôts: Carénage on Saint-Lucia and Saint-Nicolas on Saint-Domingue. These entrepôts increased smuggling and failed to improve provisioning even in peacetime. Expanding French colonial commerce seems to have emboldened royal administrators to try again.

Negotiations for a commercial treaty with England encouraged French commercial elites from Dunkerque to Marseille to justify their opposition with reference to the provisions of Oliver Cromwell's navigation act of 1651. They also emphasized Adam Smith's approbation of England's monopoly of colonial commerce. Bordeaux led the attack on 1784's "pernicious" ordinance as an expression of false principles: "The general liberty of commerce seems to be, especially in the last few years, the favorite illusion of elevated spirits and sensitive souls, but practical developments soon embarrass the flattering ideas of a seductive theory." The Bordelais claimed that allowing foreigners to use entrepôts destroyed the "just equilibrium" between metropole and colonies and would ensure the "triumph" of smuggling, "ruining" French commercial profits.[46] Yet for all the panic, French trade with the Antilles reached new heights in 1787–1788. Historian Paul Butel found that Bordeaux's merchants, faced with uncertainty, continued to ship the same amount of goods, accepting lower profits per unit. Increased trade volume provided adequate compensation. Doomsayers' arguments had more to do with an unwillingness to compete than any inability to do so. In commercial relations with the colonies, the privilege of liberty was an effective tool of royal policy.[47]

[45] The quotes are from *Arrêt du Conseil 'État du Roi, concernant le Commerce étranger dans les Isles Françaises de l'Amérique*, August 30, 1784 (Gallica) and cited by Butel, *Les négociants bordelaise*, 38–39.

[46] *Observations de Négocians de Bordeaux sur l'arrest du Conseil du 30 Août, qui a été connu à Bordeaux le 20 Novembre, 1784* (Googlebooks).

[47] The four previous paragraphs are based on Gaston Rambert, *Les Colonies de 1660 à 1789*, vol. 6 of Gaston Rambert (ed.), *Histoire du commerce de Marseille* (Plon, 1959), 96, 127–31, Clément (ed.), *Lettres, instructions et mémoires de Colbert*, II (2): 29–30, Pierre Bonnassieux, *Examen des cahiers de 1789 au point de vue commercial et industriel* (Berger-Levrault, 1884), 18, Pierrick Pourchasse, *Le Commerce du Nord: Les échanges commerciaux entre la France et l'Europe septentrionale au XVIIIe siècle* (Presses universitaires de Rennes, 2006), 155, Rambert, *Les Colonies de 1660 à 1789*, 107–12, *Observations de la Chambre du Commerce de Marseille sur l'arrêt du 30 août 1784 concernant le commerce des Étrangers dans les Isles françaises de l'Amérique*, January 10, 1785, AD Bouches-du-Rhône 1J 989, and *Lettre du Parlement de Bordeaux au Roi au sujet de l'Arrêt du Conseil d'État du 30 Août 1784 concernant le Commerce étranger dans les îles françaises d'Amérique*, 1785. A 500-page collection of pamphlets on the admission of foreigners to the colonies was published as *Receuil de différentes pieces pour et contre l'admission des Ètrangers dans les Isles Françaises*

In this context, Calonne's April 1785 decision to revive the privileges of the East Indies Company is hard to fathom. After 1769 and the lapse of the previous company, trade through the Indian and Pacific Oceans boomed, with more ships involved and a greater volume of commerce than ever. From an annual average of 8.3 million *livres* of trade in 1725–1769, commercial volume reached 20.3 million *livres* in 1770–1777. There are serious doubts about the accuracy of these sources, but France's Asian trade at least doubled under the regime of liberty. Led by foreign minister de Vergennes, naval minister de Castries, and Calonne, the royal council asserted that the company needed to be revived because "competition, useful in other branches of commerce, is harmful here." French goods sold for low prices in Asia and the quantity and assortment of goods imported into France "are insufficient to supply the realm." To benefit from the return to peace, "His Majesty is convinced that only the resources, credit, and special protection of a privileged company can take advantage of commerce with the Indies and China."[48] Based in Lorient and Paris, the new company was capitalized at 20 million *livres*. It had an exclusive privilege to trade with Asia beyond the Levant and the eastern shore of Africa other than the islands of Bourbon and France. The liberty of French merchants to import Indian or Chinese textiles from foreign sources was also revoked.

Initially granted for seven years of peace, administrators' "satisfaction with the new company's efforts" and their desire to "consolidate" the new firm led to the extension of its privileges to fifteen years in September 1786 with an increase of capital to 40 million *livres*.[49] The company seems to have made good faith, relatively effective efforts to stimulate trade. By working with the new company, mercantile elites in ports like Marseille maintained or even increased their commercial activities in Asia despite the imposition of the monopoly.

The revival of the Indies Company was hugely controversial. Although Calonne also sponsored the creation of a West African and a Northern trading company, the Indies Company's extensive privileges and enormous capitalization occasioned serious political problems and

d'Amérique, 1785 (both found on Googlebooks.) The essential source on this subject is Jean Tarrade, *Le commerce colonial de la France à la fin de l'Ancien Régime: L'évolution du régime de "l'exclusif" de 1763 à 1789*, 2 vols. (Presses Universitaires de France, 1972). See also Paul Cheney, *Revolutionary Commerce: Globalization and the French Monarchy* (Cambridge, MA: Harvard University Press, 2010), 168–94.

48 *Arrêt du conseil d'Etat portant établissement d'une nouvelle Compagnie des Indes*, April 14, 1785 (Gallica).

49 *Arrêt du conseil d'Etat qui porte à 40 millions les fonds de la Compagnie des Indes, et qui prolonge à 15 années de paix la durée de son privilège fixé à 7 années par l'arrêt du conseil du 14 avril 1785*, September 21, 1786 (Gallica).

contributed to a major credit squeeze in 1785. So why do it? It is possible that the ministers believed the reasoning found in the edict announcing the company's revival, but a more convincing explanation is that Calonne needed the support of Parisian bankers to borrow the tremendous sums required to meet France's financial obligations. These court capitalists appear to have insisted that the state provide an exclusive privilege to the company and favored access to shares as quid pro quo for helping Calonne raise 420 million *livres* during his four-year tenure as controller-general.[50]

Whether this claim is accurate or not, from an administrative standpoint, the creation of the privileged companies of West Africa, the North, and the Indies was profoundly at odds with the evolution of French policy after 1750. In the regulation of foreign and colonial commerce, expanding exclusive privileges while simultaneously widening the scope of the privilege of liberty demonstrates the limited application of ideologies of improvement. Until the outbreak of the Revolution of 1789, privilege in all its forms remained essential to French policymaking. Constraints imposed by French political economy explain the gap between ideology and praxis.

The realities of market fragmentation: the privilege of liberty and domestic commerce

Which France? From Edward Fox to Tim Blanning and Liliane Pérez, historians have emphasized the disparity between maritime, commercial France and "the other France," dominated by subsistence agriculture and isolated from the currents of international trade. The distinction is overdrawn but highlights crucial divisions and obstacles to competition impinging on the French economy that mercantilism struggled to overcome. This book emphasizes the shift from the liberty of privilege to the privilege of liberty after 1750, but privilege's persistent role in fragmenting French markets and inhibiting French industry must not be minimized or ignored. The privilege of liberty proved relatively successful in stimulating industry and foreign trade. With regard to domestic commerce, however, financial constraints and lack of political

[50] The three previous paragraphs are based on Jean-François de Tolosan, *Mémoire sur le Commerce de France et de ses Colonies* (Moutard, 1789), 96–99, Bonnassieux, *Les grandes compagnies de commerce*, 313, Shovlin, *The Political Economy of Virtue*, 157–59, Liliane Hilaire-Pérez, *L'expérience de la mer: Les Européens et les espaces maritimes au XVIIIe siècle*, 2nd printing (Seili Arslan, 1997), 231, and Pourchasse, *Le Commerce du Nord*, 163–64. For a thorough discussion of the context of the revival of the Indies company, see Weber, *La Compagnie des Indes*, 616–46, and Frederick L. Nussbaum, "The Formation of the New East India Company of Calonne," *American Historical Review*, 38: 3 (1933), 475–97.

will were high hurdles to jump. Entrenched privileged interests limited the application and effectiveness of privileges of liberty. In domestic commerce, the state failed to take advantage of the conflict between privileged interests. Trade within France did not realize its full potential, seldom attaining the threshold of "useful commerce."[51]

Privileged obstructions to domestic commerce were under assault by mercantilistic Bourbon administrators, but enough barriers remained to slow growth considerably while giving credence to the notion of two Frances. Because the roads were in rather sorry shape and tolls numerous, with very rare exceptions, even relatively light bulk goods rarely traveled more than fifteen miles by land. River transport was more economical, but the pattern of the river network and the paucity of canals accentuated the regional nature of the French economy. No wonder the state and entrepreneurs focused on the ports, maritime trade, and smuggling.

Tolls were hard to escape, legally. In 1567, 120 separate tolls obstructed the Loire River and its tributaries. A load of salt traveling from Nantes to Nevers paid four times the value of the cargo in taxes. Although tolls were regularly challenged and revoked, it was only in 1724 that the royal government took systematic action. The royal commission examining the legal basis of tolls achieved some reductions. In the province of Languedoc alone, 154 tolls were eliminated between 1729 and 1782. On the Dordogne River and its tributaries, thirty of thirty-eight tolls were abolished in 1730–1745. Despite this progress, in 1789, 600 separate tolls based on privilege remained to encumber French roads and rivers. When a shipment of wood from Lorraine to Sète paid thirty-four tolls at twenty-one sites and a ton of wine worth 500 *livres* shipped from Muret southwest of Toulouse to Paris paid 501 *livres*, 7 *sols* in tolls, production for other than local or at most regional consumption was frustrating and rarely profitable. Beyond foodstuffs like grain and flour or vital commodities like wood, enduring tax privileges limited domestic commerce to meeting local and regional needs. The differing economic function of the privilege of exacting tolls from the privilege of liberty deserves emphasis; the latter is focused on development, while the former is rent-seeking.

Unlike England, France had no "national" market until well into the nineteenth century. Even the vast territory encompassed by the general tax farm was fragmented by burdensome river and road tolls as well as a welter of provincial, urban, and seigneurial privileges regulating the

[51] For an overview, see Silvia Marzagalli, "Commerce," in William Doyle (ed.), *The Oxford Handbook of the Ancien Régime* (Oxford University Press, 2012), 252–66.

import, export, or exchange of certain goods. Thanks to the sad state of the transportation network, the early modern French economy can best be characterized as a set of privileged regional markets yoked together politically. In the manner pioneered by Sidney Pollard, I argue that the manipulation of privilege benefited regional economic development more than protectionism. Such manipulation worked best when applied to industry and international trade. As the push for the single duty project demonstrates, royal administrators realized that tax and transport privileges were obstacles that the privilege of liberty could not mitigate or overcome. Bourbon France had neither the financial resources nor the political will to create more "modern" economic structures. Officials granted privileges of liberty to improve the situation, but, unlike in other sectors, they found little success in domestic commerce. The evolution of domestic trade confirms that the privilege of liberty was no institutional cure-all for France's economic ills.[52]

In the English-speaking world, early modern French trade policy is associated with mercantilism. This chapter makes three chief arguments about that characterization. First, Anglo-Saxon critiques of French mercantilism portray it, both ideologically and institutionally, as static and based on a zero-sum conception of economics or, even more negatively, as regressive. Such critiques apply ideological readings of the contemporary era to the work of Adam Smith.[53] These interpretations of mercantilism do not accurately reflect either the totality of Smith's thinking or the realities of French commercial practice.

[52] The previous three paragraphs are based on Edward Whiting Fox, *History in Geographic Perspective: The Other France* (New York: W.W. Norton, 1971), Blanning, *The French Revolution*, 10, Hilaire-Pérez, *L'expérience de la mer*, 65–68, Anne Conchon, *Le Péage en France au XVIIIe siècle: Les privilèges à l'épreuve de la réforme* (Comité pour l'histoire économique et financière de la France, 2002), Marcel Marion, *Dictionnaire des Institutions de la France aux XVIIe et XVIIIe siècles* (New York: Burt Franklin, 1968 [1923]), 436–37, Lucien Bély, *Dictionnaire de l'Ancien Régime* (Quadrige-PUF, 1996), 972–73, Pierre Goubert, *The Ancien Régime: French Society, 1600–1750*, trans. Steve Cox (New York: Harper Torchbooks, 1974 [1968]), 58–62, Judith A. Miller, *Mastering the Market: The State and the Grain Trade in Northern France, 1700–1860* (Cambridge University Press, 1999), Steven Laurence Kaplan, *Provisioning Paris: Merchants and Millers in the Grain and Flour Trade during the Eighteenth Century* (Ithaca, NY: Cornell University Press, 1984), Jean-Yves Grenier, *L'économie d'Ancien Régime: Un monde de l'échange et de l'incertitude* (Albin Michel, 1996), 269–321, Sidney Pollard, *Peaceful Conquest: The Industrialization of Europe 1760–1970* (Oxford University Press, 1981), 111–22, Rick Szostak, *The Role of Transportation in the Industrial Revolution: A Comparison of England and France* (Montreal: McGill-Queen's University Press, 1991), Dominique Margairaz, *Foires et marches dans la France préindustrielle* (EHESS, 1988), Daudin, *Commerce et prosperité*, 107–88, and Bosher, *The Single Duty Project*.

[53] For an authoritative view on this subject focused on the English-speaking world, see Pincus, "Rethinking Mercantilism," 3–34.

Second, French commercial policy from 1660 to 1789 may be termed mercantilistic so long as mercantilism is understood as a system that blended privilege and liberty in the pursuit of development. Mercantilism was more than a set of ideas; it was also an economic system. The impressive success of French foreign trade after 1713 both absolutely and comparatively requires emphasis especially to English-speaking audiences, but this success should not be conflated with the overwhelming power of the Bourbon state. Limits to state power were revealed by the difficulty of eliminating tolls, improving roads, or repressing smuggling, all of which explain why the privilege of liberty was so much more effective in stimulating foreign than domestic commerce. The greater success of entrepôts than either chartered companies or experiments in free trade in stimulating exchange provides an important corrective to standard accounts. "Mercantilist" royal officials deployed privilege, liberty, and the privilege of liberty to expand French commerce in a context framed by shifts in both domestic and international political economy.

Third, between 1660 and 1789, the praxis of mercantilism demonstrated remarkable continuity, on both flanks of the Channel. England's navigation acts preceded equivalent French measures just as Dutch and English chartered companies inspired the creation of France's. With the establishment of two free ports, it might even be argued that France under Louis XIV was more willing to experiment with liberty of international enterprise than its English rival. By the mid-eighteenth century, the thinking of policymakers and economic theorists emphasized the potential of liberty to stimulate economic development. Before the late 1780s, however, the ideas of these improvers had a limited impact on policy because of constraints stemming from both British and French political economy. Privilege continued to dictate the terms of domestic commerce and its sway in foreign trade seemed on the upswing after the revival of the East Indies Company. At the same time, the trepidations of British entrepreneurs about signing the Anglo-French commercial treaty remind us of their continuing dependence on protectionism. To paraphrase the title of economist Albert Hirshman's provocative book, liberal passions could not overcome privileged interests.[54]

[54] The previous three paragraphs are based on the following works. This interpretation was expressed influentially by Eli F. Heckscher in *Mercantilism*, rev. ed., 2 vols., ed. E. F. Söderlund (London: Allen and Unwin, 1955). For a critique discussing some of those who followed this view, see Donald C. Coleman, "Mercantilism Revisited," *The Historical Journal*, 23: 4 (1980), 773–91. See also John E. Crowley, "Neo-mercantilism and *The Wealth of Nations*: British Commercial Policy after the American Revolution,"

Early modern French commerce confirms the enduring power of privilege. From 1664 to 1785, the habit of establishing chartered companies to advance French interests abroad despite their general lack of success points to royal administrators' reliance on privilege in commercial policymaking. Colonial commerce with the Americas supplied opportunities for the application of policies embodying both privilege and liberty. Most administrative initiatives failed due to the dislocations of war, but the long-term improvement of France's trade index compared to Britain's suggests that these "failures" must be placed in international context. If French domestic trade and foreign commerce with India and the Americas lagged behind the English and Dutch institutionally and in building linkages with the metropolitan economy, that was not always the case. As we shall see in the next chapter, the free port of Marseille took advantage of a monopoly of trade with the Levant and privileges granted to Languedocian woolens producers to beat the English and Dutch at their own game.

The Historical Journal, 33: 2 (1990), 339–60, Robert E. Wright, "The Transition from Feudalism to Capitalism: The Role of Mercantilism" (PhD dissertation, University of York [Canada], 2003), Bradley B. Andrew, "Unfair Trade, Mercantilism and Economic Development, Great Britain: 1660–1800" (PhD dissertation, University of Connecticut, 2002), R. B. Outhwaite, *Inflation in Tudor and Early Stuart England*, 2nd ed. (London: Macmillan, 1982 [1970]), Horn, *The Path Not Taken*, 61–63, and Albert O. Hirschman, *The Passions and the Interests: Political Arguments for Capitalism before Its Triumph* (Princeton University Press, 1977). An overly intellectualized version can be found in Philip J. Stern and Carl Wennerlind (eds.), *Mercantilism Reimagined: Political Economy in Early Modern Britain and Its Empire* (Oxford University Press, 2013).

5 Privilege, liberty, and managing the market

Trading with the Levant

> Commerce ought to be free, but it is too dangerous for the man of commerce to be absolutely free, indefinitely . . . Liberty of commerce is the power to profit from trade, but must always take place within the rules while paying reasonable attention to consequences. Liberty of commerce is not the ability of an individual to do what they want, but rather for an individual to do freely what they ought.
>
> Chamber of commerce of Marseille (1757)[1]

Bourbon policy in the Levant made use of both privilege and liberty. French mercantilism in the Mediterranean successfully nurtured commercial expansion and industrial development. From the era of Jean-Baptiste Colbert, the royal administration's regulatory approach emphasized steady, long-term profits and protecting foreign customers. France recaptured a dominant position in Levantine markets from the English and Dutch and held onto it for more than a century. This pattern differed markedly from state management of trade and manufacturing in the Atlantic world. Current English-language accounts of early modern Europe's economic development pay almost exclusive attention to the role of the Americas. Such a focus must not, however, be permitted to crowd out other narratives and other trajectories. The Levant may have been a secondary market for Europe, but, in the Mediterranean, Bourbon mercantilism beat the English and Dutch at their own game. Successfully blending privilege and liberty to manage trade with the Levant, French state action closely paralleled British and Dutch actions in the Atlantic. Yet the measures taken by their North Sea rivals are lauded as essential to the emergence of "the first modern economy" or "the Enlightened economy," while France's approach is perceived to be inferior, irrelevant, or obsolete. French trade patterns provide a corrective to such perspectives and broaden

[1] Chamber of Commerce of Marseille, *Précis pour la ville de Marseille contre la Province du Languedoc*, n.d. [1757], AD Bouches-du-Rhône C4636.

our understandings of the emergence of a world economy focused on early modern Europe.[2]

The Levantine conundrum: quality goods, empty hulls, and foreign competition

Mid-seventeenth-century France experienced a major trade decline in the Mediterranean.[3] Based on consular and ambassadorial reports, when France intervened in the Thirty Years' War in 1635, annual trade with the Levant ran between 25 and 30 million *livres tournois*. By the 1660s, the annual value of French commerce had fallen 90 percent to 2.5–3 million *livres*. As a result of the diversion of East Indian goods from overland to sea routes and trade dislocation caused by wars between the Turks and Persia, the total value of Europe's trade with the Levant declined to about 20 million *livres*, with the Dutch responsible for 10–11 million *livres*, the English 3–4 million, and the Venetians the rest. Although these statistics are highly suspect, French trade with the Levant was undoubtedly in crisis.[4]

[2] On the Atlantic/Mediterranean division, contrast Paul Cheney, *Revolutionary Commerce: Globalization and the French Monarchy* (Cambridge, MA, Harvard University Press, 2010) with Junko Takeda, *Between Crown and Commerce: Marseille and the Early Modern Mediterranean* (Baltimore: Johns Hopkins University Press, 2011). Jan de Vries and Ad van der Woude, *The First Modern Economy: Success, Failure, and Perserverance of the Dutch Economy, 1500–1815* (Cambridge University Press, 1997), Joel Mokyr, *The Enlightened Economy: An Economic History of Britain 1700–1850* (New Haven, CT: Yale University Press, 2009), François Crouzet, *Britain Ascendant: Comparative Studies in Franco-British Economic History*, trans. Martin Thom (Cambridge University Press, 1990 [1985]), and Margaret C. Jacob, *Scientific Culture and the Making of the Industrial West* (Oxford University Press, 1997). For extreme views of the national and/or religious "winners" and "losers" of early modern economic development, see Joyce Appleby, *The Relentless Revolution: A History of Capitalism* (New York: Norton, 2010), Roy Porter, *The Creation of the Modern World: The Untold Story of the British Enlightenment* (New York: Norton, 2000), and Jonathan Israel, *Democratic Enlightenment: Philosophy, Revolution, and Human Rights 1750–1790* (Oxford University Press, 2011).

[3] A version of some of the material on Levantine trade appeared in Jeff Horn, "Marseille et la question du mercantilisme: privilège, liberté et l'économie politique en France, 1650–1750," *Histoire, économie & société* (2011/2), 95–112.

[4] Charles Wilson, "Cloth Production and International Competition in the Seventeenth Century," *The Economic History Review*, 13: 2 (1960), 209–21, Robert Paris, *Le Levant*, vol. 5, Gaston Rambert (ed.), *Histoire du commerce de Marseille* (Plon, 1957), 543–74, Pierre Duparc (ed.), *Recueil des instructions données aux ambassadeurs et ministres de France depuis les traités de Westphalie jusqu'à la Révolution française, Turquie*, vol. 29 (Éditions du CNRS, 1969), 71, Mehmet Bulut, "The Role of the Ottomans and Dutch in the Commercial Integration between the Levant and the Atlantic in the Seventeenth Century," *Journal of the Economic and Social History of the Orient*, 45: 2 (2002): 197–230, 215, and Charles Carrière, *Négociants Marseillais au XVIIIe siècle: Contribution à l'étude des économies maritimes*, 2 vols. (Marseille, Institut historique de Provence, 1973), 320–23.

European trade with the Ottoman Empire was based on diplomatic concessions known as "capitulations." Several Mediterranean powers attempted to attract the declining volume of east–west commerce by establishing free ports. The creation of such ports in Leghorn, Genoa, Barcelona, Nice, and Villefranche in the 1650s and 1660s inspired France to grant similar status to Marseille in March 1669.[5] The following year, Colbert founded a chartered company tasked with reinvigorating Levantine trade and selling French manufactures abroad. By themselves, however, these institutional responses did not address the underlying sources of France's commercial woes.

For France, the basic problem was one of exchange. The French traded manufactured goods, especially woolens and paper, along with hard currency for Levantine silks and cottons as well as raw materials such as silk, wool, cotton, olive oil, wax, and leather. Intermittently, grain was also a major object of trade.[6] However, in the first half of the seventeenth century, Turkish customers increasingly turned to France's competitors for woolens and paper. Poor treatment by merchants and their agents upset the Turks, but, even more significantly, Levantine customers eschewed French manufactures because of their declining quality. Inability to sell manufactured goods in restricted markets meant that empty ships headed east. French merchants had to purchase their goods with hard currency, draining the realm of specie.

In 1665, Colbert sent detailed instructions to Denis de la Haye, baron de Vantenay, the new ambassador to the Ottoman Porte. The post had been vacant for seven years, much to the detriment of French interests. Colbert wrote that the "ruin and decay of all of France's manufactures" left Levantine trade "in the hands of the English and Dutch which has reduced French commerce to paying in cash. This has caused an inconceivable prejudice to the state." He lamented the "bad faith" and "poor commercial practices of Marseillais merchants: they have a poor reputation throughout Europe" because "all the bankrupts, dirty-minded people, and condemned criminals of France retire to Levantine ports." Only government intervention could restore France's trade position.[7]

[5] Mireille Zarb, *Histoire d'une autonomie communale: Les privilèges de la ville de Marseille du Xe siècle à la Révolution* (A. et J. Picard, 1961), 250, Duparc (ed,), *Turquie*, xxii-iii, and Paris, *Le Levant*, 11.

[6] Commercial statistics from the mid-seventeenth century for Levantine trade do not exist: the product mix is also hard to establish. These are the best estimates available. Paul Masson, *Histoire du commerce française dans le Levant aux XVIIe siècle* (Hachette, 1896), 504, 514–15 and Paris, *Le Levant*, 499–502.

[7] Pierre Clément (ed.), *Lettres, instructions et mémoires de Colbert publiés d'après les ordres de l'empereur*, 10 vols. (Imprimerie impériale, 1861–1873), II (2): 679–80. The second quote is from 1673. See also Philip McCluskey, "Commerce before Crusade? France, the

Bourbon administrators believed that reversing this commercial collapse required three major changes. First, shipping and transaction costs had to be lowered to match France's rivals. Second, French merchants and their agents must treat Turkish buyers better: no longer could customer complaints be ignored or fraud perpetuated. Last and most importantly, France had to make quality goods and offer them at competitive prices. Identifying the components of success was a necessary start, but deciding how to accomplish these goals and imposing the government's will on recalcitrant merchants and manufacturers proved far more difficult tasks, requiring decades to accomplish.

Step 1: The intervention of the state: commercial privileges for Marseille

Improving shipping and transaction costs in the Mediterranean required state intervention. Although other ports littered the coasts of Languedoc and Provence, none could compete with Marseille in wealth, ties to the Levant, or potential for east–west trade. Between 1660 and 1682, about 60 percent of all French ships coming from the Levant or the Barbary Coast docked first at Marseille – only 13 percent went to another Mediterranean port. The central state, the estates of Provence, and the municipality of Marseille agreed that international competitiveness required lower and simplified taxes on commercial transactions. Officials, diplomats, and merchants alike agreed that the trading community required greater oversight and that only cooperation could limit shipping costs and improve customer relations. This consensus led the state to provide Marseille with new institutions and new privileges of liberty.

Efforts to limit taxes on Marseille's commerce predated the reign of Louis XIV and picked up steam after the noble-dominated Consulate which ran the city rebelled in 1659–1660. The consuls resolved their long-running conflict with the chamber of commerce (established in 1599) dominated by wholesale merchants (*négociants*) by abolishing the body and absorbing its functions. Louis XIV reimposed royal authority by sending 6,000 men to breach the walls, quickly ending this last gasp of the Fronde.

Louis XIV's authority in Marseille rested on his position as seigneur. A new municipal charter eliminated the nobles' political power in the name of their privileges. Marseille's consulate was abolished. Nobles were

Ottoman Empire and the Barbary Pirates (1661–1669)," *French History*, 23: 1 (2009), 1–21, 5 and Duparc (ed.), *Turquie*, 29–30.

exempted from municipal taxes, which meant that they could no longer serve as aldermen charged with city administration. Until the end of the old régime, wholesale merchants dominated the municipality. At the same time, the chamber of commerce was restored and emancipated from municipal tutelage. Letters-patent of March 1660 gave the chamber of commerce wide-ranging authority over Marseille's trade and port. Royal military intervention and institution-building inaugurated an era of collaboration between Marseille and the Bourbon state that improved France's trade position in the Levant.[8]

Designating Marseille a free port was part of a broader effort to stimulate Levantine trade. Because certain taxes lingered, the not-quite-free port did not offer a competitive advantage. The March 1669 edict, however, served as a kind of navigation act for trade with the Turkish Empire. In addition to loosening restrictions on immigration and naturalization for foreign entrepreneurs (see Chapter 6), the edict created a 20 percent ad valorem surcharge on goods from the Levant unloaded in ports other than Marseille or Rouen. This measure signaled the royal government's desire to funnel commerce through Marseille, but allowed other ports to trade with the Levant. The chamber of commerce established offices in other ports and on the customs frontiers to collect the tax. The 20 percent figure derived from the English Levant company's charter which levied that same imposition on traders who were not part of the association. Like their English competitors, the French used both privilege and liberty to encourage trade. In the case of the Levant, the privilege of nearly free trade for Marseille was supplemented by further incentives to stimulate private initiative.

French commercial ties to the Ottoman Empire dated from 1528 when François I of Valois acquired special rights of protection and navigation. Along with certain trading prerogatives acquired later in the sixteenth century, these concessions were delegated to Marseille. In 1609, Henri IV granted the city the right to import silks from the Levant. This monopoly infringed on the rights of the powerful East Indies Company, but for over 180 years, Marseille defeated repeated attempts by chartered Indies companies to appropriate this lucrative trade. In the seventeenth

[8] The three previous paragraphs are based on Zarb, *Histoire d'une autonomie communale*, 136, 163, 281–83, 289, Carrière, *Négociants marseillais au XVIIIe siècle*, 213, Orest Ranum, *The Fronde: A French Revolution* (New York: W.W. Norton, 1993), 346, Louis Bergasse and Gaston Rambert, *De 1599 à 1789*, Gaston Rambert (ed.), *Histoire du commerce de Marseille*, vol. 4 (Plon, 1954), 78–83, Paris, *Le Levant*, 7, and *Reglement fait par le Conseil de la maison commune de cette ville de Marseille pour la chambre établie pour le fait du commerce*, November 3, 1650, AN AE BIII33.

century, additional monopolies in pepper, ginger, cinnamon, nutmeg, and cloves swelled Marseille's wealth of privileges. The city also had the sole right to traffic in Turkish *piastres*, the essential coinage for Levantine trade. Combined with a levy of 50 *sols* per ton on ships that did not disembark cargo in its port, Marseille enjoyed a de facto stranglehold if not a de jure monopoly of trade with the Levant.

The French state supported competitiveness in other ways. A year before establishing the free port, Colbert moved a squadron of galleys back to Marseille. An arsenal was constructed to build and outfit the squadron. The royal military budget funded the dredging and deepening of the main harbor channel. By 1673, the harbor could accommodate the entire merchant fleet and twenty-eight royal galleys. A royal official oversaw the port's military functions which ensured upkeep while the galleys helped to protect commercial traffic. Colbert and his successors searched assiduously for ways to develop trade with the Levant.

Louis XIV's revival of French power was expressed diplomatically and through reform of the consular service. In a June 1670 instruction to the new ambassador Charles de Nointel, Colbert complained that the Netherlands, England, and Genoa enjoyed 3 percent customs rates, while the French paid 5 percent. Nointel was ordered to make the case that trade with France would divert East Indies traffic away from the sea route around the Cape of Good Hope. As this route deprived the Turks of tax revenue on the transit of goods, France sought concessions that would also swell Ottoman trade.

Nointel successfully negotiated a new set of capitulations in 1673 that restored France's privileged place in the Levant. French merchants now paid 3 percent in customs fees and all countries without their own treaty rights were obliged to use French ships. Louis XIV's ambassadors to the Porte took advantage of his growing repute to obtain further concessions: the tariff for Mamluk Egypt fell from 20 percent in 1684 to 3 percent in 1687 leading to booming trade with Alexandria. France also expanded its commercial network into the Balkans after receiving authorization to establish a trading station at Salonika in 1685.[9]

Reform of the consular service enhanced French merchants' ability to take advantage of diplomatic concessions. Consuls for each region were selected by the king from a list of three candidates submitted by Marseille's chamber of commerce. In the 1670s, Colbert repeatedly

[9] The five previous paragraphs are based on Paris, *Le Levant*, 11, 506, Bergasse and Rambert, *De 1599 à 1789*, 204–09, Zarb, *Histoire d'une autonomie communale*, 341, Duparc (ed.), *Turquie*, xxiii, 70, 80–81, *Èdit pour l'affranchissement du port de Marseille*, March 1669, AN AE BIII252/1, and *Délibérations de la Chambre du commerce de Marseille 1660 à 1671*, ACCIMP B3, 469.

authorized the ambassador to remove corrupt or ineffective consuls. Two later measures completed the professionalization of the consular service. In December 1685, consuls and port tax collectors in the Levant were forbidden to trade on their own behalf. Instead, they received a regular, fairly generous salary from the chamber paid for with taxes collected in Marseille. Consuls soon dominated merchants and oversaw the merchant community's finances. They also verified and recorded the composition and quality of arriving ship cargos.

Bourbon administrators seconded by Marseille's chamber of commerce imposed standards of conduct on French merchants in the Levant. From October 1685, a merchant had to be certified by the chamber of commerce before trading in the Levant. Applicants had to make a substantial surety deposit and merchants were limited to a ten-year residence in the Levant. Married men were not allowed to bring their wives or daughters, and single men were forbidden to marry Turkish subjects. Consuls could expel merchants for "poor conduct." This term was defined broadly to include marriage to a Turkish subject, adulterating coins, or swindling Levantine customers by selling inferior goods.[10]

Marseille's ability to quarantine ships coming from the Levant was vital to its success. Disease impeded European trade with the Near East. In 1476, fear of epidemic led the independent county of Provence to turn Marseille's leper hospital into a lazaret where ships from the Levant or Barbary Coast were detained for up to forty days. In 1526, the plague hospital became a quarantine center on the island of Pomègues. Ships were also quarantined on the islands of Jarros and Frioul. This lazaret was so useful and so commercially well situated that, in 1622, the *parlement* of Aix forbade ships coming from the Levant or Barbary Coast to be quarantined other than in Marseille or Toulon, where the navy operated a lazaret. Marseille's monopoly on quarantining commercial shipping in Provence was reinforced by an ordinance of the intendant in September 1672. Although Toulon's lazaret was permitted to accept civilian ships in 1690, it was with the proviso that their cargos must be unloaded in Marseille. A 1709 royal edict limited quarantine to Marseille for *all* the coasts of France. After the plague outbreak of 1720–1722, Marseille recaptured its monopoly and held onto it until the 1750s when Sète in Languedoc built a lazaret. In 1762, the laxity of Sète's lazaret led the royal council to limit quarantine to the ports of Marseille and Toulon: this

[10] The two previous paragraphs are based on François Charles-Roux, *Les Èchelles de Syrie et de Palestine au XVIIIe siècle* (Paul Geuthner, 1928), 13–16, Duparc (ed.), *Turquie*, 28–113, and *Èdit du Roi*, December 25 1685, AN AE BIII192.

restriction outlasted the old régime (see Chapter 8). Marseille's lazaret strengthened its control over French trade in the Mediterranean.[11]

By themselves, these privileges and liberties did not accomplish the administration's aims. France recovered only slowly from a mid-century nadir of thirty ships engaged in a Levantine trade worth less than 3 million *livres*. Until the mid-1670s, trade remained uncertain, as the 1674 failure of the first Levant company confirms. Although it fluctuated wildly, from 1676 to 1688 France's median annual trade with the Levant was 5.6 million *livres* and, in 1683, about seventy ships left Marseille for Near Eastern ports. Until 1683, the sale of French woolens in the Levant actually fell due to Dutch dumping intended to drive out French competition. Given France's enormous investment of time, money, and privilege in the Levantine trade, these results disappointed.

Colbert blamed the Marseillais and particularly the chamber of commerce for the slow pace of improvement. In 1669, he painted the chamber of commerce with the same broad brush of dishonesty applied to consuls serving in the Levant: "Abuses and corruption can be found among everyone involved in this commerce." Four years later, he observed bitterly that the Marseillais "do not care if the volume of trade increases, but only that all of it pass through their hands in the way they wish." Naval intendant Nicolas Arnoult complained that if an inhabitant of Marseille "has even the least bit of personal interest involved in an affair, [say] goodbye to reason" and that the Marseillais "do not wish to give up their old errors. They always want to act freely on their whims." Frequently, these whims involved fraud. Colbert was forced to issue an edict in May 1671 to "very expressly forbid all merchants and shipowners from lending their name to foreigners" and imposed a heavy penalty of 1,000 *livres*. Despite these frustrations, Colbert and his successors recognized that for French trade with the Levant to flourish, the city's privileges required reinforcement to undermine incentives for fraud.[12]

Even with free port status, Marseille's tax regime grew more confounding after 1669. In September 1684, the chamber of commerce complained that "ship manifests from the Levant frequently omit

[11] Xavier Daumalin, Nicole Girard, and Olivier Raveux (eds.), *Du Savon à la puce: L'industrie marseillaise du XVIIe siècle à nos jours* (Marseille: Jeanne Laffitte, 2003), 24, Paris, *Le Levant*, 23–24, Léon Dutil, *L'État économique du Languedoc à la fin de l'ancien régime (1750–1789)* (Hachette, 1911), 385–86, Bergasse and Rambert, *De 1599 à 1789*, 424–25, Guillaume Rostagny, *Lettre*, January 20 1775, AN AE BIII188, *Arrêt du Conseil d'État concernant le Commerce des Marchandises du Levant*, September 14, 1721, ACCIMP J1578, *Avis des députés du commerce*, September 9, 1757, AN F12 711, and *Avis des députés du commerce*, May 14, 1762, AN AE BIII186.

[12] Clément (ed.), *Lettres, instructions et mémoires de Colbert*, VII: 287 and II (2): 679. The second quote is cited by Bergasse and Rambert, *De 1599 à 1789*, 209, note 3.

information or are defective, which allows the tax collector to argue with native merchants or citizens of the city as to which taxes they are exempt from." Disputes caused "significant harm" because they led to "shipping delays" and cargos were "often refused their freedom [from taxation]" on "the pretext that ship captains, owners, or agents do not have a copy of the royal declaration creating the free port." A month later, Alexandre Morant, intendant of Provence, supported the chamber of commerce's version of how tax and customs officials impinged on commerce with the Levant. Royal administrators could grant a privilege, but enforcing it proved extremely difficult.[13]

Morant's ordinance had little effect on royal tax farmers and customs officials. Joseph Fabre, the representative at court of Marseille's chamber of commerce, emphasized the problems caused by widespread Anglo-Dutch smuggling of woolens for the Levant through France's Atlantic ports. He suggested that the best means of cutting off this clandestine trade was to impose the 20 percent tax on every port other than Marseille. The establishment of a third chartered company in July 1685 with extensive privileges in the Levant prompted the central government to take action. In August, Rouen and Dunkerque became liable to the 20 percent tax. Continuing fraud led the royal council to issue an edict in December 1685 "for the good of commerce" to "remedy the abuses undertaken by French subjects in the Levant." This measure repeated Morant's ordinance exactly and added a threat of criminal prosecution.[14]

Wartime financial needs and lobbying by other ports and provinces soon led Bourbon officials to impose new taxes and other restrictions on Marseille's liberty. Entry taxes were imposed on pewterware (1681) and white and brown sugar (1690). The countrywide bans on importing blue or white calicos, muslin cloth, salt cod, or tanned leather were applied to Marseille in 1691. Despite these wartime necessities, controller-general of finance Louis Phélypeaux, count de Pontchartrain, still sought to protect Marseille. In July 1691, the royal council "suppressed all taxes levied by consuls in the Levant." Merchants from Rouen and Dunkerque

[13] The quote is from *Extrait des Registres de la Chambre du Commerce de Marseille*, September 7, 1684, ACCIMP C1557. The three previous paragraphs are based on Paris, *Le Levant*, 19, 544, 568, Masson, *Histoire du commerce française dans le Levant*, 363, *Affiche des Commissaires delegué par Sa Majesté sur l'Affranchissement du Port de la Ville de Marseille*, November 2, 1669, ACCIMP D23, *Les commissaires et deputés par Sa Majesté pour l'établissement du Port Franc de la Ville de Marseille*, March 10, 1671, and *Les commissaires et deputés par Sa Majesté pour l'établissement du Port Franc de la Ville de Marseille*, April 28, 1671, both in ACCIMP D24.

[14] Joseph Fabre, *Lettre*, April 18, 1685, AN AE BIII259, *Extrait des Registres du Conseil d'État*, August 15, 1685, ACCIMP D24, and *Édit du Roi*, December 25, 1685, AN AE BIII192.

complained, but Pontchartrain reiterated Marseille's legal monopoly of imports from the Levant and the Barbary Coast in January 1692. The royal council also noted that "the majority of captains and shippers" are "passing English and Dutch woolens as Venetian or Genoese goods," which "usurped the privileges and exemptions that France enjoys in the Levant." This practice was formally prohibited in April 1693. From a median annual trade of 5.6 million *livres* in 1676–1688, the value of median annual trade reached 7.6 million *livres* in 1688–1690 despite the onset of war with the league of Augsburg. In 1690, more than ninety French ships engaged in Levantine trade.[15]

Notwithstanding the state's dedicated attempts to clamp down on fraud and smuggling, contemporary accounts agree that clandestine trade rose markedly in the last fifteen years of the seventeenth century, impinging on Marseille's commerce. A September 1693 requirement that Languedocian woolens be inspected and certified a second time in Marseille before being shipped east only encouraged greater creativity by fraudulent merchants and smugglers. In June 1700, the newly established council of commerce composed of deputies from the major trading cities initiated a broadly based discussion of the utility of Marseille's privileges and France's terms of trade with the Near East.

The Atlantic ports led by Nantes, the province of Languedoc, and Toulon joined forces to challenge Marseille's privileged position. Bordeaux's deputy wrote "because Marseille is better situated for the Levantine trade, there is no valid reason to exclude or forbid other cities"; "this limitation damages the commercial interests of other maritime cities that ought to enjoy the same advantages." Michel Poncet de la Rivière, bishop of Uzès and general syndic of the estates of Languedoc, emphasized that the free port was separate from the monopoly of trade with the Levant. Languedocians wanted to sail directly to the Near East. This would lower shipping and transaction costs (by avoiding inspection!) and minimize how long manufacturers waited for payment. Poncet de la Rivière grudgingly conceded that returning ships had to stop in Marseille, at least until Sète built a lazaret. He concluded that "if the city of Marseille had allowed the merchants of Languedoc to do what they wanted to do, French commerce in the Levant would have grown so much that the English and Dutch would have less ability to destroy it."[16]

[15] *Extrait des registres du Conseil d'État*, July 31, 1691, AN AE BIII192, *Édit du Roy*, April 29, 1693, AN AE BIII192, Bergasse and Rambert, *De 1599 à 1789*, 73, 208–15, and Paris, *Le Levant*, 18 and 568.

[16] The quotes are from Paris, *Le Levant*, 25–26 and *Adresse à Nosseigneurs les Intendants de Languedoc et de Provence*, n.d. [1701], ACCIMP J1578.

Joseph Fabre directed Marseille's response. He reminded the deputies that Atlantic ports had conducted little Levantine commerce when Rouen and Dunkerque were allowed to do so. Merchants in these ports preferred to buy Levantine goods from the English or Dutch rather than make the hazardous voyage themselves. Fabre claimed that "the deputies of the Atlantic ports are motivated solely by their own interests which are prejudicial to other subjects of the king" and benefit the English and Dutch. "This competition would create such disorder in the Levant that in two years the trade would be lost to foreigners," who could take advantage of Article 3 of the treaty of Ryswick (1697), which equalized the taxes paid by French and Dutch merchants in the Levant. Nearly two years of discussion, a flood of memoirs, personal letters, and visits from Fabre and Marseille's other defenders complemented lavish expenditures of money by the chamber of commerce to sway the council.[17]

In July 1703, on the recommendation of the council of commerce, the royal council issued a new edict that structured French trade with the Levant for the next fifty years. It "suppressed many taxes levied in Marseille on merchandise" and restored the port's 1669 status. Moreover, Marseille was now the sole port exempt from the 20 percent tax and all ships coming from the Levant had to stop in Marseille. The 1703 edict also eliminated some restrictions on what goods could be brought into the port and extended entrepôt rights to additional goods. Tax farmers were banished to Marseille's customs borders. Rigorous inspection of goods headed east was intended to earn the confidence of Turkish customers. Officials responsible for making these checks were empowered to "seize prohibited merchandise disembarked from ships or that entered fraudulently and to prosecute those who broke the rules." The royal council expressly rejected arguments that Marseille's privileges of liberty were detrimental either to "the good of commerce" or to "the good of the state."[18]

[17] See the letters of Joseph Fabre dated August 28, 1701 and September 10, 1701, both found in AN AE BIII259 and the report quoted by Paris, *Le Levant*, 27–28.

[18] *Arrêt du Conseil d'État du Roy*, July 10, 1703, AN AE BIII192, *Extrait des Registres du Conseil d'État*, July 19, 1703, AN AE BIII252/1, *Instruction donné par nous Michel Chamillart, ministre et secrétaire d'état, contrôleur général des finances, au Sieur Louis Cauvière, Inspecteur des manufactures à Marseille pour l'exécution de l'arrêt du Conseil du dix juillet 1703 concernant la franchise du port de Marseille*, September 11, 1703, ACCIMP D25 and Paris, *Le Levant*, 29. On the terms, see David Kammerling Smith, "'Au bien du commerce': Economic Discourse and Visions of Society in France" (PhD dissertation, University of Pennsylvania, 1995) and *Observations de Messieurs les Députés du Commerce sur les Mémoires donné au Conseil par M. Fabre, deputé de Marseille et par Messieurs les fermiers généraux au sujet de la franchise du port de Marseille*, February 16, 1702, AN F12 1646.

It took thirty-five years for the French state to determine how best to apply commercial privileges of liberty to Marseille. Until 1750, the utility of these privileges was unquestioned though not unchallenged, primarily by representatives of Languedoc. As we have seen, French attitudes about privilege and liberty shifted after mid-century. Yet even as the Physiocrats and their fellow travelers and later the Revolutionaries assaulted privilege, they recognized that some of Marseille's privileges were too useful to eliminate. Certain of Marseille's prerogatives outlived the old régime and even survived the Revolution. Marseille's lazaret kept its monopoly until 1821 and the chamber of commerce's exclusive role in certifying merchants before they could reside in the Levant endured until 1835. This latter right was the era's single longest-lasting economic privilege (see Chapter 8). Commercial privileges, especially the privilege of liberty, were essential to French mercantile success in the Levant.[19]

Step 2: Privilege, regulation, and the industrial development of Languedoc

The woolens trade was the key to Levantine commercial exchange. Beginning with Colbert and continuing for nearly a century, the French state believed that it had to oversee woolens production to maintain quality and protect customers: market mechanisms alone were insufficient in so vital a sector. For Bourbon administrators, a combination of privilege, liberty, and regulation was required to improve Languedocian woolens sufficiently to conquer and hold Turkish markets.

State intervention responded to the declining quality of Languedocian woolens in the second half of the seventeenth century. Diplomats, merchants, and shippers agreed that the quality of woolens from Languedoc had fallen, making it impossible for France to compete with the English, Dutch, Venetians, or Genoese in the Levant. Freefalling sales confirmed such attestations. French administrators understood the issue as one of *police*: masters and men refused to follow the rules. In March 1669, Colbert commented, "The majority of workers in the realm's manufactures excuse themselves from the exact observation of the statutes and regulations promulgated in each city and establishment." Officials were ordered to publicize the rules on the proper length and

[19] There was a brief hiatus in 1791–1792. John Macauley Eager, *The Early History of Quarantine: Origin of Sanitary Measures Directed Against Yellow Fever* (Washington, DC: Government Printing Office, 1903), 24 and Zarb, *Histoire d'une autonomie communale*, 164.

width of bolts of woolen cloth and to ensure that merchants and manufacturers knew that they were to be followed. Before sale, fabric was to be inspected and confiscated "if it was not of the required quality."[20]

A new woolens regulation for the entire realm was issued in August 1669. For Colbert, quality products offered at competitive prices would always sell. Only strict adherence to the regulations could produce those goods. The administrative challenge was to get French manufacturers and workers to agree with this assessment of both the market's and the state's role in it. As shown in previous chapters, when left to their own devices, producers often preferred fraud and smuggling to complying with rules. The Colbertian paradigm committed the state to enforcing regulations governing the production process. National rules on dyeing were promulgated the same day. Royal agents, who soon became known as inspectors, were specifically designated to confirm that goods conformed to the regulations.[21]

Languedoc's woolens producers resisted government interference. This province began producing woolens for the Levant in the thirteenth century. From the sixteenth century, Carcassonne predominated, but production was scattered widely in the Cévennes. Languedocians believed that price alone determined sales. They skimped on thread count, fabric size, and the quality of wool and/or dye to keep costs down. Woolens producers also avoided inspection, gave kickbacks to merchants, bribed local officials, and by selling lower-quality goods as better stuff, committed outright fraud.

The state endorsed Paris merchant Guillaume de Varennes' 1665 proposal to bring Dutch workers to Languedoc to make woolens for the Levant (see Chapter 6). His workshop was called Saptes and received the title of "royal manufacture" the following year. The first of twelve royal manufactures, Saptes was intended to excite "emulation" among Languedoc's woolens producers. After two weeks of consultation with local manufacturers, Colbert issued a regulation for Carcassonne's woolens industry in October 1666. It imposed strict controls on guild production, but allowed masters to subcontract work to small workshops and domestic workers. A partner in the Levant Company, Louis Reich de Pennautier, exercised state oversight. Languedocians were encouraged to imitate English wares by making *londrins seconds*, a light woolen broadcloth dyed in vibrant shades of red and blue suitable for warm

[20] Clément (ed.), *Lettres, instructions et mémoires de Colbert*, II (2): 459–60.

[21] Philippe Minard explored Colbert's vision of economic development convincingly and with nuance. See *La fortune du colbertisme*, 17–21ff.

climates. By emphasizing medium-priced, good-quality products, Colbert recognized that France was not price competitive at either the high or low end of the Levantine market.[22]

Colbert was frustrated by local response to regulation. In March 1671, he wrote the intendant of Languedoc: "I have always found manufacturers dogged in keeping to the errors and abuses they commit." But Colbert was undeterred: "when authority is employed to get producers to execute the new regulations on length and width, good quality and dyeing, they see their sales increase appreciably as foreigners come and buy in France more abundantly than before."[23] Clearly, however, issuing a regulation was not enough. Getting Languedocians to produce quality goods required state recourse to both the carrot and the stick.

Royal administrators first dangled the carrot. With large stocks of Languedocian woolens unsold in the Levant, Colbert sought to encourage sales. The first two Levant companies founded in 1670 and 1678, respectively, were tasked specifically with selling French manufactures. To complement privileges of liberty, Colbert spent money. The first chartered company received an export subsidy of 10 *livres* (a *pistole*) per bolt of Languedocian woolen cloth, exemption from nearly all local taxes, and, for its sailors, eight years of immunity from the naval draft. To attract French consumers, in 1667–1668 Colbert bought 770 bolts of woolen cloth from Carcassonne worth 39,000 *livres* through intermediaries to be resold at bargain prices to Parisian taste-makers. Another 2,000 bolts were purchased in 1670–1671 and additional procurements were later exported to the Levant. Despite the state's commitment and repeated infusions of capital, the first Levant company failed in 1674 and the second in 1682. These companies miscarried because Turkish customers would not buy Languedocian woolens that were lower quality and more expensive than Dutch wares.

The collapse of the institutional structure intended to develop the woolens trade touched off a series of discussions involving Colbert, local administrators in Languedoc, and other concerned parties about how to improve production. Intendant Henri d'Aguesseau noted that the

22 The two previous paragraphs are based on Horn, *The Path Not Taken*, 273–88, Pierre Boissonnade, "Colbert: son système et les entreprises industrielles d'état en Languedoc (1661–1683)," *Annales du Midi*, 14 (1902), 11, Anette Smedley-Weill (ed.), *Correspondance des Intendants avec le Contrôleur Général des Finances 1677–1689: Naissance d'une administration Sous-Série G7. Inventaire analytique*, 3 vols. (Archives Nationales, 1989–1991), II: 87, Remy Cazals and Jean Valentin, *Carcassonne: ville industrielle au XVIIIième siècle* (Carcassonne: Service Educatif - Archives de l'Aude, 1984), 8, 17, 31, and Dutil, *L'État économique du Languedoc*, 344.

23 Clément (ed.), *Lettres, instructions et mémoires de Colbert*, II (2): 614–15 and Bergasse and Rambert, *De 1599 à 1789*, 543.

province's large size made it impossible for one inspector to enforce the regulations. He blamed manufacturers' laxity on the unwillingness of guild wardens and municipal authorities exercising *police* powers to impose penalties for failing to meet requirements. Colbert's frustration boiled over. He criticized the greedy, short-term perspective of Languedoc's producers, who "generally want complete liberty . . . and they always want to change and shorten the lengths and widths. They make goods that earn them a small profit but leads to the complete ruin of the industry."[24]

To force the Languedocians to follow regulations and to minimize both fraud and the outright bribery of state officials, Colbert appointed three additional inspectors. Their independence was insured by a generous salary paid from inspection fees. For similar reasons, Languedoc's inspectors always came from other parts of the country. Colbert and his successors recognized that Languedocians could not be trusted to inspect their own handiwork.[25]

Despite his exasperation, Colbert dangled more carrots in front of the Languedocians. Through the intendant, he worked with the provincial estates to reinvigorate the royal manufactures by providing additional incentives to export Languedocian woolens to the Levant. Colbert asked the estates to extend an interest-free loan of 100,000 *livres* to the royal manufactures and to pay their rent. He also solicited an export subsidy of 10 *livres* for each bolt composed of 380 meters of cloth (320 *aunes*) shipped to the Levant. In exchange, royal manufactures were to follow regulations, operate at least thirty machines year-round, and whenever possible, expand the number of machines in production to provide jobs. After considerable debate, the estates funded all of Colbert's requests. In 1694, producers other than royal manufactures could get an export subsidy at half the rate of the privileged enterprises. By 1713, the estates spent more than 115,000 *livres* annually to support the province's woolens trade in the Levant. Only in 1729 did the estates stop paying rent for royal manufactures. Export subsidies were halved before being eliminated in 1758.

Colbert and his successors supplemented local funds with state money and privileges. The central government matched the estate's export subsidy and, for ten years, added an annual subvention of 6,000 *livres* to

[24] Smedley-Weill (ed.), *Correspondance des Intendants avec le Contrôleur Général des Finances 1677–1689*, II: 71.

[25] The three previous paragraphs are based on *Délibérations de la Chambre du commerce de Marseille 1660 à 1671*, ACCIMP B3, 599, 601, 620 and *Arrêt du Conseil d'État*, July 18, 1670, ACCIMP J1566, Boissonnade, "Colbert," 11, Bergasse and Rambert, *De 1599 à 1789*, 233, and Clément (ed.), *Lettres, instructions et mémoires de Colbert*, II (2): 728.

royal manufactures with thirty machines in operation. Upon his death in 1683, Colbert had spent more than 400,000 *livres* in state money to encourage Languedocian woolens manufacture. He had also lavishly expended his influence to convince the estates to make their financial pledge. His successors continued his efforts.[26]

French sales in the Levant waxed. In 1685, Augustin Magy, an experienced merchant and former director of two Levant companies, affirmed that "Dutch woolens do not have the same reputation as before. Since the French began to compete with them, the Dutch sell 30% less than they did in 1670 and we sell 12–15% more than our competitors" despite persistent complaints about the quality of Languedoc's wares. A 1699 royal edict sought to cut down on fraud. It noted the increased "quantity of defective bolts of cloth rejected by either the chamber of commerce or by the inspector in Marseille that manufacturers and merchants have gotten to the Levant anyway, where they discredit French manufactures and diminish sales."[27]

Renewed emphasis on inspection spurred a spectacular rise in Levantine woolens sales. Royal administrators insisted that Languedocian manufacturers who took advantage of export subsidies and protected access to Near Eastern markets did not have the liberty to break quality guarantees embodied by state industrial regulations. To prevent privileged workers, workshops, and regions from counterfeiting the seals of manufacturers with better reputations, a November 1687 edict ordered all producers to mark their goods, but no penalties were mandated, seemingly because the royal council recognized that they would not be imposed. To combat fraud practiced on or by guild wardens and the repeated bribery of inspectors in Languedoc, in September 1693, Pontchartrain granted Marseille the privilege of conducting an unprecedented *third* round of inspection of woolens headed to the Levant. Another edict in October 1697 set standards for the quality of wool and thread count to be used in each type of fabric and specified how raw materials were to be cleaned and prepared.

State determination to inspect goods headed to the Levant culminated in yet another new industrial regulation promulgated in November 1708. In addition to regulating the quality of raw materials and manufacturing

[26] The two previous paragraphs are based on Cazals and Valentin, *Carcassonne*, 18–19, Boissonnade, "Colbert," 22–27, Smedley-Weill (ed.), *Correspondance des Intendants avec le Contrôleur Général des Finances 1677–1689*, II: 72–75, 87–90, 95–103, *Rapport fait au Bureau de Commerce par M. De Montaran en 1753*, AN AE BIII190, and Bergasse and Rambert, *De 1599 à 1789*, 233–35.

[27] The quotes in this paragraph are from Paris, *Le Levant*, 544 and *Édit du Roi*, September 23, 1699, ACCIMP H153.

methods, this measure also established clear penalties for rule breakers. Woolens of insufficient quality or that differed from its seal were confiscated. The same penalty applied to producers who bought undyed fabric or allowed others to sell goods under their name. Woolens lacking seals spelling out the name and address of the producers ("without abbreviation"!), the quality and thread count of the bolt, or whose seals had been "removed or effaced" were penalized 12 *livres per bolt*. Goods for the Levant were to be inspected three times by guild wardens. Beginning in 1714, a woolens inspector in Montpellier also certified the contents of bales of woolens, creating a *fourth* level of inspection before it left the province for Marseille and another inspection.[28]

The 1708 regulation was not always enforced and was modified on several occasions, but for eighty years, it structured the industry. Shippers, merchants, consuls, and customers alike attested that the quality of French woolens brought to the Levant improved in the second decade of the eighteenth century. That the state needed to repeat its regulatory efforts so frequently and in such detail highlights the difficulty of changing producers' attitudes and habits. Even determined "improvers" backed by a powerful, "absolutist" state apparatus were stymied by local intransience, adherence to custom, and preference for different approaches to profit-taking.

Commercial arbiter of the Levant: how the French beat the English and Dutch at their own game

Louis XIV and Colbert laid the foundations for French predominance in the Levant between 1665 and 1683, but neither lived to see it. Colbert's successors spent less money but devoted even greater attention to regulating French industry through inspection and to supporting Marseille through privilege. Trial and error discovered effective means of accomplishing state goals. Local interests were consulted and coopted. French mastery of Levantine markets resulted from sustained, creative effort: there was no preconceived plan imposed from on high. Given historians' denigration of early modern France's economic achievements, the most surprising aspect of mercantilist action in the Levant is its very success.

[28] The two previous paragraphs are based on *Arrêt du Conseil d'État du Roi*, November 4, 1687, *Extrait des Registres du Conseil d'État*, 1 September 1693, *Arrêt du Conseil d'État du Roi*, October 22, 1697, and *Arrêt du Conseil d'État du Roy*, November 20, 1708, all found in ACCIMP H153, and Bergasse and Rambert, *De 1599 à 1789*, 544.

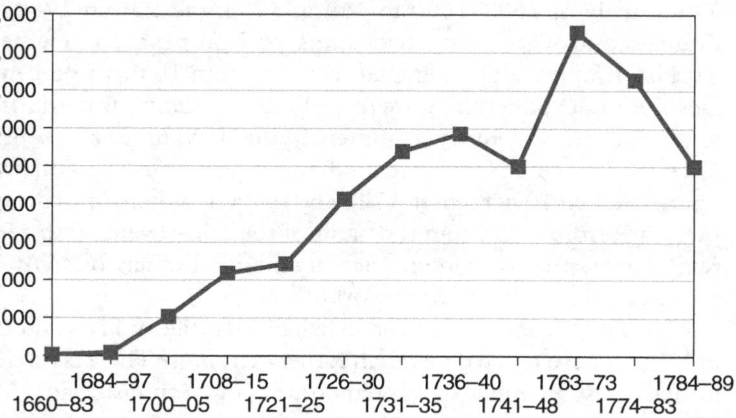

Figure 1 Average annual exports of woolens to the Levant (in bolts)[29]

France's trade position in the Levant improved dramatically. Available statistics remain approximations at best, but, as shown in Figure 1, the trends are clear. Between 1666 and 1683, France sent only 4,500 bolts of fine woolen cloth to the Levant, an average of less than 280 bolts a year. Anglo-Dutch annual exports were more than 12,000 bolts. From 1683, the export of Languedocian woolens jumped to 700–800 bolts annually. In 1698, spectacular growth commenced with 3,200 bolts sold for almost 1 million *livres*. Average annual exports jumped to 10,300 bolts in 1700–1705. In 1708–1715, as the Turkish court abandoned English goods for Languedocian, annual exports of woolens averaged 21,800 bolts. Exports remained at that level until 1725, when breathtaking growth began once again. Average sales of 41,400 bolts in 1726–1730 skyrocketed to 58,650 bolts in 1736–1740. The war-torn era from 1741 to 1762 witnessed regression to about 50,000 bolts a year before reaching an apogee of 85,300 bolts in the decade after 1763. For reasons we shall soon explore, from this summit, sales declined steadily to 50,000 bolts in 1784–1789. Despite the decline after 1773, this was impressive growth in a highly competitive market.

Sustained by the astonishing success of Languedocian woolens, total trade with the Levant expanded from 6.7 million *livres* in 1685 to 11.2 million *livres* in 1700 and to 14 million *livres* in 1717. Rapid growth followed. In 1739, total trade reached 35 million *livres* and 50–60 million in the 1780s. The number of ships involved grew from

29 Paris, *Le Levant*, 545.

94 annually in 1688–1690 to 159 in 1753 and 236 in 1789. By 1750, France controlled nearly two-thirds of European commerce with the Turkish Empire, a phenomenal recovery from 10 to 15 percent in 1660. Despite the exponential growth of French Atlantic trade in the realm's total eighteenth-century commerce, the Levant easily kept pace. In 1716–1720, the Levant generated about 3 percent of French trade: this figure reached 10 percent in 1748 and remained there until the wars of the French Revolution. From the nadir of the mid-seventeenth century, this remarkable spurt of economic activity merits comparison to Anglo-Dutch achievements in the Atlantic world.[30]

Why did state intervention on behalf of Marseille in 1703 and Languedoc in 1708 work so much better than earlier measures? There is no clear answer to that question either by contemporaries or from historians. My reading of the evidential record, both from the decades in question and from arguments made after 1750, suggests five major factors. First, commercial practice improved, while reduced taxes on goods shipped through Marseille lowered costs and improved profits. Second, French diplomacy won new concessions, affording many profitable opportunities. Third, the industrial competition, particularly the English and Dutch, had their own difficulties. Fourth, export subsidies, even generous ones, do not guarantee profits to producers, but they make them far more likely. Subsidies meant that manufacturers were not forced to skimp on materials or engage in fraud or smuggling to make a profit; many did anyway, but they did not *have* to because of market conditions. Fifth, state insistence on enforcing regulations by repeated inspection not only in Languedoc but also on the docks of Marseille and by consuls in the Levant made lawful manufacture more competitive and led to steadier profits despite massively increasing delays and bureaucratic annoyances. More efficient commercial interaction helped to maintain east–west trade after the quality of Languedoc's woolens declined and Anglo-Dutch competition revived. But building the initial commercial relationship relied on state inspections and subsidies. It is hard to escape the conclusion that the eighteenth-century success of France's woolens trade with the Levant was achieved despite rather than because of the efforts of Languedoc's producers.[31]

[30] The two previous paragraphs are based on Boissonnade, "Colbert," 16–17, 27, Paris, *Le Levant*, 545, 569, 578–79, Masson, *Histoire du commerce française dans le Levant aux XVIIe siècle*, appendix, xv, Panzac, "Maritime Trade in the Ottoman Empire," 191, Eldem, *French Trade in Istanbul*, 34–40, and Ambroise-Marie Arnould, *De la balance du commerce et des relations extérieures dans toutes les parties du globe*, 3 vols., 2nd ed. (Buisson, Year 3 [1795]), III: 27–31.

[31] Bulut, "The Role of the Ottomans and Dutch," 197–230, Paris, *Le Levant*, 544, Dutil, *L'État économique du Languedoc*, 346, and Richard Tilden Rapp, *Industry and Economic Decline in Seventeenth-Century Venice* (Cambridge, MA: Harvard University Press, 1976).

In both Languedoc and Provence, the men and women who made Levantine commerce bloom were usually immigrants to the region. Chapter 6 investigates the economic involvement of Jews, Protestants, and foreign residents, but the outsized contribution of these groups in the development of Levantine commerce deserves some comment here. In Languedoc, Dutch workers and entrepreneurs played vital roles in establishing royal manufactures. Infusing Dutch skill and diffusing their weaving techniques to local workers enabled French woolens to compete. State preference for investors from Paris and Lyon to form the first two Levant companies attracted talented entrepreneurs from those cities who remained enmeshed in the woolens trade, in some cases for decades.[32]

Marseille benefited even more profoundly from an influx of outsiders. The 1669 edict establishing the free port granted all residents some access to the city's commercial privileges. Foreigners who brought sufficient capital could marry a woman from Marseille and become a bourgeois of the city. The free port attracted merchants who relocated from Spanish and Italian ports. Groups of Greeks, Armenians, Dutch, "Americans," Scandinavians, and especially Swiss set up shop and became the backbone of Levantine trade. Religious affiliation did not seem to matter, either to Colbert or to the Marseillais: Protestants of every denomination, Greek Orthodox, Armenians, and Jews were welcomed in hopes of diverting traffic from Leghorn.

The city's industries benefited from the influx of foreign workers who brought needed craft expertise and transferred new technologies. Four hundred Armenians came in the 1670s and taught the Marseillais how to dye with madder and indigo as well as the proper use of mordants to "fix" dyed colors in woven cloth. Jacomo Bellouzo from Sicily received a privilege to establish a royal silk manufacture in 1678. He joined the Mediterranean company in 1685; his mill soon employed 2,000. Swiss immigrants dominated the calico industry and were the single largest group of foreign nationals to come to Marseille between 1669 and 1789.

Marseille's tolerance for immigrants dwindled after 1680. The following year, Jewish merchants were accused of funneling trade to other ports. In 1682, Jews were formally expelled, though it is unclear

For a very different view of Languedocian entrepreneurship, see James K. Thomson, *Clermont-de-Lodève, 1633–1789: Fluctuations in the Prosperity of a Languedocian Cloth-making Town* (Cambridge University Press, 1982).

32 Smedley-Weill (ed.), *Correspondance des Intendants avec le Contrôleur Général des Finances 1677–1689,* II: 98, Jean-Michel Minovez, "Les Manufactures royales de draps fins du midi toulousain et leurs entrepreneurs au XVIIIe siècle," *Annales du Midi,* 112: 229 (April–June 2000), 22–23, Cazals and Valentin, *Carcassonne,* 8, and Paris, *Le Levant,* 232–33.

whether anybody actually left. Jewish merchants certainly were present in the eighteenth century, but in diminished roles. After the revocation of the edict of Nantes in 1685, a number of Protestant merchants, entrepreneurs, and workers, especially in the calico industry, emigrated. Some merchants converted to Roman Catholicism but most Protestants remained – unmolested – in Marseille. A Protestant economic elite endured until the end of the old régime. Armenians were also accused of divided loyalties in the 1690s; their commercial and industrial position in Marseille soon ebbed. In addition, state policy limited Marseille's ability to welcome emigrants. Controller-general of finance Michel Chamillart imposed a tax on foreign residents in 1697. In 1704, he added a levy on naturalized citizens.

In the eighteenth century, first-generation immigrants became more involved in the Antilles trade. Immigrant merchants and shippers also invested in industry, especially silk. More than half of Marseille's 500 non-French residents were either Swiss or Italian. The recovery of Marseille's and France's position in the Levant was in no small part due to the arrival, acclimation, and retention of this large cadre of entrepreneurs and workers.[33]

Thus far this chapter has emphasized the Mediterranean roots of Marseille's spectacular growth. However, other regions also played major roles. The Atlantic world contributed strongly to the ongoing expansion of France's Levantine trade. The creation of entrepôts (see Chapters 2 and 4) for various foreign (i.e. not including France's colonies) goods including tobacco (1671), brown sugar (1690), cotton (1691), and coffee (1693) supported new commercial linkages by providing both institutional means and a physical site to exchange goods. Marseille was the sole French port where foreign coffee and tobacco could enter. The seeming redundancy of an entrepôt in a free port stemmed from wartime restrictions aimed at raising revenue by taxing imports. In an entrepôt, foreign goods paid no import or export fees but they had to be reexported. Goods entering French territory paid all taxes. To protect the colonial trade, stiff taxes remained on cotton and

[33] The previous four paragraphs are based on Paris, *Le Levant*, 14–16, 204–06, 498–503, 508, 523, 528, 537, Zarb, *Histoire d'une autonomie communale*, 253–55, Bruce Masters, *The Origins of Western Economic Dominance in the Middle East: Mercantilism and the Islamic Economy in Aleppo, 1600–1750* (New York University Press, 1988), 90, Olivier Raveux, "Espaces et technologies dans la France méridionale d'Ancien Régime: l'exemple de l'indiennage marseillais (1648–1793," *Annales du Midi*, 116: 246 (2004), 157–63, Carrière, *Négociants marseillais au XVIIIe siècle*, I: 273–86, Dumaulin, Girard, and Raveux (eds.), *Du Savon à la puce*, 40–41, 49, 82–83, and Francesca Trivellato, *The Familiarity of Strangers: The Sephardic Diaspora, Livorno, and Cross-Cultural Trade in the Early Modern Period* (New Haven, CT: Yale University Press, 2009), 100, 209.

coffee though a sizeable proportion still entered France, mostly illegally. Entrepôts kept commerce alive in wartime: foreign nations used neutral shipping to deliver goods. After 1703, only tobacco retained entrepôt status; other commodities were suspended and then abolished in 1717. These opportunities and limitations both helped and hurt the city's trade.

As part of a general loosening of the reins on colonial commerce, Marseille received a privilege to trade freely with France's colonies in the Antilles in February 1719. Goods from the Antilles flowed not only to the Levant but also to the papal enclave of the Comtat Venaissin. Silks from Avignon, salt beef, brown sugar, chocolate, cork, and ginger were given entrepôt status. Coffee was added in 1732. These privileges of liberty established a complex system of global exchange that lasted until the Revolution. Although privilege complicated policing and tax collection, it enabled Marseille's swelling volume of trade.[34]

The end of Louis XIV's wars and the opening-up of the Antilles helped Marseille develop from France's major Mediterranean port into a true world port. From a minimal Atlantic presence in 1717, Marseille became a major player in French commerce from Canada to the Antilles. After the dissolution of the Indies Company in 1769, ships from Marseille traded in China and across the Indian Ocean. Marseille's port tonnage increased about 50 percent from 1710 to 1790, or 1.6 percent annually. With the Levant, tonnage grew 0.8 percent, for Barbary Coast 1.7 percent, Canada and Asia 2 percent, and for the Antilles 3.8 percent per annum. By 1789, the value of Marseille's seaborne commerce reached 230 million *livres*; 54 million was with the Antilles (surpassing Nantes!) (23 percent). Of that 54 million, 25 million was reexported, constituting 11 percent of Marseille's total commerce. Despite the deep uncertainty of these statistics, the Antilles contributed impressively to Marseille's growth. Tropical goods, especially coffee, sugar, and indigo, shifted trade balances. Turkish customers' burgeoning taste for coffee from Martinique filled hulls headed east and limited the deepening chasm between French exports and imports. Products from the Antilles eventually equaled Languedocian woolens as mediums of exchange. Marseille's liberty to trade freely with the Antilles and its privileged

[34] The two previous paragraphs are based on Bergasse and Rambert, *De 1599 à 1789*, 215, 221–24, Paris, *Le Levant*, 559–60, Carrière, *Négociants marseillais au XVIIIe siècle*, I: 359–65, *Arrêt du Conseil d'État pour le Commerce des Colonies Françaises*, January 11, 1719, AD Bouches-du-Rhône 1F48a, and Emmanuelli, *Vivre à Marseille sous l'Ancien Régime*, 74. See also Jeff Horn, "A Different Triangular Trade – from the Antilles to the Levant via Marseille," in Joelle Neulander and Robin Walz (eds.), *Proceedings of the Western Society for French History: Selected Papers of the 2012 Annual Meeting* 40 (2014), 37–44.

entrepôts effectively supported the development of the port of Marseille and facilitated trade with the Levant.[35]

Commerce with the Near East was uneven and hard to sustain. Certain factors were beyond the control of European merchants, manufacturers, or officials such as the Ottoman Empire's military posture around the Black Sea or toward Persia. European conflict also damaged trade in the Mediterranean, especially the war of Spanish Succession and the Seven Years' War. Administrative intervention could and did support commercial exchange. Incentives for Levantine woolens led many entrepreneurs and workers to abandon production for the domestic market. By the late 1720s, twelve royal manufactures received the *pistole* per bolt and 157 other recognized producers got half that subsidy. As trade recovered once the plague in Marseille ebbed, there was a shortage of skilled labor. Producers constantly enticed workers from each other. In January 1725, Carcassonne's woolens guild was forbidden to accept new masters who were not taking over an existing workshop. Initially lasting three years, this measure was prolonged and applied to Saint-Chinian and Clermont-en-Lodève. Although intended to limit output and maintain quality, manufacturers responded by subcontracting to increase production. This approach undermined inspection by pushing manufacture outside the *corporate* system. In good years, 60,000–70,000 men, women, and children labored for guild producers. Half were located in and around Carcassonne. Other centers emerged at Clermont-en-Lodève, Saint-Chinian, and Mazamet. In 1740, royal manufactures made 22 percent of the woolens sent to the Levant, but this percentage declined by half in the mid-1760s. Guild producers – some large-scale and reliant on subcontracting and others organized more traditionally – manufactured the bulk of woolen exports to the Levant. Once the estates scaled back its subventions, competition and declining profit margins led Languedocian producers to rely once again on skimping and fraud.[36]

Documentary evidence attesting to the declining quality of Languedocian woolens after 1725 is too overwhelming to ignore. For example, a series of complaints from merchants in the Levant

[35] This is the theme of Charles Carrière, *Richesse du Passé Marseillais: Le port mondiale au XVIIIe siècle* (Marseille: Chambre de Commerce et d'Industrie de Marseille, 1979). The statistics are from Carrière, *Négociants marseillais au XVIIIe siècle*, 59, 65, 72 and Rambert, *Les Colonies de 1660 à 1789*, 363.

[36] Cazals and Valentin, *Carcassonne*, 8–66, Rémy Cazals, *Les révolutions industrielles à Mazamet 1750–1900* (Toulouse: Privat, 1983), 36, *Rapport fait au Bureau de Commerce par M. De Montaran en 1753*, Dutil, *L'État économique du Languedoc*, 346, and *Avis des Députés au Conseil de Commerce*, September 12, 1735, AN F12 701.

corroborated by consuls and the ambassador led Marseille's chamber of commerce to testify that the high number of "defects" in dyeing and skimping on size and thread count caused "disputes between French merchants in the Levant who sell woolens and those who buy their goods." The Marseillais provided technical details to show that they understood the production process. They claimed that manufacturers were not fulling the cloth either sufficiently or fast enough. Leaving soap in the fabric prevented fixing by both blue and red dyes. The colors were not as vivid as they were supposed to be and ran when bundled together with other shades.[37]

Languedocian guild wardens disputed these reports. A few wardens acknowledged the issue but blamed workers for all shortcomings. They asserted that only more thorough control over skilled labor could improve matters. Workers "stole wool from their employers" and "ignored the regulations" so frequently that "the costs of judicial expenses were too considerable to prosecute them." To remedy the situation, Carcassonne's wardens sought permission for manufacturers to discipline workers without recourse to the judicial system.[38]

Contemporaries complained that there were too many French merchants in the Levant. After a mid-1730s inspection tour, Benoît Maillet, a former consul in Algiers and Cairo, confirmed the commercial and manufacturing problems reported by others. For Maillet, the system favored large-scale merchants who could purchase an entire ship's cargo. However, the need for inventory sometimes forced merchants to bid up the cost of arriving goods. Exorbitant prices could usually be passed along to consumers, but they also led to bankruptcies, unsettling the long distribution chain. As a result of overproduction, quality defaults, and hyper-competitive, yet inefficient circulation, unsold woolens piled up in Levantine ports. They either rotted or had to be sold at such substantial discounts that manufacturers earned no profit. This backlog tied up vast amounts of capital and heightened market uncertainty.[39]

Every state official involved in the Levantine trade recognized the glitches in production. In response, Bourbon administrators intensified scrutiny of the woolens trade. Between 1720 and 1750, inspectors of manufacturing drafted four regulations seeking to impose order on producers outside guild control (1721, 1745, 1749, and 1750). In April and August 1750, intendant of Languedoc Jean Le Nain ordered the

37 *Avis de la Chambre de Commerce de Marseille*, May 16, 1726, ACCIMP H154.
38 *Avis des Deputés du Commerce*, May 3, 1734, AN F12 700.
39 See Paris, *Le Levant*, 325–26 and Maillet's correspondence AN AE BIII262, especially the letters dated November 28, 1735, April 30, 1736, June 1, 1736, and January 9, 1737.

execution of the existing regulations on manufacture and dyeing. In conjunction with the estates, intendants of Languedoc published eight additional measures policing the province's woolens manufacture (1731, 1732, 1735, 1741, 1743, 1746, 1748, and 1749). Six royal ordinances (1726, March and August 1727, 1729, January and November 1732) commanded Languedoc's producers to follow the guidelines and imposed new penalties on violators. A further six ordinances (1727, 1731, 1733, 1735, 1736, and 1739) added new rules for woolens production.

Penalties for contravening the regulations grew. Inspectors were ordered to seize and burn fraudulent goods. In 1727, the chief minister, cardinal André-Hercule de Fleury, allowed French consuls in the Levant to return defective woolens to Montpellier. Guildsmen who declared bankruptcy falsely lost their mastership and the right to send goods to the Levant. Financial penalties reached new heights in January 1732. Woolens without the required thread count were confiscated and manufacturers had to pay a 500-*livre* fine *per bolt*. Wardens caught approving fraudulent goods were fined 1,000 *livres*.[40]

Repeated commands to follow the regulations demonstrated the state's inability to enforce its orders. Harsh penalties did little good if unenforced. Languedoc's judges and guild wardens flatly refused to punish fraudulent manufacturers or settled for a slap on the wrist. In August 1727, the royal council acted to "forbid judges of manufacturing from moderating fines or other penalties prescribed by the regulations." That the royal council had to repeat the command in 1732 and that the intendant did it again in 1750 reveals the ineffectiveness of administrative action. Clearly, the "absolutist" state needed other ways to get Languedocian manufacturers to improve the quality of their products.[41]

France's ambassador to the Porte, Jean-Louis de Bonnac, suggested a new means of managing the market in 1720. To halt ruinous competition, Bonnac recommended that merchants in each French commercial

[40] Jean-Michel Minovez, "L'État et les draperies dans les Pyrénées centrales au milieu du XVIIIe siècle," *Annales du Midi*, 116, No. 246 (2004), 171–89, 177, 183, Bataillé, "La repression de la fraude dans le textile montalbanais," 193, Dutil, *L'État économique du Languedoc*, 299, 328, 347–48, Cazals, *Les révolutions industrielles à Mazamet*, 41 *Ordonnance du Roi*, March 26, 1727, and *Arrêt du Conseil d'État du Roi*, January 15, 1732, both in ACCIMP H153.

[41] *Arrêt du Conseil d'État du Roy*, August 10, 1726, ACCIMP H153 and *Avis des Députés du Commerce*, November 15, 1737, AN F12 702. For an example of the conflict within the administration, see *Avis des Deputés au Conseil de Commerce*, November 15, 1734, AN F12 700.

outpost buy woolens collectively at fixed prices based on market conditions rather than production costs. He feared opposition from Marseille's chamber of commerce to defend "what they call freedom of trade that could more justly be entitled disorder." Thirty-seven bankruptcies of Levantine commercial houses worth 5.5 million *livres* in 1729–1730 undermined Marseillais opposition.[42]

In 1730, Louis de Villeneuve, Bonnac's successor, ordered the French "nation" or merchant community of Constantinople to create "leagues" for the purchase and sale of woolens and sugar. The royal council made them mandatory in May 1731. Later that year, leagues were established in Smyrna and Salonica. Villeneuve ordered that old stocks of woolens be sold before new goods and limited the duration of credit lines advanced to Languedocian producers by merchants in Marseille. The council of commerce rejected both measures, but allowed Villeneuve to institute a different "sales distribution" system in January 1732. Each merchant requested a quota of newly arrived merchandise. If a commercial house could not sell its quota, it was redistributed after four to six weeks. After Villeneuve dismantled a Turkish merchant cartel that set prices below French offers, new leagues were established in Aleppo and Cairo not only for woolens and sugar but also for coffee and indigo. Cartels restored stability and profitability to Levantine markets. From 1750, each member of the league got an equal allotment of incoming goods.

New supply-side controls came in February 1737 with the application of *répartition* (allocation) to Languedoc. According to the count de Maurepas, "Sale by allocation is intended only to fix the price of woolens and to prevent contravention [of the regulations.] It favors good manufacturing and ought to induce emulation among all good producers." In 1741, a woolens quota and price fixing were instituted. Each manufacturer furnished a specific number of bolts. From an initial 3,000 bales, the quota grew to 3,800 in 1746 and 4,000 in 1748. Individual quotas rewarded manufacturers who followed the regulations and punished consistent frauds. Although distribution problems remained and high levels of fraud persisted, the backlog of woolens were sold without bankrupting either manufacturers or merchants. Prices fell significantly and quality improved. Languedocian woolens advanced enough that by 1757 the council of commerce believed that France could compete on an equal footing with England.[43]

42 The quote is cited by Charles-Roux, *Les Èchelles*, 37–38, Paris, *Le Levant*, 326–28, and *Rapport du Chambre de commerce de Marseille*, February 1733, AN AE BIII6.

43 The previous two paragraphs rely on Paris, *Le Levant*, 328–33, *Avis des Deputés au Conseil de Commerce*, February 27, 1733, AN F12 700, and *Résultat de la conference qui s'est tenue*

Regulation allowed French trade with the Levant to reach new heights and to conquer new markets, most notably in Greece and Egypt. By giving certain Languedocian producers the privilege of sending woolens to the Near East while preventing a glut on the market, the Bourbon state enabled the woolens industry to expand sales and to weather a serious English challenge during the war of Austrian Succession in 1740–1748. This conflict alone cost Marseille more than 800 ships worth 40 million *livres*. A considerable decline in the percentage of merchandise sent to the Levant that had to be remaindered as rubbish (*pacotille*) from 10 percent in the mid-1730s to 3–4 percent twenty years later confirmed the improved quality of French woolens. English competition, better manufacturing techniques, and the elimination of commercial bottlenecks combined to lower prices. In 1747, 57,000 bales of French woolens sold for about 10 million *livres*. Thirty years later, France earned only 11 million *livres* on sales of 100,000 bales. That most producers absorbed this dramatic fall in prices while avoiding bankruptcy amid two major wars attests to France's industrial competitiveness in Levantine markets. The Colbertian paradigm of privileges of liberty joined with state regulation successfully fostered economic development along France's Mediterranean basin.[44]

Liberty's victory, trade's decline: what's next?

Innovations in the 1730s and 1740s – fixed prices, Levantine commercial cartels, and Languedocian production quotas – facilitated French domination of trade with the Near East. State provision of privilege and imposition of regulation blended effectively to support economic development based on east–west Mediterranean trade. Shifts in official perceptions of the proper role of economic liberty in state policy undermined this system. After 1750, improvers' criticisms of government reliance on privilege and regulation infiltrated the council of commerce and informed the decision making of influential royal ministers. In the name of liberty, the privileges and complex regulatory apparatus that underlay French trade with the Levant were largely dismantled in the late 1750s.

Narratives stressing the importance of Physiocratic and their fellow travelers' conceptions of liberty are all too common in recent studies of French political economy in the second half of the eighteenth century.

chez M. Fagon le 4 Avril 1737 en presence de M. Le Comte de Maurepas, 1737, AN AE BIII237.

[44] Paris, *Le Levant*, 336–37, 548, 601.

France's Mediterranean trade nuances the bigger picture because trade freedoms and greater liberties in production granted in the late 1750s proved damaging in the long term. After decades of languishing behind France, English woolens made serious inroads in several Levantine markets. Within a decade, overwhelming evidence of waning French competitiveness led the same group of state officials who had championed liberty in the 1750s to restore most regulations while reviving several trade privileges. But a strict Colbertian approach proved increasingly difficult to enforce in the looser, more "rational" administrative environment that characterized the last decades of the old régime. Bourbon administrators' premature experiment with liberty weakened the foundations of their power and undermined the dominant position in the Levant earned by a century's painstaking effort.[45]

Long before the rise of the Physiocrats, Languedocian woolens producers championed free trade and liberty of production. From Colbert's initial efforts to regulate the woolens industry and privilege the port of Marseille in the 1660s, Languedocians rejected the central state's role. In the name of "the liberty of commerce," Languedocian mill owners and guildmasters seconded by their representatives in the estates doggedly resisted reform. The estates described the innovations of the 1730s as "deceitful and abusive because the woolens trade in the Levant does not have liberty in sales or in the price of woolens that it had up to now." The syndic claimed that "subjecting all merchants to uniform rules is called, with reason, disturbing to commerce and destroys it." The Languedocians believed that the liberty granted in the late 1750s was only their due.[46]

How did the Langeudocians make use of their long-sought liberties? After the conclusion of the Seven Years' War, woolens production spiked, but expansion came at a price. Contemporaries uniformly attested that fraud grew exponentially as the quality of Languedocian woolens collapsed. Manufacturers adulterated their products, unilaterally lowered their workers' wages, and cracked down on the theft of raw materials, confident that, with diminished quality expectations, they could make do with less skilled workers. Increased

[45] To take two prominent examples, Shovlin's *The Political Economy of Virtue* and Cheney's *Revolutionary Commerce* have major strengths, but, whether consciously or not, they endorse a triumphalist narrative based fundamentally on the history of ideas. On the growing rationality of administrative action, see Minard, *La fortune du colbertisme*.

[46] *Adresse à Nosseigneurs les Intendants de Languedoc et de Provence*, n.d. [1701], ACCIMP J1578, and *Mémoire sur le commerce des Draps fabriqués en Languedoc pour le Levant*, August 1737 ACCIMP H159.

sales in the 1760s and early 1770s generated significant short-term profits, but alienated many customers, endangering France's long-term trade position. In 1761, François-Emmanuel de Guignard, viscount de Saint-Priest, intendant of Languedoc, and a major proponent of instituting greater liberty just a few years before, complained bitterly that "allowing producers the liberty to make different kinds of woolens" led to widespread violations of the state's "wise regulations." For Saint-Priest, Languedocian "excessive greed" resulted in "abuses of liberty based on the need to lower prices because trade had been disturbed by war." As the actions of the French central state in the 1760s and 1770s made clear, the Languedocians' vision of an unfettered liberty in which they could cheat customers at will, exploit their workforces, and still enjoy full state support did not correspond to the more measured version of liberty espoused by French policymakers. Naively, given the Languedocian manufacturers' track record, the Physiocrats and their fellow travelers appear to have believed that opportunity without regulation was the best means of stimulating French trade and manufacture with the Levant. Apparently, these officials had not learned the right lessons from Colbert and his heirs.[47]

In September 1750, the council of commerce initiated the seismic shift in state involvement in the Levantine trade with an inquest into the effectiveness of the 1669 and 1703 measures that made Marseille a free port with special privileges in the Near East. Intendants of commerce Daniel-Charles de Trudaine and Jean-Claude-Marie Vincent de Gournay were hostile to Marseille's privileges in particular and commercial monopolies in general. The council dispatched intendant of commerce Jacques-Marie-Jérôme Maurille Michau de Montaran to investigate.

Montaran's 1753 report was a manifesto in favor of moderate liberty: "the freedom of the merchants can be more or less limited" for "the good of the state." The same motivation linked the government's "degree of protection" of commercial interests to "the utility of each branch of trade to the state." He concluded that Languedoc's privileges were ineffective and that Marseille's merchants profited inordinately at the expense of state interests. Montaran criticized merchants and shippers for excluding northern France's high-quality woolens from Levantine markets.

[47] *Avis des Députés du Commerce*, June 22, 1762, AN F12 713, *Avis des Députés du Commerce sur une lettre de M. De St. Priest, intendant en Languedoc du 2 Octobre 1761*, n.d. [1761], AN F12 712, and Dutil, *L'État économique du Languedoc*, 292–95.

Limiting the supply of French woolens meant that Turkish consumer demand went unmet, allowing competitors to seize market share.

For Montaran, fixed prices generated commercial profits only. He blamed the artificially low prices caused by repartition for every default in Languedocian production: "Forced to work to live, manufacturers compensated by adulterating their goods. To maintain their own credit and commercial relationships, merchants accept defective merchandise. That is the wrong that the council seeks to remedy with new arrangements." He stated that "Except for executing the regulations, freedom of manufacturing is necessary in Languedoc. In the Levant, complete liberty of sales and pricing is necessary to attract buyers with low prices, brush aside competition, and reduce the price of merchandise returning to France."[48]

The Marseillais responded by expressing their own conception of the "liberty of commerce." Adapting some of the same rhetoric used against their privileges, the chamber of commerce argued that "Commerce ought to be free, but it is too dangerous for the man of commerce to be absolutely free, indefinitely ... The liberty of commerce is the power to profit from trade, but must always take place within the rules and pay reasonable attention to consequences." They concluded that "The liberty of commerce is not the ability of an individual to do what they want, but rather for an individual to do freely what they ought."[49]

In addition to writing numerous memoirs defending their privileges and affirming the benefits of a restrained notion of free trade, Marseille's chamber of commerce mobilized support from the estates of Provence and patrons like the marshal de Villars, governor of the province, the prince de Condé, the count de Saint-Florentin, secretary of state of the royal household, and the bishops of Orléans and Marseille. Their most influential supporter was controller-general of finance Jean-Baptiste de Machault d'Arnouville, who feared the effects of drastic changes to the system with war on the horizon. The count de Vergennes, ambassador to the Porte, also defended the existing system. Despite Marseille's powerful protectors, the council issued a preliminary report in May 1754 endorsing Montaran's conclusions: "It is the unanimous opinion of the council of commerce that liberty should be restored to the manufacture of woolens destined for the Levant trade which should depend completely on restoring freedom of trade in the Levant and on free trade in general." Despite their

48 The three previous paragraphs rely on the *Rapport fait au Bureau de Commerce par M. De Montaran en 1753* and Paris, *Le Levant*, 37.

49 *Précis pour la ville de Marseille contre la Province du Languedoc.*

unanimity, the deputies sought political cover by consulting the other chambers of commerce. Four chambers suggested more study while six recommended ending Marseille's monopoly.[50]

Chambers of commerce strongly supported the commercial aspects of Montaran's recommendations. Further cover came from François Véron Duverger de Forbonnais' *Questions sur le commerce des français au Levant*, published in 1755. He argued that "As long as Marseille's monopoly in the Levant has existed, France has not undertaken all the trade it could." Forbonnais concluded that Near Eastern commercial competition would benefit French interests at the expense of other European nations. A privilege of liberty was the initial crack in the dike. In 1755, Languedocian woolens manufacturers and dyers were expressly permitted to break certain of the regulations of 1669, 1708, and 1732. The following year, Machault ordered merchants in the Levant to abandon repartition and price-fixing. Finally, formal lists of woolens producers allowed to export to the Levant along with the quota system were eliminated.[51]

The council of commerce issued its final decision in September 1757. The Languedocian port of Sète and any other port that built a lazaret could trade directly with the Levant. The 20 percent tax, Marseille's monopoly, and the requirement that woolens be inspected in Marseille were superseded in the name of "public utility." The council criticized the Marseillais' stubborn defense of their privileges as contrary to "common right and natural liberty which gives to all men the incontestable right to undertake the same commerce." The council asserted as policy that "competition and liberty of which one is the cause and the other the effect, today take the place of privilege ... [as] true commercial principles."[52]

In April 1757, a royal edict commanding Levantine merchants to stop repartitions and price-fixing reinforced the ordinance of the previous year. After seventy-five years, the estates of Languedoc were also permitted to conclude the expensive subsidy of woolens exports with the proviso that the money went to other commercial and industrial projects. Finally, several other districts in Languedoc were licensed to make woolens for export to the Levant.

[50] Marseille's correspondence is in AN AE BIII264. *Délibérations du Bureau du Commerce*, May 16, 1754 and the responses are found in AN AE BIII240. See also *Avis de la Chambre de Commerce de Marseille*, November 2, 1757, ACCIMPJ 1578, and Paris, *Le Levant*, 339.

[51] François Véron Duverger de Forbonnais, *Questions sur le commerce des français au Levant* (Marseille: Carapatria, 1755), 105–06 and Paris, *Le Levant*, 339, 351–52.

[52] *Avis des députés du commerce*, September 9, 1757, AN F12 711.

The Marseillais made a last-ditch attempt to demonstrate the consequences of destroying the existing system. In hopes of influencing the council's final dispositions, the city's inspection bureau seized 116 bales of "defective" scarlet cloth that "had escaped the vigilance of the inspector in Montpellier." Marseille's aldermen and commercial deputies wrote, "It is easy to imagine that these woolens dyed in contravention [of the regulations] could have gone to the Levant where they would have had a very prejudicial effect on the reputation that our manufactures have acquired." Amid the distractions of the Seven Years' War, Marseillais lobbying postponed application of the council's decision for sixteen months. In January 1759, a royal edict finally promulgated the council's decisions.[53]

State provision of greater liberty of manufacture, sale, and shipping occurred in wartime. Even without the estates' subsidy, production increased, but stocks piled up on Marseille's docks because of ship losses and the English blockade. Competition pushed prices sharply lower, squeezing profits to the vanishing point. From 1755, the manufacturing regulations seem to have been essentially a dead letter for most woolens producers. As early as 1758, Saint-Priest sought to restore a quota system to reward those manufacturers who still followed the rules. Trudaine rejected the request, asserting that "the most certain means of helping commerce to prosper is to allow liberty to reconcile good faith and the maintenance of the laws."[54]

Languedocians took advantage of their liberty. As we have seen, output for the Levant peaked in the decade from 1763 to 1772, averaging more than 85,000 bales a year. With the cost of high-quality wool rising rapidly and the sale price of woolens dropping, producers expanded output by cutting their workers, wages, systematically skimping on thread count and raw materials while ignoring the regulations.

The breakdown of inspection and quality production affected some regions more than others. Carcassonne and its surrounding districts were more committed to satisfying Levantine customers. Yet even there, where nearly half of the woolens shipped to the Levant were manufactured, rampant skimping on raw materials, thread count, and size occurred. The regulation of 1732 mandated a warp thread count of 2,600 for *londrins seconds*. Carcassonne's woolens, even those of the royal

[53] The two previous paragraphs are based on Paris, *Le Levant*, 331, 339, 354, *Copie du jugement rendu par Messieurs les Echevins et Deputé du commerce de Marseille sur saisies d'étoffes défectueses*, September 5, 1757, AD Bouches-du-Rhône C4639 and *Arrêt du Conseil d'État du Roy*, January 15, 1759, AN AE BIII192.

[54] Cited by Dutil, *L'État économique du Languedoc*, 318.

manufactures, generally had 2,200. Outside the city, producers stopped marking their goods to foil prosecution.

Other districts had far lower standards. Some newly licensed regions like Bédarieux took the high road, seeking to manufacture quality goods at reasonable prices. Others like Mazamet, Saint-Pons, and especially Clermont-en-Lodève explored the boundaries of what they could get away with. Mazamet specialized in avoiding inspection fees. Throughout the 1760s, the local inspectors examined only 4,000–5,000 bolts annually even though production was known to be 12,000–14,000 bolts. Clermont's producers were more brazen, even chasing the inspector of manufacturing out of town. When he was not replaced for some years, they switched to cheap local wool. Thread counts fell to 2,000 or even 1,800. Jean-Marie Roland de la Platière's appointment as inspector led to protests because "he speaks only of theory and we act based on practice." Dissatisfied with Roland and frustrated by the repeated seizure of their goods by scrupulous inspectors in Montpellier and Marseille, guild wardens complained "you can see the growing lack of utility of inspectors." The Clermontese even requested dispensation from the regulation of 1708, which they claimed "was never observed." As they could sell their goods, they asked why they should be held to an outdated standard. The council of commerce ordered them to follow the regulations: the order had no effect, despite Clermont's increasing difficulty finding buyers even at deeply discounted prices. In 1770, controller-general of finance abbé Joseph-Marie Terray commented that "the bad faith of these manufacturers is too obvious not to punish them for their fraud." But he then lowered the financial penalties levied on several manufacturers from Clermont "because the purpose of the law is not to ruin guilty manufacturers, especially for the first offence, but only to punish them sufficiently to prevent a second mistake." Inspectors of manufacturing, Marseille's chamber of commerce, and merchants in the Levant all believed that the poor quality of Clermont's woolens and the state's inability to enforce the regulations hurt the entire trade by alienating Turkish customers.[55]

[55] The two previous paragraphs are based on Cazals, *Les révolutions industrielles à Mazamet*, 36, Dutil, *L'État économique du Languedoc*, 355–56, *Avis des Députés du Commerce*, July 17, 1761, AN F12 712, *Avis des Députés du Commerce*, June 14, 1763, AN F12 713, *Lettre de Terray à l'intendant de la Tour*, February 7, 1770, AD Bouches-du-Rhône C4639, *Extrait d'une lettre écrite à M. de Boynes par M. Peyssonel, Consul de France*, January 5, 1773, AN F12 1379, *Copie d'une Lettre écrite par le S. Leblanc, Inspecteur général des manufacture de Languedoc à M. Le Vicomte de Saint-Priest, Intendant, le 12 mars 1776*, AN F12 1379, and Bataillé, "La repression de la fraude," 19. On Clermont's unruliness, see Olwen Hufton, "Attitudes Towards Authority in Eighteenth-Century Languedoc," *Social History*, 3: 3 (1978), 281–302.

Languedoc proved unable to capitalize on the opportunity to send woolens directly to the Levant through the port of Sète. Despite agitating for this right for nearly a century, the commercial dynamism and port infrastructure of Sète could not compete with Marseille's. According to Robert Paris, the historian of Marseille's Levantine trade, Languedocians with ships and capital were more interested in developing ties to the Antilles than with the Near East. Loopholes were punched in the 20 percent tax belt in 1759, but the levy lasted until the Revolution, funneling commerce through Marseille. Marseille's lazaret played the same role. Sète built one, but the council of commerce did not consider it adequate. After two ships were quarantined unsuccessfully in 1761–1762, Marseille's chamber of commerce convinced the council to mandate as "a precaution not a privilege" that ships could leave from Sète, but had to return to Marseille. By 1766, even Montaran supported protecting Marseille's commercial position: "the city's commerce cannot be favored too much because its [geography] conveys such great advantages."[56]

Montaran's change in attitude helps to explain how Marseille held on to its remaining privileges. In the name of liberal principles, Languedoc pushed to eliminate Marseille's remaining privileges in 1769, 1774, and 1779. The provinces of Flanders, Picardy, and Brittany also pursued further liberation of the woolens trade in the 1760s. But as Montaran's comment shows, the deputies of commerce had come to appreciate the utility of many of Marseille's privileges. After 1765, the council of commerce defended Marseille. Requests to avoid inspection or for permission to ignore the regulations on manufacturing fell on deaf ears. Yet, from the royal council to guild wardens, French officials had few effective means of implementing the rules, especially in a regulatory environment featuring the steady extension of manufacturing liberty (see Chapters 6 and 7).[57]

"Improving" officials were convinced to rethink the role of liberty by overwhelming evidence that fraudulent manufacturing stemming from ignoring the regulations was damaging France's long-term

[56] Rostagny, *Lettre*, January 20, 1775, AN AE BIII188 and Paris, *Le Levant*, 40–41.

[57] Paris, *Le Levant*, 253, *Défenses de la Chambre du Commerce de Marseille contre les Fabricans de Camelots d'Amiens et de Lille au sujet de la demande qu'ils ont faite de la réduction ou abolition du droit de 20 p. %*, 1764, ACCIMP H157, *Mémoire de la Chambre du Commerce de Marseille*, January 15, 1770, ACCIMP H161, *Copie de la lettre écrite par M. Le Contrôleur Général à M. l'Intendant de Languedoc le 6 Mai 1766*, ACCIMP H157, *Observations de MM. Les Intendants du commerce sur l'article 5 du cahier de representations présenté par les Députés des États de Languedoc en 1777*, n.d. [1777], AN F12 1379, and Bataillé, "La repression de la fraude," 199–200.

commercial position. Navy minister César Gabriel de Choiseul, duke de Praslin, remarked that shortchanging bolts "was an abuse deadly for commerce and dishonorable to the manufacturers," before concluding that "sadly, greed always sweeps away the best rules or ensures that such rules are not executed as they are supposed to be." Officials ordered Languedocian producers to follow the regulations and exempted woolens for the Levant from the liberty of manufacturing extended to rural areas in 1762. Administrative action accomplished little. By 1780, textile inspection in Languedoc had broken down almost completely – adherence to the regulations became essentially voluntary.[58]

In the Levant, ambassador Vergennes used falling woolen prices as an excuse to reimpose price-fixing. His decision was initially reversed but then upheld following an investigation by Montaran. After April 1766, each French outpost received the "liberty" to collectively decide whether to adopt price-fixing and repartition. Near Eastern commercial conditions made cooperation more effective than competition. Consular inspection was also stepped up to compensate for the collapse of inspection in Languedoc.[59]

Some Languedocians saw the problem but could not agree on a solution. In separate addresses to the estates written in 1765, guild wardens from Carcassonne, Saint-Pons, and Bédarieux stated that too much liberty was the source of the industry's problems. Bédarieux wanted to restore the restricted list of producers, Saint-Pons, the quota system, and Carcassonne sought to make each region responsible for a single item of consistent quality. All three groups of guild wardens limited local output and planned to cut back further to prop up prices and minimize competition for scarce raw materials. Using a time-honored strategy, the estates blamed all the industry's problems on Marseillais commercial practices. Like their superiors in Paris and Versailles, authorities in Languedoc either could not or would not

[58] duc de Praslin, *Lettre à la Chambre du Commerce de Marseille*, January 23, 1769, ACCIMP H154 and Dutil, *L'État économique du Languedoc*, 361–73.

[59] *Instruction relative à l'Ordonnance du Roi concernant les Consulats, la Résidence, le Commerce et la Navigation des Sujets de Sa Majesté dans les Echelles du Levant et de Barbarie, rendu le 3 Mars 1781*, ACCIMP J1561, *Copie de la lettre circulaire écrite à MM les Consuls de France établis en Levant et en Barbarie par la Chambre du Commerce de Marseille en date du 31 Janvier 1783*, AN AE BIII241/1, *Adresse des gardes-jurés du corps des Marchands Fabricants de Carcassonne à nosseigneurs des États de la province de Languedoc*, 1782, The Goldsmiths'-Kress Library of Economic Literature microfilm series, and Paris, *Le Levant*, 255.

impose strict rules on recalcitrant producers, making the issue of regulation moot.[60]

Bourbon administrators undermined France's trade position by granting greater freedom to merchants and manufacturers trading with the Near East. A policy shift after mid-century led eventually to declining sales of Languedocian woolens in the Levant. Philosophical preferences for a restrained liberty proved impossible to enforce once the mercantilist framework created by Colbert and his heirs was undermined in the 1750s. In encouraging French economic interests in the Mediterranean, liberty was far less effective than the combination of privilege and regulation it replaced.

When the Bastille fell, France still dominated trade with the Levant. Yet commerce with the Near East was in crisis for reasons that went beyond the disastrous experiment with measured liberty or the recession of 1787–1789. Defaults in French manufacturing, compounded by the effects of unsuccessful Turkish military adventures and domestic unrest in Syria, led to drastically reduced demand for European woolens. Marseille's chamber of commerce proudly reported that "In the Levant and Barbary Coast, the French nation is challenged by every foreign nation, but because of wise measures and rules that have been followed up to the present, almost two-thirds of this commerce is carried in French ships."[61] After 1665, French mercantilism defeated the English and Dutch in the Levant using tactics generally associated with these North Atlantic powers' economic exploitation of global markets. Influenced by "improvers," the intentional dismantling of mercantilist frameworks in favor of greater liberty of trade and manufacturing had the opposite effect of that intended by critics like Adam Smith. Less than a decade later, French officials restored regulation to Languedocian manufacturing, but their efforts floundered due to resistance from producers. Small wonder, then, that eighteenth-century Bourbon political economy was marked by a constant search for effective means of stimulating and regulating commerce and industry. This administrative pursuit outlived the old régime; it remains a standard problem of political economy to this day.

[60] Dutil, *L'État économique du Languedoc*, 358–59, *Avis des Députés du Commerce*, March 18, 1766, AN F12 714, and *Extrait du Registre des délibérations prises par les Gens des Trois Etats du Pays de Languedoc*, December 28, 1769, AN F12 1379.

[61] *Deuxième mémoire de la Chambre de Commerce de Marseille sur la franchise du port*, n.d. [1789], AD Bouches-du-Rhône 1J 989.

6 Outside the body politic, essential to the body economic

The privileges of Jews, Protestants, and foreign residents

> The Albigensian wars and the inquisition in Languedoc, St. Bartholomew's day, the league, the revocation of the edict of Nantes, the humiliations practiced against the Jansenists are all the product of the axiom: "one law, one faith, one king."
>
> Anne-Robert-Jacques de Turgot, "Seconde Lettre sur la Tolérance" (1754)[1]

Insiders needed outsiders. Louis XIV's public adherence to "one law, one faith, one king" notwithstanding, France's economy relied on legally excluded groups without formal status in the society of orders. Jews, Protestants, and foreign residents facilitated the exchange of goods and credit and provided essential services. At the same time, those people and groups who, because of their faith or place of birth, were outcasts from French society depended on special permission to participate in the economy. Political exclusion did not preclude economic utility. Privilege was the organizing principle of this mutual need.

Bourbon administrators granted liberties of privilege and privileges of liberty to individuals and groups on the margins of French society. When it came to fostering economic development, policymakers adopted a surprisingly flexible and pragmatic attitude to rules. Liberties of privilege granted room to maneuver to certain innovative yet monopolistic producers, while privileges of liberty provided exemptions from rules that hindered growth. In addition to stimulating exchange and gaining access to vital resources, especially in wartime, royal officials used privilege to augment France's precious stock of entrepreneurs by recruiting from these groups. Such efforts began in the sixteenth century and survived Louis XIV's desire to unite the French people under one faith as well as his wars against coalitions of largely Protestant foes. Under Louis XIV, royal administrators increasingly allowed outsiders

[1] Pierre-Samuel Dupont de Nemours (ed.), *Oeuvres de M. Turgot, ministre d'état, précédés et accompagnées de Mémoires et de Notes sur sa Vie, son Administration, et ses Ouvrages*, 9 vols. (Delance, 1804–1810), II: 386.

greater leeway if they contributed to the economy or the state's coffers, or both. This trend continued under Louis XV. After 1750, the integration of Jews, Protestants, and foreign residents accelerated, quickening still further in the decade before 1789. This chapter is organized around two intertwined arguments. First, the contributions of Jews, Protestants, and foreign residents to the French economy must be contextualized through an appreciation of how privilege functioned in the society of orders. Second, Bourbon administrators' role in recruiting and supporting entrepreneurs from among the legally excluded demonstrates both a deeper and an earlier official commitment to economic matters than historians generally acknowledge.

Previous chapters have considered privilege primarily in spatial terms. Here the emphasis is on the privileges of liberty and liberties of privilege given to individuals and collectivities whose most important characteristic was their legal exclusion from French society. Space continued to play a role in facilitating and inhibiting the economic activities of outsiders, but its role was fundamentally complementary. Jews, Protestants, or foreign residents could take advantage of a municipal privilege only if they already had a privilege to be able to dwell in that urban space and to participate economically. That privilege applied equally effectively to places, persons, and groups underscores the impressive adaptability of this policy tool.

Outsiders' lived experience varied enormously depending on their possession of privileges of liberty or liberties of privilege. As we shall see later, Jews and Protestants experienced Bourbon France as collectivities akin to the guilds and other *corporate* groups. Although their privileges and constraints depended on the locality, their economic access was as part of a larger unit. Group identity did not, however, prevent members from acquiring personal or familial privileges. In fact, such success stories helped to justify the extension of further privileges to groups as a whole. Foreign residents enjoyed solidarity with others from their country or sometimes of their faith, but their privileges did not derive from a collectivity beyond "other." They benefited from privileges of liberty for more abstract reasons that differed greatly from liberties of privilege experienced by Jews and Protestants. Local conditions mattered more for religious minorities than foreign residents: the former had fewer options in terms of where they could live, and faced far more legal constraints. Jews and Protestants were "other," but their collective identity fit more neatly into the society of orders.

On behalf of the general welfare, the French government was committed to the widest possible extension of entrepreneurship. Integrating Jews, Protestants, and foreign residents into the economy required officials to extend privileges that circumvented legal exclusion. The royal administration's willingness to ignore its political and religious obligations on behalf of economic development encourages a reconsideration of the gap between rhetoric and reality in the relationship of the Bourbon state to French society.

This understanding of early modern political economy builds on the scholarly literature illuminating the relationship of Louis XIV to Roman Catholicism in particular and to religious issues more generally. At the same time, I seek to revise historical interpretations of the French state's priorities especially with regard to the economy and entrepreneurship, broadly conceived. Evaluating the early modern economy on its own terms requires recognition that entrepreneurs had to be recruited and/or supported; they did not emerge *ex nihilo* from the void of traditional society. Far too many commentators dodge the institutional context of entrepreneurship or misrepresent the state's necessary role in encouraging individuals to contribute to economic development in favor of investigating economic systems or ideas.[2]

Ideas, of course, have an important role in economic development. That said, practice deserves pride of place. Entrepreneurship – understood as the actions of someone who makes judgments about the coordination of scarce resources – is not fundamentally about implementing the ideas of others.[3] Individual entrepreneurs' efforts to innovate or maximize profits have little to do with the goal of advancing economic modernity. From the largest wholesale merchant to the smallest peddler, entrepreneurs made decisions that animated the economy: those decisions were influenced by market institutions, by the state, and by the international economic context. Early modern

[2] Pierre Goubert began the process of complicating the policy implications of Louis XIV's growing religiosity in *Louis XIV and Twenty Million Frenchmen*, trans. Anne Carter (New York: Pantheon, 1970 [1966]), 149–62. James B. Collins follows in Goubert's wake: *The State in Early Modern France*, 2nd ed. (Cambridge University Press, 2009), 188–90. However, almost all works on Louis XIV's reign after the mid-1680s focus on the growth of monarchial and state power and war-making, even in the context of the economy and religious policy. See, for example, John B. Wolf, *Louis XIV* (New York: W. W. Norton, 1968), 383–401. For such a vision of entrepreneurship, see David S. Landes, *The Wealth and Poverty of Nations: Why Some Are So Rich and Some So Poor* (New York: W.W. Norton, 1999) and Hilton L. Root, *The Fountain of Privilege: Political Foundations of Markets in Old Regime France and England* (Berkeley: University of California Press, 1994). See also François Crouzet, *Britain Ascendant: Comparative Studies in Franco-British Economic History*, trans. Martin Thom (Cambridge University Press, 1990 [1985]), 99.

[3] Entrepreneurship is a deeply contested term. In English, a starting point to consider the vast literature on the subject is David S. Landes, Joel Mokyr, and William J. Baumol (eds.), *The Invention: Entrepreneurship from Ancient Mesopotamia to Modern Times* (Princeton University Press, 2010).

entrepreneurial decisions were messy and responded to multiple, convoluted factors. They were not made in an intellectual bubble that was somehow independent of or removed from the state. Privileges granted by royal administrators structured the choices made by entrepreneurs that shaped early modern economic development.[4]

In early modern Europe, the mercantilist state was the essential economic actor. Thanks to privileges of liberty, Jews, Protestants, and foreign residents made substantial contributions. At the same time, Bourbon officials molded how potential entrepreneurs, particularly those nominally outside the bounds of French society, participated in the economy through liberties of privilege. Privilege's dual role in expanding the pool of entrepreneurs and encouraging individuals with vital skills to apply them to the realm's economic needs demonstrates how Bourbon political economy managed the constraints and opportunities that emerged from the society of orders.

Earning their privileges: Jewish entrepreneurship and state service

France's monarchs, Europe's "most Christian kings," were not known for their warm welcome of non-Roman Catholics, especially after the revocation of the edict of Nantes. Yet those same kings confirmed and extended assorted privileges of liberty and liberties of privilege to diverse groups of Jews both before and after 1685. By performing important

[4] Predictably, different scholars stress different themes. David Landes' emphasis on "continental emulation" is founded on an analysis of the role of culture in economics. William Reddy uses the lack of free markets to evoke a productive "world without entrepreneurs." With regard to trade, the practical application of ideas engages scholars from Jean-Yves Grenier and Guillaume Daudin who focus on determining the profits to be made from commercial exchange to Istvan Hont and Paul Cheney who seek to understand trade through analyses of the writings of noted thinkers. David S. Landes, *The Unbound Prometheus: Technological Change and Industrial Development in Western Europe from 1750 to the Present* (Cambridge University Press, 1969), William M. Reddy, *The Rise of Market Culture: The Textile Trade & French Society, 1750–1900* (Cambridge University Press, 1984), Jean-Yves Grenier, *L'économie d'Ancien Régime: Un monde de l'échange et de l'incertitude* (Albin Michel, 1996), Guillaume Daudin, *Commerce et prospérité: La France au XVIIIe siècle* (Presses de l'Université de Paris-Sorbonne, 2005), Istvan Hont, *Jealousy of Trade: International Competition and the Nation-State in Historical Perspective* (Cambridge, MA: Belknap Press of Harvard University Press, 2005), and Paul Cheney, *Revolutionary Commerce: Globalization and the French Monarchy* (Cambridge, MA: Harvard University Press, 2010). For a brief yet cogent treatment of this trend, see Colin Heywood, *The Development of the French Economy, 1750–1914* (Cambridge University Press, 1992), 52–61. Some notable recent exceptions include Sheilagh Ogilvie, *Institutions and European Trade: Merchant Guilds, 1000–1800* (Cambridge University Press, 2011) and Alessandro Stanziani, *Rules of Exchange: French Capitalism in Comparative Perspective, Eighteenth to Early Twentieth Centuries* (Cambridge University Press, 2012).

services for the state and facilitating the circulation of goods and credit, France's Jews merited their privileges. These privileges varied by region and even by municipality, but, taken together, they reveal the royal administration's persistent willingness to ignore its own discriminatory laws when Jewish economic participation was perceived to be useful to the French economy.

As Jacques Savary des Bruslons (with Philemon-Louis Savary) noted,

> Jews have the reputation of being very skilled at commerce, but they are also suspected of not trading with all possible integrity and fidelity.
>
> Whatever one makes of this reproach, it is definite that even those nations that are most accusatory against the Jews and not just those nations that suffer them to live among them, pride themselves on learning their trading secrets and sharing profits with them.[5]

These observations illustrate that although discrimination continued, these outsiders were becoming economic insiders. Such repositioning refers to Jewish skills and capacities rather than their bodies, which remained off-limits. The privileges extended to Jews show that in policymaking, "profit" trumped either religious concerns or worries about "integrity and fidelity."

Only through privilege could Jews live, work, and trade in France. Barred from residence in 1394 and endangered by an edict from Marie de Medici as regent for Louis XIII "expelling the Jews," this religious group's position in early modern French society was precarious at best.[6] Loopholes established and exploited by the government allowed four geographically distinct Jewish communities to emerge. By 1789, approximately 40,000 Jews lived in France. These territorially distinct communities (Paris, northeast, southwest, and southeast) had different origins and little interaction. Divergent relationships to privilege make it impossible to generalize about "the Jews" in early modern France. Taking a step back and framing the lived experience through the politics of privilege helps to reveal common patterns and the broader significance of seemingly unrelated state actions.

Jewish privileges in southwestern France stemmed from the need to repopulate the region after the devastation of the Hundred Years' War. A succession of Valois monarchs allowed Sephardic crypto-Jews or "new Christians," commonly known as "Portuguese merchants," to settle in

[5] Jacques Savary des Bruslons with Philemon-Louis Savary, *Dictionnaire universel de commerce, d'histoire naturelle et des arts et metiers*, revised edition, 5 vols. (Copenhagen: Cl. Et Ant. Philibert, 1762), III: 460.

[6] The text is reprinted in François-André Isambert, Alphonse-Honoré Taillandier, and Decrusy (eds.), *Recueil général des anciennes lois françaises, depuis l'an 420 jusqu'à la révolution de 1789*, 29 vols. (Berlin-Le-Prieur, 1821–1833), XVI: 76–78.

France. Large communities developed at Saint-Jean-de-Luz (moving to Saint-Esprit-lès-Bayonne, a suburb of Bayonne, in the seventeenth century) and Bordeaux. Despite rumors of their adherence to the Jewish faith, Henri II issued letters-patent in 1550 offering new Christians commercial rights and freedom of personal movement along with the right to purchase real estate without having to pay fees. Three generations later, the judges of Bordeaux's *parlement* flatly refused to register the expulsion edict of 1615. After two years, the city's aldermen offered Jews the privilege of becoming a *bourgeois* of the city in exchange for a fee of 300 *livres*. Two hundred and sixty individuals paid for the privilege of naturalization, enabling them to sell goods retail as well as wholesale. New letters-patent of 1656 (registered in 1658) limited residential rights for new Christians to the province of Guyenne, where they weathered the religious crisis of the 1680s with its renewed threat of expulsion (see the section "Turning a blind eye: Protestant privileges under the 'most Christian kings'"). By the turn of the eighteenth century, "new Christians" displayed their Jewish faith more openly, founding social and charitable institutions to regulate their communities. In 1723, Louis XV accepted the Jewish presence in Guyenne comprising 1,500–2,000 people in Bordeaux and approximately 3,500 in Saint-Esprit. For a payment of 100,000 *livres*, he confirmed these communities' privileges of liberty. This legal exception – tantamount to official tolerance – expedited Jewish economic contributions in southwestern France.

Jews, presence did not go unchallenged. In 1681, Jean-Baptiste Colbert confirmed that Jews had to earn their sufferance. He wrote the intendant in Aix-en-Provence that:

> The king has the right to banish the Jews anytime it pleases him. [The intendant] is to examine circumspectly and secretly whether Marseille's Jews are useful or not. He is to be careful because commercial jealousy by other merchants makes it hard to evaluate whether the commerce undertaken by Jews is advantageous to the state and whether the French can furnish it [themselves], in which case the Jews will be banished.

Colbert ordered the intendant to expel a few families, restrict Jewish immigration, and try to slowly diminish their economic influence so that "in eight or ten years, the Jews can be banished entirely from the realm. Because the expulsion will be gradual, their commerce will pass into the hands of French merchants who are subjects of the king."[7] Ninety-three Sephardic Jewish families were duly expelled. Privileges

[7] Pierre Clément (ed.), *Lettres, instructions et mémoires de Colbert publiés d'après les ordres de l'empereur* (Imprimerie impériale, 1861–1873), II (2): 722.

could always be withdrawn. Outsiders could not rest on their laurels if they wanted to retain privileged status.

Despite periodic bouts of discrimination, state officials acknowledged Portuguese merchants' contributions. In 1625, Bordeaux's aldermen wrote, "in this city, they [the Portuguese merchants] are useful because of their commerce. They produce and sell merchandise and trade with unquestioned loyalty and fidelity. Up to now, no reproach has been heard."[8] To undercut hostility from the city's merchant community, Bordeaux's Jews regularly gave grain to the city, lent money to purchase food, or donated bread to feed the poor. Not long before his death in 1683, Colbert acknowledged their commercial importance. An instruction sent to the intendant of Guyenne concerning a case of sacrilege by two Jews stated: "His Majesty recognizes that it would be dangerous to punish the Jews rigorously for this crime because their general expulsion would follow. And because commerce is almost completely in the hands of these people . . . [this would be] dangerous."[9]

Residential and commercial privileges afforded Guyenne's Jews economic opportunities shared by few other outsiders in French society. Until their status was confirmed in 1723, the Jews of Bordeaux and Saint-Esprit were largely confined to small-scale exchange with the Iberian peninsula. Bordeaux's Jews also engaged in light manufacturing, primarily of soap, chocolate, and snuff, to complement the output of various artisanal trades for local consumption. Saint-Esprit's Jews focused almost exclusively on manufacturing for and trade with Spain and Portugal.

Bordeaux's Jews far surpassed the community outside Bayonne in wealth if not in numbers. In Bordeaux, bourgeois status enabled certain Jews to benefit from the port's privileged position in Atlantic commerce. With easy access to capital through links to the London and Amsterdam Jewish communities and the right to lend money at interest (nominally) denied to Christians, a substantial number of Jews became bankers and insurers. By 1751, almost a third of Bordeaux's Jews, including a few women, engaged in banking or large-scale commerce. Most Jewish merchants and shippers traded with the Caribbean, exchanging wine, liquor, and desperately needed foodstuffs for sugar and indigo. Several Jewish traders also developed extensive ties to Quebec through the Société du Canada established in 1748. During the Seven Years' War,

[8] Cited by Arnaud Detcheverry, *Histoire des israélites de Bordeaux* (Bordeaux: Balarac jeune, 1850), 57.
[9] Cited by Jonathan I. Israel, *European Jewry in the Age of Mercantilism 1550–1750* (Clarendon Press, 1985), 162–63.

some Jews even armed privateers on behalf of the crown. The port's privileges in Atlantic commerce were essential to Jewish success.

Nearly half of Bordeaux's "Portuguese" were involved in medium- or small-scale commerce within the region or to Spain. Eleven percent owned shops or worked as artisans, and 8 percent toiled in the service sector. In 1773, nearly one-quarter of Bordeaux's total *capitation* tax on merchant shippers was paid by Jews. These statistics point, first and foremost, to the privileged position of Bordeaux's Jews. Liberties of privilege such as residence and retail trade, which allowed artisanal production as well as the privilege of liberty to engage in wholesale commerce, afforded these Jews opportunities available to only a handful of outsiders. The ability to purchase land and the stability that followed Louis XV's recognition of the community also encouraged investment. Bordeaux's Jews, however, made the most of their prospects. They tapped into international commercial and credit networks of Sephardic Jews and took full advantage of their privileges of residence and bourgeois status. For this Jewish community, successful entrepreneurship linked privilege to opportunity. Bordeaux's Jews contributed robustly to the development of French commercial capitalism while also performing vital services to the Bourbon state.[10]

The trajectory of the well-known Gradis firm demonstrates how privilege unleashed Jewish entrepreneurialism and allowed outsiders to contribute to the defense of France's Atlantic empire.[11] Founded in 1695 with a capital of 5,000 *livres*, by the eve of the Revolution, its working capital surpassed 4 million *livres*. The firm still exists as the Société française pour le commerce avec l'outre-mer (SFCO). The success of this enterprise depended on the Gradis family's access to liberties of privilege and privileges of liberty.

[10] The seven previous paragraphs are based on Esther Benbassa, *The Jews of France: A History from Antiquity to the Present*, trans. M. D. DeBevoise (Princeton University Press, 1999 [1997]), 41–72, 50, Paula E. Hyman, *The Jews of Modern France* (Berkeley: University of California Press, 1998), 1–15, Ronald Schechter, *Obstinate Hebrews: Representations of Jews in France, 1715–1815* (Berkeley: University of California Press, 2003), 18–34, Richard Menkis, "The Gradis Family of Eighteenth-Century Bordeaux: A Social and Economic Study" (doctoral dissertation, Brandeis University, 1988), 47–87, Paul Butel, *Les dynasties bordelaise de Colbert à Chaban* (Perrin, 1991), 134–44, and John F. Bosher, *The Canada Merchants 1713–1763* (Clarendon Press, 1987), 168. Henri II's letters-patent are reprinted in Théophile Malvezin, *Histoire des juifs à Bordeaux* (Bordeaux: Charles Lefebvre, 1875), 106–08.

[11] Francesca Trivellato's superb study provides the template for this analysis. See her *The Familiarity of Strangers: The Sephardic Diaspora, Livorno, and Cross-Cultural Trade in the Early Modern Period* (New Haven, CT: Yale University Press, 2009).

In the seventeenth century, the Gradis family exploited the commercial rights accorded to Portuguese merchants to build capital reserves and expertise. Contracting with "new Christian" artisans for goods they thought would sell in Bordeaux was possible only because of the privileges of production and exchange that went with bourgeois status. Early in the eighteenth century, the family invested in seaborne trade, exchanging grain from Brittany and textiles from Picardy up and down the Atlantic coast. Access to international networks of Sephardic Jews headquartered in Amsterdam and London helped the Gradis family to expand rapidly and earn windfall profits. The family borrowed on favorable terms to purchase and outfit ships to engage in the burgeoning Caribbean trade. Ready access to foreign capital continued even in wartime. During the war of Spanish Succession, David Gradis was able to borrow large sums from Jews living in the Netherlands and England. By providing the privilege of liberty to Guyenne's Jews, networks of "Portuguese merchants" provided France with capital and commercial opportunities that Roman Catholics could not, especially in wartime.

The more secure position of Bordeaux's Jews after 1723 was reflected in the diversification of the Gradis family's enterprises. In addition to Caribbean trade, the Gradis family ultimately became the driving force in the Société du Canada's efforts to provision Quebec and the Île Royale (Cape Breton Island).[12] The family also purchased a large estate and seigneury in Talence, where they planted vines to make wine. A plantation in Martinique was also acquired on the cheap from a debt-ridden magistrate. These purchases, which ensured the long-term survival of the firm, were possible only because of Jewish privileges in Guyenne. During the Seven Years' War, David and Abraham Gradis put the firm's capital on the line to supply French forces in Canada. They advanced huge sums to the royal administration and sent their own vessels into harm's way (along with those of their Huguenot allies) when no other shippers would. Thanks to these efforts, the firm received state contracts to supply military garrisons at Gorée in West Africa and at Cayenne on the northern coast of South America. In recognition of the firm's reliability and wartime sacrifices, Étienne-François, duke de Choiseul, granted it a hefty 8 percent commission on hundreds of thousands of *livres* worth of trade. The firm possessed these contracts from 1763 to 1780 while also acting as commission agents for high-placed colonial officials including the intendant of Cayenne.

[12] The Gradis' role suggests a revision of the Huguenot-centric findings in Bosher, *The Canada Merchants*.

Privilege allowed the Gradis family's firm to become one of France's most successful enterprises. Phenomenal profit margins reveal the scale and scope of their success. According to historian Richard Menkis' painstaking reconstruction of the costs and benefits of the voyages of the *Renommée*, on two voyages for the Société du Canada in 1749 and 1755, net profits were an impressive 54,300 *livres* (41 percent) and 181,000 *livres* (63 percent), respectively, and 27 percent and 53 percent after depreciation. Although one of the *Renommée*'s other voyages earned profits of only about 10 percent, Menkis' findings suggest that the Gradis family's endeavors for the Société generally enjoyed far higher margins. Such fabulous profits enabled the family to weather massive wartime ship losses and the write-off of a considerable investment in Law's scheme. The Gradis family benefited from privilege along with access to investment capital furnished by Sephardic Jews at home and abroad, but the magnitude of their success stemmed from what the family did with those opportunities. The firm earned profits far in excess of those cleared by other prominent Bordelais shippers in the same era. To take just one example, François Bonnaffé earned only 11 percent profit on two voyages of *le Magnifique* in 1753–1756. Providing Bordeaux's Jews with privileges allowed them to participate in the Atlantic economy, germinating some of France's most successful entrepreneurs.

Success on this scale enabled these noted Jews to become true insiders. State service earned the Gradis family their own privileges in August 1779. Family members were allowed to inherit (not just possess) property in France's American colonies, superseding the ban on Jews. Their privilege noted the "integrity and most marked distinction" of father and son in "many important activities for the good of the military that were accomplished with zeal and, one might say, a disinterestedness of which there are very few examples."[13] The family became so prominent that when Abraham Gradis lay dying in 1780, the count de Provence and the count d'Artois (the future Louis XVIII and Charles X), who were visiting Bordeaux, each sent their personal physician to attend him.

In practice, the public commitment of the "most Christian kings" to "one law, one faith, one king" counted for little. The opportunities afforded by the privileges of liberty given to Bordeaux's Jews and the liberties of privilege possessed by that port enabled the Gradis family's remarkable success. The family's acquisition of a personal privilege represents the pinnacle of entrepreneurial achievement. But that

[13] The letters-patent are reprinted in Jean de Maupassant, *Un grand armateur de Bordeaux: Abraham Gradis (1699?-1780)* (Bordeaux: Feret et fils, 1917), 143–44.

summit rested on the firm foundations of the collective privileges granted to the city of Bordeaux and the Jews of Guyenne.[14]

In the south of France, Jewish liberties of privilege were linked closely to the territorial privileges of liberty enjoyed by the Comtat Venaissin. From 1624, Jews were allowed to live in ghettos in Avignon, Carpentras, Cavaillon, and Isle-sur-la Sorgue. Between 2,500 and 3,000 Jews lived in southern France from the mid-seventeenth century until the Revolution. Jewish merchants were also permitted to reside in Marseille from 1669 until 1682. In this region, residence carried no additional rights, but enterprising Jews flourished thanks to the Comtat's transit privileges (see Chapter 4) and their close ties to Sephardic financial and commercial networks in northern Italy, Switzerland, and the German lands.

Lacking privileges that would enable them to manufacture goods or retail merchandise comparable to those possessed by Guyenne's Jews, Comtadins relied on privileges of liberty associated with their place of residence. They became southeastern France's primary cattle and horse-traders, providing saddle and draft horses to the army, the nobility, and the clergy as well as for general use. Jews lent money to elites and for commercial purposes. Jewish peddlers and small-scale merchants also distributed woolens and silks along with jewelry and other luxuries across the length and breadth of the Midi, at very competitive prices. With horses to ease and speed travel, and the right to visit important fairs from Beaucaire in July to Bordeaux in October and to trade, both along the way and afterward for a specific period, enterprising Jews distributed goods to small towns and isolated markets neglected by other traders.

Comtadin Jewish commercial success attracted new clients. Faced with declining or stagnant foreign markets in the mid-eighteenth century, silk and woolens manufacturers throughout the Midi needed to increase domestic sales. Jewish entrepreneurialism was the solution. An 1808 memoir addressed to the minister of the interior recalled that "the confidence of the region's manufacturers led them to entrust a great part of their merchandise to Jews, who peddled it all over the realm."[15] Those same manufacturers also had difficulty acquiring sufficient stocks of raw silk and high-quality wool to keep their mills in operation. By tapping into international networks to supply raw materials, Jews provided essential

[14] The six previous paragraphs are based on Paul Butel, *Les négociants bordelaise, l'Europe et les Îles au XVIIIe siècle* (Aubier, 1974), 252–77, Butel, *Les dynasties bordelaise*, 134–40, Menkis, "The Gradis Family of Eighteenth-Century Bordeaux," 95, 156–57, and 212–19, and Bosher, *The Canada Merchants*, 180. Menkis provides detailed accounting of the family's various commercial transactions.

[15] Cited by Solomon V. Posener, "The Immediate Economic and Social Effects of the Emancipation of the Jews in France," *Jewish Social Studies*, 1: 3 (1939), 276–80

service to the manufacturing economy. The transit privileges of Orange and the Comtat along with the ease of smuggling or selling fraudulently made goods facilitated Jewish entrepreneurs' low prices.

Jewish entrepreneurialism spawned a host of complaints from inspectors of manufacturing, the deputies of commerce, guild wardens, and merchants from Aix and Lyon in the east to Bordeaux and Nantes in the west. They sought to eliminate or reduce Jewish mercantile presence by enforcing exclusionary laws. Aix's *parlement* renewed its injunctions on Jewish commerce except during fairs, but the measure had little effect. The Comtat's privilege of liberty and the liberty of privilege that permitted Jewish residence allowed these outsiders to fill vital economic niches. By promoting and distributing French manufactures while furnishing raw materials and other needed goods in underserved markets through the Midi, Comtadin Jews earned their privileges.[16]

[16] The four previous paragraphs are based on Benbassa, *The Jews of France*, 41–47, Hyman, *The Jews of Modern France*, 5–8, Léon Dutil, *L'État économique du Languedoc à la fin de l'ancien régime (1750–1789)*, thèse – Université de Paris (Hachette, 1911), 744–45, Jean-Michel Minovez, *La Puissance du Midi: Drapiers et draperies de Colbert à la Revolution* (Presses universitaires de Rennes, 2012), 208–15, Bruce Masters, *The Origins of Western Economic Dominance in the Middle East: Mercantilism and the Islamic Economy in Aleppo, 1600–1750* (New York University Press, 1988), 90, *Avis des Deputés au Conseil de Commerce sur deux mémoires envoyés à M. Le Contrôleur général, le 22 Novembre et le 13 de ce mois par le Sieur de Lan, Inspecteur des manufactures à Bordeaux*, January 27, 1733, AN F12 700, Dubroeuil, *Mémoire de la plus grande consequence pour l'état au sujet de la manufacture de Lyon expirante et que l'on propose à tous Citoyens pour parvenir en lui administrant les plus prompts secours, la remettre sur pied lequel concerne les commissionnaires étrangers qui y font établis, les courtiers et le juif qui ne peuvent que le rendre d'un détail un peu long, mais que l'on reconnaîtra d'une absolue nécessité pour y remedier dans tous les points et par lequel on y d'autre intérêt que de rendre à la nature ce qu'on lui doit y*, 1768, AN F12 647–648, *Arrêt du Parlement de Provence portant défense à tous Juifs de hanter ni fréquenter en cette ville d'Aix, ni faire aucun commerce, vendre et débiter aucuns marchandises, ni friperies, excepté les tems des Foires*, November 18, 1775, AD Bouches-du-Rhône 1F48a, *Observations du Deputé de Nantes sur la requete des Gardes du corps des marchands de draps de soye de la ville de Nantes contre les juifs fréquentans, vendants et débitants dans les foires de ladite ville en conséquence des ordonnances de M. L'Intendant et du lieutenance de police qui leur ont permis d'y faire commerce pendant lesdites tems des foires*, September 17, 1745, AN F12 705, *Avis des Deputés du Commerce sur la lettre de M. L'Intendant d'Auvergne, par laquelle il s'informe M. Le Controlleur général qu'on se plaint que les Juifs et colporteurs tiennent dans son département pendant toute l'année des boutiques et magasins ouverts sous prétexte des privileges qu'ils disent avoir: comme ils lui sont inconnus, il demande des ordres précis à cet égard*, July 1, 1729, AN F12 699, *Avis des Deputés du Commerce sur la lettre de M. De Fontamieu, au sujet des juifs qui font leur demeure et residence dans la ville et principauté d'Orange*, March 24, 1739, AN F12 699, and *Arrêt du Conseil d'État du Roi qui casse deux Arrêts rendus au Parlement de Dijon les 22 Juin 1724, et 29 Juillet 1730 par lesquels il a été permis aux nommé Joseph Raphael de Lazia, et autres Marchands Juifs établis à Bordeaux, de trafiquer, vendre et negocier pendant un mois de chaque saison de l'année, dans toutes les Villes, Bourgs et Lieux de ressort de ce Parlement. Et fait deffenses aux Juifs de trafiquer, vendre et debiter des marchandises dans aucunes Villes et Lieux du Royaume, autres que celles où ils sont domicilé*, February 20, 1731, AD Bouches-du-Rhône 1F48a.

In eastern France, the Jews' acquisition of privilege was more tortured and far more expensive. A larger population shaped access to privilege. By 1789, there were 500 families in Lorraine, 3,500 individuals in Metz, and about 22,500 Jews in Alsace. Various rulers granted limited numbers of Jews the privilege of residence in exchange for substantial annual payments. From 1715, Metz' Jews paid 40,000 *livres* annually to live in a de facto ghetto. For 10,000 *livres* a year, duke Léopold of Lorraine issued letters of toleration in 1721. The fee rose to 14,300 *livres* in 1737, a hefty sum for a mere 180 families to pay. When Lorraine became French in 1766, Louis XV's officials confirmed the Jews' status, but demanded 16,000 *livres* annually as payment for the privilege. Alsace's Jews did not have to contribute a lump sum. Instead, starting in 1657, they paid substantial fees (increased in 1674 and 1681) for royal protection. They were also subject to an additional head tax and further levies to their seigneur. To visit or stay overnight in Strasbourg, Jews shelled out high fees. They also had to wear either a yellow patch or some other distinguishing mark such as a special ring to indicate their faith.

Few liberties were associated with the privilege of residence in eastern France. In Lorraine, toleration conveyed only limited rights to engage in retail trade or wholesale commerce. These privileges allowed Jews to earn meager livings as itinerant peddlers and small-scale moneylenders, though the duchy also boasted a few successful bankers, manufacturers, and merchants. Metz' Jews had no privileges beyond the right to engage in wholesale commerce. Alsace, however, had been part of the Holy Roman Empire where each community determined the terms of Jewish residence. Some tolerant seigneurs – including France's kings – granted Jews extensive commercial rights.

Jews advanced funds, supplied military garrisons, and circumvented wartime trade embargos by the House of Bourbon's many enemies. A 1698 memoir by the intendant of Metz noted that "by means of their agents" in other lands, Jews could import "all sorts of merchandise" "more quickly and more cheaply than Christians."[17] Herz Cerf-Berr, a former agent of the duke of Hesse-Darmstadt, used his contacts in the Rhineland to bring enough grain to Strasbourg to alleviate shortages in 1770–1771. Cerf-Berr later became a major military supplier for Louis XVI, which earned him a personal privilege to live in Strasbourg, trumping the municipal prohibition.

Jewish entrepreneurialism in Alsace was valuable enough to the state that an edict exempted Alsace's Jews from the head tax in January 1784. Letters-patent promulgated that July allowed Jews to engage in banking,

[17] Schechter, *Obstinate Hebrews*, 24,

commerce, and manufacturing as long as they did not employ Christians to do the work. France accrued sufficient economic benefits from extending limited liberties of privilege that the royal government granted privileges of liberty to Alsace's Jews.[18]

Jews inhabiting Guyenne, the Comtat Venaissin, and northeastern France depended on privilege. In these three regions, residence was a liberty of privilege that allowed Jewish entrepreneurs to take advantage of privileges of liberty possessed by municipalities or parishes, as in Bordeaux and Alsace, or larger geographical entities such as those of Alsace, Guyenne, and Lorraine. The ability to tap into the broader framework of privilege was not, however, a given in the society of orders. In Paris, the Jewish experience reveals the lofty barriers that the privilege of residence and willing entrepreneurs sometimes confronted. Paris' Jews were too constrained to achieve economic success comparable to France's other Jewish populations.

Paris' 500–600 Jews had no permanent right to residence. The expulsion of seventy-three families in 1749 shone a spotlight on that particular sword of Damocles. De facto toleration came only in 1755. Beyond a few "Portuguese" who possessed naturalization papers, Jews required a passport or temporary residence permit issued by the police, who kept them under surveillance. Temporary privileges of residence did allow the Jews of Paris to engage in trade. Most operated outdoor stalls, but a few supplied horses for the army or jewelry to the royal family.

The city's Jews understood that privilege was the only way to escape the economic margins. Paris' powerful six corps were, however, adamantly opposed to Jewish economic participation; they excluded enterprising Jews from those aspects of commerce and industry overseen by the guilds. An opportunity to circumvent the religious restrictions on their economic participation came in 1767. Unable to acquire collective privileges of liberty, individual Jews sought access to the liberty of privilege embodied by guild membership.

A royal edict of March 1767, clarified in June and August, created "letters of privilege," which established masterships in guilds across France. The number varied according to the size and economic importance of the urban area (see Chapter 3). The June edict expressed the royal council's "intention to employ every means to enable the commerce of the realm to

[18] The four previous paragraphs are based on Zosa Szajkowski, *The Economic Status of the Jews in Alsace, Metz and Lorraine (1648–1789)* (New York: Editions Historiques Franco-Juives, 1954), 18–22, 29–30, 50–54, 57–63, Benbassa, *The Jews of France*, 58–70, Schechter, *Obstinate Hebrews*, 18–26, Posener, "The Immediate Economic and Social Effects," 279, and Hyman, *The Jews of Modern France*, 14.

flourish by favoring foreigners, both resident and potential, to live in safety and to profit from their industry."[19] Five Portuguese Jews living in Paris, along with a number of Protestants, purchased these privileges for 1,400 *livres* each. Guild opposition, nominally on religious grounds, eventually succeeded in annulling the privileges bought by Jews. In August 1774, the royal council ordered the Jews' fees to be reimbursed, "forbade them from engaging in the clothing trade," and renewed the 1615 prohibition on Jewish commerce in Paris.[20] This measure reinforced the outsider status of Paris' Jews and challenged the trends in state policy toward both greater liberalism and broader access to economic privileges.

Nineteen months later, French officials offered a more wide-ranging opportunity for Jewish economic participation in Paris. The edict promulgating Turgot's limited abolition of the guilds allowed "All persons of whatever quality and condition, even all foreigners ... to espouse and practice throughout the kingdom whatever sort of commerce or craft they may choose."[21] (See Chapters 2 and 7.) Jews, Protestants, and foreign residents embraced the opportunity. Turgot's fall, however, eliminated the possibility that these outsiders could participate in the economy on the same footing as French Catholics.

Individual Jews continued to seek access to liberties of privilege. When "new communities" of guilds were created in August 1776, six Parisian Jews (including the five excluded in 1774) paid the fee to join the merchants' guild. Citing anti-Jewish measures from across the realm as precedents, the royal council ousted them in February 1777, although they were allowed to continue practicing their trade for two more years. Both Jews and Protestants renewed efforts to join Paris' guilds in 1787 after the promulgation of the Edict of Toleration, but were again rebuffed.

Paris' deeply entrenched guild system was protected by the *parlement*. The city also enjoyed a vibrant economy and an ample supply of energetic entrepreneurs. Privileged enclaves like the faubourg Saint-Antoine provided loopholes for outsiders to exploit. In Paris, state officials maintained the Catholic monopoly on trade and industry. Jews failed to acquire access to either collective privileges of liberty or individual liberties of privilege. Paris' Jews remained outsiders in ways that France's other major Jewish communities did not.[22]

19 *Arrêt du Conseil d'État du Roi, et lettres patentes sur icelui*, June 23, 1767 (Gallica).

20 Quoted in Posener, "The Immediate Economic and Social Effects," 277.

21 *Édit du Roi portant suppression des Jurandes & Communautés de Commerce, Arts et Métiers*, February 1776 (Gallica).

22 The seven previous paragraphs are based on Benbassa, *The Jews of France*, 70–71, Schechter, *Obstinate Hebrews*, 31, and Posener, "The Immediate Economic and Social Effects," 271–326, Steven L. Kaplan, *La fin des corporations*, trad. Béatrice Vierne (Fayard, 2001), 357, as well as *Édit du Roi concernant les Arts et Métiers*, March 1767,

Legal Jewish residence in early modern France required a privilege. As the experience of Paris demonstrated, the privilege of residence was not enough to enable a Jewish community to prosper. Where entrepreneurs could tap into additional privileges, Jewish entrepreneurialism had greater opportunity. Individual Jews and entire communities earned their privileges by providing much-needed revenue or broader economic benefits. In practice, where entrepreneurs were at a premium, the state's military supply needs unfulfilled, or access to foreign capital was required for development, the prohibitions on Jewish residence and commerce were either removed or ignored. At the end of the eighteenth century, French Jews remained outsiders, but in some places, officials added privileges of liberty to liberties of privilege granted earlier. Taken together, privileges allowed the Jewish communities of Bordeaux and Alsace to approach the status of insiders.

Turning a blind eye: Protestant privileges under the "most Christian kings"

In early modern France, Protestants were insiders turned into outsiders. This shift is not particularly surprising in light of the dictum established at the 1555 peace of Augsburg and modified in the treaties of Westphalia of 1648: *cuius regio eius religio* ("whose realm, his religion"). Although their religious records deserve to be nuanced, it should be remembered that both Louis XIV and Louis XV enacted draconian measures to ensure a Roman Catholic monopoly over production. As demonstrated in the previous section, before 1784 Jews infringed on that privilege only in Bordeaux and Saint-Esprit. Most Jewish privileges of liberty involved commerce and moneylending. Protestants, however, had a far more significant position in French capitalism and therefore in Bourbon political economy. Not only were there up to a million Protestants in early modern France, but also thanks to those following up on the insights of Max Weber, their many contributions to the emergence of an industrial economy have been delineated by an enormous scholarly literature. Privilege's role in bridging the gap between Protestant entrepreneurs' legal rights and their contributions is this section's central concern.

Protestant economic participation depended on privilege. The edict of Nantes, promulgated in 1598, confirmed or conveyed vital economic privileges. Huguenots or Calvinists were generally referred to as

Arrêt du Roi, August 12, 1767, and *Arrêt du Conseil d'État du Roi*, February 7, 1777, all available on Gallica.

adherents of the RPR or *Religion Prétendue Réformée* ("so-called reformed religion"). They could live (although not always worship publicly) where they wished and could hold public office or join a guild "without being constrained to participate in any ceremonies contrary to their religion. When called to take oath, they have only to raise their hand, swear and promise to God that they will speak the truth" (Article 24).[23] In the 1648 treaty of Münster, France agreed to respect the liberty of "commerce" for Lutherans and Calvinists in territories like Alsace that had been part of the Holy Roman Empire (Articles 28, 49, 70). Even 1685's edict of Fontainbleau revoking that of Nantes expressly stated that "liberty is granted to the said persons of the R. P. R ... to remain in the cities and places of our kingdom, and the lands, and territories subject to us, and there to continue their commerce, and to enjoy their possessions" (Article 12).[24] These privileges of liberty breached the religious monopoly of legal economic participation enjoyed by Roman Catholics in Bourbon France. Trade was clearly permitted by these privileges. But in practice, the Catholic productive monopoly was far more limited than the vicious treatment of Huguenots by Europe's "most Christian kings," emphasized by most historians, would suggest.[25]

In the name of a Roman Catholic monopoly, Louis XIV's administration began to shrink Huguenots' productive liberties a generation before the revocation of the edict of Nantes. First, the royal council attempted to make sure that guild oaths included observance of Roman Catholicism. This 1664 measure was, however, withdrawn in 1669. Instead, territorially based measures chipped away at Calvinist privileges of liberty.

A royal edict allowed Paris' seamstress guild to exclude "women of the R. P. R." in 1665. Two years later, a general regulation for the city of Lyon excluded Protestants from guild membership. In 1669, another measure "expressly forbade all judges, officials, and others from allowing the reception of any masters of the R. P. R. by masterwork or other means without a direct order from the king" in the Protestant haven of La Rochelle. That same year the *parlement* of Paris, "banned master embroiders of the reformed religion from training apprentices." A 1673

[23] Henri IV, *Édit de Nantes en faveur de ceux de la religion prétendue réformée* (April 13, 1598) reproduced on HuguenotsWeb, http://huguenotsweb.free.fr/histoire/edit_nantes.htm (accessed June 23, 2013).

[24] "Revocation of the Edict of Nantes," October 22, 1685, Internet Modern History Sourcebook, http://www.fordham.edu/halsall/mod/1685revocation.asp (accessed June 23, 2013).

[25] For a sense of older historiographical currents, see William F. Church, *Louis XIV in Historical Thought* (New York: Norton, 1976), 81–84.

court case filed in the privileged enclave of Saint-Germain-des-Près outside Paris involving the seizure of a few bales of woolen stockings resulted in a general decision that "the edict of July 21, 1664 will be executed according to its form and content. Letters of mastership for all guilds that are contrary to its provisions are nullified." Huguenot guild membership was not outlawed, although some jurisdictions, like Paris, made their participation harder than others.[26] However, in much of France, a de facto legal barrier was erected by requiring journeymen and masters to join Catholic religious brotherhoods and by forbidding the training of Huguenot apprentices.

Colbert also shifted stance. For sixteen years, he protected Josse Van Robais, the innovative woolens manufacturer near Abbeville (see below) from harassment for his Calvinist faith. But in 1681 Colbert directed the intendant of Amiens to devote himself to converting Van Robais "because in this manner instead of this manufacture remaining in Huguenot hands, we can achieve the conversion of all those who work there."[27] Van Robais' state-granted privilege guaranteeing his freedom of worship was seemingly irrelevant.[28]

The legal basis of Protestant economic involvement before, during, and after the edict of Fontainbleau has been poorly understood. Notoriously, the revocation of the edict of Nantes triggered a Huguenot exodus of about 200,000 (within a decade) out of a population of around 730,000. Most Huguenots remained. Forced to abjure their faith, at least in public, they became known as "new converts" or "new Catholics." That Protestants played vital roles in French economic development and technology transfer after 1685 is an equally well-told tale.[29] When

[26] The measures of 1664, 1665, 1669, 1673, 1673bis, and 1681 are reprinted in Jacques Lefebvre, *Nouveau Recueil de tout ce qui s'est fait pour et contre les Protestans, particulièrement en France* (Frederic Lenard, 1696), 424–35 (Googlebooks).

[27] Cited by Clément (ed.), *Lettres, instructions et mémoires de Colbert*, VI: 97.

[28] The five previous paragraphs are based on "Peace Treaty between the Holy Roman Emperor and the King of France and their respective Allies," October 24, 1648, Avalon Project-Yale University Law School, http://avalon.law.yale.edu/17th_century/westphal.asp (accessed June 23, 2013), Émile Coornaert, *Les corporations en France avant 1789*, 5th ed. (Gallimard, 1941), 193, Émile Levasseur, *Histoire des classes ouvrières et de l'industrie en France avant 1789*, 2nd ed., 2 vols., (Arthur Rousseau, 1901), II: 341, and Savary des Bruslons with Savary, *Dictionnaire universel de commerce*, III: 693–94.

[29] Warren C. Scoville played a major role in that integration. See his magisterial *The Persecution of Huguenots and French Economic Development 1680–1720* (Berkeley: University of California Press, 1960). For a contrary view of the effects of discrimination against Protestants, see David S. Landes, *Revolution in Time: Clocks and the Making of the Modern World* (Cambridge, MA: Harvard University Press, 1983), 97. See also Bosher, *The Canada Merchants*, and Robert Forster, *Merchants, Landlords, Magistrates: The Depont Family in Eighteenth-Century France* (Baltimore: Johns Hopkins University

privilege frames the explanation bridging these two narratives, it encourages a new understanding of the possibilities and constraints on Protestant economic participation.

The edicts of 1598 and 1685 guaranteed commercial rights and the ability to engage in finance to French Calvinists, who comprised nearly the entire Protestant population outside Alsace. During the famines of 1694 and 1709, Louis XIV swallowed his pride and appealed for help from Huguenot bankers in Rouen, who promptly borrowed vast sums from their religious brethren abroad. Protestant financiers were essential long before John Law. Jacques Necker and Étienne Clavière continued that tradition.

Protestant participation in industry was more complicated. Huguenots' ability to belong to a guild had been whittled away even before the edict of Fontainbleau. Despite lacking de jure privileges, Protestants unmistakably participated in French industry in places and sectors subject to the guilds. This seeming contradiction not only exposes the limits of state power but also suggests a more penetrating analysis. Bourbon administrators openly favored Protestant manufacturers and inventors, granting them privileges and even naming many of their enterprises "royal manufactures." Perhaps more significantly, the French government allowed – and by inaction even encouraged – Protestants to contravene the privileges of guilds, cities, and provinces. The state also declined to use inspection to stop the distribution of goods made by Protestants (often through subcontracting or by using the trademarks of Catholic producers) as it tried to do with fraudulently made manufactures. This de facto permission was never openly discussed. In light of the tremendous degree of state oversight of industry inaugurated by Colbert and added to by his successors, the flouting of the law by Nîmois hosiers, Van Robais woolens manufacturers, and Parisian calico printers was too systematic to have been accidental.

Such tacit consent to breaking the rules is striking to anyone who has explored the workings of the early modern economy: it represents a form of the privilege of liberty. In this case, state action was negative rather than positive as with other varieties of the privilege of liberty. By ignoring laws

Press, 1980). Recent studies of the fate of Protestants in industry include Gérard Gayot, *Les draps de Sedan 1646–1870* (Éditions de l'École des Hautes Études en Sciences Sociales, 1998) and Alain Becchia, *La draperie d'Elbeuf (des origins à 1870)* (Publications de l'Université de Rouen, 2000), 30–46. On population, see Philip Benedict, "The Huguenot Population of France, 1600–1685: The Demographic Fate and Customs of a Religious Minority," *Transactions of the American Philosophical Society*, 81: 5 (1991), 1–164, esp. 77.

mandating a Roman Catholic monopoly of production, French officials extended the privilege of liberty to a considerable number of Huguenots.

Why did the regime choose not to enforce its own rules? By allowing, facilitating, and encouraging Protestant involvement in production, the House of Bourbon recognized the Huguenots' contributions as well as European economic realities. As Jeffrey Merrick explained in a quite different context, royal administrators ignored the existence of non-Catholics by assuming religious uniformity even when there was overwhelming evidence to the contrary. In their treatment of outsiders in French society, Bourbon monarchs from Henri IV to Louis XVI steadfastly pursued policies exemplifying *raison d'économie*. As economic and financial power were intimately linked to a state's ability to make war, such tactics should also be understood as *raison d'état*. In practice, economic usefulness trumped the French kings' dedication to either a universal monarchy or a universal church.

This practical accommodation ran counter to state rhetoric. A declaration of March 1715 asserted that "the former Protestants ... had embraced the Catholic religion." It voided Article 12 of the edict of Fontainbleau granting Huguenots the liberty to worship in private.[30] Legal elimination of French Protestantism outside of Alsace was confirmed by ordinances of May and August 1716 as well as by Louis XV's edict of Versailles of May 1724. This legal façade, however, concealed a deeply furrowed religious terrain fertilized by privilege.

De facto privilege of liberty was evident because royal administrators knew that nearly all Huguenot conversions were only for show. Intendant of Languedoc Nicolas Lamoignon de Basville remarked, "The change in the religion of the principal merchants of Nîmes changed nothing in their commercial dealings. They are flourishing more than ever. If these merchants are still bad Catholics, at least they have not ceased to be good traders."[31] The government's blind eye also protected shippers engaged in the Canada trade, which officially excluded Protestants and was closely supervised by the state. Samuel Bernon was allowed to purchase a vessel around 1690; this noted Huguenot was described as "the Merchant who has carried on the greatest trade in Canada" because he supplied commodities to other towns from his warehouses in Québec.[32] In 1710, an anonymous observer wrote that since 1685,

[30] Cited by Henri Hauser, "The Characteristic Features of French Economic History from the Middle of the Sixteenth to the Middle of the Eighteenth Century," *The Economic History Review*, 4: 3 (1933), 257–72, 263.

[31] Cited by Levasseur, *Histoire des classes ouvrières*, II: 346.

[32] Cited by John F. Bosher, "Huguenot Merchants and the Protestant International in the Seventeenth Century," *The William and Mary Quarterly*, 52: 1 (1995), 77–102, 95.

all persons of the [Protestant] religion have made their conversion, either real or feigned, to the true and Catholic religion. Since that time no master has been received who did not say he was Catholic, but they are taken at their word, and on that of the guild officials, without any demand for a certificate from their parish priest or other proof ... and whenever the zeal of certain priests has led them to denounce these stubborn Huguenots ... the now deceased President de Harlay and Monsieur de la Raynie [sic] always believed that they should cover things up.[33]

Such practices left only scattered traces in the archives, but they appear to have been relatively widespread in the decades after 1685.

Historian David K. Smith explores a controversy over the introduction of guild statutes into Nîmes' hosiery industry between 1706 and 1712 that demonstrates how de facto privileges of liberty worked. In Nîmes, abjured Protestants seemingly opposed statutes, and "old Catholics" supported them. Of the "new converts," intendant Basville observed that "few are effectively Catholic ... Nearly all of them hold in their hearts to their evil [*mauvaise*] religion."[34] Yet, at the conclusion of the controversy, the city's hosiers enjoyed a privileged monopoly empowering them to dominate rural producers. No masterships were introduced. This framework allowed former Huguenots considerable liberty and negligible constraint. As the conflict occurred soon after the bloody war of the Camisards (1702–1704) in which perhaps 100,000 people perished, it is difficult to avoid the conclusion that such solutions were intended to facilitate the return of economic normalcy by permitting the participation of "new Catholics." Hosiery was too vital to the region and had too much export potential to be allowed to collapse amid the economic devastation that took place during the war of Spanish Succession. By 1744, hosiery employed more than 5,000 people in and around Nîmes. Most of them were Protestant. About 5,100 stocking frames produced nearly five million pairs of silk, woolen, or cotton stockings valued at an average of a *livre* per pair. Most of this output was shipped to European markets from Spain and the Italian states to various Swiss polities and assorted German and northern European countries. The privilege of liberty afforded to Nîmes' Protestant hosiers permitted them to develop one of France's most valuable industries.

To ensure civil peace and economic development, Basville allowed the veneer of Catholicism to shield abjuring Huguenots from the letter

[33] Cited by David Garrioch, "The Protestants of Paris and the Old Regime," in Vesna Drapac and André Labelet (eds.), *French History and Civilization. Papers from the George Rudé Seminar*, 2 (2009), 16–24, 19.

[34] Nicolas Lamoignon de Basville, *Mémoires pour servir à l'histoire de Languedoc* (Amsterdam: J. Ryckoff, 1736), 79.

of the law. "New converts" became nominal Catholics, but in places like eastern Languedoc where Huguenots were numerous, militarily dangerous, and economically essential, the state permitted them to wear the yoke lightly.[35] This realistic approach helps to explain how Protestantism survived to make those well-known later contributions. A secret census in 1728 revealed that there were 120 churches and 200,000 Protestants in Languedoc and Dauphiné, nearly as many as before 1685. By 1761, there were 350,000 Huguenots in Languedoc alone. Nîmes had Protestant lawyers, and Huguenot judges even sat on the presidial court thanks to sham "certificates of Catholicity." A majority of city councilors were also Protestant. In 1789, Languedoc's Huguenots made up at least half of France's 600,000 to 700,000 Protestants. About 200,000 were Lutherans in Alsace. Protestants did not simply disappear in 1685 or even in 1724. Nor did they suddenly immigrate to France or abandon Catholicism on the eve of the Revolution. Economically, privilege linked to *raison d'économie* made possible the survival of Protestantism in France.

Privileges of economic participation were extended despite ongoing legal discrimination. The revocation of the edict of Nantes contained an "express prohibition to all our subjects of the said R. P. R ... against leaving our kingdom" (Article X). Three months later, in January 1686, the royal council issued an edict permitting "all merchants and other foreign Protestants ... to enter the realm with their wives, children, servants and others of their nation, samples and merchandise. They may stay, come, and go from cities and other places and leave with the same liberty that they have had in the past."[36] Historians have described Louis XIV as increasingly determined to implement the doctrine of "one law, one faith, one king" from the late 1670s. Both contemporaries and later critics blamed him for ruining the French economy by pushing out the Huguenots. But on the ground, the situation looks rather different. Protestants often had to claim to be something they were not, but they continued to be able to earn a living.[37]

35 It is possible to view the state's economic empowerment of Protestants so long as they did not press their religious views in public as an example of the type of social collaboration detailed by William Beik, *Absolutism and Society in Seventeenth-century France: State Power and Provincial Aristocracy in Languedoc* (Cambridge University Press, 1985). Privilege provides a more convincing explanation because of even greater inequality in the power relationship and because the degree of legal oppression was so different in scale and scope. I owe this point to David K. Smith.

36 The royal edict is reprinted in François-André Isambert, Alphonse-Honoré Taillandier, and Decrusy (eds.), *Recueil général des anciennes lois françaises, depuis l'an 420 jusqu'à la révolution de 1789* (Berlin-Le-Prieur, 1821–1833), XIV: 540–41.

37 For a survey of contemporary views, see Scoville, *The Persecution of the Huguenots*, 12–21.

The nature of this de facto privilege of liberty shifted in the 1740s as local administrators began to allow Huguenots to profess their faith openly. In light of the central state's close oversight of provincial officials and the multiple sources of information flowing into policymakers' hands, the right hand surely knew what the left hand was doing. Perhaps it is difficult to conceive of living a lie as a privilege, de facto or otherwise. But in the confessional context of early modern Europe, the state's tacit policy of allowing those lies to stand was of great significance and went beyond a mere practical accommodation. Toleration and the ability to earn a livelihood were privileges of liberty in the sense of liberty from oppression so fundamental to the *Declaration of the Rights of Man and Citizen*.[38]

The Van Robais family received a variety of encouragements over the course of a century. This manufacturing dynasty's relationship to the government demonstrates not only the vast array of possible privileges at the state's disposal but also how an entrepreneur's Protestantism was systematically ignored. In the 1660s, Colbert attempted to improve the quality of French manufactures, especially woolens, by bringing in a number of foreigners with needed skills and technical knowledge. Among these emigrants was Josse Van Robais, a Calvinist draper from Middelbourg in the Netherlands. He, along with his wife, several members of his family, forty workmen, with "a load of machines, presses and tools" to make fine woolens in the "Dutch style," set up shop outside Abbeville in Picardy.

Van Robais received a stupendous level of state support including many privileges. Letters-patent of 1665 included exemption from all local and municipal taxes as well as the quartering of troops, a gratification of 12,000 *livres*, and an interest-free loan of 80,000 *livres* (never fully repaid) to establish a mill which became a "royal manufacture." His privilege included exemption from customs duties

[38] For the eleven previous paragraphs, I rely on Jeffrey Merrick, "Conscience and Citizenship in Eighteenth-Century France," *Eighteenth-Century Studies*, 21: 1 (1987), 48–70, esp. 51, David Kammerling Smith, "The Nîmes Hosiery Guild and the Statutes Controversy of 1706–1712," *French Historical Studies*, 22: 4 (1999), 493–533, Michael Sonenscher, "The Hosiery Industry of Nîmes and the Lower Languedoc in the Eighteenth Century," *Textile History*, 10 (1979), 142–60, 142, 154, Roland E. Mousnier, *The Institutions of France under the Absolute Monarchy 1598–1789: Society and the State*, trans. Brian Pearce (University of Chicago Press, 1979 [1974]), 383–412, Arno J. Mayer, "The Perils of Emancipation: Protestants and Jews," *Archives des sciences sociales des religions*, 90 (1995), 5–37, and Raymond Birn, "Religious Toleration and Freedom of Expression," in Dale Van Kley (ed.), *The French Idea of Freedom: The Old Regime and the Declaration of Rights of 1789* (Stanford University Press, 1994), 265–99 esp. 282–98. John Bosher believes that the oppression of Protestants began to lessen in the mid-1720s, at least in La Rochelle: *The Canada Merchants*, 134.

on the import of Spanish merino wool and on the export of finished goods. For twenty years, Van Robais had carte blanche to ignore guild rules and requirements: Josse could organize production as he wished. Van Robais' monopoly encompassed the city of Abbeville and ten leagues in every direction. Inside this territory, he had the exclusive right to make fine woolens. His privilege specified that "no one can use a large spinning wheel or card either wool or cotton either for warp or weft without having first obtained Van Robais' permission."

Van Robais, his family, and his workers were authorized "to continue to profess the so-called reform religion, which is tolerated in our kingdom."[39] Colbert told the bishop of Amiens to "moderate the zeal of a monk who pressed the Van Robais to convert" hoping that "if they are content and satisfied with their treatment, they will attract other manufacturers to the realm."[40] The firm's workers also got seemingly trivial but welcome exemptions like tax-free salt and the right to brew their own beer. Furthermore, Colbert defended Van Robais from attempts to restrict these privileges by diverse Abbeville guilds ranging from woolen drapers to brewers.

Van Robais' privileges were renewed and extended in 1681 because the enterprise far exceeded expectations. Instead of the required thirty looms, Van Robais operated sixty-five. The firm employed 1,500–1,600 workers, half in several mills and half female domestic spinners. Their products set the benchmark for French woolens. Most Van Robais woolens were exported to Spain and its colonies, but they also found ready markets in France.

The revocation of the edict of Nantes did not undercut Van Robais' family privilege even after the death of the firm's founder later that year. Two sons, Isaac and Josse, took over the firm and when Josse junior died in 1733, his nephews seized the reins. In 1686, the royal council specifically ordered missionaries not to trouble either the family or Van Robais' workers. Minister of war François-Michel Le Tellier, marquis of Louvois, withdrew soldiers who had been quartered in the fulling mill. He even commanded them to return money or goods they had requisitioned. This protection was broadened in 1698. Van Robais received new and even more extensive privileges in exchange for keeping first 80, then 90, and finally 110 looms in operation. Eventually the firm employed between 2,500 and 3,000 workers. Between 1740 and 1745, Van

[39] The quotes in the three previous paragraphs about 1665 are from *Lettres-patentes du Roi qui continuent pendant vingt années, à commencer du premier Octobre 1725, le Privilège accordé aux Sieurs Vanrobais, de la Manufacture des Draps et autres Étoffes, établie à Abbeville*, September 11, 1724 (Gallica).

[40] Cited by Clément (ed.), *Lettres, instructions et mémoires de Colbert*, VI: 97, n. 1.

Robais family's average annual production was 1,272 bolts of fine woolens worth 636,000 *livres*.

Protected by privilege, Van Robais family focused on producing high-quality woolens. Early in the eighteenth century, the Van Robais family constructed a large mill of 1,000 square meters where nearly every aspect of production (except fulling and spinning) was centralized "under the same key." From father to son to nephews, the Van Robais family was famed for keeping close control of the production process to ensure the manufacture of superior goods. The deputies of commerce reported that there was "no faulty work or insubordination by their workers in Abbeville who are controlled by severe regulations."[41] These workers were not well paid, but they kept their jobs during industrial downturns when most employers furloughed their employees. Despite the deputies of commerce's rising distaste for exclusive privileges, the Van Robais family's were renewed in 1724, 1769, and partially in 1784. No mention was made of their faith, only their industrial and entrepreneurial successes. A number of Van Robais family's Calvinist foremen or their children, including Daniel Scalogne, set up their own enterprises. It was at Scalogne's mill that Englishman John Kay naturalized the flying shuttle in 1747. The "emulation" that Colbert hoped for when Josse Van Robais received his initial privilege seems to have occurred.

How was this success possible? Josse Van Robais enjoyed both royal favor and detailed letters-patent guaranteeing freedom of worship. The family's privileges infringed on those of Abbeville's guilds and flouted various measures taken against Protestants. That these privileges were continued and even extended after 1685 despite the family's open observance of Calvinism is striking. Colbert's shift toward seeking to convert the family shows that the faith of the Van Robais family concerned the highest levels of policymakers.

The state's extraordinary provision of privilege applied equally to the associates and children of the initial group of emigrants. The government decreed that Josse Van Robais, Jr., and the rest of the family along with "all their associates and foreign workers employed in their manufacture will be counted and reputed naturalized Frenchmen" in 1724, the same year that Louis XV confirmed the edict of Fontainbleau.[42] Throughout the eighteenth century, the family supported a resident Calvinist pastor who baptized each

[41] *Avis des Députés du Commerce sur la demande en continuation de privilege des Sieurs Vanrobais d'Abbeville*, March 7, 1766, AN F12 714.

[42] *Lettres-patentes du Roi*, September 11, 1724.

succeeding generation. Yet, French administrators not only overlooked the faith of the Van Robais family and many of their key workers, but they also naturalized them and provided new privileges that surpassed those granted before the revocation of the edict of Nantes.

Protestants frequently received letters of naturalization, according to historian Peter Sahlins. But here no overworked secretary filled out routine paperwork. Louis Phélypeaux, count de Pontchartrain and secretary of state for the royal household, personally signed the letters-patent. The document was then registered by the *parlement* of Paris, the court of auditors (*chambre des comptes*), and the tax appeal court (*cour des aides*). Sahlins quotes the royal solicitor of the court of auditors, Jean-Jacques-Auguste Lefebvre de la Planche: "letters of naturalization are accorded to all foreigners who come to France with the desire to establish themselves here, provided they practice Catholicism."[43] There can be no doubt that the state knew of the family's Calvinism. The firm's and thus the family's usefulness to the economy furnish the only viable explanation for the inconsistency. In 1766, the deputies of commerce summed up their endorsement of the Van Robais family's request to maintain the firm's privileges: "their manufacture is the only one that today, as in 1665, provides an example of superior fabrication." The Van Robais family took advantage of their privileges to furnish "a model that other manufacturers ought to emulate."[44] Seemingly, this example merited an exception to the laws excluding Protestants from production. In the case of the Van Robais family firm, Bourbon administrators clearly favored *raison d'économie* over their religious convictions.[45]

The Van Robais family demonstrates that the privilege of production enjoyed by "useful" Protestants began under Louis XIV and continued until the eve of the French Revolution. This tale of continuity must be balanced by the changes that took place after 1740 when the treatment

[43] Peter Sahlins, *Unnaturally French: Foreign Citizens: Foreign Citizens in the Old Regime and After* (Ithaca, NY: Cornell University Press, 2004), 83–84.

[44] *Avis des Députés du Commerce*, March 7, 1766.

[45] The previous nine paragraphs are based on Jean-Michel Chaplain, "Avoir ce qui manque aux autres: la manufacture de draps fins Van Robais, d'Abbeville au XVIIIe siècle face au milieu local," *Le Mouvement social*, 125 (1983), 13–24, 14, Jules Mathorez, *Les Étrangers en France sous l'Ancien Régime*, 2 vols. (Champion, 1921), II: 266–69, Scoville, *The Persecution of Huguenots*, 227–28, Georges Ruhlmann, *Les corporations, les manufactures et le travail libre à Abbeville au XVIIIe siècle* (Sirey, 1948), 74–79, and Fernand Braudel, *Civilization and Capitalism 15th–18th Century*, vol. 2, *The Wheels of Commerce*, trans. Siân Reynolds (Berkeley: University of California Press, 1992 [1982, 1979]), 335, 338.

of Protestants began to shift. If Van Robais exemplified the liberty of privilege, Christophe-Philippe Oberkampf exhibited the possibilities of the privilege of liberty.

Oberkampf (1738–1815) was born to a long line of dyers in Wiesenbach, in the German-speaking marquisat of Anspach. He learned the trade from his father, who set up a printed cotton or calico (*indiennes*) mill in Aarau, Switzerland. At eighteen, Oberkampf worked briefly as an engraver for the famous Koechlin and Dolfuss printing works in Mulhouse. He was recruited by French entrepreneurs seeking to take advantage of the accelerating cotton craze and moved to Paris in 1758. His Lutheran faith seems to have been of small concern. In Paris, Oberkampf worked for a guild master who made cotton cloth in the Arsenal. His skill earned him high wages, allowing him to rapidly save 600 *livres*. Along with several partners, including his younger brother Étienne-Fréderic, Oberkampf began making his own printed cottons in a house in Jouy-en-Josas near Versailles beginning in 1760. He had technical help and design assistance from relations in Switzerland. From the outset, the various iterations of the firm flourished. Oberkampf made 3,600 bolts of printed cotton cloth in 1761. Production swiftly rose to more than 81,000 bolts in 1779 and 164,000 in 1805 (See Chapter 8). Early on, he brought an engraver and two printers from Switzerland (also Protestant), who became long-time collaborators in the rapidly expanding enterprise.

Profits were stupendous. In the first year, the firm earned 36,000 *livres* in net profits (10 *livres* per bolt), of which half went to the Oberkampf brothers. Hard work, perseverance, and skill led to success, but Christophe-Philippe did not rest on his laurels. He developed two important technical breakthroughs: copper-roller printing for multiple colors on cotton and the first machine to print wallpaper. Another mill at Corbeil run by Étienne-Fréderic made a variety of cotton fabrics to supply the printing mill. Jouy's products found favor with customers ranging from the royal family to well-to-do artisans and shopkeepers. During the Revolution, 2,000 workers labored for Oberkampf. He became mayor of Jouy in 1790 and kept the firm thriving. After winning a gold medal at the 1806 industrial exposition, Napoleon inducted him into the legion of honor. Jouy closed during the occupation of 1814–1815. His son Émile reopened the mill after the founder's death but sold it in 1822.

Oberkampf's success was based on the state's policy shift from deploying the liberty of privilege to the privilege of liberty. From 1686 to 1759, it was "illegal to import, manufacture, sell or wear … printed cottons from the Indies or to imitate them within the realm."[46] The vogue for this fabric led to extensive smuggling and widespread illicit sales. Clandestine supply of printed cottons bled France of specie and cost jobs. At the request of several intendants and entrepreneurs, the bureau of commerce punched a number of spatial loopholes in the thick legal belt (two edicts and eighty rulings of the royal council between 1686 and 1748) prohibiting printed cottons. Spaces exempted from the prohibition included Paris' Arsenal, where Oberkampf was first employed. A national debate about the prohibition on printed cottons initiated by the circle of Jacques-Claude Vincent de Gournay with the Physiocrats' aid led to greater provision of the privilege of liberty, ostensibly to cut down on smuggling and to encourage import substitution. In September 1759, the royal council tentatively lifted the prohibition on manufacturing printed cottons and imposed taxes of 10–15 percent on foreign-made printed cottons. Thus protected and encouraged, policymakers hoped that French manufacturers would create new enterprises to satisfy demand. The measure was confirmed by edict in November.

Because the expertise for making printed cottons did not exist in France, experienced foreigners were recruited to fill the gap. Serge Chassagne counted 1,600 foreign workers who came to France in the century after 1760 to work in the printed cotton industry. Most of these "experts" were either Swiss or had worked there or in Mulhouse. The first group of skilled workers took advantage of their networks in Switzerland and the German lands to bring in yet more laborers with essential technical knowledge. Almost everyone involved in this step migration was Protestant. The Seven Years' War seems to have had little effect on the ability of these skilled workers to come and go. Pent-up demand ensured sales and allowed capable entrepreneurs to earn exceptionally high profits. This privilege of liberty afforded sufficient opportunity for the hardworking, innovative Oberkampf to succeed.

Success led to new privileges. The brothers Oberkampf received naturalization letters in August 1770. No mention was made of their faith. Solicitor Jean-Baptiste Denisart claimed that "foreigners who request these letters are never refused."[47] Peter Sahlins confirms this assertion for the era from 1661 to 1789. By the twilight of Louis XV's reign, naturalization ignored the injunction against non-Roman Catholics. The mill at Jouy became a royal manufacture in 1783. Four years later, Oberkampf was awarded the sine qua non of privilege,

[46] *Arrêt du Conseil d'État du Roi, et Lettres Patentes sur icelui, Registrées en Parlement concernant les Toiles de coton blanches et les Toiles peintes, teintes et imprimées*, September 5, 1759 (Gallica).

[47] Cited by Sahlins, *Unnaturally French*, 72.

a patent of nobility, nine months *before* the promulgation of the Edict of Toleration.

As with the Van Robais family, Oberkampf's Protestantism was no secret. Oberkampf wrote that "The enemies of the mill roused the parish priest against it. He said nothing until its third year of existence. The priest said that I was a bad example in the region because I do not go to mass and neither do my workers. Twice, the archbishop demanded that I do so."[48] Oberkampf became a well-known member of Paris' Protestant community. Both his wives were from prominent Protestant families and they were married in the Swedish and Dutch embassies, respectively. In fact, Oberkampf's second marriage (in 1785) was authorized explicitly by a brevet from Louis XVI. All of Oberkampf's six children were baptized openly as Protestants. Oberkampf reached the pinnacle of French society despite the legal prohibition on Protestant nobles contained in the edict of Fontainbleau.

The privilege of liberty conveyed by the edict of 1759 on printed cottons enabled this exceptionally capable Protestant to become one of the most famous entrepreneurs in France. The government certainly knew that he was a Lutheran and that he did not live in Alsace or another privileged territory. Yet, Oberkampf received letters of naturalization and then a patent of nobility. Neither legal injunctions nor Roman Catholicism was permitted to get in the way of industrial development. Royal administrators allowed Christophe-Philippe Oberkampf to ignore the rules: his de facto privilege symbolizes the early modern French state's mounting commitment to economic matters.[49]

[48] Alfred Labouchère, *Oberkampf (1738–1815)*, 3rd ed. (Hachette, 1878), 37.

[49] The seven previous paragraphs are based on Serge Chassagne, *Oberkampf: Un entrepreneur capitaliste au Siècle des Lumières* (Aubier, 1980), 9–150, 340–41, 9, Sahlins, *Unnaturally French*, 66–69, Serge Chassagne, "La mobilité des ouvriers qualifiés de l'indiennage (1760–1860)," in Gérard Gayot and Philippe Minard (eds.), *Les ouvriers qualifiés de l'industrie (XVIe-XXe siècle. Formation, emploi, migrations: Actes du colloque de Roubaix, 20–22 1997* (Presses de l'Université Charles-de-Gaulle-Lille 3, 2001), 65–81, Eugène Haag and Émile Haag, *La France protestante; ou, Vies des protestants français qui se sont fait un nom dans l'histoire depuis les premiers temps de la réformation jusqu'à la reconnaissance du principe de la liberté des cultes par l'Assemblée nationale; ouvrage précéde d'une notice historique sur le protestantisme en France, suivi de pièces justificatives, et rédigé sur des documents en grand partie inédits*, 10 vols. (J. Cherbuliez, 1846–1859), VII: 27–29, and Labouchère, *Oberkampf*, 3–73. See also Alain Dewerpe and Yves Gaulupeau, *La fabrique des prolétaires: Les ouvriers de la manufacture d'Oberkampf à Jouy-en-Josas 1760–1815* (Presses de l'École normale supérieure, 1990). Sahlins notes that the clause of Catholicity was left off the patents given to the marshal de Berwick and his family in 1703 and John Law in 1716 because their services were so great that they "effaced the stain of heresy" but that many Protestants were refused. Peter Sahlins, "Fictions of a Catholic France: The Naturalization of Foreigners, 1685–1787," *Representations*, 47 (1994), 85–110, 94.

Outsiders on the inside: the privileges of foreign residents

The privileges given to foreign residents were essential to other outsiders' ability to live, trade, and manufacture in France. Throughout the early modern era, royal administrators understood that privileging foreigners was its most effective and, in many cases, sole means of transplanting new technologies or techniques. Some workers, entrepreneurs, and inventors who received privileges became naturalized, but most did not. Protected by privilege, these foreign residents had no urgent need to become French. The provision of privilege to foreign residents was a vital part of French industrial policy.

When Louis XIV came to the throne, foreign residents enjoyed most of the same economic rights as Frenchmen. The chief exceptions were that foreigners could not join guilds and required the king's permission to hold office. The royal right of escheat (*droit d'aubaine*) confiscated all property from foreigners who did not have French-born heirs. This death tax strongly encouraged foreigners to limit their term of residence and investments.[50] Foreign residents were also subject to special duties levied in 1639, 1646, 1657, and 1697. A sort of forced loan was imposed on wealthy foreign residents in 1709. Based on this right of escheat, a naturalization law promulgated in 1697 revoked every grant made since 1600, while imposing new taxes on immigrants and their descendants. Foreign residents, who had taken advantage of specific territorial privileges such as those of the free ports of Marseille and Dunkerque (see Chapter 5), were taxed. In 1703, the royal council confirmed the commercial privileges of Marseille's foreign residents to stop the hemorrhage of talented and wealthy entrepreneurs.

By granting privileges to individuals and small groups of foreign residents, the French state circumvented discriminatory legal limitations. Colbert employed this policy instrument widely. As we saw in Chapter 5, a Parisian merchant, Guillaume de Varennes, brought Dutch workers to Carcassonne in 1665 to improve technique in Languedoc's woolens industry. These workers were essential to Saptes' designation as a royal manufacture in 1666. Experienced workers taught new techniques, brought fresh skills, and stimulated best-practice manufacturing through "emulation." A second category of privileged residents

[50] Royal officials frequently granted exemptions to the *aubaine*. Included in the exemptions were merchants in Bordeaux, artisans at the Gobelins and Beauvais tapestry works, foreign ambassadors, and mercenary troops like the Swiss Guards. Michael Rapport, *Nationality and Citizenship in Revolutionary France: The Treatment of Foreigners 1789–1799* (Clarendon Press, 2000), 35.

included Josse Van Robais, who was recruited to establish a model enterprise. Although the Van Robais family was discussed in the context of Protestantism, their experience is equally revealing with regard to the state's efforts to foster entrepreneurialism by privileging exemplary foreigners. Inventors comprised a third category. To receive privileges, however, inventors had to satisfy the kingdom's economic needs. Privileged inventors were pushed to create enterprises that either directly supported French producers – as with machine-builders and dyers – or made innovative goods such as hardware and cotton textiles. In manufacturing, French policymakers considered such provisions of privilege to be so successful and so necessary to economic development that this ad hoc tactic was expanded into a more general policy.

In preparation for the Anglo-French commercial treaty, the royal council issued letters-patent in January 1786 "to favor the establishment of foreign manufacturers." Entrepreneurs in "muslins of all types, white linen, printed and cotton fabrics, leather, woolens, and every kind of hardware" gained tax-exemption to import all "necessary raw materials ... machines, and tools." They, along with any "foreign workers brought by them," were relieved of royal taxes for three years. Nor did these foreign manufacturers have to perform personal services like militia duty or pay guild reception fees. They and their children were "freed from the right of escheat and have the ability to acquire and sell inheritances and all other property."[51] The only significant restriction on enterprises created under this new policy was that, to enjoy these privileges of liberty, the manufacture had to be situated at least seven leagues from the border. Although this measure was not a generalized privilege for foreign manufacturers, it represented a significant widening of the opportunities available to them. By allowing outsiders to function as insiders, the 1786 letters-patent represented the next step in a long trend in French industrial policy.[52]

The exact number of foreign workers and entrepreneurs who resided in early modern France will never be known. John Harris believed that about

[51] Isambert, Taillandier, and Decrusy (eds.), *Recueil général des anciennes lois françaises*, XXVIII: 138–39.

[52] The four previous paragraphs are based on Sahlins, *Unnaturally French*, 5–6, 38–42, *Arrêt du Conseil d'État du Roy qui ordonne que les Habitans de la ville de Marseille, et les Marchands et Négocians, tant Sujets de Sa Majesté qu'étrangers, et autres Personnes de toutes Nations et qualités, jouiront dans l'étendue de la Ville, Port et Territoire de Marseille, des Exemptions, Privileges et Franchises accordées en faveur du Commerce et portées par l'Edit du mois de mars 1669*, July 10, 1703, AN AE BIII192. On the commercial treaty, see Jeff Horn, *The Path Not Taken: French Industrialization in the Age of Revolution 1760–1830* (Cambridge, MA: MIT Press, 2006), 51–88. The 1697 law is reprinted in Isambert, Taillandier, and Decrusy (eds.), *Recueil général des anciennes lois françaises*, X: 296–301.

1,000 English came between 1715 and 1800, but the correct figure is at least twice as high. English, Irish, and Scots colonies existed in several places. Brittany's ports and Normandy, especially in and around Rouen, Le Havre, Honfleur, and Dieppe, had large expatriate communities. Other communities existed in Paris, Sens, Amiens, Dunkerque, Saint-Étienne and Saint-Chamond, Marseille, La Rochelle, and Bayonne, with the largest group inhabiting Bordeaux. But the British Isles did not furnish the largest cadres of foreign workers. Far from it. Swiss textile printers, ribbon makers, and merchants were numerous in northeastern France, in the Forez, and in the Rhône valley. Coal miners, arms and other metal workers, along with seasonal laborers from what became Belgium were common in the Forez and along the northern frontier from Flanders to Champagne. "Italians" were found in Lyon, all over Dauphiné, and across the Mediterranean littoral, while many Spaniards crossed the Pyrénées. Up to 40,000 Savoyards did France's dirty work, especially in Paris and Lyon. Dutch merchants and workers in paper and woolens such as the Van Robais family were plentiful in several spots across the Midi and in ports from Marseille to Dunkerque as well as in Picardy. "Germans" like the Oberkampfs provided essential expertise in mining, metallurgy, and textile production in many places, especially in eastern France. Hambourgeois and other Hansa merchants were found in all the Atlantic ports, most commonly at Bordeaux, Le Havre, and Dunkerque. Smaller or more temporary groups from other parts of Europe and the Mediterranean such as the Armenians of Marseille could also be itemized. John Holker's appointment as "general inspector of manufacturing principally of those imitating foreigners or with foreign workers" in 1755 along with a letter of naturalization the following year shows the clear direction of administrative thinking. The negotiation of 34 treaties and edicts eliminating or limiting the right of escheat for various groups between 1774 and 1789 was considered as a means of encouraging economic growth much like abolishing tolls on waterways. While foreign residents were quite rare in large swaths of the country, especially in agricultural areas, they were rather common in regions linked to broader currents of production and exchange. The privileged participation of foreign residents demonstrated France's growing economic cosmopolitanism.

Liberties of privilege, both de facto and de jure, encouraged both male and female foreign workers to come to France. Most foreign residents had state-granted privileges conveying basic economic rights. In many cases, the government sidestepped enforcement of religious restrictions. In the second half of the eighteenth century, dozens of English, Irish, Belgian, and Swiss women were recruited to teach French women superior spinning techniques such as proper use of the reel or how to handle a large spinning wheel to make finer cotton thread. Manchester spinning mistresses surnamed Law and Heyes were recruited by Holker in 1756 to go from region to region and enterprise to enterprise at state expense. Law married a Frenchman and trained girls at the royal manufacture at Sens for almost thirty years, while Heyes travelled the highways and byways of Dauphiné and Languedoc. Other women were brought to France to assist at a particular mill and yet more came to work at charity "spinning schools" for girls sponsored by reform-minded nobles like François-Alexandre-Frédéric de La Rochefoucauld, duke of La Rochefoucauld-Liancourt. A succession of intendants of Burgundy dedicated to improving spinning technique in the Beaujolais employed roving foreign spinning instructors. The central government subsidized these efforts heavily, even providing pensions for some women. In 1788, the encouragement bureau of Upper Normandy established three prizes for female spinners who produced the finest, the most uniform, and the greatest quantity of linen thread in a ten-hour day. The prizes were almost always awarded to women and girls who used "English" methods. Female foreign workers clearly had skills to teach their French sisters; liberties of privilege recruited these women in particular and foreign workers more generally.

Workers with rarer talents received greater privileges, but such skilled workers were usually recruited by their employers. We have seen that Dutch workers at the Van Robais family's mill were given privileges equivalent to those granted to the founding entrepreneur and his family. These privileges ranged from tax and service exemptions to protection from guild interference and from naturalization to the ability to brew their own beer. Skill earned foreign workers, often Protestant, significant access to privilege, but their rights were linked to the site of production instead of being attached to individuals.

Inventors or entrepreneurs seeking privilege to facilitate technology transfer had to be able to run their own businesses. At the request of Daniel-Charles de Trudaine, the intendant of Rouen submitted a project to improve French dyeing methods in December 1762. Holker recruited James Morris and James Hope, his relatives from Lancashire, who claimed to have "the secret ... of heating cotton cloth or fabrics of different kinds of thread in vats to fix the blue dye better and more cheaply than any French dyer. Their secret seems an attractive investment as a means of obtaining commercial preference by diminishing labor costs without altering the quality of the merchandise"

(See Chapter 3). High demand for blue cotton cloth to supply the African slave trade encouraged the royal council to offer considerable privileges to Morris and Hope. They were authorized to set up a dyeworks in or near Rouen despite "all the contrary privileges." The royal council "prohibited anyone from troubling their dyeworks and also prohibited the wardens of the dyers guild from inspecting them under any pretext." Morris and Hope's children would be naturalized if they remained in the country. The entrepreneurs and three of their workers, "French or foreign," were exempted from militia service.[53] Thanks to Holker, the dyeworks was established in Saint-Sever. In 1788, the firm remained under Hope's direction and had eighteen employees. Chemist Claude-Louis Berthollet along with several shippers involved in the Africa trade vouched for the quality of his dyeing, but noted that his cost advantage disappeared as other dyers in and around Rouen adopted the same process. Despite the impressive but not unusual degree of nepotism at work and the firm's uneven profitability, royal officials' provision of privileges of liberty enabled foreign entrepreneurs to spread best practice in France's most important textile center.[54]

The Bourbon state made thorough use of privilege to increase the supply of entrepreneurs, often by ignoring its own laws. By granting privileges to Jews, Protestants, and foreign residents, royal administrators facilitated French access to networks of much needed credit, commercial exchange, and technical knowledge that crisscrossed Europe, the Mediterranean basin, and the Atlantic world. Although limited, privileges of residence, trade, and production granted to entrepreneurial outsiders benefited the French economy.

Privileges granted to Jews, Protestants, and foreign residents encroached on long-standing privileges held by, among others, the *corporations*. Many privileges also infringed on the Roman Catholic monopoly of production

[53] *Arrêté du Conseil d'état du Roi*, December 18, 1762, AN F12 1341A.

[54] The four previous paragraphs are based on John R. Harris, *Industrial Espionage and Technology Transfer: Britain and France in the Eighteenth Century* (Aldershot, UK: Ashgate, 1998), 69–72, 107–08, 552, Serge Chassagne, *Le coton et ses patrons: France, 1760–1840* (Éditions de l'École des Hautes Études en Sciences Sociales, 1991), 71–72, André Rémond, *John Holker: Manufacturier et grand fonctionnaire en France au XVIIIe siècle 1719–1786* (Marcel Rivière, 1946), 92, Rapport, *Nationality and Citizenship*, 36, 79–80, duc de Liancourt, *Mémoire*, January 13, 1784, AN F12 1339, John Holker, *Lettre à Pottier*, August 3, 1762, AN F12 1365, *Journal de Guienne*, 193 (July 11, 1788), 773, Jeannette Law, *Mémoire à Joly de Fleury, Directeur général des finances*, December 13, 1782 and Guillaume Hall, *Lettre à M. de Montaran*, January 4, 1783, both in AN F12 1340, *Arrêté du Conseil d'état du Roi*, December 18, 1762, and Claude-Louis Berthollet, *Rapport sur un mémoire de M. Hope rélativement aux teintures de coton en bleu*, September 5, 1788, AN F12 1341A.

established by Louis XIV. The ability of the Gradis and Van Robais families to join France's economic elite indicates the opportunities available to successful entrepreneurs. Without privileges, "Portuguese merchants," "new Christians," and "foreign manufacturers" could not live and work in France. But privilege alone does not explain the success of exemplary individuals like Herz Cerf-Berr or Christophe-Philippe Oberkampf. Although privileged, Jews, Protestants, and foreign residents were outsiders who relied on entrepreneurialism to overcome discriminatory laws, rules, and regulations. The state's perception of the value of the contributions made by Jews, Protestants, and foreign residents is revealed by the steady increase in the privileges of liberty granted to these groups in the last decades of the old régime. The Enlightenment certainly played a role in this policy development, but the flow of readily apparent economic benefits was essential. Where such benefits were not as evident, as with the Society of the Friends of the Blacks' efforts to end the slave trade, improvers were stymied. In contrast, the Jews of Alsace received extensive privileges of liberty in 1784, the state welcomed numbers of foreign manufacturers in 1785, and the Edict of Toleration for Protestants was promulgated in 1787. These measures were consistent with the evolution of policy since the age of Louis XIV.

Privileges extended to "outsiders" were both formal and informal in nature. The privilege of liberty added 40,000 Jews, hundreds of thousands of Protestants, and tens of thousands of foreign residents to France's population. More importantly, these populations had to rely on entrepreneurialism because of the strictures of a Roman Catholic society of orders. Barred from agricultural pursuits in most of the realm, Jews, Protestants, and foreign residents turned to commerce and finance along with industry (in some places) to earn a living and merit the continuation of their privileges. In terms of total output, state provision of privileges to Jews, Protestants, and foreign residents was more significant than the privileges granted to royal manufactures, inventors, and for mining to be discussed in the next chapter. Political marginalization was quite separate from economic exclusion: the law cut both ways. Privileges granted by the early modern state bypassed or compromised religious and political measures constraining or oppressing Jews, Protestants, and foreign residents.

State provision of privileges to legally excluded groups began long before Louis XIV came to the throne. The practice survived, albeit in drastically different forms, that monarch's efforts to create a polity marked by "one law, one faith, one king." Louis XV reaffirmed his great-grandfather's religious and political commitments, but, in practice, the same intellectual currents that enabled improvers to rise to positions of power around 1750 led to shifts in the attitudes of many royal officials. Increasingly, administrators went beyond mere tacit acceptance of the privileged yet inferior positions of Jews, Protestants, and foreigners to cautiously extend more formalized legal recognitions. This trend culminated in the 1787 Edict of Toleration and the extension of citizenship to Protestants and Jews in 1789–1791 (see Chapter 8).

Through the prism of privilege, Bourbon policymaking revealed its true colors. By maintaining and even extending privileges to legally proscribed Protestants and "outsiders" like Jews and foreigners, the French state demonstrated its commitment to supporting the economy at all costs, even at the expense of its religious and political principles. Official dedication to economic matters has been conspicuously absent from the literature on early modern France. At the same time, the willingness of many decision makers to make outsiders into insiders when they made useful economic contributions exhibits the flexibility and pervasiveness of privilege as an instrument of policy. Royal officials effectively used privilege to recruit and integrate additional groups of entrepreneurs and workers. Over the long term, this tactic stimulated the French economy and made it more internationally competitive. This is not to say that Bourbon France did not seriously discriminate against Jews, Protestants, and foreigners. It did. Nor am I arguing that this discrimination did not have serious, sometimes devastating economic consequences. But this chapter uncovers how the state deployed both the privilege of liberty and the liberty of privilege to limit that intolerance for the greater economic good. With regard to Jews, Protestants, and foreign residents, *raison d'économie* became synonymous with *raison d'état*. As a frame of analysis, privilege underscores how fundamental the economy was to French administrative action from Louis XIV to Louis XVI.

7 Privilege, innovation, and the state

Entrepreneurialism and the lessons of the old régime

> That France could prosper and grow rich, given the inequality of taxation, the vagaries of local laws, internal customs barriers, feudal rights, the trade corporations, the sales of offices, and all the rest, may well seem hardly credible. Yet the fact remains that the country did grow richer and living conditions improved throughout the land, and the reason was that though the machinery of government was ramshackle, ill regulated, inefficient, and though it tended to hinder rather than to further social progress, it had two redeeming features which sufficed to make it function and made for national prosperity. Firstly, though the government was no longer despotic, it still was powerful and capable of maintaining order everywhere; and secondly, the nation possessed an upper class that was the freest, most enlightened of the day and a social system under which every man could get rich if he set his mind to it and keep intact the wealth he had acquired.
>
> The American war did not check this upward movement; though the State fell yet more heavily into debt, private persons went on making fortunes; also they worked harder than in the past, showed more initiative and resourcefulness.
>
> Alexis de Tocqueville, *The Old Régime and the French Revolution* (1856)[1]

Privilege was not a panacea. From the days of Jean-Baptiste Colbert, officials recognized privilege's liabilities as well as its potential. Eighteenth-century Bourbon administrators relied on policies based on privilege even though many Enlightened "economists" believed – or wanted to believe – that its economic effectiveness was on the wane. Privilege nurtured many industrial triumphs, but those achievements did not fully realize the state's increasingly lofty developmental goals. Liberty was increasingly identified as the objective of policymaking but proved extraordinarily difficult to put into practice. Avoiding the web of overlapping and conflicting privileges embodied in the society of orders was complicated by the *parlements*' steadfast defense of privilege as intrinsic to

[1] Alexis de Tocqueville, *The Old Régime and the French Revolution*, trans. Stuart Gilbert (Garden City, NY: Random House, 1955 [1856]), 173–74.

the French constitution. Ongoing conflicts with the judges severely limited policymakers' ability to turn their aspirations into realities.

Despite a growing though abstract desire to apply liberty to production, in practice, privilege remained the lifeblood of almost all economic policy. Privilege retained pride of place even after "improvers" rose to positions of power around 1750. The persistent clamor for "unrestrained liberty" articulated by Enlightened officials should be regarded mainly as a rhetorical strategy intended to justify minimizing liberties of privilege in favor of privileges of liberty. In the 1770s, however, more fundamental reforms were executed. The few exceptions to this policy trajectory involved commercial rather than industrial liberty. Liberty unconstrained by privilege was a chimera that led Bourbon policymakers to embrace the privilege of liberty as a necessary step toward a more competitive, more efficient economy.

Royal administrators did not shape policy in a vacuum. Decision makers' knowledge and understanding of broader macroeconomic trends was, however, profoundly limited. Economic decisions were constrained by the quality and quantity of available information. Although the Bourbon government had a web of officials and other informants that crisscrossed the realm, incoming data varied enormously in accuracy, depth, and relevance to the economic issues at hand. The state relied on local informants to report grain prices and food shortages. The government also collected a great deal of information from customs levies and via inspection of manufactured goods. Non-serial data required even more explanation, interpretation, and assessment.

Political considerations aside, royal officials of elite background frequently asked the wrong questions about economic developments. Furthermore, mayors', subdelegates', and bailiffs' responses were often deeply flawed. Overreliance on one source, misunderstanding how to calculate profits, or failing to recognize the steep capital requirements involved in long-distance trade represent just a few of the problems that afflicted information flows. Although the Bourbon state employed various "experts" such as the inspectors of manufacturing, the applicability of their observations was limited by the complexities of French political economy and the fragmented nature of economic conditions and markets stemming from the welter of overlapping industrial and commercial regulations. In sum, early modern policymakers were swamped by an enormous amount of specific information that did not necessarily coalesce into an accurate picture of regional, much less national economic trends. Even the most professionalized royal officials relied on certain informants, paid closer attention to some places and economic activities, and had little more than an intuitive grasp of the flood of data that crossed their desks.[2]

A hazy sense of broader economic trends complicated the efforts of French officials to shift the policymaking balance toward liberty. In large measure, that meant moving the application of privilege from the particular to the general. Royal administrators developed procedures to select which individuals or firms to support with liberties of privilege and privileges of liberty. Their goal was to maximize returns on invested money, effort, protection, and the various exemptions and rights encompassed in privileges. In practice, these procedures were far from foolproof, but they did weed out many unlikely projects. We have already seen that geographical spaces received privileges based on unique resources, strategic location, or a record of previous industrial success. In the initial quote, Alexis de Tocqueville noted that France's expanding wealth relied on increasingly hardworking, creative, and resourceful entrepreneurs. The two-step problem facing eighteenth-century Bourbon policymakers was how to engage larger groups in industrial activities and how to ensure those efforts' competitiveness.

In a policymaking environment characterized by incomplete information, resolving that two-step problem focused on guilds. As one of the largest and broadly diffused sets of privilege-holders, *corporations* provoked considerable opposition. Although they produced most of France's industrial output, their contributions were undervalued, especially by Enlightened improvers who embraced the cause of liberty and had only a partial grasp on guilds' role in the economy. The massive, and frequently unsuccessful, administrative effort required to ensure that guild masters followed regulations, submitted to inspection, and took advantage of economic opportunities frustrated officials at every level of government.

In the *Encyclopédie*, Joachim Faiguet de Villeneuve emphasized the guilds' "degeneration" since Colbert's era. He called for drastic revision or elimination of "these institutions which are ruinous for the public" because "masterships are the result of arbitrary laws . . . favorable to some

[2] The archives reveal these limitations and constraints by comparing what was reported to the central state with the information gathered at the local levels. In large or densely populated generalities like Guyenne or Upper Normandy, subdelegates' reports vary enormously in quality and depth. The council of commerce struggled with uneven reliability of information. This data can be found in series C in the Seine-Maritime and Gironde's departmental archives and in series F12 in the Archives Nationales in Paris. A superb example of the variability of the data available to French policymakers based on the same set of questions is Christiane Demeulenaere-Douyère and David J. Sturdy (eds.), *L'Enquête du Régent 1716–1718: Sciences, Techniques et Politique dans la France pré-industrielle* (Turnhout, Belgium: Brepols, 2008).

and harmful to a great number." Instead, Faiguet de Villeneuve endorsed "the general liberty of commerce and the trades." "Protecting the economy" should be "the principal business of government." The "secret" was to ensure that "every man can work, manufacture, and sell." Such critiques were widely echoed and encouraged improvers to consider how productive liberties not only could but also should replace guild privileges. This consideration began early in the eighteenth century and picked up steam around 1750.[3]

Although a number of influential improvers endorsed economic liberty and sought a more *laissez-faire* state, we must not forget that most eighteenth-century government officials feared the consequences of unfettered economic liberty. Jean-Emmanuel de Guignard, viscount of Saint-Priest and intendant of Languedoc, wrote an aggressive report insisting on the need for liberty in both commerce and industry. Saint-Priest sought to undermine Marseille's monopoly in the Levant, while simultaneously unshackling Languedoc's woolens producers (see Chapter 5). The deputies of commerce responded in 1753:

> Monsieur de Saint-Priest, intendant of Languedoc . . . observes that there are two basic commercial principles. The government ought to protect and encourage commerce and ought to allow merchants the liberty to trade . . . But it is perhaps an abuse of the word "liberty" to give it too great an extent in its effects or to pretend that commerce should not submit to any impediments. There is an important distinction between commerce in general relative to the advantages that the state ought to collect and commerce by individuals from that state.[4]

Keeping such "important distinctions" in mind, for most of the eighteenth century, the deputies of commerce and like-minded bureaucrats recognized that in commerce and especially in industry, privileges of liberty were safer, more manageable, and ultimately more effective than an unrestrained "liberty."

Until mid-century, most of the "liberties" afforded to industrial producers were actually privileges of liberty because they were given to some and not to others. The success of printed calico production after 1758 encouraged policymakers to "think big." The 1762 measure liberating the rural population to produce textiles was, however, limited by privilege (see Chapters 3, 5, and 6). The state continued to police urban industry, and rural residents could only make textiles if they followed the regulations, not any goods they wished. As we shall see

[3] Joachim Faiguet de Villeneuve, "Maitrises," Denis Diderot and Jean Le Rond d'Alembert (eds.), *Encyclopédie ou Dictionnaire raisonné des sciences, des arts et des métiers, par une Société de Gens de lettres*, 28 vols. (1751–1772), IX: 911–15 (ARTFL).

[4] *Avis de Messieurs les Députés du commerce sur le commerce du Levant*, 1753, AN AE BIII191.

below, provision of these kinds of "liberties" became more common after 1775.

Improvers voiced growing dissatisfaction with liberties of privilege and the need for constant government intervention. The move toward privileges of liberty reflected Bourbon policymakers' shifting mindset. They searched for an alternative to the economy's dependence on state use of privilege to recruit and encourage entrepreneurs. Officials' preference for liberty expressed their rising confidence in French entrepreneurship.

This chapter traces three major themes. First, it investigates certain opportunities privilege afforded to entrepreneurial "insiders." Then, I explore how the Bourbon state abandoned much of the regulatory edifice governing French industry, long identified with Colbert, in favor of liberating entrepreneurialism from government control. Finally, this chapter considers what effect the changes – both philosophical and concrete – that occurred in the last fifteen years of the old régime had on the possibility of an industrial revolution in late eighteenth-century France.

In tracing these themes, this chapter underscores the changing relationship between the state and entrepreneurs. Thus far, I have emphasized the state's successful application of privilege, but failures and mediocre results are also essential parts of the puzzle. As officials learned from experience, the second half of the eighteenth century witnessed an important realignment in the balance between government regulation and entrepreneurialism. In previous chapters we established that it was the philosophical perspectives of key policymakers that changed after 1750. At the highest levels of the state, growing preference for liberty was inspired more by political and intellectual imperatives than economic realities. Decision makers expected to liberate entrepreneurs from state oversight, but difficulties in application usually led them to extend privileges of liberty rather than implement a more "liberal" political economy. This chapter examines how the royal administration loosened its regulatory yoke after 1775 and argues that this new direction marked a crucial turning point in the old régime's attitudes toward entrepreneurialism and the economic role of the state.

Investigating how guild authority was limited and access to the *corporate* system broadened after 1776 illuminates the difficulties involved in the practical application of this evolution of state policy. To foster competitiveness, officials unchained textile entrepreneurs, transforming the manufacture of textiles between 1779 and 1781. Inventors and royal manufactures continued to receive state support though not in the same manner as had been the case under the Colbertian paradigm. Decision makers increasingly sought to cut the cord by requiring recipients of government aid to become better entrepreneurs. But desiring liberty is not the same as being able to apply it. In the context of French economic policymaking, the privilege of liberty was a compromise between philosophical objectives and practical realities. After 1776 the rationale behind state action was more fluid than it had been in generations.

Insider privilege: royal manufactures, inventors, and mining

As a tool of economic development, privilege was awarded to groups and firms, both large and small, as well as to individuals. In the previous chapter, we explored how Jews, Protestants, and foreigners expanded France's precious stock of entrepreneurs, making important contributions to production and exchange, by taking advantage of de facto and de jure privileges. Individually and collectively, these groups benefited from different aspects of the privilege of liberty. At the same time, officials extended privileges to key individuals and sectors as well as to spaces with vital resources or in strategic locations. These privileges, and the policies that underlay them, represented a far better-known aspect of state-sponsored economic development. A host of merchants, manufacturers, and inventors directed their entrepreneurialism toward tapping into the wealth of privileges available from the state.

Recipients of liberties of privilege, however, rarely accomplished the state's broader economic goals even if they enriched or ennobled the entrepreneur. Relatively few innovative, profitable enterprises emerged, especially in sectors where French technology lagged behind its competitors, as in metallurgy or coal mining. This lack of success came despite the administration's best efforts and experts' increasing involvement in the decision-making process. Bourbon administrators' disappointment with the liberty of privilege motivated the post-1750 shift toward the privilege of liberty.

In previous chapters, the provision of privilege to manufacturers has been shown to emerge from a dialogue between potential entrepreneurs and state officials. Some enterprises received honorific privileges (that, of course, conferred certain economic and political advantages), such as being able to call a firm a "royal manufacture." Others collected exemptions from various taxes, duties, and rules. Enterprises perceived to offer the greatest economic or technological benefits or that were the shakiest obtained exclusive rights to make or market a specific product in a certain area (ranging from a radius of five leagues to a province or even the entire realm) for a limited amount of time (from five to thirty years). Privilege was a flexible instrument that allowed Bourbon officials to adapt the size of the potential market to the capacity and potential of the enterprise.

These limitations remind us that, unlike their British counterparts, domestic entrepreneurs rarely had tax-free or privileged access to the entire French market. Only a very few entrepreneurs like John Holker or the initial group of printed-cotton manufacturers collected loans, grants, subsidies based on performance, or the rent-free use of sufficient space to house their enterprise. On occasion, firms with perceived artistic value like the Saint-Gobain glassworks were taken over by the government. The state also guaranteed (and usually monopolized) sales by vital military suppliers like Saint-Étienne's gunsmiths to maintain quality production. In certain cases, a privilege was extended to all producers of a particular product such as woolens in carefully defined urban spaces like Elbeuf or Carcassonne. According to historians Pierre Deyon and Philippe Guignet, who wrote the only significant English-language study of the royal manufacturers, other than the title itself, "the exclusion of competition was the most sought-after privilege."[5] My findings, however, suggest that whatever entrepreneurs may have requested, what they received most frequently and what they made the best use of were privileges of liberty such as exemptions from guild rules (that may or may not have prevented competition), customs dues, or royal taxes.

According to Prosper Boissonnade, 574 royal manufactures were created in the first two centuries of Bourbon rule. Henri IV founded forty royal manufactures, twenty were established under Louis XIII and Mazarin, and 113 by Colbert. Of the enterprises recognized by Colbert, 49 percent were in textiles and 45 percent were in some form of metallurgy. An additional 243 royal manufactures were launched between 1683 and 1753, 61 percent in textiles, 9 percent in glassmaking, and 8 percent in metallurgy. From 1753 to 1789, a further 158 royal manufactures were founded with textiles declining to 47 percent and metallurgy, especially related to armaments, increasing to nearly one-quarter of new grants. Charted by decade, after the spike under Colbert, the high point of the provision of privilege came during the final decades of the old régime when partisans of liberty dominated royal administration. This pattern underlines French officials' continuing reliance on privilege even when its use challenged their aspirations.

[5] Pierre Deyon and Philippe Guignet, "The Royal Manufactures and Economic and Technological Progress in France before the Industrial Revolution," *Journal of European Economic History*, 9: 3 (1980), 617.

Colbert's role in establishing royal manufactures is well known. Beginning with the reorganization of Paris' "royal upholstery manufacture for the crown," commonly known as the Gobelins, in 1661–1662 Colbert founded a multitude of privileged enterprises. While acknowledging the need for state involvement in creating and supporting these enterprises, he always considered government association with entrepreneurs to be temporary. Colbert understood that fledgling ventures required state participation to attract able entrepreneurs and elite investment. Government involvement defrayed start-up costs and allowed firms a far greater degree of vertical integration. Beyond military or artistic establishments, Colbert limited the extension of privileges to enterprises engaged in import substitution or the transfer of techniques or technology, or that provided large numbers of jobs. Exciting emulation by other entrepreneurs was an important though sometimes unstated objective.

From its creation in 1700, the council of commerce adopted and applied these principles, but this body focused less on supporting employment. The council witnessed the shift in industrial competition from the Dutch to the English. The rise of the Hanoverian state to the position of France's chief economic competitor was late but swift. English competition forced France to compete in different goods and in different markets with serious repercussions for Bourbon political economy.

England's perceived competitive advantages inspired a 1762 royal declaration regulating industrial privileges. This measure limited their duration, reduced unrestrained grants to fifteen years, and revoked privileges that were not continuously exploited, because royal manufactures "have not always had the success that one should anticipate." Although "failures stem from the exercise of privilege which causes inconveniences and hampers liberty without providing the public with the resources they ought to expect," the number of enterprises created in succeeding decades demonstrates that French policymakers sought to improve the performance of royal manufactures, not eliminate them.[6] Letters-patent issued in 1779 declared that future royal charters would be granted exclusively to "the sole manufactures of their type."[7]

[6] *Déclaration du Roi concernant les Priviléges en fait de Commerce*, December 24, 1762, AD Bouches-du-Rhône 1F48a.

[7] Charles Ballot, *L'Introduction du machinisme dans l'industrie française*, ed. Claude Gevel, (Geneva: Slatkine Reprints, 1978 [1923]), 12–13 cites the 1779 quotation. The seven previous paragraphs are based on Deyon and Guignet, "The Royal Manufactures," 611–32, Prosper Boissonnade, *Colbert: Le Triomphe de l'Étatisme, La Fondation de la Suprématie Industrielle de la France, La Dictature du Travail (1661–1683)* (Marcel Rivière, 1932), 37–122, 229–42, and Michael Sonenscher, *Work & Wages: Natural Law, Politics*

A privileged manufacture's location and the international economic context mattered almost as much as the quality of entrepreneurship. In Chapters 2, 3, and 5, we saw that Colbert sought to develop certain spaces like Louviers and to recruit and support "outsiders" such as Josse Van Robais. Here greater attention is paid to how privilege realized state industrial policy.

The success of many privileged manufactures was balanced by failed initiatives. Historians tend to overemphasize either the achievements of French technology and industry or its shortcomings, but it is the balance, the uncertainty, that most profoundly influenced royal policymakers. In textiles, privileges afforded to Elbeuf and to Holker's various enterprises facilitated the creation of productive, lasting firms that introduced new techniques and incited emulation. On the other hand, Carcassonne's royal manufacture succeeded primarily in maintaining employment. Workplace innovation – other than in finding novel ways to cheat – was basically nonexistent and the quality of Carcassonne's woolens declined steadily (although they were still superior to their local competitors). The effects of rising raw material costs and stable or falling sales and prices for finished goods in the Levant were compounded by lax inspection and widespread smuggling. Carcassonne's royal manufacturers augmented meager profit margins by skimping on raw materials. The state either allowed these manufacturers to get away with cheating or had no effective means of stopping this type of fraud. As shown in Chapter 5, this entrepreneurial approach represented a setback to royal policy, which devoted so much long-term attention to acquiring and maintaining France's dominant position in Levantine markets.

Economic context influenced the fate of royal manufactures far more than the contours of their privileges. The ordinances, edicts, and letters-patent creating royal manufactures demonstrate that Bourbon administrators understood that a firm's use of technology and the ability of its director strongly shaped its ability to compete. Over the course of the eighteenth century, policymakers increasingly took institutional and economic factors into account in evaluating potential royal manufactures. During this era of transition, the ever-greater professionalization of

and the Eighteenth-century French Trades (Cambridge University Press, 1989), 137. For Colbert's views on royal manufactures, see the "Privilège accordé au Sieur Guichard pour la manufacture des basins de Saint-Quentin," of February 17, 1671 in Pierre Clément (ed.), *Lettres, instructions et mémoires de Colbert publiés d'après les ordres de l'empereur*, 10 vols. (Imprimerie impériale, 1861–73), II (2): 859–60. On French policymakers' vision of England, see Jeff Horn, *The Path Not Taken: French Industrialization in the Age of Revolution, 1750–1830* (Cambridge, MA: MIT Press, 2006), 53–63.

policymaking was reflected in added attention to political economy and to broader conditions.

Sectors using coal as fuel most clearly demonstrate this evolution. In glass, steel, and earthenware, for example, the French state pursued import substitution through technology transfer. As in textiles, granting privileges to foreigners with needed skills was a basic element of government strategy. Peter Mitchell, the son of an Irish Jacobite, worked as a barrel maker before becoming a merchant. His privilege to establish Bordeaux's first glassworks in 1723 restricted him to making wine bottles. To avoid depleting the city's precious wood supplies, Mitchell's glassworks was obliged to use coal. The greater economic goal was to replace bottle imports from Hamburg, England, and the Netherlands. Mitchell designed the bottle now known as "bordelaise." His sales were strong, though he found it hard to secure consistent supplies of English coal, and his glassblowers, mostly brought from England or northern France, struggled to adapt their techniques to local materials.

The mediocre quality of his wares and the difficulty of resolving the technical aspects of coal use led Mitchell to try to protect his turf. In 1730, he appealed unsuccessfully to annul a privilege granted to a glassworks located in Bourg. Eight years later, Mitchell petitioned to have his establishment named the "royal glassworks of Bordeaux" with an exclusive privilege for ten leagues around the city. The deputies of commerce approved the title and granted the monopoly, but did not extend customs exemptions or any of the other privileges of liberty Mitchell requested. Burgeoning demand and the difficulty of establishing large-scale glass production in the southwest due to shortages of skilled labor and raw materials allowed the firm to earn substantial profits without innovating. Administrative dissatisfaction with the state of affairs was reflected in his widow's inability to prevent another privileged glassworks from being established at Libourne (within the reserved area) by a Dutch emigrant in 1748. Yet, at the end of the old régime, the firm was France's largest bottle producer. It remained in operation until 1930.

The government protected privileged manufacturers by deliberately limiting competition in glassmaking in the province of Guyenne. Three bottlemakers (Bordeaux, Bourg, and Libourne) supplied only part of the vintners' needs: more bottles were imported in 1789 than before Mitchell's first privilege in 1723. Instead of expanding production to achieve state economic goals, the glassworks owners' close ties to administrative and social elites enabled three generations of entrepreneurs to enter other, more lucrative forms of glassmaking from which they had initially been excluded. They used their profits to drive out potential competitors in bottlemaking. According to local administrators, Mitchell's enterprise damaged innovative royal manufactures like Jacques Hustin's earthenware works by monopolizing scarce coal, sand, and water supplies as well as skilled workers. In the vast province of Guyenne, production techniques in glassmaking stagnated. Two noble glassmakers used coal, but they relied on step migration by foreign workers, slowing the naturalization of this essential craft knowledge. Mitchell's privileged enterprise "crowded out" competition, frustrating the administration's aims when they named the glassworks a royal manufacture.[8]

In creating royal manufactures in metallurgy, the eighteenth-century French state prioritized import substitution and technology transfer. The limited successes and expensive failures of noted English emigrants like Michael Alcock and William Wilkinson along with French entrepreneurs, such as Jean-Baptiste Sanche and his various partners, are familiar to historians of technology. Pedestrian results came despite the state's provision of extensive privileges of liberty and liberties of privilege. Alcock was supposed to replicate Birmingham's "toy" industry, first at La Charité-sur-Loire and later at Roanne. He was also expected to teach English steelmaking methods. He and his sons converted to Catholicism and founded a prosperous button-making enterprise that employed around 200 workers from the early 1760s until the late 1780s. It survived into the nineteenth century, but steelmaking, the key to Alcock's recruitment, fell by the wayside despite some promising early trials.

[8] The three previous paragraphs are based on Jean-Pierre Poussou, "Recherches sur l'immigration anglo-irlandaise à Bordeaux au XVIIIième siècle," *Revue historique de Bordeaux et du departement de la Gironde*, 23 (1974), 163–80, Muncipality of Bordeaux, *Bordeaux: Aperçu historique, sol, population, industrie, commerce, administration,* 3 vols. (Bordeaux: Librairie Feret et fils, 1892), I: 440–41, "Requête de Jacques Hustin au subdélégué Thomas Sorlus demandent qu'on prenne des mesures pour empêcher l'envahissement par les eux de sa faiencerie," 1745, reprinted in *Archives historiques du département de la Gironde*, 41 (1906), 317, "Délibération de la Chambre de commerce sur une question de concurrence, intéressant les manufactures également privilégiées des sieurs Fonberg et Mitchel," August 17, 1730, AD Gironde C4253 and "Délibération de la Chambre de Commerce déterminant les conditions auxquelles un privilège exclusif pourra accordé 'aux manufactures de bouteille de gros verre' de Bordeaux et de Bourg," January 23, 1738, AD Gironde C4254, both reprinted in *Archives historiques du département de la Gironde*, 45 (1910), 565–66, 572–73, *Avis des Deputés du commerce sur la requête presentée au Roi par Pierre Michel proprietaire de la manufacture de verrerie établie à Bordeaux*, February 25, 1738, AN F12 702, Mitchell, Meynard l'aîné, Gilbert-Dés-Audineau, Lanabathie, Nicolas Fourcaud, *Lettre à M. Calonne*, n.d. [1785], AD Gironde C1596, du Chesne, *Avis du Subdélegué de Bordeaux*, July 21, 1785, and Devin de Gallande, *Lettre à Camus de Néville, intendant à Bordeaux*, August 23, 1785, both in AD Gironde C1597.

French officials intended the multitalented Wilkinson to be "the Holker of metallurgy." After a visit in 1768, Wilkinson emigrated in 1781. He pioneered the use of coke in ironmaking. With partners like François-Ignace de Wendel, Wilkinson helped to establish innovative blast furnaces at Indret-sur-Loire and Le Creusot to cast naval cannon. Although these enterprises were relatively well funded and received extensive administrative support, they did not naturalize or spread new steelmaking techniques. Not only did Indret and Le Creusot make few cannon, but they also failed to stimulate French competitiveness. Only in the 1830s under the Schneider family did Le Creusot begin to fulfill its potential as a steelmaking site.

Sanche's "fine steel" royal manufacture at La Charité was intended to disseminate a new process of making files "superior to those of Germany." Instead, it went bankrupt within a decade. A royal manufacture's privileges did not ensure either technology transfer or the establishment of competitive firms capable of import substitution. For reasons related to technical capacity and natural resources, in steelmaking, France lagged badly – though not inevitably – behind its competitors.[9]

Official determination to achieve technology and skill transfer in the use of coal through the establishment of royal manufactures seemed more promising in Saint-Sever. In 1781, another émigré Irishman, William Sturgeon, received permission to coal-fire fine earthenware. This authorization is striking because Rouen's *parlement* had restricted the use of coal to minimize industrial pollution just a few years before. Letters-patent promised Sturgeon a bonus for each worker trained in his methods. Two years later, Sturgeon petitioned to become a royal manufacture. He wanted to escape harassment by the generality's seventeen other earthenware-makers. His competitors admitted their fear of being forced to switch to coal if Sturgeon's claims about energy savings proved justified. At the same time, Sturgeon requested a number of other privileges and asked to be named "general inspector of manufactures using coal [*à feu*]."

[9] The three previous paragraphs are based on John R. Harris, *Industrial Espionage and Technology Transfer: Britain and France in the Eighteenth Century* (Aldershot, UK: Ashgate, 1998), 173–74, 180–86, 208–09, 248–53, John R. Harris, "Michael Alcock and the Transfer of Birmingham Technology to France before the Revolution," *Journal of European Economic History*, 15 (1986), 7–57, and Denis Woronoff, *L'Industrie sidérurgique en France pendant la Révolution et l'Empire* (Éditions de l'École des hautes etudes en sciences sociales, 1984), 27, 209, 257, 316–17, 352, 426. The documentary evidence on Sanche is found in AN F12 656, most notably Louis-Casimir Brown, *Procès-verbal des opérations faites à la Manufacture Royale d'aciers à Amboise*, March-April 1788, and Claude Berthollet, *Rapport sur la manufacture d'acier établie à Amboise*, July 9, 1788.

From the intendant to Rouen's chamber of commerce to the *parlement* to the deputies of commerce, the state took Sturgeon seriously. A team composed of two investigators named by the municipality, two by the chamber of commerce, two earthenware retailers, and two earthenware manufacturers visited his works to assess his grandiose claims for efficiency and cost savings. Two separate, carefully monitored tests of his new ovens precisely measured the use of coal as fuel. Sturgeon passed with flying colors. His ovens saved between 17 and 30 percent on fuel costs depending on the type of earthenware. Local officials rejected "earthenware manufacturers' mendacious efforts to undermine the results" and endorsed Sturgeon's requests.[10] Impressed, intendant Louis Thiroux de Crosne awarded 10,000 *livres* as an additional bonus for training masons to make ovens and workers to regulate heat. Sturgeon's training enabled his techniques to spread to other sectors. He instructed workers until the Revolutionary wars made acquiring sufficient high-quality English coal impossible.

The state's role is the most remarkable element of this account. By assigning experts to make a detailed, accurate cost-benefit analysis, the decision whether or not to provide a privilege was made by increasingly professionalized French officials who combined old and new means of fostering economic growth. Of course, the development of expertise in judging inventive and industrial activity was never strictly a French phenomenon, rather it is part of a broader evolution of state practice common to western Europe.[11]

Privilege structured France's exploitation of inventive activity. Liliane Perez explicated the process by which inventors did or did not seek and

[10] *Extrait des registres de la Société royale d'Agriculture de Rouen*, May 15, 1783, AD Seine-Maritime C144.

[11] The three previous paragraphs are based on Jean-Pierre Bardet, *Rouen aux XVIIe et XVIIIe siècles: Les mutations d'un espace social*, 2 vols. (Société d'Édition d'enseignement supérieur, 1983), I: 205, Patrick Clarke de Dromantin, *Les réfugiés jacobites dans la France du XVIIIe siècle* (Presses Universitaires de Bordeaux, 2005), 339–41, *Journal de la ville de Rouen*, November 20, 1784, Jean-Baptiste Goy, *Mémoire général sur les bureaux de visite et de marque établis dans la ville et généralité de Rouen, sur ses différentes fabriques, et sur ses principaux établissements de commerce, avec quelques observations en conséquence des tournées de l'inspection des manufactures de la généralité en 1787*, December 15, 1787, AN F12 1365, Jean-Barthélémy Couteulx de Canteleu and Elie Lefebvre, *Avis*, March 31, 1785, William Sturgeon, *Lettre à de Crosne*, November 15, 1784, and de Belbeuf, *Lettre au comte de Vergennes*, September 7, 1783, all found in AD Seine-Maritime C144. On the evolution of western European administrative practice regarding invention, see Margaret C. Jacob, *Scientific Culture and the Making of the Industrial West* (Oxford University Press, 1997) and the essays by Lissa Roberts, Usula Klein, and William Ashworth in Lissa Roberts, Simon Schaffer, and Peter Dear (eds.), *The Mindful Hand: Inquiry and Invention from the Late Renaissance to Early Industrialization* (Amsterdam: Koninklijke Nederlandse Akademie van Weternschappen, 2007), 197–220, 247–78, and 349–78.

did or did not receive protection for their discoveries. She detailed the perceptions as well as the realities of France's scientific and technological inventiveness. Her study supports Joel Mokyr's influential resumé of the era's key technological breakthroughs. Perez and Mokyr, among many others, emphasize that, compared to Britain, France's major stumbling blocks stemmed from regulatory and market institutions. Christine MacLeod, for example, argues that the British patent system provided more effective encouragement to inventors. Since T. S. Ashton's evocation of a "wave of gadgets," historians have insisted ever more strongly that "heroes of invention" enabled Britain to make more and better use of technical improvements.

My findings reinforce the importance of market and regulatory institutions, but in different ways than those articulated by historians of science and technology. For inventors, liberties of privilege were less valuable, less useful than the privileges of liberty given to innovative manufacturers. In early modern France, privileges pushed pioneering entrepreneurs toward production. Market orientation, in a country with real strengths in innovation, was eminently rational. In this context, institutions refer to diverse rights, duties, and powers ranging from seigneurial control over *police* to judicial enforcement of monopolies and state inspection of manufactured goods. Institutional approaches have also been applied to even more seemingly tangential actions like dueling or the purchase of army commissions. The French state's strategic approach to fostering innovation nuances institutional analyses of scientific and technological improvement in eighteenth-century Europe.

Until the creation of "brevets" of invention in 1791 (see Chapter 8), innovators sought privileges. Royal administrators used privilege to support and sustain inventive activity. From the 1680s, procedures to judge inventions were steadily professionalized with experts coming to play a dominant role. Keeping proprietary information secret became far more difficult and, with uneven enforcement of industrial regulations, inventors had to jump high hurdles to make privilege pay. The royal declaration of December 1762 clarified state policy and provided the basis for the 1791 law. For Perez, the depth of state involvement meant that "in France, to invent meant to go into politics." In many ways, this observation applied to almost every innovative entrepreneur in France, both before and after 1791.[12]

12 The three previous paragraphs are based on Liliane Hilaire-Pérez, "Invention and the State in 18th-Century France," *Technology and Culture*, 32: 4 (1991), 911–31, 931, which anticipates *L'invention technique au siècle des Lumières* (Albin Michel, 2000), Joel Mokyr, *The Lever of Riches: Technological Creativity and Economic Progress* (Oxford University Press, 1990), 294–95, Thomas S. Ashton, *The Industrial Revolution 1760–1830* (Oxford

Alexander Bonvallet personified the complex interaction of privilege and liberty found in state oversight of invention and manufacturing. Bonvallet was a successful tailor who became a wholesale merchant in Grandvilliers (Oise). He established a small dyeworks to print floral patterns on twill in 1753. Twice, the mill failed, in part because of interference from the dyers' guild which charged that leakage from Bonvallet's vats damaged his neighbors' health. To escape the guild, Bonvallet quit the jurisdiction of Beauvais' bishop who was responsible for the *police* of manufacturing for nearby Éramecourt (Somme). But the expenses involved in launching the enterprise and then moving it bankrupted him.

Bonvallet benefited from Amiens' declining textile sales. Supported by intendant Étienne Maynon d'Invault and Picardy's chamber of commerce, a group of wholesale merchants loaned Bonvallet 17,000 *livres* to establish a new dyeworks in Saint-Maurice-lès-Amiens. They gambled that Bonvallet could dye cotton cloth well enough to avoid sending goods to Beauvais or Bolbec, enabling Amiens' producers to lower prices. As Saint-Maurice lay outside the jurisdiction of the city's guilds, Bonvallet and his backers believed that the privilege of liberty, enforced by the intendant and his subdelegate, would protect him. Bonvallet brought several skilled workers with him. Because these workers skipped out on their employers, Bonvallet's protectors had to intervene before he even set up shop. It was worth it. Dyeing floral patterns on cheap cloth helped to revive Amiens' industry.

Almost immediately, Bonvallet faced both emulation and harassment. Other dyers set up shop in this emergent enterprise zone, leading Amiens' dyers guild to seek to eliminate this threat to their monopoly. In 1762, they convinced inspector of manufacturing Joseph Imbert de Saint-Paul to impound several bales of cotton velour dyed by Bonvallet for trespassing on guild methods. The wardens wanted to force him, and by extension the other dyers in Saint-Maurice, to join their guild and follow its regulations. The intendant and the chamber of commerce interceded in the name of "liberty." Both rejected this guild's last-ditch attempt to stifle innovation and eliminate competition.

Privileges of liberty enabled Bonvallet's enterprise to flourish. Consistently innovative, Bonvallet developed new printing techniques

University Press, 1948), Christine MacLeod, *Heroes of Invention: Technology, Liberalism and British Identity 1750–1914* (Cambridge University Press, 2007), Charles Coulston Gillispie, *Science and Polity in France: The End of the Old Regime* (Princeton University Press, 1980), and Shelby T. McCloy, *French Inventions of the Eighteenth Century* (Lexington: University of Kentucky Press, 1952). See also Douglas W. Allen, *The Institutional Revolution: Measurement & the Economic Emergence of the Modern World* (University of Chicago Press, 2012).

and introduced novel designs and colors while keeping prices low. In 1787, his establishment acquired the purely honorary title of "royal manufacture of floral-pattern fabrics" (*Manufacture royale d'étoffes fleuries*). During the Revolution, Bonvallet's dyeworks thrived. At the second French industrial exposition in 1801, he received a silver medal. A visit by first consul Napoleon Bonaparte in 1803 helped the enterprise become an "imperial manufacture" a few years later. The firm remained in family hands until 1962.

A highly successful entrepreneur, Alexandre Bonvallet aspired to be an inventor. He repeatedly sought liberties of privilege to defend his dyeworks from other privileged producers. Amiens' guilds imposed "hassles of every kind" to "prevent the exercise of his talent" putting his "liberty in danger." Yet, in 1775, when he applied for government recognition of a machine to line-engrave fabric using a cylindrical press, Bonvallet insisted that he needed liberties of privilege to protect his invention and to allow him to perfect his new machine. He recognized that "limits" arose when inventors with exclusive privileges had no incentive to perfect their inventions. But, he asserted, "It is different for inventions of secondary utility or for expensive inventions that require costly trials. In such cases, entrepreneurs can only be compensated for their initial investment and uncounted trials by the assurance of being able to reap the fruit of their effort and expenditure." Bonvallet claimed to have developed fifteen different models and invested 18,000 *livres* before hitting on the most effective mechanism. He requested a twenty-five-year exclusive privilege covering the entire country. To exploit his invention "properly," Bonvallet asserted that he needed to invest a further 200,000 *livres* of start-up capital.[13]

There was no chance that controller-general of finance Anne-Robert-Jacques de Turgot would agree to this request. When consulted, Picardy's chamber of commerce criticized exclusive privileges as "contrary to reason and equity," remarking that "similar establishments had already been set up in Amiens by Bonvallet's former employees." However, the chamber noted that his machine worked; "it gives cheap fabric all the colors and vivacity of more expensive cloth" and that he deserved "some recompense and encouragement" if only because of Amiens' long-standing debt to him for revitalizing local industry.[14]

Bonvallet did not let rejection stop his campaign for state support. Several more attempts to get an exclusive privilege for this and other

[13] The quotes in this paragraph are from *Mémoire présenté à Messieurs les Présidens et membres de la Chambre du Commerce de Picardie, par Jacques-Alexandre Bonvallet, Inventeur d'une nouelle Impression en Taille-douce pour Étoffes*, February 7, 1775, AD Somme C2715.

[14] Chamber of commerce of Picardy, *Lettre à d'Agay*, February 9, 1775, AD Somme C332.

related machines followed. As a sop, inspector of manufacturing Jean-Marie Roland got Bonvallet a pension of 300 *livres*. Yet, when a disappointed Bonvallet planned to take his machines to Russia, Roland nipped this design in the bud by having him briefly imprisoned.

Frustrated, Bonvallet installed his inventions anyway. He not only kept applying for privileges, but he also kept inventing. During the Consulate, he adapted his cylindrical press to print on wool. It was this machine that won the silver medal in 1801. Noted manufacturer Guillaume-Louis Ternaux installed Bonvallet's machines in his mill at Reims.

Inventors found getting exclusive privileges arduous in eighteenth-century France. Many, like Alexandre Bonvallet, focused instead on developing their industrial interests in places where they could escape guild regulation while continuing to seek lesser privileges and prizes, mostly for their prestige value. For inventors, privileges of liberty were usually more valuable than liberties of privilege.[15]

Coal mining deepens our understanding of state use of privilege as a tool of economic development. In hopes of assuring "abundant French supplies" of this critical natural resource, Louis de Phélypeaux, chancellor de Pontchartrain, sponsored an edict in May 1698 that liberated landowners from having to acquire royal permission to open a coal mine. The edict also annulled all existing coal-mining privileges, putting mining rights in the hands of landowners. As seigneurs with the right of high justice had controlled mineral rights in their jurisdiction, this measure attacked their privileges. In 1744, the royal council adopted Daniel-Charles de Trudaine's analysis admitting that previous "dispositions have remained without effect." The new regulation recognized the rights of *hauts justiciers*, but required both seigneurs and landowners to first "obtain permission from the controller general of finance if they want to open and exploit coal mines." Potential

[15] The nine previous paragraphs are based on Ronald Hubscher (ed.), *Histoire d'Amiens* (Privat, 1986), 155–56, Albéric de Calonne, *Histoire de la ville d'Amiens*, 3 vols. (Amiens: Piteux Frères, 1899–1906), II: 359–61, Sophie Olive and Xavier Daugy (eds.), *Fonds Bonvallet: Sous-série 75 J Répertoire numérique détaillé* (2003), http://www.somme.fr/oldpdf/application/1eb0797fd81496835d1630fdbd02ddaf.pdf, (accessed July 15, 2013), Georges Durand (ed.), *Inventaire sommaire des Archives Départementales antérieures à 1790: Somme*, vol. 2 (Amiens: Imprimerie picarde, 1888), v–vi, Pierre Bonnassieux and Eugène Lelong (eds.), *Conseil de Commerce et Bureau du Commerce 1700–1791: Inventaire analytique des process-verbaux* (Imprimerie nationale, 1900), 402, Hyacinthe Dusevel, *Histoire de la ville d'Amiens, depuis les Gaulois jusqu'à nos jours*, 2nd ed. (Amiens: Caron & Lambert, 1848), 525, and *Seconde exposition publique des produits de l'industrie française: Procès-verbal des opérations du Jury nommé par le Ministre de l'intérieur pour examiner les Produits de l'Industrie française mis à l'Exposition des jours complémentaires de la neuvième année de la République*, 1802 (Gallica), 20.

entrepreneurs had to "indemnify the landowners to their liking or to agree to the judgment of experts named by the intendant ... who also judges any disputes that arise between landowners and entrepreneurs, their representatives, employees, and workers." The edict included guidelines for how to maintain pits, safeguard miners, and preserve shafts for future exploitation in case of bankruptcy.[16] Reissued in 1783 with additional safety rules, this edict bolstered the economic influence of certain seigneurs but subordinated their authority to the needs of industrial policy.

Emmanuel, duke du Croÿ and prince of Solre, exploited his seigneurial rights, both for his own profit and to benefit his vassals. Soon to be named a field marshal, du Croÿ enjoyed tremendous influence at court. In 1749, he received the right to mine anywhere on his extensive properties scattered across the province of Hainault. (Although he had been digging since 1741, he only sought permission five years after the edict was promulgated.) Du Croÿ used his powers of high justice to expand his control over Condé's rich coal seams. Anticipating the expiration of the long-time concessionaire's privilege in 1760, du Croÿ sought exclusive mining rights for the entire county in 1756.

Royal administrators devoted significant attention and invested tens of thousands of *livres* at several reprises between 1717 and 1730 to developing Hainault's coal resources. The concessions they granted, however, overlapped and ran afoul of seigneurial authorities. Experts considered these concessions too small and too fragmented for effective exploitation. Du Croÿ claimed that his request was not solely on his own behalf but also to support the claims of "all other seigneurs with high justice."[17] The deputies of commerce endorsed the specific request, but not the principle. They asserted that "concessions to exploit coal mines are granted by the king" and then limited the span of du Croÿ's privileges.[18]

Partly rebuffed, du Croÿ pressured three companies to amalgamate their small and intersecting claims to form the Anzin Mining Company in 1757. He became the largest shareholder. Du Croÿ's privileges and concessions were essential to the new firm, but his contribution went beyond mining rights. He also invested 30,000 *livres* and pushed the

[16] *Arrêt du Conseil d'État du Roi portant règlement pour l'exploitation des Mines de Houille, ou Charbon de terre,* January 14, 1744 (Gallica).

[17] This and the next quote are from Emmanuel Henri de Grouchy and Paul Cottin (eds.), *Journal inédit du duc de Croÿ, 1718–1784,* 4 vols. (Flammarion, 1906–1907), I: 468.

[18] *Avis des députés du commerce sur la demande de M. le Prince de Croÿ pour faire exploiter exclusivement à toutes autres personnes les mines de charbons du terre decouvertes et à decouvrir dans ses terres,* February 3, 1756, AN F12 710.

directors to deepen the pits and install steam engines that enabled Anzin to become France's largest coal producer. Two years later, his mining privileges were extended to forty years: "ten years more than I asked for. It was given out of consideration for me."

Despite this administrative encouragement, du Croÿ resented the efforts of improvers like Trudaine and his son Jean-Charles-Philibert Trudaine de Montigny to limit certain of his privileges because of their "outrageous principle of complete liberty. They confound cases where strong companies are necessary with those where that necessity does not exist."[19] Once he became Hainault's provincial governor in 1763, du Croÿ protected the rapidly growing and ever more profitable firm by scaring off potential challenges from other seigneurs with extensive mining rights. In the 1780s, du Croÿ earned 50,000 *livres* annually from his investment in Anzin which, in 1789, produced almost 300,000 tons of coal. Economists might observe that despite this impressive output, du Croÿ's actions did not maximize coal production. While certainly accurate, that observation is beside the point. Without du Croÿ's rent-seeking behavior, Anzin would never have existed in the first place and certainly not on the scale that it attained. For the first half of the nineteenth century, Anzin was France's biggest private company. It remained in operation until 1949. In the case of du Croÿ and Anzin, entrepreneurial vision, seigneurial rights, and the state's provision of privilege combined effectively to fulfill a vital aim of French industrial policy.[20]

The French state deployed privilege to create or co-opt several groups of insiders. Privilege was deployed by royal officials to channel entrepreneurial energies toward desired goals. Some objectives in specific places were more attainable than others, as demonstrated by the experiences of Peter Mitchell and William Sturgeon. At the same time,

[19] Grouchy and Cottin (eds.), *Journal inédit du duc de Croÿ*, II: 235.

[20] The five previous paragraphs are based on Marie-Pierre Dion, *Emmanuel de Croÿ (1718–1784): Itinéraire intellectuel et réussite nobiliaire au siècle des Lumières* (Brussels: Editions de l'Université Bruxelles, 1987), 92–99, Marcel Rouff, *Les mines de charbon en France au XVIIIe siècle 1744–1791* (F. Rieder, 1922), 1–8, 423–24, John Shovlin, *The Political Economy of Virtue: Luxury, Patriotism, and the Origins of the French Revolution* (Ithaca, NY: Cornell University Press, 2006), 69, *Arrêt du Conseil d'État du Roi portant Réglement pour l'exploitation des Mines de Charbon de Terre*, March 19, 1783, AD Bouches-du-Rhône 1F12, and *Avis des Députés du Commerce sur l'instance pendante au Conseil entre M. Le Prince de Croÿ et Consors et M. Desmaizière, seigneur, haut-justicier de Trith, Maing et Verchineul près de Valenciennes au sujet de l'extraction du Charbon de Terre*, June 2, 1767, AN F12 714. The various concessions are reprinted in *Mémoire pour la compagnie d'Anzin concernant son origine et son droit de propriété sur les divers concessions qu'elle exploite* (J. Claye, 1863), 44–84.

Alexandre Bonvallet's successes and failures suggest that certain privileges were more effective than others in achieving the government's aims.

Fostering development through the provision of privilege experienced mixed results. These undertakings highlight the creativeness and frustrations of generations of talented and increasingly professionalized officials captured so well by Tocqueville. Certainly the precision and focus of the trials testing Sturgeon's methods were unimaginable a century earlier. But the central state still had to balance developmental efforts with local interests and to rein in or co-opt the ambitions of powerful seigneurs like the duke du Croÿ. Through privilege or its absence, thwarted inventors like Bonvallet were steered toward the practical application of their ideas. As we saw in earlier chapters, after 1750, royal policymakers recognized that while the liberty of privilege retained many attractions, the privilege of liberty was more effective in aiding development, especially in sectors where France was more internationally competitive, as in textiles. In eighteenth-century France, insiders accomplished many goals, but providing the privileges of liberty to more and more people became an increasingly important goal of Bourbon political economy.

Betwixt and between: *corporate* reform, textile deregulation, and the limits of privilege

Corporations were the largest group of privileged producers in early modern France. In Chapter 2, we saw that until about 1750 Colbert and his successors viewed guilds in a generally positive light, although there were a number of exceptions to that rule. Official frustration with the status quo stemmed both from perceived competitive shortcomings of guild-made goods and from the restiveness of journeymen who appeared to pose a threat to the socioeconomic order. To stop their "harmful abuses," the royal council issued paternalistic letters-patent in January 1749 that firmly subordinated journeymen to their masters in hopes of improving the quality of guild output and minimizing conflict in the world of work.[21] Unsurprisingly, commands from on high were frequently modified or ignored at the local level.

Over the next twenty-five years, improvers' mounting influence was reflected in the provision of greater privileges of liberty. Allowing the production of printed cottons in 1758 and rural textile manufacture in 1762 were the biggest leaps, but numerous smaller steps along this path

[21] Jacques Peuchet (ed.), *Collection des lois, ordonnances et règlements de police depuis le 13e siècle jusqu'à l'année 1818*, 2nd series, vol. 5, *1739 à 1749* (Lottin, 1818), 419–22.

such as the curbs on Marseille's de facto monopoly on Levantine trade passed in 1759 (see Chapter 5) also indicated the direction of royal policy. Turgot's liberation of the grain trade in 1774 and his partial abolition of the guilds in 1776 fulfilled many "economists'" goals regarding liberty.

Not enough commentators – then as now – acknowledge the limits of Turgot's attack on the guilds. *Corporate* structures for "crucial" professions such as the pharmacists, goldsmiths, booksellers, and printers were retained. New guidelines for the butchers, bakers, and apothecaries were promulgated, while barbers and wigmakers were exempted. In principle, French subjects (of any faith) and foreign residents could now exercise whatever trade or trades they wished. Occupation(s) still had to be registered with the police, which allowed local authorities a means of excluding potential entrepreneurs. Employers had to keep written records on each employee. Although these particular guilds were unconnected to the industrial economy, their exemption demonstrates the difficulty of generalizing about privilege, liberty, or the *corporate* world in early modern France.

Turgot's system was never really tried. Only its negative elements were implemented and only in some places. His positive policies did not survive long enough to yield results. Crop failures, grain riots, and intense opposition from entrenched privileged interests pushed Turgot from power in less than a year. Partial abolition of the guilds occurred only in the jurisdictions of the *parlements* of Rouen, Nancy, Metz, Roussillon, and Paris. Other *parlements* successfully rebuffed the royal government's offer of liberty from the *corporations*.

For most policymakers, Turgot's tenure demonstrated that France was not ready for an abrupt loosening of the state's hold on the reins guiding the economy. In August 1776, controller-general of finance Jean-Étienne-Bernard Ogier de Clugny restored a modified guild structure intended to make these institutions more inventive and more competitive as well as less exclusionary. The royal council resolved:

> to preserve the freedom of certain types of trades and businesses which should not be subjected to any particular regulation ... and to establish guild rules that will favor their interior discipline. Masters' domestic authority will be maintained without which commerce, talent, and industry will be deprived of the advantages attached to this liberty. [These changes] ought to stimulate emulation without introducing fraud and license.

The council lowered the costs of joining guilds and widened access by stipulating that "women and girls will not be excluded from them," although Protestants and Jews were. Producing a *chef d'oeuvre* or serving an apprenticeship was no longer required to become a master.[22] Other reforms changed how guilds were governed, how to join them, and who controlled their finances. These measures took years to wend their way past the roadblocks thrown up by provincial *parlements*, those inveterate defenders of *corporations* and their privileges. For example, an edict issued in February 1778 and amended in April 1779 imposed similar regulations on a number of small cities in Normandy, but exempted Rouen. Influential seigneurs with rights of high justice in the suburbs also lobbied successfully to keep their powers. As we shall see, only in February 1783 did another edict emerge to apply these same reforms to Rouen and the high justices girdling the city, effectively destroying their separate *corporate* structures.

Guilds never recovered from Turgot's carnival. Without guild inspection to enforce the rules, producers, especially in textiles, ignored the regulations. Shoddily made goods poured out of French workshops, raising a hue and cry from customers at home and abroad and heightening doubts about the realm's international competitiveness. Royal officials worried about the slow pace of gaining judicial approval to restore the revised guilds and the difficulties of reestablishing regulatory observance. *Corporate* privileges persisted in law, but in practice their hold had been severely weakened. As a result, exemptions from guild oversight and rules became far less useful. Both privileges of liberty and liberties of privilege were not as valuable after 1776.

Swiss-born financier Jacques Necker, a Protestant, emerged as the royal administration's leading figure on industrial matters after being appointed director-general of finance in October 1776. He became convinced of the need for a different approach to regulating textiles. In hindsight, Necker observed that having tried "indefinite liberty as the only reasonable idea, after a time, regulations resumed their advantage. During the more or less lengthy battles between the rules and liberty, commerce and manufacturing were continually disrupted."[23]

Beginning with an edict issued in May 1779, the royal administration charted a course between "indefinite liberty" and stringent regulation. What emerged was a middle or third way. Producers were permitted to make textiles as they pleased, but goods made according to the regulations could also be inspected and receive a state seal of approval. These choices expressed the state's faith in the ability of most textile

[22] François-André Isambert, Alphonse-Honoré Taillandier, and Decrusy (eds.), *Recueil général des anciennes lois françaises, depuis l'an 420 jusqu'à la révolution de 1789*, 29 vols. (Berlin-Le-Prieur, 1821–1833), XXIV: 74–89

[23] Jacques Necker, *Compte Rendu au Roi*, 1781 (Gallica), 116.

manufacturers to improve competitiveness while also providing a means for high-end producers to retain hard-won consumer confidence.

Implementing Necker's "intermediate" system required an additional three years. Overhauling guilds, massively extending the privilege of liberty in textile production, and the ongoing transformation of key privileged enclaves into enterprise zones combined to overwhelm the state's ability to oversee the textile industry. These overlapping initiatives enabled some French manufacturers to become more competitive, but other sectors and regions experienced sharp declines, at least in the short run. The decade before the outbreak of the French Revolution demonstrated that, as a tool of royal policy, the privilege of liberty was a step along the way to greater economic changes.

The May 1779 letters-patent relaxed the state's supervisory role in France's largest industry. This measure and follow-up clarifications issued on June 1, 4, and 28, 1780, removed direct oversight of textile production by government experts such as inspectors of manufacturing. Inspection of finished goods was the sole remaining administrative means of evaluating regulatory compliance. Although the letters-patent established a dual system, in practice, almost all textile producers rejected the deeply held preference of most French administrators for quality goods (see Chapters 2–5). Instead, French producers overwhelmingly chose liberty from regulation. Entrepreneurs alone selected fabrics and styles. Statistics gathered at Rouen's cloth hall reveal that, in the six months before September 1783, only 2,198 bolts (1 percent) were made according to the rules, while 191,420 bolts (99 percent) were made "in arbitrary sizes." For the next six months, only 856 bolts were made according to the regulations, versus 159,361 bolts made arbitrarily. Similar figures were reported from across the length and breadth of the realm.

The intermediate system also lessened the *corporations*' role in the manufacture of textiles. Entrepreneurs could ignore guild regulations (which needed to be thoroughly rewritten in light of the changes), and rural producers were liberated from *corporate* domination. In Normandy, the royal council anticipated that rural textile producers who chose to conform to the regulations would be inspected by Rouen's guild wardens (see Chapter 3). Their "repugnance" for this time-consuming and poorly paid task contributed to the collapse of inspection in this key province.[24] Monopolies for producing a particular type or style of textile were jettisoned, ending uncounted liberties of privilege. Over a six-year period, the regulatory edifice begun by Colbert and extended by his

[24] Jean-Baptiste Goy, *Lettre à M. Necker*, January 6, 1780, AN F12 676B.

successors was dismantled, but only in textiles, marking this important initiative, somewhat paradoxically, as a (particularly extensive) privilege of liberty.

State provision of privileges of liberty to textile producers did not apply to workers. The royal council decided to "add precautions which they thought capable of maintaining *police* and subordinating workers." Workers had to register with the police and were forbidden to leave their masters without finishing tasks in progress, reimbursing advances, and providing eight days' notice. Only then could a leave notice (*billet de congé*) be issued. No worker could be offered a job without one. Employers who lured workers from other jobs were liable to be fined 100 *livres*. Laborers were banned from assembling for any reason. Masters' domination of men was perceived to be necessary for France to compete in international markets both in price and in quality.[25] Privileges of liberty granted to the textile industry should be understood as expressing faith in both the paternalism and the entrepreneurship of French producers.[26]

Alexis de Tocqueville devoted a chapter to "How revolutionary changes in the administrative system preceded the political revolution and their consequences." Tocqueville focused on the establishment of provincial assemblies in 1787, but he begins with the observation that "The suppression of the trade and craft corporations, followed by their partial restoration, had entirely changed the old relations between worker and employer." In the economic sphere, "revolutionary changes ... preceded the political revolution," beginning in 1776 with the six edicts.[27] Just as the intendants' diminished authority facilitated the outbreak of Revolution in 1789, so too the much-reduced powers of royal officials and guild wardens in economic matters enabled

[25] Isambert, Taillandier, and Decrusy (eds.), *Recueil général des anciennes lois françaises*, XXVII: 78–80.

[26] For this section, consult the following sources. I have written about these topics in Horn, *The Path Not Taken*, 17–45, but the foremost historian of these reforms is Steven L. Kaplan. See his *La fin des corporations*, trans. Béatrice Vierne (Fayard, 2001). Production figures are in Jean-Baptiste Goy, *État des pièces d'étoffes fabriquées et présentées aux Bureaux de visite et de marque de l'inspection de Rouen pendant le premier semestre de l'année 1783 avec la comparaison du pareil Semestre*, September 20, 1783 and Jean-Baptiste Goy, *État des pièces d'étoffes fabriquées et présentées aux Bureaux de visite et demarque de l'inspection de Rouen pendant le 2eme semestre de l'année 1783 avec la comparaison du pareil Semestre*, March 25, 1784, both in AN F12 650. See also *Édit du Roi concernant les Communautés d'Arts et Métiers des villes du resort du Parlement de Rouen*, April 1779 AN F12 786, *Mémoire pour le seigneur de la haute-justice de Belbeuf, et pour les habitants des hautes-justices de la banlieue de Rouen*, n.d. [1779], AN F12 786, and *Déclaration du Roi, concernant les Communautés d'Arts et Métiers du resort du Parlement de Rouen*, February 6, 1783, AD Seine-Maritime C122.

[27] Tocqueville, *The Old Régime and the French Revolution*, 193.

entrepreneurs and workers to push for fundamental change, though often in opposite directions.

These privileges went too far and did not go far enough. Production in Bordeaux was not as firmly under guild control as in other large cities (see Chapter 2) and the *parlement* of Guyenne flatly refused to register Turgot's reforms. Yet this booming city still suffered growing laxity in production. Increasingly confrontational relations between masters and men slowed industrial expansion and technological change.

Guild masters were on the offensive in Bordeaux. They succeeded in establishing certain controls over the world of work in the privileged enclaves of Saint-Seurin and Saint-André in 1759. Through creative deployment of their powers of inspection, masters appropriated scarce supplies of raw materials and skilled labor. Bordeaux's guilds also used inspection to dominate unincorporated trades. Except for the relatives of masters, joining a guild became ever more difficult. Enhanced legal powers provided to masters by the letters-patent of 1749 and 1781 fueled considerable pushback from other privileged producers and from skilled workers. Legal authority must not be confused with the realities of power. Bordeaux's guilds overreached, precipitating a significant decline in their day-to-day authority.

Bordeaux's journeymen were a restive, combative lot. The letters-patent of 1749 legally established masters' "domestic authority," but the capital of Guyenne must then be regarded as a broken home. The city's rulers reiterated the ban on worker meetings and *compagnonnage* several times, with the same lack of effect. A 1769 edict ordered Bordeaux's militia and city watch to arrest all groups of more than *three* workers. Because bands of armed journeymen "run through the city and countryside" attacking "the homes of individuals or those of bakers," the *parlement* mandated capital punishment for anyone convicted of participating in these "mobs" in 1773.[28] Until banned in 1781, religious brotherhoods also brought together groups of potentially riotous journeymen. Workers' continuing devotion prompted the archbishop to forbid clergy from "allowing journeymen of the city's different trades to assemble" for any "motive" whatsoever.[29] Bordeaux's skilled workers imposed their collective will on employers through violence and by walking off the job en masse. Legal prohibition had little effect on either practice. With jobs plentiful, Bordeaux's political elites recognized the masters' inability to control their

[28] *Arrêt de la cour de Parlement, qui ordonne l'exécution des Ordonnances portant défenses à toutes Personnes de faire des Attroupements sous peine de mort*, May 14, 1773, AM Bordeaux FF68.

[29] Cited in *Archives Historiques du département de la Gironde*, 19 (1879), 83–84.

journeymen and apprentices. Municipal officials feared that workers' "plots" to raise piece rates represented "a threat to public authority" that their masters could not quell.[30]

Bordeaux's city fathers' were unable to enforce the September 1781 letters-patent requiring workers to present a leave notice from a previous employer before hire. In 1783, the aldermen wrote, "Journeymen naval carpenters and other construction workers rose up, left their work, assembled by the port, tore down notices of the law, and insulted their masters. Work was suspended for several days." To entice workers to return, several masters announced that they would not ask for leave notices. The *parlement* supported the masters: the judges feared for public order. The aldermen were powerless to stop journeymen's "usurpation of authority."[31] Inability to enforce laws subordinating workers to their masters had serious consequences. Worker resistance in Bordeaux either prevented or drastically slowed workplace and technological innovation. This productive logjam heightened Bordeaux's reliance on goods made elsewhere, lessening the price competitiveness of France's largest port.

Guild interference hampered entrepreneurs in the privileged enclaves of Saint-Seurin and Saint-André. Encouraged by the government's restructuring of Paris' *corporations* in 1776 that left the faubourg Saint-Antoine largely to its own devices, Saint-Seurin's entrepreneurs asked "to be able to work the same way as Parisians in the same position."[32] Saint-Seurin's master locksmiths, masons, cabinetmakers, tailors, and ropemakers complained that Bordeaux's guilds continually lobbied the authorities to compel them to join the city's guilds. The subdelegate, mayor, and aldermen joined forces to stall the execution of reforms on the Paris model, forcing the inhabitants of Saint-Seurin to spend time and money justifying their independence. According to Saint-Seurin's masters, Bordeaux's guild wardens lied about the ancillary expenses of joining: "to use a vulgar expression, one could say that the city's masters pay more for the sauce than for the fish."[33] Guild inspection required the enclaves' entrepreneurs to expend considerable effort petitioning various authorities to recover unjustly confiscated raw materials and

30 *Requête des Bayles de la communauté des Maîtres Cloutiers de Bordeaux aux Messieurs les Maire, Lieutenant de Maire te Jurats, Gouverneurs de Bordeaux, Juges Criminels et de Police*, August 1788, AM Bordeaux HH 80.

31 *Lettre des Jurats de Bordeaux à M. Joly de Fleury, Ministre des Finances*, September 23, 1783, AM Bordeaux BB179 registre, 152–54.

32 Delessart, *Lettre à M. de Cotte*, February 28, 1780, AN F12 757A.

33 *Mémoire pour les maitres serruriers sans jurandes habitants la ville et fauxbourgs de Bordeaux responsif à celui des maitres jurandés dans la même ville*, n.d. [1780], AN F12 757A.

goods. “The guild masters’ tyranny results in the most distressing calamities,” they declared.[34] Harassment played havoc with these entrepreneurs’ business commitments and profit margins, undermining the privileged enclaves’ ability to innovate.

Royal officials had difficulty enforcing reform because the *parlement* of Guyenne protected the guilds. Controller-general of finance Charles-Alexandre de Calonne intervened in 1784 after the *parlement* quashed several royal edicts permitting various entrepreneurs who had suffered from masters’ interference to join Bordeaux’s guilds for either one-quarter of the regular fee or for free. Most were masters from Saint-Seurin and Saint-André. Money was the rub: the wardens wanted applicants from the privileged enclaves to pay full price. By tacking on several additional fees and by maintaining the tradition of putting on lavish banquets for the membership, guild wardens hoped to soak the applicants to enfeeble their rivals.

Calonne tried to convince the judges to change their minds by detailing the “multiple abuses” introduced by the guilds. He noted that “especially at Bordeaux, a large number of individuals who exercise different professions complain of the wardens’ vexations, especially the excessive price of masterships and the expenses associated with joining.” He warned that “it will be difficult to allow the *parlement* to persist in its opposition to His Majesty’s intentions,” but declined to take more definitive measures.[35] Masters persevered in using their privileges to try to control production in Bordeaux. Other than delay and aggravation, they seemed to have accomplished little on their own behalf. But Bordeaux’s guild masters did succeed in curtailing opportunities both in the privileged enclaves and those stemming from the central government’s reform of the *corporate* world. In Bordeaux, the state’s goal of unleashing the populace’s entrepreneurial spirit by extending privileges of liberty was foiled by the guilds’ obstinate defense of their liberties of privilege.[36]

34 *Adresse à Monseigneur Necker, Contrôleur Général des finances*, March 29, 1780, AN F12 757A.

35 Charles-Alexandre de Calonne, *Lettre à Boutin et de Boisguilbert*, October 13, 1784, AD Gironde C3689.

36 The eight previous paragraphs are based on Bernard Gallinato, *Les Corporations à Bordeaux à la fin de l’ancien régime: Vie et mort d’un mode d’organisation du travail* (Presses Universitaires de Bordeaux, 1992), 334–35, *Édit des Maire, lieutenant de Maire et Jurats, Gouverneurs de Bordeaux, Juges Criminels et de Police*, July 25, 1769, AM Bordeaux HH70, *Lettre des Jurats de Bordeaux à M. de Castries*, October 11, 1783, AM Bordeaux BB 179 registre, 162, *Pétition à Monseigneur Camus de Néville, Intendant de la Généralité de Guienne*, n.d., [1784?], AD Gironde C3689, and two documents entitled *Adresse à Nosseigneurs de Parlement*, one undated from 1783 and another from February 21, 1785, both in AD Gironde 3J E703.

In Normandy, guilds were weaker, government stronger, and workers more cowed. Here the results more closely resembled the royal council's reformist intentions. Differing results stemmed largely from the impetus provided by the enterprise zones located in privileged enclaves. Yet, in Normandy too, the conflict between and among privileges constrained entrepreneurialism and undermined pressure for innovation generated by competition.

Three deaths cast a pebble in the pond whose ripples changed the rules governing the productive environment in and around Rouen. In Darnetal, a high justice on the edge of Rouen, a master draper named Delamarre, his wife, and son all died in 1782. The couple left behind three daughters and heavy debts. Only by continuing their father's business could the three women, aged twenty-four, twenty-three, and twenty-one, hope to earn enough to meet their father's financial obligations. Described by Alexandre, the deputy chief of Rouen's guild of merchant haberdashers (*merciers*) as "filled with honor and integrity," the sisters petitioned the guild to keep the business open longer than the six months allowed by law.[37] They offered to pay a fee of either 100 *livres* if they could operate the shop long enough to settle their father's debts or 400 *livres* (rather than the 300 set by law) if the oldest daughter was accepted into the guild.

The Delamarres were "surprised by an exceptionally definitive refusal."[38] No reason for the wardens' action survives. The sisters' attempt to find a way to overcome this rejection sparked implementation of *corporate* reform in Rouen's high justices. On the Delamarres' behalf, Alexandre wrote to secretary of state Henri Bertin suggesting that the real issue was the *parlement*'s delay in registering the edict reforming the *corporations*. Bertin involved the intendant, Louis Thiroux de Crosne. Rebuffed by the masters, de Crosne corroborated Alexandre's report and recommended proceeding by edict. Days later in December 1782, the royal council commanded that "Miss Delamarre immediately be received as a mistress in the community of drapers in the bourg of Darnetal." She was to pay the regular provincial rate.[39]

The drapers rejected Delamarre yet again and seized her goods. The community met and declared that without the *parlement*'s approval, they would only obey their seigneur, the duke de Montmorency. On the spot, they contributed large sums to send a delegation to Versailles to seek the edict's nullification. Commissioners investigating the affair reported that

[37] Alexandre, *Lettre à M. De Bertin*, October 30, 1782, AD F12 760.
[38] Louis Thiroux de Crosne, *Rapport à M. Tolozan*, n.d. [1782], AN F12 786.
[39] *Arrêt du Conseil d'État du Roi*, December 3, 1782, AN F12 786.

"the masters' conduct seems to stem more from aversion and entitlement than any true reasons for opposition."[40] Two weeks later, in February 1783, the royal council imposed *corporate* reform on Rouen and its suburbs, ending the separate existence of Darnetal's drapers' guild, among others. The drapers' intransience prompted the integration of this privileged enclave into Rouen's guild structure.

A few weeks later, inspector of manufacturing Jean-Baptiste Goy attended a hearing in Rouen. It was run by guild wardens who, days before the promulgation of the new declaration, had seized a half-bolt of Delamarre's stiff lacy woolens used to cover furniture because it did not display the required information about the maker, place of manufacture, or quality. The wardens ordered it marked properly and then returned. The sisters were to pay all expenses. For Goy, "this judgment is fair . . . At first, the wardens wanted to treat the young Delamarres more harshly. The wardens were motivated more by jealousy against manufacturers received [in the guild] against their will by edict of the council than by any desire to maintain a wisely established rule."[41]

This is not just a heartwarming story of gallant royal officials coming to the aid of a trio of deserving young women. At issue was the unwillingness of Darnetal's drapers to accept outside regulation. In 1782 alone, the royal government ordered the drapers to affix their mark to the fringe of each bolt of woolens on three separate occasions. Masters who wanted to produce according to the regulations were required to submit to inspection before the seal was fastened. The Darnetalais rejected both requirements as contrary to their privileges, making their seizure of Delamarre's goods even more ironic. Deputy of commerce Jean-Baptiste Tolozan noted "frankly" that "those manufactures who wish to cheat are the ones most interested in avoiding inspection." He asked de Crosne to "examine closely all their [the drapers of Darnetal] work." The royal council's intervention in the high justices surrounding Rouen was intended to force Darnetal's drapers to follow the few remaining rules.

What effects did these changes in *corporate* structure have on the production of woolens in particular and textiles more generally? At first glance, putting Rouen's drapers in charge of Darnetal's made little sense. The former's output was in decline, the latter's booming. In 1787, the formerly privileged enclave of Darnetal had nearly 450 woolens manufacturers whose annual output of more than 8,000 bolts sold for 3

[40] Jean-Baptiste Goy, *Lettre*, February 6, 1783, AN F12 1365.

[41] Jean-Baptiste Goy, *Mémoire général sur les bureaux de visite et de marque établis dans la ville et généralité de Rouen, sur ses différentes fabriques, et sur ses principaux établissements de commerce, avec quelques observations en conséquence des tournées de l'inspection des manufactures de la généralité en 1787*, December 15, 1787, AN F12 1365.

million *livres*. Dyeing and finishing also earned large sums. A few masters operated on a large scale, but most did not. Producers generally avoided inspection (both before and after that became legal). Although Darnetal's woolens outshone Rouen's, Goy reported that competition from "English merchandise" depressed sales of their goods: "The English send over about the same merchandise, but at a lower price. Their goods are not as well-made, but the lower price gives them the [customers'] preference."[42]

Darnetal's drapers responded by investing in mechanization to lower labor costs. Contemporaries emphasized the restiveness of Darnetal's woolens workers, particularly when food prices were high, but the competition for scarce jobs usually kept the workforce far more docile than Bordeaux's. The potential for violence was, however, quite real. As mentioned in Chapter 3, on July 14, 1789, a mob from Darnetal touched off a series of major machine-breaking riots in and around Rouen. Machines in Darnetal were also destroyed by crowd action in August and October. Entrepreneurs responded to the "threat from below" by slowing the pace of technical change. These events were in the future, but the central state perceived the Rouennais to be far less likely to engage in fraud or to avoid inspection, which justified putting them in charge. Exchanging one privilege for another could have positive effects on competitiveness, at least in the short term.[43]

Textile regulation did not disappear. Elbeuf and Louviers demonstrate that the royal council's growing commitment to greater liberty in production and exchange did not apply to the high end of the market. A February 1780 edict regulating the woolens manufactures of Elbeuf and Louviers was precipitated by escalating shopfloor theft of "trimmings, string, and waste." The preamble states:

> The king judges it necessary to prevent inconveniences that might result from these thefts while taking essential precautions to prevent these manufactures from degrading and losing imperceptibly the reputations that they have justly acquired in foreign lands as well as within the realm.

[42] Goy, *Mémoire general*, December 15, 1787.

[43] The previous eight paragraphs are based on Alexandre, *Lettre à Bertin*, January 10, 1783, Henri Bertin, *Lettre à de Crosne*, January 21, 1783, both in AN F12 786. See also Jean-Baptiste Goy, *Observations sur la requête des fabricans du Bourg de Darnetal*, January 8, 1782, AN F12 1365, Jean-Baptiste Tolozan, *Lettre à de Crosne*, September 18, 1782, AD Seine-Maritime C126, Comité régional d'histoire de la Révolution française (Haute-Normandie), *La Révolution en Haute-Normandie 1789–1802* (Rouen: Editions du P'tit Normand, 1988), 16, Harold T. Parker, *An Administrative Bureau during the Old Regime: The Bureau of Commerce and Its Relations to French Industry from May 1781 to November 1783* (Newark: University of Delaware Press, 1993), 102, and Horn, *The Path Not Taken*, 33, 39–41, 107–08.

Accordingly, the king is pleased to see that there are no longer guilds in these two cities and that the exercise of arts and trades is entirely free. Therefore, it is even more vital to establish a good *police* of these manufactures which are so important commercially.

The manufacturers were to convene each year and elect wardens to "execute exactly the general regulations and the particular regulations for each [royal] manufacture."[44]

The edict was soon overturned. As duke d'Elbeuf, the prince of Lambesc complained that the edict "deprived him of the right to exercise through his officers the *police* of those workers and entrepreneurs who make up the manufacture of Elbeuf." Necker backed down in September 1780. He directed that the prince be "reestablished in this right until it is ordered otherwise."[45] Elbeuf's masters remained in control of production (see Chapter 3).

In Elbeuf and Louviers, the *corporate* system remained in place, both because of the influence of their seigneurs and because it worked. In 1787, inspector of manufacturing Goy reported that wages were falling because of competition from abroad. Daily wages were steadily replaced by pay based on performance. In the 1780s, Elbeuvians also took the first steps toward mechanizing the spinning process for wool. Goy warned, however, that although "manufacturing [quality] is generally good at Elbeuf," shoddy woolens were on sale in many places. After complaining of the effects of "liberty," he reported that "more entrepreneurs follow the regulations today than when the new regulations began."[46]

It was hard to argue with success. In 1786, Elbeuf made 18,300 bolts of woolens worth more than 9,600,000 *livres*. Louviers produced more than 4,100 bolts of fine woolens whose value surpassed 3,300,000 *livres*. From these two cities, Goy announced, spinning jennies were spreading across the generality. These enclaves retained their original privileges as well as the privilege of keeping their *corporate* structures; their success shows the potential of Norman enterprise zones.

Deputies of commerce made Elbeuf the centerpiece of their argument rejecting Necker's intermediate system. They reasoned that "the quality of Elbeuf's woolens is such that the least alteration is noticeable. It lowers the price more than the small economy that the manufacturer gains ... What we say about Elbeuf applies to all the realm's manufactures." After

44 *Arrêt du Conseil d'État du Roi concernant la police d'observer dans les Manufactures de Drap d'Elbeuf et de Louviers*, February 14, 1780, AN F12 786.

45 *Lettre de Necker, Directeur général du commerce à M. De Crosne, intendant à Rouen*, September 10, 1780, AN F12 786.

46 Goy, *Mémoire general*, December 15, 1787.

a lengthy resumé of trends in trade and manufacturing, the deputies claimed that

> unlimited liberty of trade, manufacturing, and shipping is only a beautiful madness that has never arisen among people who are jealous of their law and order, natural advantages, and rights ... A careful examination of the many branches of industry reveals that they ... are almost everywhere secured by precision of manufacture which is the surest means of keeping customers and acquiring new ones.

The letters-patent of May 1779 were unnecessary, the deputies stated, because "liberty and protection are the real encouragements that commerce and manufacturing need from the administration." They concluded that liberty should consist of:

1. The ability to acquire raw materials in abundance and at the best possible price. Domestic raw materials should have preference over foreign;
2. Equality of treatment; and
3. The ability of manufactured goods to circulate and to be exported.[47]

This political economy defended certain forms of privilege: it was consistent with the evolution of royal policy until the mid-1770s but not with the drastic shift inaugurated by Turgot.

Turgot's tenure as controller-general marked a number of turning points. Perhaps most importantly, the highest levels of French officialdom endorsed entrepreneurialism as the key to future competitiveness. Turgot and those who followed in his wake built on François Quesnay's advocacy of "agricultural entrepreneurs" as agents of economic improvement. After 1776, royal administrators sought to liberate the inventive and entrepreneurial capacities of French manufacturers and traders more systematically than ever before. Growing industrial and commercial competition at home and abroad motivated this revision. Perhaps more fundamentally, however, policymakers at the highest level accepted that "the fortune of Colbertism," to borrow Philippe Minard's apt phrase, was nearly bankrupt. Based on this belief, decision makers moved faster and farther than experts responsible for implementing policy advised.

This triumph of philosophy over expertise is a deeply revealing statement about French political economy. Executive action between 1776 and 1789 reflected a budding consensus that change was needed

[47] *Avis des Députés du Commerce sur un Mémoire qui leur a été communiqué par Monseigneur le Directeur Général des finances, dans sa lettre du 8 mars 1778*, n.d. [1779], AN F12 719. Part of the first block quote appeared in Jeff Horn, "'A Beautiful Madness': Privilege, the Machine Question and Industrial Development in Normandy in 1789," *Past & Present*, 217 (November 2012), 162.

and that greater liberty was the direction that change should take. By reducing the place of regulation, royal administrators intended liberated entrepreneurs to stimulate French production and exchange. This intention entailed abandoning the generally successful policies of the previous 125 years. The significance of that shift for French economic development, both actual and potential, is the subject of the next section.[48]

Privilege and the possibility of an industrial revolution in France

Commentators on the British industrial revolution generally dismiss the prospect of a similar phenomenon occurring in France. I challenged that view in *The Path Not Taken: French Industrialization in the Age of Revolution, 1750–1830.*[49] Through the lens of privilege, however, I see the issue a bit differently. Rather than rehearse past arguments, I will articulate a set of interlinked conclusions based on this book and then consider their significance in relation to France's potential for an industrial revolution.

First of all, as a tool of economic development, the institution of privilege effectively fostered Smithian growth (see Chapter 2), though, naturally, it was more effective in some places than in others. Secondly,

48 The seven previous paragraphs are based on the following sources. The works of Philippe Minard are essential to understanding this transition. See, in particular, *La fortune du colbertisme: État et industrie dans la France des Lumières* (Fayard, 1998) and "'France colbertiste versus 'Angleterre libérale'? Un myth du XVIIIe siècle," in Jean-Philippe Genet and François-Joseph Ruggiu (eds.), *Les idées passent-ils la Manche? Savoirs, representations, pratiques (France-Angleterre, Xe-XXe siècles)* (Presses de l'Université Paris-Sorbonne, 2007), 197–209. See François Quesnay, "Fermiers" and "Grains" (ARTFUL), VI: 528–40 and VII: 812–31, and José M. Menudo and José M^{a} O'kean, "A.-J.-R. Turgot and the Construction of an Economic Agent Called Entrepreneur," Universida Pablo de Olavide, Department of Economics Working papers series, 6: 25 (2006), http://www.upo.es/serv/bib/wps/econ0625.pdf (accessed July 29, 2013), 1–19. See also Maurice Veyrat, *La haute justice des archevêques de Rouen, comtes de Louviers 1197–1790*, thèse de doctorat en droit (Rouen: Éditions Maugard, 1948), 179, *Mémoire pour les fabriquants d'Elbeuf*, May 27, 1783, AN F12 760, and Jeffry Kaplow, *Elbeuf during the Revolutionary Period: History and Social Structure* (Baltimore: Johns Hopkins University Press, 1964), 36.

49 The denigration of French industrial potential received new impetus with David S. Landes, *The Unbound Prometheus: Technological Change and Industrial Development in Western Europe from 1750 to the Present* (Cambridge University Press, 1969), 124–92 and then with François Crouzet, *Britain Ascendant: Comparative Studies in Franco-British Economic History*, trans. Martin Thom (Cambridge University Press, 1990 [1985]). See also Robert C. Allen, *The British Industrial Revolution in Global Perspective* (Cambridge University Press, 2009), 135–44. For a more balanced view, see Leandro Prados de la Escosura (ed.), *Exceptionalism and Industrialisation: Britain and its European Rivals, 1688–1815* (Cambridge University Press, 2004) and Horn, *The Path Not Taken*, 1–9.

privilege played an important role in the professionalization of the French state's economic and technical management. Thirdly, challenges to privilege's economic function emerged during the reign of Louis XIV but intensified around 1750. In response to those challenges, officials increasingly provided privileges of liberty rather than liberties of privilege. Although a growing number of policymakers championed liberty, especially after mid-century, privilege's relative effectiveness slowed a faster shift in that direction. For either philosophical or political reasons, a succession of high-level administrators starting with Turgot sped up the process, overriding the views of engaged bureaucrats and industrial experts. The practical results of this change were uneven at best. At issue is whether the institution of privilege allowed or impeded an industrial revolution in late eighteenth-century France.

Privilege clearly helped France develop sufficient capital, expertise, skilled labor, and entrepreneurs along with the requisite commercial and administrative institutions to embark on an industrial revolution. Yet, market fragmentation, legal hindrances, shortages of key raw materials, transportation deficiencies, institutional immaturity, worker intransigence, and the rent-seeking aspects of privilege ensured that if France commenced the transition to "modern" economic growth, it would not be on the same terms as its cross-channel rival. As Tocqueville implied in the quote at the beginning of the chapter, France might have been able to embark on what has been termed "labor-intensive industrialization."[50] A British-style industrial revolution based on coal, cotton, and iron was out of the question.

State decision making was shaped by economic matters to a far greater degree than has been recognized by most historians or economists, as was demonstrated in Chapter 6. In considering economic policy, royal officials weighed privilege's diminishing returns against liberty's mostly empty promises. Neither government credit nor state debt was the essential factor in industrial, commercial, or technological decision making until the American war (1777–1783). Contemporary economists and economic historians laud how post-1688 Britain managed its debt and disparage the Bourbon state's growing debt.[51] Yet, for all the scholarly

[50] On this concept and its application, see Gareth Austin and Kaoru Sugihara (eds.), *Labour-Intensive Industrialization in Global History* (New York: Routledge, 2013).

[51] This view is developed by Douglass C. North and Barry R. Weingast, "Constitutions and Commitment: The Evolution of Institutions Governing Public Choice in Seventeenth-Century England," *Journal of Economic History*, 49: 4 (1989), 803–32. The most influential articulations of the importance of debt and credit to policymaking are Philip T. Hoffman, Gilles Postel-Vinay, and Jean-Laurent Rosenthal, *Priceless Markets: The Political Economy of Credit in Paris, 1660–1870* (University of Chicago Press, 2000), Michael Sonenscher, *Before the Deluge: Public Debt, Inequality, and the Intellectual*

consideration of financial matters, remarkably little attention has been paid to policymaking where credit and debt related to industry, commerce, shipping, or mining. That said, debt *was* a major concern at several junctures, most notably during the war of Spanish Succession (1702–1713) and the Seven Years' War (1756–1763), as well as after the collapse of Law's system (early 1720s). I seek to call attention to the gap between public discourse and public policy.

In the forty years leading up to 1789, improvers successfully "liberated" several facets of the French economy. But from the grain trade to commerce with the Levant and the manufacture of textiles, liberty's tangible economic benefits were few and far between. Without privilege to mitigate and restrain its effects, greater liberty did not have the desired effects on production or exchange. Market realities made clear liberty's limitations. Policymakers and bureaucrats may not have had sufficient information or understanding to judge why these measures did not succeed, but they could recognize the meagerness of the results. Eighteenth-century "economists" also learned from their mistakes. We should acknowledge that their use of the term "liberty" was not generally intended to advocate for concrete action. Rather, liberty frequently served as a bludgeon that allowed the economists to score political points or to develop their theories. In short, liberty is a term, a concept, and a set of policy choices that cannot be understood either as synonymous with progress or taken at face value.[52]

The French had an intimate understanding of England's economic transformation. They realized that Adam Smith's *The Wealth of Nations* articulated an approach to improving British performance; it was not a description of current practice. After all, Britain's economy was undeniably mercantilist until well into the nineteenth century. How else

Origins of the French Revolution (Princeton University Press, 2007), and Thomas J. Sargent and François R. Velde, "Macroeconomic Features of the French Revolution," *Journal of Political Economy*, 103: 3 (1995), 474–518, esp. 480–82. Interestingly, Sargent and Velde's own analysis of the debt explains why that was the case. See also Eugene N. White, "Was There a Solution to the Ancien Régime's Financial Dilemma?" *Journal of Economic History*, 49: 3 (1989), 545–68.

52 For an example of this use of liberty, see David S. Landes, *The Wealth and Poverty of Nations: Why Some Are So Rich and Some So Poor* (New York: W.W. Norton, 1999), 218–20. On its origins, see Donald Winch, *Riches and Poverty: An Intellectual History of Political Economy in Britain, 1750–1834* (Cambridge University Press, 1996). Too frequently, recent historians' consideration of liberty on either side of the Channel seems limited to the liberty to consume. See, for example, William H. Sewell, Jr., "The Empire of Fashion and the Rise of Capitalism in Eighteenth-Century France," *Past & Present*, 206 (2010), 81–120, Maxine Berg, *Luxury & Pleasure in Eighteenth-Century Britain* (Oxford University Press, 2005), and Jan de Vries, *The Industrious Revolution: Consumer Behavior and the Household Economy, 1650 to the Present* (Cambridge University Press, 2008).

can we understand the liberties of privilege enjoyed by the East Indies Company, among others, or the privileges of (English!) liberty embodied in the navigation acts? We should also remember that eighteenth-century Britain had guilds, even if their liberties of privilege were much less effective than in France. British economic privileges far outlasted their French counterparts and were even added to in the nineteenth century with the passage of the Corn Laws in 1815.[53]

Smith's rejection of British practice is often overshadowed by the drastic changes to political economy that came with the Revolution. As we shall see in Chapter 8, economic "liberty" came to mean something quite different than it did before 1789. We should not apply that later meaning to the previous era. A major purpose of this book is to situate this multivalent concept in the context of practice to better understand early modern economic development on its own terms.

In hindsight, decisions scaling back the provision of privilege were based on philosophical and political concerns rather than economic performance. Institutions influenced but did not determine policymaking. In an economy with such a large and pervasive illicit sector, we must also pay particular attention to the informal consequences of actions taken by formal institutions. Structures, in the sense used by Douglass C. North, tell only part of the story.

The assault on privilege in favor of liberty had long roots, but a turning point came in 1776 with Turgot's carnival rather than the publication of Smith's magnum opus. Contemporary critics of French economic performance in general and specific institutions such as markets tend to idealize British practice. Such critics overlook the similarity of institutions on both sides of the Channel. Policies based on liberty had great potential but limited success. Both the theory and the practice were known and understood long before the publication of *The Wealth of Nations*.[54] This book demonstrates that the goal of using liberty to determine economic policy was a perverse problem for French political economy rather than the solution to its economic woes.

Far too frequently, the looming presence of the Revolution shades evaluations of Bourbon France. Institutional restructuring in 1776–1781 constituted a major policy shift with the promise of more to come. Despite

[53] Crouzet, *Britain Ascendant*, 127–48 and Horn, *The Path Not Taken*, 53–63. See also Kenneth Carpenter, *The Dissemination of* The Wealth of Nations *in French and in France: 1776–1843* (New York: Oak Knoll Press, 2002).

[54] Sargent and Velde, "Macroeconomic Features of the French Revolution" and Hilton R. Root, *The Fountain of Privilege: Political Foundations of Markets in Old Regime France and England* (Berkeley: University of California Press, 1994).

the guilds' financial usefulness, their authority was unmistakably on the wane. Extending the privilege of liberty to textile producers was clearly a transitional step toward greater liberty. The Anglo-French commercial treaty of 1786 and the single duty project (pushing customs to the frontiers to create a true national market) were the next steps in that shift. By changing course, Bourbon policymakers sought to transcend what today would be termed "path dependence." The economic effectiveness of that effort, undertaken primarily for political and ideological reasons, will be evaluated in the next chapter.[55]

Although these issues were considered in *The Path Not Taken*, focusing on privilege as a policy tool underscores the interrelated issues of entrepreneurialism and state regulation. By gutting the authority of officials like the inspectors of manufacturing and limiting the power of the guilds, the royal council expressed its faith in French entrepreneurs. The measures of 1776–1781 conclusively proclaimed the state's conviction that French industrial entrepreneurs could and would make decisions to help the realm become more competitive. Although reducing the *police* power held by both royal and local officials made controlling workers an ever more difficult proposition, this choice can also be read as a mark of confidence. The royal council seemed to believe that French entrepreneurs could manage their labor forces if given appropriate legal tools and sufficient economic opportunities.

The royal council anticipated that these opportunities would emerge from the raft of sixteen commercial treaties or conventions signed under Louis XVI, the opening up of the colonies to foreigners with the expectation of being able to trade with the colonies of other European states (see Chapter 4), and the creation of a unified national market. In the short run, French entrepreneurs were unable to take advantage of these initiatives. A near "perfect storm" of international, climatological, and administrative problems allowed English goods to flood French markets, while the latter's best foreign customers were distracted by domestic concerns. Unemployment soared just as food prices spiked. The economy played *a* major if not *the* major role in the crisis of 1789.

Generally, I find counterfactual supposition to be a sterile exercise. In this case, I believe it can emphasize certain characteristics of the early modern economy. Had the policies initiated in the 1770s and 1780s been

55 For an example of the outsized presence of the Revolution in analyses of the old régime, see Paul Cheney, *Revolutionary Commerce: Globalization and the French Monarchy* (Cambridge, MA: Harvard University Press, 2010). On customs reform, see John F. Bosher, *The Single Duty Project: A Study of the Movement for a French Customs Union in the Eighteenth Century* (London: the Athlone Press, 1964) and Horn, *The Path Not Taken*, 51–88.

given longer to work, might the Bourbon administration have been able to extend the liberties given to entrepreneurs enough to make the transition from Smithian growth to an industrial revolution? My answer to that counterfactual question is a resounding no: if Britain could not do it, France certainly could not.

The eighteenth-century British state was by no means *laissez-faire*. The island kingdom just handled regulation and social control in distinctly different fashion than continental governments. During the early industrial revolution, many British workers endured a harsher discipline and more thorough state control than the worst-off French guild apprentices. The British navigation acts remained in force at a time when the French were opening up markets. As shown in Chapters 3–5, France's lack of a unified market and transportation shortfalls, along with its inefficient and insufficient taxation system, constrained opportunities for entrepreneurs to earn legitimate profits. French merchants and manufacturers up and down the socioeconomic spectrum responded by cheating, smuggling, and defrauding. Without thoroughgoing state involvement, French entrepreneurs generally chose not to compete. Instead they took profits in different, but eminently rational ways. The government's inability to mimic the British state's effectiveness in overawing workers also undercut innovation and investment.[56] In the late eighteenth century, greater liberty was a stumbling block not a path to an industrial revolution, at least in the short run.

France's structural impediments endured until the completion of the railroad network fifty years later. To put it bluntly, France did not lack the scientific and technical knowledge, understanding of liberal policies, institutions, or raw materials needed for an industrial revolution. These factors mattered, deeply, but they were sufficient rather than necessary causes. Structural reasons provide the best explanation for why France did not commence an industrial revolution at the same time as Britain.

The events of 1789–1794 fundamentally and irrevocably shifted the trajectory of French political economy and the nature of French capitalism. In the wake of the Revolution, it became clear that if an industrial revolution took place, it would have to be on quite different terms from what might have emerged organically out of Bourbon

[56] Patrick K. O'Brien, "The State and the Economy, 1688–1815," in Roderick Floud and Donald McCloskey (eds.), *The Economic History of Britain since 1700*, vol. 1 (Cambridge University Press, 1994), 204–37, 451–64, Prados de la Escosura (ed.), *Exceptionalism and Industrialisation*, 1–14, 111–26, 145–69, 261–82, and Emma Griffin, *A Short History of the British Industrial Revolution* (New York: Palgrave, 2010), 126–43. See also Horn, *The Path Not Taken*, 89–125 and Horn, "'A Beautiful Madness,'" 179–85.

reformist efforts. As we shall see in the next chapter neither privilege nor the *corporate* mentality disappeared after 1789 – far from it – but their heyday at the center of economic policy ended with the old régime. France had to wait for institutions and structures to change before an industrial revolution became possible.

8 The reign of liberty?
Privilege after 1789

> The word "privilege" ought to irritate the restorers of French liberty. They see the privileged as the spoiled children of arbitrary power and as parasitic branches which absorb the sap which invigorate commerce.
>
> Joseph Dupré, deputy of the city of Carcassonne and representative of Languedocian industry (1790)[1]

The year 1789 was a watershed in French political economy just as much as it was in French political culture. As previous chapters demonstrate, the Bourbon government believed that privilege had reached its limit as a tool of economic development, but policymakers remained convinced that privilege still had a major role to play in paving the way for greater economic liberty. This belief drove the post-1750 shift from reliance on the liberties of privilege to the privilege of liberty. The trends in policymaking toward providing greater liberty, supporting entrepreneurialism, and competing internationally are clear and incontrovertible. Without a crisis of the magnitude and depth of the French Revolution, it seems likely that the royal government would have continued this organic policy evolution, which had been underway since the end of the age of Louis XIV. In the same fashion as its cross-channel rivals, France might have developed a political economy that relied increasingly on liberty and competition but retained many elements of mercantilism until well into the nineteenth century.

As Joseph Dupré's scapegoating of privilege and the privileged makes clear, that economic policy tool became impractical because of shifts in public opinion. In a distinct departure from the political situation, the accelerating vilification of the privileged did not result in the immediate demolition of the cornerstones of the edifice supporting economic privilege in favor of a system based fundamentally on liberty. In 1789–1791, privilege's slowly receding tide reveals how deeply imbricated privilege

[1] Joseph Dupré, *Mémoire sur le Commerce en général et celui du Languedoc dans les rapports avec les Echelles du Levant, la Compagnie des Indes, les Colonies et la Traité des Noirs*, 1790, ACCIMP J1562.

was as a policy tool. The rebirth of some privileges as "exemptions" also reminds us of the lack of viable alternatives to fostering economic growth. The profound shifts in political economy and the role of the state in society inaugurated by the French Revolution required and perhaps even necessitated the elaboration of new approaches to economic regulation and development.

In *The Path Not Taken: French Industrialization in the Age of Revolution, 1750–1830*, I argued that Revolutionary political economy rendered French state and society incapable of imitating the British approach to industrialization. Amid intense domestic upheaval and, after 1792, with war on every frontier, Revolutionary policymakers experimented with liberal political economy and then, during the crisis of the Year II (1793–1794), with a statist command economy. Although privilege did not completely disappear until halfway through the decade after 1789, its role was drastically curtailed. The French inability to consolidate the republic politically undermined economic development, and vice versa. Taking advantage of acute uncertainty, Napoleon Bonaparte and his co-conspirators seized power in November 1799 and managed to found a powerful and popular state that actively sought to stimulate economic development.[2]

Between 1799 and 1820, economic privilege reemerged as a tool of state policy, albeit in far different roles. State-granted privileges represented exceptions to the reign of liberty and violated Revolutionary principles. Under the Consulate and Empire and continuing well into the nineteenth century, the French state deployed privilege almost solely to protect public order and consumers rather than to foster development. Early modern Bourbon administrators certainly favored some over others and they paid careful attention to issues of public order, but they almost always maintained a sense of the broader purposes of economic policymaking. Although Dupré's defamation of privilege was aimed at these paternalistic but development-minded royal administrators, the bureaucrats who deployed privilege on behalf of the nineteenth-century state deserved the criticism far more.

This trajectory of economic policymaking raises questions related to path dependence. Were France's economic problems in the 1790s related inextricably to the difficulty of shifting approach rather than more standard explanations based on the upheavals of war and revolution? Did the slow dismantling of liberties of privilege and privileges of liberty

[2] Jeff Horn, *The Path Not Taken: French Industrialization in the Age of Revolution, 1750–1830* (Cambridge, MA: MIT Press, 2006).

in 1789–1791 and their revival after 1799 uncover the deep roots of French political economy or merely the difficulties of executing so many changes at once? And finally, by abandoning British-style industrialization, did Revolutionary policymakers doom the country to a second-class economic position? These big questions have profound implications not only for French and European history but also for understanding the uneven, drawn-out global transition to an industrial economy.

Path dependence has been an important but implicit theme of this book. The Revolutionary break, however, was significant enough that the concept deserves pride of place. Understanding economic decision making historically, rather than fundamentally in mathematical terms, has wide application in a variety of subdisciplines and subfields in economics. Paul A. David usefully defines the term, both negatively and positively. Negatively, path dependence refers to a dynamic resource allocation process that cannot escape from earlier decisions and the structures developed to implement them. More positively, path dependence occurs when the "branching" processes relating to probabilities of change are constrained by previous states of the system of resource allocation.[3]

In light of this definition and in the context of French economic decision making between 1650 and 1830, path dependence means (1) that France could not escape, or could only escape with dire consequences, the economic strictures of a society of orders based on the notion of privilege, and (2) that French policymakers were limited so greatly by previous decisions and structures that profit maximization and fully "rational choices" were simply not options. I reject both these formulations as fundamentally ahistorical. To be true not only to the archival record but also to what people actually did – as opposed to what they wrote or said about it – historians of political economy must accept the notion that trying to shift "paths" could have profoundly negative consequences. This was a particular concern for an economy competing for customers, for sources of raw materials, and ultimately for the mastery of Europe. French economic policymaking between 1789 and 1815 was both facilitated and constricted by the legacies of the old régime's reliance on liberties of privilege and privileges of liberty.

[3] See Paul Krugman, "Increasing Returns and Economic Geography," *Journal of Political Economy*, 99: 3 (1991), 483–99, Carolina Castaldi, Giovanni Dosi, and Evita Paraskevopoulou, "Path Dependence in Technologies and Organizations: A Concise Guide," Eindhoven Center for Innovation Studies: Working Paper 11.04 (2011), http://ideas.repec.org/p/dgr/tuecis/wpaper1104.html (accessed December 19, 2013), and Paul A. David, *Path Dependence and the Quest for Historical Economics: One More Chorus of the Ballad of QWERTY*, University of Oxford: Discussion Papers in Economic and Social History 20 (November 1997), http://www.nuff.ox.ac.uk/economics/history/paper20/david3.pdf (accessed December 19, 2013), 1–48, esp. 13–14.

Recognizing that multiple political transitions made use of different elements of privilege takes path dependence out of the realm of the theoretical by bringing to life the possibilities and potentialities of French political economy in the Revolutionary era.

This interpretation of path dependence with the goal of recovering economic possibilities in light of the constraints on economic systems on the cusp of industrial society responds to the multilayered debate on British exceptionalism, divergence, and globalization. In the past fifteen years, a distinguished collection of scholars have advanced diverse explanations for *why* these linked, but essentially separate, processes took place. These interpretations can be grouped according to whether they emphasize (1) what might be termed "purely" economic factors, (2) the role of technological innovation, or (3) differences related to political economy. As the policies that granted the liberty of privilege and the privilege of liberty were fundamentally matters of political economy, I will engage related interpretations of the economic transition that took place during the age of Revolution.[4]

Through the lens of France's old régime, arguments about the causes of British exceptionalism and the growing gap between "the West" and "the rest" consistently underestimate the intensity of the transformation of European political economy inaugurated by the French Revolution. "Political economy" is the key term here because the changes that shaped French, continental, and ultimately Western development were neither fundamentally political nor essentially economic, but rather melded the two. Tracing privileged enterprises, entrepreneurs, *corporate* groups, and regions during the decade from 1789 to 1799 while considering the evolution – and diminution – of privilege as a tool of state policy allows us to glimpse the depth of the Revolutionary cataclysm. This

[4] The first category includes David S. Landes, *The Wealth and Poverty of Nations: Why Some Are So Rich and Some So Poor* (New York: W.W. Norton, 1998). The second can be represented by Robert C. Allen, *The British Industrial Revolution in Global Perspective* (Cambridge University Press, 2009), Margaret C. Jacob, *Scientific Culture and the Making of the Industrial West* (Oxford University Press, 1997), and Joel Mokyr, *The Gifts of Athena: Historical Origins of the Knowledge Economy* (Princeton University Press, 2002). The third grouping includes Joseph E. Inikori, *Africans and the Industrial Revolution in England: A Study of International Trade and Economic Development* (Cambridge University Press, 2002), Prasannan Parthasarathi, *Why Europe Grew Rich and Asia Did Not: Global Economic Divergence, 1600–1850* (Cambridge University Press, 2011), Kenneth Pomeranz, *The Great Divergence: China, Europe, and the Making of the Modern World Economy* (Princeton University Press, 2000), Jean-Laurent Rosenthal and R. Bin Wong, *Before and Beyond Divergence: The Politics of Economic Change in China and Europe* (Cambridge, MA: Harvard University Press, 2011), and the various scholars who honored Patrick O'Brien in Leandro Prados de la Escosura, (ed.), *Exceptionalism and Industrialisation: Britain and Its European Rivals, 1688–1815* (Cambridge University Press, 2004).

boulder was sufficiently large to force a detour in every path leading up to it. Nineteenth-century state policies were affected by France's experiences during the Revolution far more than they were by what came before. In other words, paths could be and are dependent on multiple variables that can be grouped in different ways in different times and different places: oversimplifying the equation robs it of explanatory value.

Privilege and the Revolution

Privileges – political, tax, economic, and honorific – played a vital role in the outbreak of the Revolution of 1789. Debates about the proper format and structure of the Estates-General in 1788–1789 expressed most famously by the abbé Emmanuel-Joseph Sieyès centered on the position of privilege in French society. Applied to economic matters, these fundamentally political arguments resonated throughout the *cahiers de doléance* written in March–April 1789. Amid an industrial slump that followed the Anglo-French commercial treaty of 1786, growing unemployment fueled popular dissatisfaction with economic privileges. In regions dependent on manufacturing for the domestic market, economic uncertainty helped to radicalize public opinion. From the fall of the Bastille through the Great Fear, widespread violence against economic, social, and political privilege took the form of machine-breaking primarily in and around Normandy's privileged enclaves. I have argued that the rising "threat from below" visible in these popular movements and the inability of the French state to control the laboring classes undermined the confidence of entrepreneurs in mechanization and innovation, thereby slowing down and altering the character of French industrialization.

Until late summer 1789, the French were deeply conflicted when it came to privilege. Repeated and long-lasting clashes between liberties of privilege and privileges of liberty discussed in previous chapters, along with the struggles among territories, groups, and the guilds (a very different kind of group), were reflected not only in public discourse but also in public action. This inconsistency is to be expected in any consideration of such a complicated and multifaceted institution that varied so widely according to place and space.

Troyes, capital of the province of Champagne, was a major textile producer. Hard hit by the post-1786 industrial depression, the *cahier* of the Third Estate of the city of Troyes demanded that urban *police* powers should supervise the economic activities of the suburbs, privileged or not, and that "all privileged places be closed to that crowd of bankrupts who, from these sanctuaries, lay down the law and insult their creditors," before concluding that "privileged enclaves for manufacturing in the cities, inner suburbs [*faubourgs*], and outer suburbs [*banlieues*] should be eliminated." The *cahier* is internally inconsistent. After observing that "nearly all the trades of the city and suburbs of Troyes request to be continued as communities," the concluding summary stated "that some *corporations* demand the elimination of workshops in the countryside and the continuation of the guilds, while others ask for complete and indefinite liberty. Since each group believes that they have the means to support their request, it seems prudent to leave the decision to the Estates-General." Both the privilege of liberty and the liberty of privilege were contentious subjects in the spring of 1789.[5]

Privilege divided economic elites in southern Champagne. In a pamphlet published five weeks after the meeting of the Third Estate,

> The wholesale merchants representing Troyes' trade and craft guilds were astonished to learn that the commissioners named by the general assembly to write the list of grievances had claimed that the Third Estate of the bailliage requested the abolition of the guilds and indefinite liberty to exercise any trade or profession.

After referring to "abuses without number" occasioned by Anne-Robert-Jacques de Turgot's suppression of the guilds in 1776 and their reestablishment soon afterward (see Chapter 7), the sixty signers of the pamphlet remarked that the opinions expressed in the *cahier* were not "the view of the Third Estate" but rather those of "rural inhabitants who would abandon agriculture to take refuge in the cities if the professions of the arts and crafts were open."[6]

Actions speak louder than words. Sometimes they shout. On September 9, 1789, a subsistence riot turned into an assault on innovative English-style textile machines. The riot culminated in the murder of the champion of mechanization, the royal mayor, Claude Huez. His head was put on a pike and paraded around the city. This bout of machine-breaking and ongoing threats of its recurrence effectively delayed Troyes' entrepreneurs from mechanizing or improving their production processes for over a decade. Attacks on those who enjoyed the privilege of liberty by those with liberties of privilege demonstrated both how important privilege was to the French economy and the ambiguities involved in attempts to reform.[7]

5 Jules-Joseph Vernier (ed.), *Cahiers de doléances du bailliage de Troyes (principal et secondaires) et du bailliage de Bar-sur-Seine pour les États généraux de 1789*, 3 vols. (Troyes: Nouel, 1909–1911), III: 250, 265, 285–86. On the *cahiers* as a source and for the most complete investigation of their content based on all available documentation, see Gilbert Shapiro and John Markoff, *Revolutionary Demands: A Content Analysis of the Cahiers de Doléances of 1789* (Stanford University Press, 1998).

6 *Protestations des corporations de la Ville de Troyes*, April 17, 1789 (Gallica).

7 The five previous paragraphs are based on Jeff Horn, "'A Beautiful Madness': Privilege, the Machine Question and Industrial Development in Normandy in 1789," *Past &*

Pressured by the rural Great Fear and the initial wave of municipal revolutions, the deputies of the National Assembly eliminated the privileges of the old régime during the frenzied night of August 4–5. Or did they? Such a potted version of events has been taught to many an undergraduate, but it obscures both the nuances of the deputies' actions and the survival of most economic privileges until 1791. Michael P. Fitzsimmons described August 4, 1789, as "The Night the Old Regime Ended": in economics, that claim might overshoot the mark.

That fevered night many privileges were abolished or renounced, in particular those related to the feudal system. The resulting decree published on August 11 eliminated feudalism, but made most dues redeemable. It also established compensation for aspects of the feudal system unrelated to personal serfdom or servitude. On the other hand, "pecuniary privileges, personal or real, in the payment of taxes are abolished forever." So too were the "peculiar privileges, pecuniary or otherwise, of the provinces, principalities, districts, cantons, cities and communes."[8] The National Assembly intended that privileged enclaves either be annexed to existing municipalities or form their own elected municipal governments. The only major exceptions to the elimination of spatial privileges were free ports, colonial entrepôts, and the Comtat Venaissin. The August 1789 obliteration of most spatially demarcated privileges of liberty shattered one of the chief pillars of state developmental policies based on privilege.

Liberties of privilege based on *corporate* and/or group identity or held by individuals largely survived the Revolutionary events of August 1789. Article 1 of the *Declaration of the Rights of Man and Citizen* asserts that "Men are born and remain free and equal in rights. Social distinctions may be founded only upon the general good." But Article 17 mitigates those rights and distinctions when it comes to economic privileges, "Since property is an inviolable and sacred right, no one shall be deprived thereof except where public necessity, legally determined, shall clearly demand it, and then only on condition that the owner shall have been previously and equitably indemnified."[9] Although guild privileges were eliminated on the night of August 4, that action was left out of the final list of the Assembly's decisions. When queried by constituents as to why the guilds had been left alone, deputy of Le Havre Jean-François Begouen-

Present, 217 (November 2012), 149–85 and *The Path Not Taken*, 89–125, esp. 102–03 and 114–16.

8 The decree spelling out the *Abolition of Feudalism*, August 11, 1789, www.chnm.gmu.edu/revolution/d/366 (accessed December 19, 2013).

9 *Declaration of the Rights of Man and Citizen*, August 25, 1789, www.chnm.gmu.edu/revolution/d/295 (accessed December 19, 2013).

Demeux wrote, "guilds have been deliberately set aside as demanding scrutiny and the taking of various precautions. Thus, nothing was decided on their account."[10]

Amid widespread labor unrest and worker militancy, this hesitancy seems prudent if not entirely consistent with the measures proposed on the night of August 4 and enacted into law over the course of succeeding weeks and months. Thus, individual privileges – other than tax immunities – along with those of the guilds and the *police* powers of seigneurs in the high justices survived the storied destruction of privilege in August 1789. Even the hated East Indies Company retained its trade monopoly until April 1790 and lingered until it was liquidated in 1794. Avignon and the Comtat Venaissin kept many of their privileges until late 1791.[11]

That privileged economic institutions endured until 1791 is not a new insight. Yet, in the developmental context of the privilege of liberty and the liberty of privilege, this survival takes on new meaning. The first step taken that fateful year was the creation of a new patent system in January, and revised in March, which allowed inventors who exploited their innovations exclusive ownership for five, ten, or fifteen years. Patents became a right for all who met the criteria rather than a privilege. Inclusion in a widely distributed registry entailed the payment of a rather steep fee ranging from 500 to 1500 *livres* depending on the length of protection sought. In September 1791, the Legislative Assembly designated a large fund to compensate inventors who released their discoveries to the public domain to spread French technical prowess. The state could and did provide funds or other forms of support for inventors and/or industrial enterprises in key sectors. However, the ad hoc nature of this encouragement, especially in light of the chronic shortage of funds for economic development in an era scarred by war, made the new patent system less attractive than privilege to potential inventors or investors.

The Allarde Law in March 1791 suppressed *corporations* and royal manufactures. Anyone could enter any trade. Entrepreneurs had only to

[10] Cited by Michael P. Fitzsimmons, *From Artisan to Worker: Guilds, the French State, and the Organization of Labor, 1776–1821* (Cambridge University Press, 2010), 23.

[11] The four previous paragraphs are based on Michael P. Fitzsimmons, *The Night the Old Regime Ended: August 4, 1789 and the French Revolution* (University Park: Pennsylvania State University Press, 2003), 63, 178–84 and *From Artisan to Worker*, 20–25, Léopold Duhamel, *Documents sur la Réunion d'Avignon et du Comtat-Venaissin à la France (1790–1791)* (Picard, 1891), and Jacques Le Scene-Desmaisons, *Compte Rendu à l'Assemblée Nationale*, September 10, 1791 (Gallica). Gail Bossenga posed a number of the questions raised here in "Capitalism and Corporations in Eighteenth-Century France," in Alain Plessis (ed.), *Naissance des libertés économiques: Liberté du travail et liberté d'entreprendre: le décret d'Allarde et la loi Le Chapelier, leurs conséquences, 1791-fin XIXe siècle* (Institut d'Histoire de l'Industrie - Ministère de l'Industrie, 1993), 13–31.

register their occupation and pay a reasonably small tax based on the rent on their stores, workshops, or other properties. In conjunction with the elimination of inspectors of manufacturing (in September) and the Le Chapelier Law passed in June, which outlawed either worker or producer coalitions, the Allarde Law eradicated the last liberty of privilege. By eliminating intermediary institutions, these measures increased state economic regulation albeit at a substantially reduced level.[12]

Freedom of enterprise was limited almost immediately. Initially restrictions were confined to occupations that dealt with scarce resources or influenced public health, such as the goldsmiths and silversmiths, who were supervised by the police (law of April 3, 1791). Only "those who had been received as pharmacists according to the [guild] statutes and regulations of that profession" in existence before March were allowed licenses after April 14 because of "abuses" that "undermined the confidence of the citizens in the preparation, sale, and distribution of drugs and medicines." A law of July 22 maintained locksmith guild regulations.

The significance of these practical, limited measures, however, should not be overstated. "Privilege" meant something different after 1789 than it had before. In the course of parliamentary discussion regarding the regulation of brokers on April 14, 1791, François Buzot of the Eure asked, "We speak a great deal about public confidence. Should it not be given freely to individuals rather than granted to a privileged class of individuals? Those who earn that confidence will soon gain a reputation. The reputation earned by their integrity and wisdom will be their 'privilege.'" Buzot's speech led immediately to the elimination of all offices related to brokering in "exchange, banking, commerce and insurance." Privilege was rapidly disappearing in fact, if not in the perceptions of the public.[13]

Corporate groups and individuals witnessed the steady erosion of their privileges in 1789–1791. This assault did not eliminate all privileged spaces, but it did transform how the existence of de facto privileges was justified. As mentioned above, provincial or territorial privileges were eradicated in August 1789 with one exception. The Comtat Venaissin

12 The two previous paragraphs are based on Horn, *The Path Not Taken*, 169–77.

13 The two previous paragraphs are based on Jean Imbert, "Lé 'décret' d'Allarde et ses suites immédiates," in Alain Plessis (ed.), *Naissance des libertés économiques: Liberté du travail et liberté d'entreprendre: le décret d'Allarde et la loi Le Chapelier, leurs conséquences, 1791-fin XIXe siècle* (Institut d'Histoire de l'Industrie - Ministère de l'Industrie, 1993), 103–10, 104. The quotations are from Jerôme Mavidal and Émile Laurent (eds.), *Archives parlementaires de 1787 à 1860, recueil complet des débats législatifs et politiques des Chambres françaises*, 1st series *(1787 à 1799)*, vol. 25 (Paul Dupont, 1886), 64, 98–99.

was incorporated into France in September 1791 only after a plebiscite. Municipal privileges were also jettisoned in August 1789, but again, there were significant exceptions, namely Marseille's Levantine rights and the free ports of Bayonne and Dunkerque.

The National Assembly expressly eliminated the free ports of Lorient and Bayonne in 1790 citing the decrees of August 1789 eliminating territorial privileges. Reporting on Bayonne, the vice president of the Committee of Agriculture and Commerce, François-Pierre Lasnier de Vaussenay of the Maine, referred to deep divisions in the city and in the region. As well he might. On June 11, 1790, crowds attacked the customs barriers separating the free port. Considerable amounts of tobacco and English merchandise were brought into the city. The municipality offered to send the national guard to restore order, but according to a report written by the city's Chamber of Commerce in 1802, the customs service declined. Order was only restored along with the city's free port on December 30, 1790. Bayonne kept its exemption until 1793, when it was removed due to wartime pressures.[14]

Dunkerque retained its *franchise* (exemption) without recourse to popular action. The National Assembly imposed serious conditions, including new spatial limits that required massive new construction in and around the old quays. This construction was paid for by the city and was intended to facilitate regulation and inspection. The legislature also specifically exempted colonial goods from the liberties of this privilege.

The substitution of *franchise* for "privilege" is telling: it explains the National Assembly's justification of Dunkerque's free port. Pierre-Antoine-Charles Herwyn of Dunkerque, secretary of the Committee of Agriculture and Commerce, argued that "The interests of the nation support the continuation of Dunkerque's exemption. Those same interests demand that this exemption be full and entire." Where Bayonne's and Lorient's exemptions damaged French manufacturing, commerce, and agriculture, Dunkerque's were "in the general interest of the realm."[15] Herwyn's detailed exposition of the long history and specific nature of Dunkerque's economic contributions based on the free port seemingly made for a more convincing argument.

[14] The nine previous paragraphs are based on François-Pierre Lasnier de Vaussenay, *Rapport à l'Assemblée Nationale sur la franchise de Bayonne*, 1790, (Gallica), *Réponse du Conseil de Commerce de Bayonne aux Objections faites par la Regie des Douanes contre la Franchise du Port de cette Ville*, Frimaire 25, Year XI [December 16, 1802], AN F12 1646.

[15] Pierre-Antoine-Charles Herwyn, *Rapport à l'Assemblée Nationale au nom de la Comité d'Agriculture et de Commerce sur la franchise de Dunkerque*, 1790 (Gallica).

Marseille's situation was, as usual, more complicated. The economic stakes were also far higher for France's second port, the kingdom's major outlet on the Mediterranean and its chief link to the Near East and North Africa. As Marseille's port did not enjoy "absolute exemptions," its defenders concentrated on maintaining the city's other privileges, namely the entrepôt, a near monopoly on providing quarantine for vessels returning from the Levant, and the 20 percent tax on goods shipped directly to other ports or that arrived in foreign ships. Marseille's claim to keep its *ci-devant* privileges was based on international competitiveness.

Étienne-David Meynier of the Gard presented the Committee on Agriculture and Commerce's recommendations to the National Assembly:

> If the exemptions accorded to a port, to a city, were only the particular privileges of that port, of that city, there is no question that those privileges no longer exist according to Article 10 of the edicts of August 1789. The questions facing the Committee of Agriculture and Commerce are whether it is in the realm's interest to have free ports and whether the disadvantages of those exemptions are counterbalanced by the advantages.

He concluded that "the great advantages gained for the realm by Marseille's exclusion" from the customs and conversely the threat to the nation's economy if the system were changed convinced the Committee that "Marseille's commercial system should be maintained."[16] By emphasizing the role of geography, the competition from other free ports in the Mediterranean, and the broader needs of the French economy, Meynier and the Committee justified preserving Marseille's entrepôts and maintaining lower tariffs on many goods entering and leaving the port.

The fate of Marseille's Levantine privileges was decided the following year. On July 21, 1791, on behalf of the Committee on Agriculture and Commerce, Pierre Roussillou from Toulouse distinguished between old régime rights granted as privileges and exemptions made in the national interest. He denigrated the "odious privileges of the former government," but Marseille's privileged role in trade with the Levant was different. He observed that "If, for political considerations, the exclusion of the port of Marseille did not exist, it might be necessary to create it for return voyages from the Levant." The 20 percent tax on goods in foreign hulls or those French ships that did not go through quarantine in Marseille also served "the national interest," Roussillou determined. The Committee's recommendations were endorsed by the legislature.

[16] Étienne-David Meynier, *Rapport à l'Assemblée Nationale au nom de la Comité d'Agriculture et de Commerce sur le régime à donner au port et au territoire de Marseille, quant aux droits de douane*, 1790 (Gallica).

Reborn as "exemptions" that benefited not just the city, but the entire nation, Marseille retained its privileges when most other places did not.[17]

Commercial exemptions attached to particular places were the most likely "privileges" to survive the Revolutionary changes of 1789–1791. In keeping with the arguments about the impact of machine-breaking discussed above, I suspect, but cannot prove, that industrial privileges were eliminated because of their potential threat to employment. On June 27, 1791, the National Assembly decreed that "exemptions accorded to fairs are more a favor for the realm's commerce than the particular privilege of a city."[18] This decision left those vital institutions of exchange intact and contributed to the transmutation of certain commercial privileges into exemptions, a term devoid of baggage inherited from the old régime.

These practical arrangements were swept away in the egalitarian tide of 1793–1795. Trade dislocations stemming from European war, the needs of the Maximums (wage and price controls) instituted during the Reign of Terror, and runaway inflation undermined economic justifications lingering from the old régime. At the same time, the Terror magnified the political penalty of resisting the dictates of the central state. Marseille, Dunkerque, and Bayonne lost their exemptions with the law of Nivôse 11, Year III (December 31, 1794), though all three ports retained their entrepôts.[19] After January 1795, the economic privileges of the old régime were gone, but as we shall see in the next section, they were not forgotten.

The doom of privileged individuals, groups, and places during the Revolution demonstrates the depth of the economic cataclysm of the decade after 1789. The failure of most formerly privileged enterprises and the significant declines in commerce and industry that occurred during this period can be attributed less to the shift to a different economic pathway and more to the Anglo-French commercial treaty, the outbreak of war in 1792 attended by blockade leading to the collapse of foreign trade, the dislocations of the Maximum, and the effects of the societal focus on politics and war-making. Therefore,

[17] *Rapport du comité chargé par l'Assemblée générale du commerce du 12 Août, de traiter de la franchise du Port de Marseille et de tout ce qui concerne les avantages du Commerce*, November 16, 1790, ACCIMP D26.

[18] Odilon Barrot, Antoine-François-Henri Lefebvre de Vatismesnil, and Jacques-Guibert Ymbert (eds.), *Recueil général annoté des lois, décrets, ordonnances, etc. etc. depuis le mois de juin 1789 jusqu'au mois d'août 1830*, vol. 5 (Bureau de l'Administration du Journal des Notaires et des Avocats, 1835), 428–29.

[19] Jerôme Mavidal and Émile Laurent (eds.), *Archives parlementaires de 1787 à 1860, recueil complet des débats législatifs et politiques des Chambres françaises*, 1st series *(1787 à 1799)*, vol. 28 (Paul Dupont, 1887), 492–503.

tracing particular industries, groups, or firms across the Revolutionary divide must be contextualized by the era's economic tribulations and opportunities. The shift away from reliance on the liberty of privilege and the privilege of liberty was less traumatic for French producers and traders than the massive falloff in foreign trade and the reduction of industrial output by one-third that occurred between 1789 and 1799.

Religious minorities did not immediately receive citizenship. In December 1789, Protestants acquired full rights, but Jews had to wait until September 1791. In economic terms, Protestants seem to have taken advantage of citizenship to integrate even more thoroughly into French practice. Nîmes' Protestant hosiers, for example, experienced troubled times at the end of the 1780s. Production fell by half during the Revolutionary decade primarily due to the loss of export markets, but rebounded strongly early in the nineteenth century thanks to a switchover to cotton facilitated by the Jacquard loom and the steam engine. The Continental Blockade (1807–1813) caused another major decline, but hosiery recovered under the Restoration. The industry's slow decline had little to do with the loss of privilege.

Christophe-Philippe Oberkampf, perhaps France's most economically important Protestant (see Chapter 6), became mayor of Jouy-en-Josas in 1790, in large measure because his employees constituted one-third of the voters. Exports, government contracts, and the Directory's taste for luxury allowed him to remain open throughout the Revolutionary decade, employing up to 2,000 men, women, and children. In 1792, Oberkampf sensed opportunity. He decided to build a massive factory costing 280,000 *livres* to house all aspects of the production process. Oberkampf continued to enjoy state protection, an arrangement he cemented with more than 166,000 *livres* of contributions to the war effort. The Committee of Public Safety requisitioned his labor in April 1794 and detailed him to run his own factory. Oberkampf's integration into French society, which began so successfully under the old régime, was completed during the Revolution.[20]

[20] For the three previous paragraphs, I rely on Jeff Horn "Lasting Economic Structures: Successes, Failures, Legacies," in David Andress (ed.), *Oxford Handbook of the French Revolution* (Oxford University Press, 2015), 607–24 and Jean-Pierre Gross, *Fair Shares for All: Jacobin Egalitarianism in Practice* (Cambridge University Press, 1997). On Oberkampf, see Serge Chassagne, *Oberkampf: Un entrepreneur capitaliste au Siècle des Lumières* (Aubier, 1980), 151–82, esp. 155, 164, Albert Labourchère, *Oberkampf (1738–1815)*, 3rd ed. (Hachette, 1878), 82–88, 107, 113, and Bertrand Badré and Philippe Colombet, *Entreprises en Révolution* (Jean-Claude Lattès, 1990), 183–88. On Nîmes, see Armand Cosson, "L'industrie textile à Nîmes: la fin d'une hégémonie (1790–1850)," *Le Mouvement social*, 133 (1985), 5–24, esp. 6–7, and Léon Dutil, "L'Industrie de la soie à Nîmes jusqu'en 1789," *Revue d'histoire moderne et contemporaine*, 10: 4 (1908), 318–43, esp. 341–43.

In 1789, Jewish lobbyists from Bordeaux sought de facto not de jure citizenship. They got their wish – in a privilege. On December 24, 1789, "The National Assembly decrees that all Jews known as Portuguese, Spanish and Avignonais, will continue to enjoy the rights that they have exercised until now and which will be established in their favor by letters-patent. In consequence, eligible Jews will have the rights of an active citizen." The "privileged" position of Sephardic communities in 1789–1791 reflected their greater wealth and degree of assimilation. The provision of citizenship to all French Jews in September 1791 completed the process. The substitution of citizenship for privileged status facilitated economic participation by religious minorities and laid the foundation for greater contributions in the nineteenth century.[21]

The loss of privilege was harder for individuals, firms, groups, and regions that faced heavier competition. Older firms dependent on privilege for competitive advantage like Van Robais (see Chapter 6) and royal manufactures such as Saint-Gobain and the Gobelins (see Chapter 7) limped through the Revolutionary decade with minimal state support. They did so by partnering with experienced workers and exporting a much-reduced output. As late as 1790, Van Robais employed between 3,000 and 3,200 men, women, and children in and around Abbeville. They made woolens worth about 1.5 million *livres*, but war and Revolution terminally wounded the firm. With raw materials and other inputs like soap increasingly scarce and cut off from many traditional export markets, Van Robais survived on government contracts to make uniforms. To compete on price, the firm lowered wages and skimped on raw materials, which destroyed the firm's long-standing reputation for quality. The appropriation of 600,000 *livres* worth of woolens during the Terror prevented investment and, in many ways, doomed the enterprise. By the end of the decade, both the value of output and the number of employees had fallen about 90 percent. Van Robais closed definitively in 1804. The loss of privilege was less damaging than the collapse of the domestic luxury market and foreign trade.[22]

[21] The quote is cited by Théophile Malvezin, *Histoire des juifs à Bordeaux* (Bordeaux: Charles Lefebvre, 1875), 261–63. More generally, see Paula E. Hyman, *The Jews of Modern France* (Berkeley: University of California Press, 1998), 33–34.

[22] André Dumont, "Lettre du sous-préfet au préfet," in *Extrait du registre de la correspondance du sous-préfet de l'arrondissement d'Abbeville*, Messidor 3, Year VIII [June 22, 1800], AD Somme 99M 107423. On the formerly royal manufactures, see Badré and Colombet, *Entreprises*, 175–83, Maurice Hamon and Dominique Perrin, *Au coeur du XVIIIe siècle industriel: Condition ouvrière et tradition villageoise à Saint-Gobain* (Mesnil-sur-l'Estrée: Editions P.A.U., 1993), 660–83, Maurice Hamon, *Du Soleil à la Terre: Une*

Guild producers and regional manufactures reliant on privilege for their competitiveness faced the same fate. In the Midi, Languedoc and Marseille suffered greatly from the elimination of their privileges. As we saw above, Marseille retained its commercial privileges in the Levant, but Languedocian woolens producers did not. Both royal manufacturers and guild masters in Carcassonne and Clermont-de-Lodève lost their exclusive rights to produce for Levantine markets even before war and blockade shut off access. Military orders filled much of the gap. Some centers of innovation and entrepreneurship like Bédarieux and Mazamet bucked the general trend, but the impact of the loss of privilege is clear.

Marseille's industry also suffered from the loss of privilege, especially tax-free use of imported raw materials from the Levant to manufacture goods for export. The termination of this privilege in 1790 multiplied the difficulties endured by Marseille's guild producers, who depended on Levantine tallow, leather, silk, cotton, or angora wool, and whose hold over their labor forces was increasingly precarious. Without the protections and opportunities inherent in both liberties of privilege and privileges of liberty, export-driven industries in Languedoc and Marseille lost their competitive edge after 1789.[23]

Newer enterprises and regions based on innovation often survived the loss of their privileges. During the Revolution, Alexandre Bonvallet's dyeworks in Amiens (see Chapter 7) expanded. He achieved great financial success under the Empire when his enterprise became an "imperial manufacture." Elbeuf's royal manufacture (see Chapter 3) faced stiff competition and falling sales at the end of the 1780s, but rebounded in 1790–1791 despite their loss of privileges. The fine woolens industry both in Elbeuf and nationally suffered from the onset of war and the imposition of the Maximum. The entire sector was buffeted by a succession of economic crises during the Revolutionary decade and Napoleonic era. Elbeuf's output declined dramatically. Despite peaks in 1791, 1796, 1801–1802, and 1807–1810, by 1815 Elbeuf made only one-third to one-half as many woolens as in 1789.

histoire de Saint-Gobain (JC Lattès, 1994), 40–42, and Charles-Axel Guillamot, *Notice sur l'origine et les travaux de la manufacture impériale de tapisseries des Gobelins*, 2nd ed. (Marchant, 1804).

23 For Languedoc, the essential source is Christopher H. Johnson, *The Life & Death of Industrial Languedoc, 1700–1920* (Oxford University Press, 1995), 3–22. On Marseille, see *Extrait des Registres du Comité des Manufactures et du Commerce de France à Paris du 20 Avril 1790*, ACCIMP D26, *Mémoire de MM. Les Négociants de Marseille*, 1791, ACCIMP J1562, Les fabricants de Chandelle de Marseille, *Adresse au Comité de Commerce*, June 1, 1792 and *Mémoire de divers fabriquants des départements des Bouches-du-Rhône, du Var et des Basses Alpes au sujet de la franchise du port de Marseille*, June 15, 1791, both in AN F12 1646.

Yet all the chief manufacturers remained in operation. The loss of their diverse privileges seems to have had little effect on Elbeuf's woolens. Rather, this former royal manufacture required only peace and access to far-flung markets and sources of raw materials to return to pre-Revolutionary levels of production. Almost all of Elbeuf's major firms recovered after 1815. Louviers' entrepreneurs faced the same cycle of boom and bust, but they earned more consistent and greater profits by mechanizing production and by switching back and forth between wool and cotton depending on market conditions. Over the long term, for the entrepreneurs of Elbeuf and Louviers, liberty proved more profitable than either the liberty of privilege or the privilege of liberty.[24]

Privilege did not disappear in 1789, or even in 1791. National debates over the role of privilege in 1789–1791 reveal the deep-seated ambivalence toward privilege expressed in French political economy. Among decision makers, political principles based on liberty conflicted with the undeniable efficacy of privilege as a means of promoting economic development. The lack of viable alternatives also influenced the dialogue. The reign of liberty had clear limits, both in theory and in practice. Reborn as "exemptions," some privileges were justified by the Revolutionaries as being in the "national interest."

Commercial privileges outlived their industrial counterparts. Trade privileges granted to the free ports of Bayonne and Dunkerque, cities with fairs like Beaucaire and Caen, and Marseille for the Levant lasted, in some cases, until 1795. Nearly all industrial privileges were swept away in 1789–1791, perhaps because trade privileges appeared to support employment while privileges in manufacturing seemed to cost France jobs. During the French Revolution, the "threat from below" exercised decisive influence on political economy when it came to determining the fate of commercial and industrial privileges. France's economy was far more path dependent on the course of the Revolution than it was on previous approaches to economic policymaking based on privilege. But, as the next section will demonstrate, the legacy of privilege's effectiveness as a tool for economic development proved impossible to escape amid the trials of war in the aftermath of the Terror.

[24] Alain Becchia, *La draperie d'Elbeuf (des origins à 1870)* (Publications de l'Université de Rouen, 2000), 363–437, Jeffry Kaplow, *Elbeuf during the Revolutionary Period: History and Social Structure* (Baltimore: Johns Hopkins University Press, 1964), 100–26, and Jean-Michel Chaplain, *La Chambre des Tisseurs: Louviers: cite drapière 1680–1840* (Champ Vallon, 1984), 136–44.

In service to the Empire: privilege under Bonaparte

Alexis de Tocqueville contended that the Napoleonic regime completed the project of state centralization begun by Louis XIV.[25] The rebirth of limited economic privileges preceded the revival of political privileges that began with the "senatories," the large landed properties granted to senators in January 1803. Bonaparte and his chief economic policymakers were heirs of the Revolution: they granted economic privileges rarely and only in the "national interest." Following in the footsteps of Colbert (see Chapter 2), the Consulate restored certain *corporate* structures as a means of protecting consumers and maintaining order. As we shall see, the Napoleonic administrators were more pragmatic than path dependent in their use of privilege. Ideology was increasingly subordinated to other concerns, but the regime was not limited to or by the legacy of privilege when it decided on what policies to implement. Other options were equally if not more attractive.

The Napoleonic regime's relationship to privilege was complex and, in some ways, contradictory. In October 1801, Paris' Prefect of Police Louis-Nicolas-Pierre-Joseph Dubois established a quasi-*corporate* organization to regulate the city's bakers. The edict responded to both worker unrest and the difficulties of provisioning the capital. Dubois sought to ensure a sufficient supply of quality bread at reasonable prices. Bakers needed "special permission" from the Police Prefect to set up shop: they also had to keep in stock between fifteen and sixty sacks of "first-quality" flour, each weighing 325 pounds, depending on how many ovens they operated. In addition, "as a guarantee," they had to depose fifteen sacks of first-quality flour at the Sainte-Elizabeth warehouse. Nor could bakers allow an oven to remain cold or leave the profession without permission. Paris' butchers were regulated in similar fashion in September 1802.

That same year, several other cities established "police regulations for bakers" to avoid "abuses." Ensuring quality and limiting windfall profits through skimping were the foremost considerations for the municipal council of Nice. Bakers could use "only pure wheat flour," which had to be "washed and sifted for all rocky or grainy materials." "Master bakers" were allowed "the same profit as under the old régime, namely three francs per load."[26] Establishing these quasi-*corporate* organizations as French arms forced the elimination of guilds across much of western

[25] Alexis de Tocqueville, *The Old Régime and the French Revolution*, trans. Stuart Gilbert (Garden City, NY: Doubleday Anchor, 1955), 209.

[26] Mairie de Nice, *Règlement pour les boulangers*, Nivôse 15, Year XI [January 5, 1803] (Googlebooks).

and central Europe confirms yet again that the Consulate was immune to irony. French administrators revived semi-privileged organizations in the "national interest" because they worked and because they lacked cheap alternatives to control the food supply.

Did such organizations constituted a privilege? Licensed bakers enjoyed a government-enforced monopoly in France's largest city; their limited numbers almost assured profitability. Flour brought to the city through official channels was divided by "quota" according to the bakers' declared number of ovens in operation. Paris' bakers also had some small element of self-government. The twenty-four most senior bakers were allowed to nominate syndics. However, the syndics' sphere of activity was restricted to "oversight and administration of the flour deposed as a guarantee." Without formal masterships, the (sometimes tacit) quality guarantee of the masterpiece, and exclusive control over apprenticeship, bakers did not "own" their position and could not automatically pass their profession on to their heirs. The state also did not regulate how the butchers or the bakers (much less the candlestick makers) crafted their wares; it just held them responsible for what they made and sold. Bakers gained considerable financial security and protection by allying with the state, but they had no recourse if the police took away their license. These quasi-*corporate* organizations satisfied the state's need to assure the food supply and control labor, but they did not revive privilege, the essence of the guilds.[27]

The Napoleonic regime never took the next step. Despite strong administrative support and constant lobbying by merchants and manufacturers from a number of major economic centers, especially those dependent on the troubled woolens industry, the guilds were not revived. In his 1803 report on how to reform manufacturing, Michel-Louis-Étienne Regnaud de Saint-Jean d'Angély noted that before the Revolution:

> The communities of arts and trades succesfully acquired more influence and also committed more abuses.
>
> These communities were formed to defend themselves from the tyrannical excesses and exactions of the privileged.

[27] For the previous two paragraphs, see the following sources. The text of the 1801 edict is reprinted in Antoine-Auguste Carette (ed.), *Lois annotées: ou Lois, décrets, ordonnances, avis du Conseil d'État avec notes historiques, de concordance et de jurisprudence,* 1st series, *1789–1830* (Sirey, 1843), X: 567. See also Fitzsimmons, *From Artisan to Worker*, 139–43, Michael David Sibalis, "Corporatism after the Corporations: The Debate on Restoring the Guilds under Napoleon I and the Restoration," *French Historical Studies*, 15: 4 (1988), 723–26, and Judith A. Miller, *Mastering the Market: The State and the Grain Trade in Northern France, 1700–1860* (Cambridge University Press, 1999), 197–218.

> They themselves became usurpers of privileges which they abusively conserved, fortified, and maintained up to the present. Like all institutions based on prejudice and particular interests, these communities opposed the attacks of reason and the general interest with the longest and greatest resistance.

The Consulate was determined not to revive such dangerous and destructive institutions. To the negative reputation of guilds must be added the fundamental changes in French political economy that occurred during the Revolutionary decade and a deep unwillingness to cede decision-making authority to any group of citizens. Although it adopted some elements of old régime economic privilege, the Bonapartist state stayed true to its Revolutionary roots and never restored the guilds.[28]

The Consulate's hesitancy to resuscitate privilege can be glimpsed in the lobbying effort to restore free ports. Officials in the departments of the Basses-Pyrénées (Pyrénées-Atlantiques), Bouches-du-Rhône, Lys, and Nord on behalf of Bayonne, Marseille, Ostend, and Dunkerque led the campaign. These cities marshaled all their arguments, mobilized all their supporters, and requested help from all their patrons. They succeeded in convincing Pierre-Alexandre-Laurent Forfait, the Minister of the Navy and the Colonies, to propose "the reestablishment of the free ports of Marseille, Bayonne and Dunkerque" in 1801. The General Commercial Council rejected the idea on the grounds that it was "not in the public interest."

The battle had probably been lost before it was begun. The General Commercial Council's report began, "In the times of destruction, the free ports were abolished as an exclusive privilege incompatible with the principles of equality." After a lengthy cost-benefit analysis, the Council "distinguished the abusive and unlimited exemptions that existed at Dunkerque and Bayonne from the limited version established at Marseille which had been further restrained by the law of Nivôse 11, Year III [December 31, 1794]." However, they concluded, "all discussion of a suitable system for this port and entrepôts for the others should be postponed until the return of peace." Under the Consulate, the "public interest" prevailed, especially in wartime.[29]

[28] Michel-Louis-Étienne Regnaud de Saint-Jean-d'Angély, *Exposition des motifs du projet de loi concernant les manufactures, arts et métiers*, 1803 (Gallica). On French actions vis-à-vis the guilds under Napoleon, see Jeff Horn, "La police des ouvriers sous l'Empire: vers un ordre social européen?" in François Antoine, Jean-Pierre Jessenne, Hervé Leuwers, and Anne Jourdan (eds.), *L'Empire napoléonnien: une expérience européenne?* (Armand Colin, 2014), 323–31, and on the regime's legacy of Jacobinism, see Isser Woloch, *Napoleon and His Collaborators: The Making of a Dictatorship* (New York: W.W Norton, 2001).

[29] *Réponse du Conseil de Commerce de Bayonne aux Objections faites par la Regie des Douanes contre la Franchise du Port de cette Ville*, Frimaire 25, Year XI [December 15, 1802], AN F12 1646, Maximin Isnard, *Aperçu de l'État commercial de Marseille relativement au Port*

The short-lived ceasefire inaugurated by the Peace of Amiens signed in March 1802 witnessed the formalization of a system of entrepôts. Once conflict resumed, these commercial institutions were revised constantly as France attempted to wage economic warfare against Britain. The Napoleonic regime crafted several different kinds of entrepôts. Twenty-eight cities from Nice to Sète and from Bayonne to Ghent were allowed to trade with the colonies. Seven categories of colonial products liable to reexport could be warehoused for up to a year. In these amusingly but accurately named "fictitious" entrepôts, cargo owners had to declare the quantity and quality of their goods. They faced stiff penalties for moving goods without permission. Sugar, coffee, and chocolate were taxed when shipped to another country. Other goods paid half the rates of foreign goods. It is hard to see these commercial institutions as privileged, despite the use of a term introduced under the old régime.

Sixteen maritime cities – Marseille, Sète, Bayonne, Bordeaux, La Rochelle, Lorient, Nantes, Saint-Malo, Cherbourg, Rouen, Le Havre, Honfleur, Dunkerque, Ostend, Bruges, and Anvers (thirteen from inside pre-1789 borders) – were granted "real" entrepôts to handle "foreign merchandise and commodities, whether colonial or otherwise." At the chief border crossings in the Rhineland, "real" entrepôts were also established in the ports of Strasbourg, Mainz, and Cologne. In "real" entrepôts, goods were warehoused in "buildings locked with two keys, one held by a customs agent and the other by the owners."

Marseille gained an entrepôt for foreign merchandise "whose entry is or will be prohibited." In addition, tobacco, salted fish, wine, brandy, liqueurs, oils, sugar, coffee, indigo, and chocolate could be warehoused for up to two years and then reexported. Mainz and Cologne could warehouse "foreign merchandise and commodities, prohibited or non-prohibited, colonial or otherwise." The ability to accept prohibited goods is the only aspect of this impressively detailed law that resembles a privilege in the old régime sense of the term. The legal provision of the right to break state proscriptions is more reminiscent of the circumlocutions devised by creative Bourbon administrators than the uniformity sought by the Revolutionaries and their heirs. The revival of

franc, au Commerce de Turquie et à la Peste, Year X [1801], AN AE BIII 252/1, *Adresse des membres du Conseil de Commerce séant à Marseille ay Citoyen Ministre des rélations extérieures*, Nivôse 4, Year X [January 4, 1802], AN AE BIII 252/1, and Claude-Anthelme Costaz, *Essai sur l'administration de l'agriculture, du commerce, des manufactures et des subsistances. Suivi de l'Historique des moyens qui ont amené le grand essor pris par les arts depuis 1793 jusqu'en 1815* (Huzard, 1818), 197–201. The quotes are from *Rapport du Conseil général de Commerce*, Thermidor 9, Year IX [July 28, 1801], AN F12 1646.

limited commercial privileges responded to widespread smuggling more than to a lack of other means of encouraging trade.[30]

The Napoleonic regime's major provision of economic privilege involved trademarks. The Allarde and Le Chapelier Laws eliminated the right of royal manufacturers, guilds, cities, and regions to brand their wares. The very first article of the Allarde Law "abolished the taxes on marks and seals that manufacturers and artisans had to affix to fabrics and other products made in their workshops and manufactures."[31] Entrepreneurs and firms continued to put their names and the place of origin on their goods. But entrepreneurs and firms were not required to follow any special method, use any particular materials, or adhere to any specific quality standard. Unsurprisingly, these informal trademarks were counterfeited so widely that they fell into general disuse other than at the very top of the market.

Revolutionary administrators obliged some manufacturers to trademark their goods but that obligation did not constitute a privilege. Public display or distribution of printed materials required "the name of the author or authors and the name and residence of the printer" from April 1796 (Germinal 28, Year IV). In November 1796 (Brumaire 20, Year V), an edict mandated that French-made cotton goods have a "distinctive sign" to differentiate them from smuggled English wares. Three laws passed in 1797–1798 forced goldsmiths and silversmiths to add a "particular mark" to protect consumers from skimping on precious metals. These requirements were clearly in the "general interest": they benefited the public rather than the producer.

Under the Consulate, trademarks protected consumers and limited smuggling in the name of the defense of property. Makers of cutlery and hardware were allowed to trademark their goods in January 1801 (Nivôse 23, Year IX). A few months later, in August (Fructidor 3, Year IX), the government repeated the directive about a "national mark" for a wide variety of cotton fabrics. Goods without the mark were "deemed of English manufacture and liable to be confiscated." The infamous law of Germinal 22, Year XI (April 12, 1803), that outlawed all coalitions and created the *livret*, the hated "workbook" for laborers, also contained "penalties" and "damages" for those guilty of "forging the particular

[30] The three previous paragraphs are based on Jean-Charles Magnier-Grandpré, *Code des douanes de l'Empire français, au courant depuis le mois de novembre 1790 jusqu'en juin 1806 avec deux traités, l'un sur toutes les questions en matière contentieuse, l'autre sur les acquits-à-caution*, 3 vols. (Strasbourg: Berger-Levrault, 1806), I: 528–65.

[31] Jerôme Mavidal and Émile Laurent (eds.), *Archives parlementaires de 1787 à 1860, recueil complet des débats législatifs et politiques des Chambres françaises*, 1st series (*1787 à 1799*), vol. 23 (Paul Dupont, 1886), 625–30, 625.

trademarks that every manufacturer or artisan has the right to place on the objects he has made." These limited measures avoided either the rhetoric or the reality of privilege in favor of an explicit protection of property.[32]

But the first crack in the dike had already appeared. Émile Levasseur reported that an edict of March 1802 (Germinal 7, Year X) authorized a hosiery manufacturer in Orléans to place a particular mark on goods produced for export and stipulated that forgers would be punished. This exception came three days after the Treaty of Amiens allowed France full access to seaborne commerce. The fact that the Consulate issued no further exceptions – despite many requests to do so – suggests the enduring clout of the Revolutionary attitude toward privilege.[33]

Trademark privileges made a comeback under the Empire. Echoing the policies of Colbert, Napoleonic administrators used trademarks to guarantee the quality of French manufactures goods to protect consumers both at home and abroad. In September 1807, woolens for the Levant were the first category of manufactured goods to receive its own trademark, to "guarantee good quality, the dimensions and the nature of the manufacture." Specifically referring to the regulations of 1697, 1708, and 1732 (see Chapter 5), the decree established distinctive borders for twelve different types of woolens, each with a minimum thread count and minimum size. Every bolt had to be marked with the name of the manufacturer, the production site, and its quality. Cities that made

[32] The two previous paragraphs are based on Jean-Baptiste Duvergier (ed.), *Collection complète des lois, décrets, ordonnances, réglemens et avis du Conseil d'état, publiée sur les éditions officielles du Louvre, de l'Imprimerie nationale par Baudouin et du Bulletin des lois, de 1788 à 1824 inclusivement*, 24 vols. (Guyot et Scribe, 1825), IX: 94–95 for the law on printers, Claude-Anthelme Costaz, *Lois et instructions ministérielles sur les manufactures, les ateliers, les ouvriers et la propriété des auteurs de découvertes dans les arts (brevets d'invention)* (Firmin-Didot, 1819), 256–68 on arms and hardware, Jean-Hippolyte Bénard, *Table générale analytique et raisonnée du Receuil général annoté des lois, décrets, ordonnances, etc., etc.: depuis le mois de juin 1789 jusqu'au mois d'août 1830* (Administration du Journal des Notaires et des Avocats, 1840), III: 220, and *Loi du 22 germinal an XI (12 avril 1803): MANUFACTURES, FABRIQUES ET ATELIERS* http://histoire.comze.com/loi12avril1803.pdf (accessed January 6, 2014). On trademarks more generally, see especially Philippe Minard, "Réputation, norms et qualité dans l'industrie textile française au XVIIIe siècle," and Jean-Yves Grenier, "Une économie d'indentification: Juste prix et ordres des marchandises dans l'Ancien Régime," in Alessandro Stanziani (ed.), *La qualité des produits en France (XVIIIe-XXe siècles)* (Belin, 2003), 69–89, 25–53.

[33] Émile Levasseur, *Histoire des classes ouvrières en France depuis 1789 jusqu'à nos jours*, 2 vols. (Hachette, 1867), I: 291–93. For official responses to requests to restore the guilds and their regulations, see *Lettre du Préfet du département de la Loire au Ministre de l'Intérieur*, Thermidor 29, Year IX [August 17, 1801], AN F12 1569, Scipion Mourque, *Rapport au Ministre de l'Intérieur*, Messidor 1, Year XI [June 20, 1803], AN F12 654, Claude-Anthelme Costaz, *Rapport présenté au Ministre de l'Intérieur*, April 7, 1809, AN F12 2337, and Vital Roux, *Rapport sur les jurandes et maîtrises et sur un projet de statuts et règlements pour MM. les marchands de vin de Paris* (Stoupe, 1805).

woolens for the Levant were to have a controller (*vérificateur*) assisted by "the oldest manufacturers with the best reputations." Woolens were to receive "a detailed examination" after manufacturing was complete. If the bolt passed inspection, it received a mark, stamp, and seal reading "Imperial Stamp." The type and quality of the fabric was then written on the bolt in French and Arabic. Woolens headed for the Levant were required to pass through checkpoints at Marseille, Genoa, Anvers, Turin, or Mainz, where the stamps were to be checked for forgeries and the composition of the bolt verified. The manufacture of woolens for the Levant was restricted to the departments of Ardèche, Aude, Gard, Haute-Garonne, Hérault, Lozère, and Tarn; in other words, to pre-1789 Languedoc. In December 1810, another decree raised standards for the controllers' expertise and sought to insure their independence from manufacturing interests.[34]

A sign of the Languedocian producers' weak competitive position came in December 1810. Verviers, Eupen, Montjoye, and Aachen were permitted exemption from the French national stamp and the restrictions that went with it, but they could still manufacture woolens for the Levant. According to Ministry of the Interior bureau chief Claude-Anthelme Costaz, these cities' "manufacturers could be allowed the liberty to make goods as they judged suitable to their interests." Producers in the Midi had to imitate "the machines and processes" of these Belgian, Rhenish, and Swiss producers if they hoped to compete in quality and price.[35]

With this shift in approach, trademarks again assumed a vital position in French industrial policy. I have no documentary smoking gun to explain why the Napoleonic state rejected the Revolutionary legacy. Geographical limitation on production, regulation of the thread count and size of various types of woolens, reliance on inspectors, and inspection guaranteed by a combination of trademarks and certification undertaken by qualified civil servants and experienced manufacturers are all startlingly reminiscent of the system in place from 1708 to 1759. The revival of the system in operation at the height of quality woolens production for the Levant demonstrates the practicality, flexibility, and rejection of ideological strictures that marked Napoleonic industrial policy.

Administrators recognized the need for change by woolens producers in the Midi. Compared to other industries and regions, Languedocian

[34] "Décret impérial contenant Réglement pour la fabrication des draps destinés au commerce du Levant," *Bulletin des lois de la République française*, 4th series (September 21, 1807), 286–92 and C.-M. Galisset, *Corps du droit français, ou recueil complet des lois, décrets, ordonnances, arrêtés, senatus-consultes, règlemens, avis du conseil d'État, publiés depuis 1789 suivi par la Table générale du Corps de droit français*, 14 vols. (Bureau des Corps du Droit français, 1833), XIV: 281.

[35] Claude-Anthelme Costaz, *Mémoire sur les moyens qui ont amené le grand développement que l'industrie française à pris depuis vingt ans*, (Firmin Didot, 1816), 13–14.

woolens production was in obvious decline. Between 1790 and 1810, the region's share of a sharply diminished national output of woolens fell from 30 to 23 percent. Relying on military orders for survival did not encourage competitiveness: high profits attracted entrepreneurs and workers, but only slowly trickled into funding innovation. As Jean-Michel Minovez remarked, this industrial trajectory did not represent an encouraging form of path dependence. Christopher Johnson estimates that, in 1810, 80 percent of Languedoc's broadcloth woolens satisfied military demand. Nationally, the military purchased more than half of French output. Total woolens production in the region fell from an estimated 140,000 bolts in 1781 to no more than 100,000 in 1810, a decrease of almost 30 percent.

Napoleonic officials did not have full knowledge of the depth of the decline, but they recognized that a serious problem existed. This recognition encouraged them to revive successful models from the past. The closure of the last former royal manufacture of Levantine fine woolens in 1806 might have been the straw that broke the camel's back. The regime could have let Languedoc's woolens industry continue to decline. But to revive that industry, in that place, at that time, Napoleonic administrators recognized that restoring the system of privilege was the most effective means at their disposal.

The timing was also favorable. The treaties of Tilsit with Russia and Prussia signed in July 1807 reopened the land route to the Levant and eased naval pressure on France in the Mediterranean. With the Atlantic ports still blockaded by the English and the Continental System in place and generating opposition within the Empire, the Levant represented an important economic opportunity for France in 1807. Like their predecessors under the old régime, Napoleonic administrators sought to use privilege to capitalize on that prospect.[36]

Louviers' woolens industry was the first to recover a municipal trademark based on quality. The impetus for this privilege came from a visit by Napoleon and Empress Marie-Louise. On their honeymoon, they visited the Ternaux brothers' innovative woolens mill on June 1, 1810. According to the prefect, Rolland de Chambaudoin, "Their Majesties … admired the 'perfection' of the mill and the machines designed to lessen the labor and increase the output as well as the reconciliation of

[36] The previous three paragraphs are based on Johnson, *Life & Death*, 18–19, Jean-Michel Minovez, *L'industrie invisible: Les draperies du Midi XVIIe-XX siècles: Essai sur l'originalité d'une trajectoire* (CNRS, 2012), 104–15, and Emmanuel Crétet, "Exposé de la situation de l'Empire française: 1806 et 1807," in *Recueil des lettres circulaires, instructions, programmes, discours et autres actes publics, Émanés en 1807 du Ministère de l'Intérieur*, vol. 7 (Imprimerie Nationale, 1808), 237–75, esp. 255–59.

traditional processes with new ones of their own invention."[37] Napoleon presented Guillaume-Louis Ternaux, who operated mills in Reims, Sedan, and outside Paris (among other places), with a medal of the Legion of Honor. He also purchased a dozen of Ternaux's famous cashmere shawls designed by the painter Jean-Baptiste Isabey, "which surpass all those made in England," for his new bride.

This seemingly commonplace event led to a July 1810 decree reinstating an edict issued in December 1782 that gave Lovériens an exclusive privilege to affix a yellow and blue border to their bolts of woolen cloth. In 1810 as in 1782, bolts of woolens made in other places found with the yellow and blue border were to be seized and confiscated. This inexpensive gesture granted a request on a lengthy list of appeals submitted by the municipal council on the eve of the Imperial visit. But what appears as an example of rather straightforward patronage politics deserves further consideration as an act of industrial policy.

Under the Empire, Louviers' woolens industry underwent a burst of technological innovation. The Eure River and a canal opened in 1808 were harnessed to power industrial machinery of ever-growing efficiency and complexity. Water power allowed the Lovériens to capitalize on technological opportunities. The finishing process for woolens was mechanized in 1808, and spinning followed two years later. All three of Louviers' mechanized cotton spinning mills converted to wool, the first two in 1806 and 1811. From two mechanized water-powered woolens spinning mills in 1810, the area in and around Louviers boasted eight by 1813. The installation of water-powered machinery did not boost total production; rather it pushed out uncompetitive producers who did not keep up technologically. In 1790, 430 machines produced 5,450 bolts of fine woolen cloth. By 1802, the output of 140 machines had fallen to 1,800 bolts.

The conjuncture again points to why the Empire applied the lessons of the old régime. In 1810, 309 machines were in operation employing 4,600 workers. The crisis of 1811 cut woolens employment in half. As with the revival of the system regulating woolens for the Levant, the restoration of Louviers' trademark helped to maintain high prices, thereby rewarding technical innovation and spurring further development.

The Ternaux brothers played a major role in the development of Louviers' woolens industry. They led the way by innovating, pressing for the trademark, and expanding once the trademark had been granted.

[37] Quoted in Maurice Collignon, "Ternaux 1763–1833," *Bulletin de la Société d'études diverses de l'arrondissement de Louviers*, 7 (1903), 63–111, 73–74.

The Ternaux set up a small-scale water-powered mill in 1802. Four years later, Guillaume-Louis and Étienne-Nicolas-Louis purchased land that included a double water fall and built a three-story brick building. This fully integrated mill is accounted as one of the first French factories. Its three waterwheels powered more than 100 machines and employed up to 600 workers. The factory could produce an astonishing 40,000 bolts annually, but it did not ramp up to that level of output for another twenty years. In September 1810, the Ternaux bought a large mill (visited by Bonaparte in 1802 and again in 1810) and fulling workshop from Jean-Baptiste Decretot, one of the city's leading manufacturers. Today, it is a regional woolens museum. A third mill was acquired in 1813. Rapid expansion by the Ternaux and by Louviers more generally took advantage of an opportune moment for woolens, as the cotton industry went into crisis in 1811 because of the scarcity of raw material. The delivery of a privileged trademark encouraged the Ternaux brothers' to invest their time, capital, and technical expertise in woolens.[38]

The Napoleonic regime supplied other trademarks to serve as an incentive for quality woolens production. In December 1812, a decree proclaimed that "All the woolens manufactures in the Empire may share in the preferential treatment accorded to Louviers. As a consequence, each of them may obtain authorization to place a unique border on their products." Once accepted, all manufacturers in the specified area were required to use it. Applications had to be approved by a local Chamber of Commerce or Consultative Chamber of Arts and Manufactures. From there it went to the prefect and then on to the Minister of Manufacturing and Commerce, who brought the request before the Council of State.[39]

Jean-Antoine Chaptal, the leading figure in French industrial policy for the first third of the nineteenth century, articulated the political economy of trademarks. He asserted that fraudulent use of other people's trademarks "deceives the public and compromises the reputation of accredited manufacturers." Defense of trademarks by the state was

[38] The five previous paragraphs are based on Maurice Collignon, "Napoléon Ier dans l'Eure," *Bulletin de la Société d'études diverses de l'arrondissement de Louviers*, 12 (1909–1910), 59–60, 66–68, 70, 144–49, L. M. Lomüller, *Guillaume Ternaux 1763–1833: créateur de la première integration industrielle française* (Les Éditions de la Cabro d'Or, 1977) 119–23ff, http://sedlouviers.pagesperso-orange.fr/patrimoine/decretot/decretot.htm (accessed January 7, 2014), Monique Lévi-Strauss, *The Cashmere Shawl* (New York: Abrams, 1988), 12, Chaplain, *La Chambre des tisseurs*, 138–48, Levasseur, *Histoire des classes ouvrières*, I: 293, and *Arrêt du conseil d'État qui ordonne qu'à l'avenir les draps de Louviers seront coiffés d'une lisière jaune ayant quatre ou six liteaux bleus; et que les draps fins d'Elbeuf seront coiffés d'une lisière rouge*, December 5, 1782 (Gallica).

[39] Quoted in Levasseur, *Histoire des classes ouvrières*, I: 292.

essential to "excite emulation among manufacturers and to protect a respected name from infringement."

The trademarks established in 1812 also encouraged quality production and technical innovation, especially for goods to be exported. Taking a long-term view that could have been expressed by Colbert, Chaptal argued that:

> good faith in contracts and accounts along with uniformity in the quality of production are the only ways to consolidate and perpetuate commercial relations. The clearly understood interest of the manufacturer requires that these conditions always be observed. Too frequently, however, the lure of a temporary profit or the desire to sell defective fabric prevails over these major considerations. By deceiving the consumer once, they discredit the manufacture forever.

For Chaptal, technological innovation, as demonstrated by woolens producers in Verviers and Aachen, was required to make French manufacturers competitive. Belgian and Rhenish goods were cheaper and better made. To equal their quality *and* price, Languedocian producers had to improve their manufacturing processes in order to satisfy consumers. Because exports of woolens to the Levant were "commercial relations based on trust" (*commerce de confiance*), the privilege of state-guaranteed trademarks made innovation potentially more profitable by protecting a brand from encroachment.[40]

The General Council of Manufactures' explicit policy was to approve trademarks for only a few production centers, that is, those known for innovation and quality. In the manufacture of woolens, these attributes were linked because the market was hyper-competitive and saturated. In the first set of applications, only Castres, Elbeuf, Malmédy (in Belgium), and Sedan were authorized and Turin was the sole approval the second time around. De facto if not precisely de jure, during the Empire, the Napoleonic regime granted the liberty of privilege for technologically innovative woolens producers.

With the precedent established, the Empire also accorded trademarks to manufacturers of playing cards and then firearms in February and December 1810, respectively. The regulation of the soap industry in 1811–1812 represented a far more significant manifestation of industrial policy. In woolens, the state first granted a trademark to an eminent, technically advanced, geographically delimited manufacturing center and then allowed other centers to apply for the same privilege of liberty. The process worked in reverse for soap.

[40] The quotes in the two previous paragraphs are from Louis Bergeron (ed.), *Chaptal: De l'industrie française* (Paris: Imprimerie nationale, 1993 [1819]), 447–51.

Following the Consulate's practice, in three decrees issued in 1811–1812 Napoleonic administrators obliged soap makers to indicate the content of every bar with a mark of "olive oil," "seed oil," "tallow," or "fat." In December 1812 – not coincidently, the exact same day that trademarks were offered to all woolens manufactures – Marseille's premium soap received a unique mark, a pentagon surrounding the words "olive oil." The manufacturer's name and "Marseille" were also to be spelled out inside the border. Perhaps a privileged position in fine soap-making was intended to compensate the city for its loss of control over trade with the Levant. Trademarks functioning in the same manner as pre-1789 liberties of privilege emerged as an important part of French economic policy under the Empire.[41]

The scale and scope of privilege's revival under Napoleon has garnered little notice. The traditional divisions of historical study between old régime, Revolution, and nineteenth century surely play some role in obscuring the linkages emphasized in this section: most studies of the old régime end in 1789 or 1791, explorations of the Revolution begin in 1787 or 1789, and examinations of the nineteenth century begin in 1799 or 1814–1815. These boundaries conceal the longer trajectory of French economic policy. Despite the recent spate of bicentennials of Napoleonic milestones, the period, and particularly its political economy, attracts relatively few scholars.

The lack of attention to these subjects may also stem from the realization that the evidence presented in this chapter reveals important limitations of the impact of the Revolution or at the very least in the consistency of Revolutionary administrative action. These examples also poke holes in myths related to the implementation of certain fundamental Revolutionary goals. The continuities between the old régime and the Napoleonic era, passed through the knothole of the Revolution, remind us that political economy is messy; there are no hard-and-fast start or end dates for most ideas and policies. Focusing on privilege does not undermine the importance of the Revolution. It

[41] The five previous paragraphs are based on the following sources. Horn, *The Path Not Taken*, 194–210, Fitzsimmons, *From Artisan to Worker*, 144–45, Bertrand Gille, *Le Conseil général des manufactures (Inventaire analytique des procès-verbaux) 1810–1829* (S.E.V.P.E.N., 1961), 29–31, Pierre-Paul Zalio, "Le 'savon de Marseille': Contribution à une sociologie économique des produits," in Alessandro Stanziani (ed.), *La qualité des produits en France (XVIIIe-XXe siècles)* (Belin, 2003), 93–122, "Décret impérial qui établit une marque particulière pour les Savons à l'huile d'olive fabriqués à Marseille," *Bulletin des lois de la République française*, 4th series, December 22, 1812, 258–60, and Bénard, *Table générale*, III: 220. On the 1810 laws, see *Receuil des Lois et Acts généraux du Gouvernement en vigueur dans le Royaume des Pays-Bas*, 1st series (Brussels: Pinchon-Bhoux, 1821), IX: 236–38.

does, however, shift and complicate how we understand the evolution of French political economy. By calling attention to the importance of durable approaches to economic policymaking, it is my hope to encourage scholars to ask different questions of the historical record.

Privilege was in a liminal position in Napoleonic political economy. Many officials and large segments of the commercial and industrial elite pushed for the revival of economic privileges, such as the free ports, the guilds, and Marseillais control over trade with the Levant. Where elements of privilege did reappear – because of their undeniable efficacy and cost efficiency as well as the lack of alternatives – the Consulate granted exclusions and exceptions solely in the "national interest," which meant to protect consumers from fraud, adulteration, or deception. For most key policymakers under the Consulate, the legacy of the Revolution precluded systematic recourse to economic policies based on privilege. At the dawn of the nineteenth century, France was not path dependent on privilege.

Under the Empire, the situation changed. The return of political privilege enabled economic privilege to reemerge as an important part of policymaking. Although the term itself was avoided, the Empire granted a number of liberties of privilege and privileges of liberty. These "privileges" referred explicitly to the past, particularly previous successes, as they revived old régime economic practices. The most notable elements of continuity were geographic delimitations on the right to manufacture certain goods in certain ways, trademarks sanctioned by the state, multiple inspections for exported woolens by state officials assisted by local experts, and special rights for technological innovators. After 1805, the Revolutionary legacy was clearly in eclipse in economic policymaking. Administrators deployed privilege, albeit under other names, as a policy tool to combat recalcitrant economic problems. The legacy of the Revolution fundamentally shifted French political economy, but the heritage of the old régime continued to influence how nineteenth-century decision makers approached economic policymaking.

Using the existence of continuities between the old régime and the Empire to test whether France was path dependent on privilege yields a false positive. To encourage the economy of an overgrown France that was constantly at war, administrators used one of their few available and effective policy tools. Yet, as we shall see, the majority of the policies resuscitating the tactics of the old régime did not outlive the Empire, most were in place for six or seven years at most, and many were implemented just as the successive crises of the disaster in Russia, the loss or defection of the continental Empire, and the invasion of France led to the collapse of the Napoleonic regime. I would suggest that French policymakers focused on effectiveness: their pragmatism outweighed their commitment to ideological positions. The Empire was also powerful enough and self-confident enough to ignore the legacy of the Revolution when it deemed necessary. In the vastly different economic environment that followed the Hundred Days, pragmatism eventually led French economic policymakers to abandon provision of liberties of privilege and privileges of liberty.

Continuity and change: privilege as a tool of French industrial policy

Privilege was an economic tool that emerged and endured, in a context of constraints. Although economic privileges had existed for centuries, only after 1650 did the liberty of privilege and the privilege of liberty became systemic and systematic elements of a coherent state economic policy focused on development. Colbert and his successors made frequent use of privilege, in part because of its relative effectiveness, and in part because of the lack of alternatives. Budget and later debt pressure, the dislocations of near-constant war-making, and the recalcitrance of entrepreneurs, workers, and local administrators along with a lack of political will were major concerns. These factors accentuated the effects of fragmented markets and the overlapping *bricolage* of boundaries and jurisdictions, transportational inadequacies, chronic shortfalls of key raw materials, and multifaceted economic competition from abroad to limit the policy choices available to Bourbon economic decision makers.

Privilege made a virtue of necessity. Privilege could turn friction points in the structure of the society of orders into potential sources of strength. The flexibility of the liberty of privilege and the privilege of liberty enabled Bourbon administrators to support entrepreneurs, firms, and groups of producers who sought to take advantage of the opportunities stemming from France's political power, geography, and the structure of the society of orders. From the 1660s until the 1750s, privilege played a major, even dominant, role in French economic policymaking. Challenges to privilege in the name of liberty were mounted at the end of the reign of Louis XIV and grew in intensity over the course of the eighteenth century. Disputes about the proper balance of privilege and liberty marked the reigns of Louis XV and Louis XVI. The pendulum swung back and forth, but the direction of French political economy was clearly toward greater liberty. Economic realities, however, restrained, and in some cases reversed, the march toward that goal.

This longer-term perspective helps to explain the post-1789 survival and then revival of certain economic policies associated with privilege. The French Revolution changed the rules of the economic game: neither the liberty of privilege nor the privilege of liberty remained acceptable policy alternatives. Yet, in the guise of "exemptions" in the "national interest," a number of old régime privileges outlived the cataclysm of 1789. Some lasted until 1791 and a few persisted until 1795. Selected "exemptions" were reborn under the Consulate and more were resuscitated during the Empire. Why? Because Revolutionary and later Napoleonic officials recognized the utility of using exemptions to encourage economic development.

After 1789, exemptions were used differently than privileges. No longer were feudal seigneurs, individuals/single firms, or associations of producers organized into *corporations* – in a bewildering welter of institutions, privileges, and customs – major recipients of state largess. Revolutionary practicality, an underappreciated aspect of economic policymaking after 1789, drastically limited the provision of exemptions. The Revolutionary state and its successors focused on fewer specific areas and sectors of need. As a consequence, the state's practice of economic patronage shifted fundamentally with important implications in the nineteenth century.

Despite the ambitious policymaking of Napoleonic officials, the use of policy tools associated with privilege was discrete and far more restrained than had been the case before 1789. This falloff is critical to understanding the economic legacy of the French Revolution. In its wake, European political economy, especially in France, could not long ignore the equality of individualism, either ideologically or practically. The nineteenth-century decline and eventual disappearance of privilege or "exemption" as a policy tool in an era generally understood to have experienced strong economic growth suggests that it was no longer perceived to be useful or effective. This chapter has argued that pragmatism trumped ideology in policymaking after 1789. That same practicality endured in the economic decisions made under Louis XVIII.

The definitive return of the House of Bourbon in 1815 gave hope to those who sought to reestablish old régime economic privileges. Some privileges were revived, but did not long endure. A more pragmatic approach that recognized the power of the Revolutionary legacy cut short most experiments with reviving privilege. Under the Restoration, French political economy moved past a reliance on policies based on privilege.

Michael P. Fitzsimmons surveyed the effort to reestablish the guilds after the fall(s) of Napoleon. Tentative steps were taken in late 1814 to early 1815 and accelerated after Waterloo. Leadership came from officials like Jules Anglès, Paris' Police Prefect, but the impetus came from cities that had been especially dependent on privilege, most notably Bayonne, Bordeaux, Dunkerque, Lyon, Marseille, Nantes, and Paris. In Fitzsimmons' detailed account, the final decision not to restore the guilds was made in 1819. Lobbying, however, continued on for more than a decade. In response to yet another request to revive the guilds, in 1821, the General Council of Commerce quoted Anne-Robert-Jacques Turgot's "remarkable" 1776 edict aimed at "suppressing the guilds and their numerous privileges," asserting that "since then its aims have been justified by [France's manufacturing] improvements and discoveries. Today, the same motives oppose the reestablishment of the guilds." In the name of industrial progress, the Restoration declined to restore this economic privilege. Although other institutions, formal and informal, licit and illicit, imitated certain guild functions and activities, geographically organized *corporations* of *industrial* producers who enjoyed government-sanctioned privileges did not return.[42]

Pragmatism strongly influenced administrative decisions when it came to trademark privileges. In April 1816, a decree required all domestic versions of "textiles of foreign manufacture whose entry into France is prohibited" to establish their "nationality" with a mark that included their name, that of the city or department where the fabric was made, and the thread count. Clarifications were passed or issued in August 1816, April and September 1818, and January 1819 to cover this vast array of goods. Although initially part of the state's campaign against smuggling, marking textiles became universal practice at the end of 1819, making it a vital part of French industrial policy. These trademarks, however, were subtly different than old régime privileges.[43]

Jean-Antoine Chaptal, now count de Chanteloup and a member of the Chamber of Peers, emphasized the differences when he presented a new

[42] The reports of the Conseil general du Commerce and the Conseil des Manufactures are reprinted in Étienne Jouy, *État actuel de l'industrie française, ou Coup d'oeil sur l'exposition de ses produits, dans les salles du Louvre, en 1819* (L'Huillier, 1821), 145–64, 157. See also Fitzsimmons, *From Artisan to Worker*, 189–239, esp. 189, 202, Francis Demier, "L'impossible retour au régime des corporations dans la France de la Restauration, 1814–30," in Alain Plessis (ed.), *Naissance des libertés économiques: Liberté du travail et liberté d'entreprendre: le décret d'Allarde et la loi Le Chapelier, leurs conséquences, 1791-fin XIXe siècle* (Institut d'Histoire de l'Industrie - Ministère de l'Industrie, 1993), 117–42, Sibalis, "Corporatism after the Corporations," 718–30, and Horn, *The Path Not Taken*, 260–73.

[43] *Circulaires, instructions et autres actes émanés du Ministre de l'Intérieur, ou relatifs à ce département, de 1797 à 1821 inclusivement*, 2nd edn, vol.3, *1816–1819 inclusivement* (Imprimerie royale, 1823), 110–13, 197–98, 314–20, 380–87, 391–92, 448–62 and Bénard, *Table générale*, III: 220.

law increasing the penalties for counterfeiting a trademark. In July 1824, he commented that "It cannot be said that this law puts a monopoly or a privilege in the hands of some manufacturers. No, there is neither a monopoly nor a privilege because manufacturers are permitted to copy any methods and processes." The law was needed because:

It is just to guarantee industrial property. I say property because nothing is more sacred than a manufacturer who by assiduous work, conduct without blemish and useful discoveries is placed honorably among the benefactors of the country and the creators of industry . . .

What I say about industries should also be said about cities where manufacturers have created industries where the superiority and the constant quality of the products have been appreciated by all consumers. Often the name of the city on products gives confidence and forms a guarantee in the eyes of the buyer.

Manufacturers from Sedan and Louviers suggested the proposed law to protect the reputations of their wares. Chaptal, however, recommended that "it be reserved to manufacturers of fine woolens, formerly known under the name of *woolens of Louviers* or of *Sedan* to add *first quality* to those denominations. The names of Elbeuf, Sedan or Louviers alone offer a guarantee to the consumer." The law passed later that month contained no provisions for a separate quality designation. It merely increased the penalty for storekeepers and commercial agents to sell goods whose trademarks had been "assumed or altered." The law's final form maintained geographic "privilege" but did not include distinctions for quality. Instead, quality continued to be associated with place.[44]

Under the Restoration, groups of manufacturers dedicated to reputation, high standards, and innovation deserved some protection but not privilege. As ably demonstrated by Alessandro Stanziani, similar arguments about how to support the economy were later applied to agricultural goods, wine in particular, with the laws on *appellation d'origine contrôlée* (AOC) beginning in 1855. Here an element of old régime economic policy was reborn in the nineteenth century as a fundamental means of protecting and maintaining the unique attributes of France's productions of the soil. The Physiocrats would have been proud. The utility, and more importantly, the salability of this branding ensured that a regional approach to managing production outlived the Revolutionary emphasis on the equality of individualism.[45]

44 Jerôme Mavidal and Émile Laurent (eds.), *Archives parlementaires, recueil complet des débats législatifs et politiques des Chambres françaises de 1800 à 1860, faisant suite à la réimpression de l'ancien "Moniteur" et comprenant un grand nombre de documents inédits*, 2nd series (Paul Dupont, 1879), XLII: 73–74, 313–14, 395.

45 Alessandro Stanziani, *Rules of Exchange: French Capitalism in Comparative Perspective, Eighteenth to Early Twentieth Centuries* (Cambridge University Press, 2012) and

The revival of the 1708–1759 system for ensuring the quality of woolens exported to the Levant did not seem to have survived the collapse of the Empire. I can find no reference to its continuation after 1814; nor does there appear to have been any specific trademark assigned to this important category of exports. The Restoration's concessions to fine woolens producers in Elbeuf, Louviers, and Sedan, however, begs the question: why not Carcassonne, Lodève, or Bédarieux? No conclusive evidence is available, but the nineteenth-century fortunes of the Midi's woolens industry are suggestive. First, as discussed above, the dramatic shift toward military production left the region far less dependent on exports. Second, exports and production in general did well after Waterloo. Nearly 5,000 bolts were sent abroad annually in 1816–1817. After a downturn, exports reached almost 12,000 bolts in 1826.

This impressive revival reminds us of the gaps in the north–south industrial division articulated by David Landes. He asserted that France's key industries shifted northward. Such a shift undeniably took place, but, following Christopher Johnson, the evidence from the woolens industry suggests that it occurred later and for different reasons than Landes believed. Many Languedocian producers mechanized at rates comparable to technological leaders in Elbeuf, Louviers, and Sedan. Military supply, with its less exacting standards and steady profit margins, shrank under the Restoration, but remained an important market. In July 1820, Lodève's manufacturers even asked for "an exclusive privilege to furnish all the woolens and other fabrics necessary to supply the royal army." Their request was refused because Lodève, with Clermont-en-Lodève, already furnished half of military requirements. The state demanded efficiency, not quality. As Johnson put it, "Privilege was won at a price." Consequently, producers in the Midi did not need trademarks as much as their northern competitors: woolens for the Levant, though still significant, had been replaced as the chief market for Languedocian producers.[46]

Corine Maitte, "Labels, Brands, and Market Integration in the Modern Era," *Business and Economic History On-Line*, 7 (2009), http://www.thebhc.org/publications/BEHonline/2009/maitte.pdf (accessed January 7, 2014).

[46] The two previous paragraphs are based on the following sources. On Languedocian woolens, see Johnson, *Life & Death*, 29–31, 38–40, 68. For the north-south divide, see David S. Landes, *The Unbound Prometheus: Technological Change and Industrial Development in Western Europe from 1750 to the Present* (Cambridge University Press, 1969), 159–62 and François Crouzet, "Les Origines du sous-développement économique du Sud-Ouest," *Annales du Midi*, 71 (1959): 3–21. The quote on Lodève is cited by Minovez, *L'industrie invisible*, 137.

Under the Restoration, privilege did not disappear from France's trade with the Levant. Instead of focusing on the production side, however, Bourbon officials after 1814 concentrated on facilitating exchange. They did so by reinstating many of Marseille's commercial privileges. The replacement of a liberty of privilege with a privilege of liberty is striking. It constitutes a fitting conclusion to this study.

Louis Becquey, director-general of commerce, justified this shift in the "public interest." In December 1814, "the franchise of the port, the city, and the territory of Marseille was reestablished," adding to and complicating the function of the entrepôt that remained in place. Customs barriers were shifted to "the limits of the territory in 1789." So long as they followed the rules, all other ports could trade directly with the Levant, although "for their return voyage, they had to conform to the realm's health regulations," which effectively meant undergoing quarantine in Marseille's lazaret (until 1821). On behalf of the council of state, Becquey claimed that the free port "contained nothing exclusive, nothing that could be called a monopoly." The "surveillance of the customs service" would prevent any "inconveniences."[47] During the Hundred Days, the Napoleonic regime left the free port in place (it had other, more pressing concerns), but an ordinance issued in February 1815 attempted to crack down on smuggled goods passing through the free port.

The matter did not rest there. Public debate focused on the free port, the role that privilege should play in facilitating trade with the Levant, and whether the entire territory of Marseille should be included in the franchise. A new ordinance issued in September 1817 retained the entrepôt established in 1802, making only minor changes. A vast assortment of manufactured items, raw materials for industry, and colonial goods could be warehoused without paying taxes so long as they were reexported. The free port was restricted to the docks "to allow [the rest of the city] access to the indefinite liberty of domestic trade without which Marseille cannot prosper" and "to protect French industry" from smuggling. As had been the case in 1789, de facto if not de

[47] Jerôme Mavidal and Émile Laurent (eds.), *Archives parlementaires, recueil complet des débats législatifs et politiques des Chambres françaises de 1800 à 1860, faisant suite à la réimpression de l'ancien "Moniteur" et comprenant un grand nombre de documents inédits*, 2nd series (Paul Dupont, 1868), XIII: 376–80. For some representative positions in this debate, see Louis Mejanelle, *Considérations sur la franchise du port de Marseille*, October 16, 1814, Pierre Perron, Pierre Plasse, and Pierre-Honoré Roux, *Mémoire concernant la franchise du Port, de la Ville et du Territoire de Marseille*, 1816, both in AN AE BIII 252/1, *Adresse de la Chambre de Commerce de Marseille au duc de Richelieu*, April 8, 1816, AN AE BIII 252/2, and Anonymous, *Mémoire sur les inconvéniens de la franchise du port de Marseille, sur la nécessité de supprimer les barrières intérieures et sur les moyens de faire jouir le commerce de cette ville de la plus grand liberté possible* (Marseille: Antoine Picard, 1816).

jure, Marseille remained the entry point for nearly all Levantine goods. The city's chamber of commerce also retained its ability to license commercial firms operating in the Levant and could nominate the consuls posted to Near Eastern and North African cities.[48] Marseille therefore enjoyed perhaps the most important geographical exemption to the uniformity of economic practice sought before 1789, created by the Revolution and maintained by Napoleon and the restored Bourbons.

In the new administrative language used after 1815, these measures – previously described as privileges – were termed "necessary special regulations." Although expressly framed with reference to old régime economic practice, the Ordinance of September 1817 pragmatically accepted and continued Revolutionary and Napoleonic "trade modifications" in the name of "liberty." "Public interest" enshrined in law was also succeeded by an executive act focused on "protection" and the "general interest" of "industry" and "domestic trade." Operating in reduced circumstances, administrators during the Restoration looked inward far more than they looked outward. The confidence of earlier eras was succeeded by more conservative, more defensive policies.

Marseille retained its "privileges" governing trade with the Levant until 1835, but after the fall of the Empire, the rules of the game had clearly changed. As a result of the evolution of French political economy, the policies associated with privilege were no longer perceived to be effective. Many practices developed under the old régime lived on, such as enterprise zones, trademarks, entrepôts, and free ports, but these methods should be viewed as pragmatic responses to specific opportunities and problems rather than fundamental elements of a reasonably coherent economic policy. In the wake of the changes in French political economy that occurred in 1789–1791, privilege was no longer acceptable as a pillar of state encouragement of economic development. The Revolution shaped France's economic path far more than the policies of privilege inherited from the old régime and refurbished by Napoleon and the Restoration.[49]

Administrative willingness to implement policies associated with privilege intensified under the Empire. But the fleeting existence of most of these ad hoc tactics illustrates how much the rules of the game

[48] The text is reprinted in *Bulletin des lois de la République française*, 7th series, September 10, 1817, V: 177–90.

[49] The four previous paragraphs are based on Bergeron (ed.), *Chaptal*, 466–69, *Manuel des entrepreneurs de bâtimens de la ville de Paris, organisés pour l'année 1813, par MM. les délégués des entrepreneurs de bâtimens* (J.-R. Lottin, n.d. [1813]), 175–77, 195, and Édouard Salvador, *L'Orient, Marseille et la Méditerranée, histoire des échelles du Levant et des colonies* (Amyot, 1854), 426.

had changed in French political economy since 1789. In governing trade with the Levant, especially in woolens, and by reviving state-guaranteed trademarks for quality producers, economic decision makers were inspired explicitly by the old régime measures. But that inspiration can be misleading. Substituting "*franchise*" for "privilege" was more than a symbolic change; it also represented a shift in approach. Thanks to the French Revolution, state support for economic development had to reflect equality of opportunity and the "public good." No longer could administrators have faith that an entrepreneur, "[b]y pursuing his own interest he frequently promotes that of the society more effectually than when he really intends to promote it." Under the old régime, this facet of Adam Smith's "invisible hand" animated state economic policy more than it did during the nineteenth century.[50] A few prominent exceptions like trade with the Levant, notwithstanding, privilege, both in form and in content, withered away after 1815.

The political economy of privilege between 1650 and 1820 sheds light on certain current debates on the process of economic development stretching from the heyday of mercantilism to the dawn of the industrial revolution. My findings suggest that French economic development was driven by the central government. Institutions that were either part of the state apparatus or operated under its imprimatur were the means by which development was conceptualized, shaped, and implemented. As reported in Chapter 3, Alexis de Tocqueville characterized the situation precisely: "It never occurred to anyone that any large-scale enterprise could be put through successfully without the intervention of the State."[51]

Yet the power of the state was by no means "absolute." Government action encountered more constraints and more limitations, than opportunities. The liberal critique of the Bourbon state's devotion to privilege strongly resembles Adam Smith's censure of mercantilism in a country whose economy was profoundly shaped by this approach to policymaking. French administrators' reliance on the liberty of privilege and later the privilege of liberty was a creative, realistic application of the art of the possible.

[50] Adam Smith, *The Wealth of Nations*, ed. Edwin Cannan (New York: the Modern Library, 2000), 485 (Bk. IV, Ch. II).

[51] Tocqueville, *The Old Régime and the French Revolution*, 69. The best summary of certain contradictions in entrepreneurial attitudes toward the state is Jean-Pierre Hirsch and Philippe Minard, "'Laissez-faire nous et protégez-nous beaucoup' pour une histoire des pratiques institutionnelles dans l'industrie française (XVIIIe-XIXe siècle)" in Louis Bergeron and Patrice Bourdelais (eds.), *La France n'est-elle pas douée pour l'industrie?* (Belin, 1998), 135–58.

Bourbon officials had relatively few additional tools at their disposal. Neither France's nor Europe's economy was path dependent; rather there were simply not that many effective means for the early modern state to stimulate the economy before the onset of the industrial revolution. The past constrained policymaking, but that reflected a set of political choices rather than economic limits. Official recourse to policies based on privilege should be understood as pragmatic responses to the realities of political economy, not adherence to the society of orders or rejection of liberal ideas.

A lack of effective tools should not be conflated with inability to implement fundamental shifts in economic pathway. The epic economic experimentation undertaken during the French Revolution conclusively demonstrates that point. Yet that example – an event of world historical importance – is often ignored, disparaged, or forgotten for fundamentally ideological reasons. Only by discounting the Revolution can the role and effectiveness of state economic intervention be downplayed.

These observations also militate against the notion, so much in vogue in the current moment, that the economy, French, British, and European, was driven by consumption during the long eighteenth century. Demand could not and did not play the developmental role assigned to it in the scholarly literature on consumption. Economic change from the bottom up, or from the middle out, was certainly possible in eighteenth-century Europe, but it occurred when hungry people demanded bread at affordable prices. Trinkets, gegaws, and the latest fashions were popular. Their manufacture and distribution encouraged technological change while providing many opportunities for profit taking. But, in many ways, their production took place on the margins of industrial society.[52]

The Bourbon state devoted far greater attention to improving the quality of products whose manufacture changed little with the decades. Administrative deployment of privilege reflected a long-standing supply-side approach to economic development that was also market sensitive. France manufactured many luxury goods, but the great majority of those products sold because of their classic style and quality. Constant innovation was a goal, and for a very few, a reality. Product innovation,

[52] Consumption has attracted inordinate attention in the last twenty years. Here I depart from the influential vision of political economy expressed by William H. Sewell, Jr., "The Empire of Fashion and the Rise of Capitalism in Eighteenth-Century France," *Past & Present*, 206: 1 (2010), 81–120 and by Michael Kwass in a series of articles including "Ordering the World of Goods: Consumer Revolution and the Classification of Objects in Eighteenth-Century France," *Representations*, 82: 1 (2003), 87–116, "Consumption and the World of Ideas: Consumer Revolution and the Moral Economy of the Marquis de Mirabeau," *Eighteenth-Century Studies*, 37: 2 (2004), 187–213, and "Big Hair: A Wig History of Consumption in Eighteenth-Century France," *The American Historical Review*, 111: 3 (2006), 631–59.

however, did not propel early modern France's impressive growth. It must not be forgotten that France was the world's largest industrial producer until about 1820; French entrepreneurs were not "free riders," but major players in the global production and exchange of manufactured goods.[53]

This interpretation has implications for current debates about the divergence of the Western economy led by Britain and the emergence of a British industrial revolution. Robert C. Allen is perhaps the most influential recent proponent of the argument that Britain industrialized primarily because of internal factors, in particular, high wages and high energy inputs. Turning the argument around clarifies the contribution of understanding French recourse to privilege. I have argued that, in terms of economic policy, France and Britain differed far less than is generally acknowledged. Yet, Britain made the shift toward an industrial society at least three generations before France. The inability of France to follow the British in a timely fashion was not founded on shortcomings of technology or resources. The political economy of privilege evokes the myriad ways that French entrepreneurs earned profits from fractured markets, from opportunities in the colonies, and by taking advantage of international networks stretching across the Atlantic world, encompassing much of Europe and stretching to the Near East, North Africa, and beyond.[54] As a result of the political economy of privilege, eighteenth-century French entrepreneurs needed the profits generated by industrialization far less than their British rivals.

After 1789, however, different reasons prevented France from industrializing on the British model. Again, these reasons stemmed from political economy rather than technological incapacity or shortfalls of key resources. Although Allen frames his argument globally, internalist explanations of the British industrial revolution dramatically underestimate the importance of comparative political economy and the exogenous factors most effectively highlighted by Patrick K. O'Brien.[55]

[53] On "free riding," see Joel Mokyr, *The Enlightened Economy: An Economic History of Britain 1700–1850* (New Haven CT: Yale University Press, 2009), 374ff.

[54] Daron Acemoglu, Simon Johnson, and James Robinson, in "The Rise of Europe: Atlantic Trade, Institutional Change, and Economic Growth" *American Economic Review*, 95: 3 (2005), 546–79 argue that Atlantic trade also played a major indirect role in promoting institutional reform. My evidence strongly supports this conclusion.

[55] For contrasting views of the British Industrial Revolution and divergence, see Robert C. Allen, *The Industrial Revolution in Global Perspective* (Cambridge University Press, 2009) and, among Patrick K. O'Brien's many contributions, see "The Contributions Of Warfare With Revolutionary And Napoleonic France To The Consolidation And Progress Of The British Industrial Revolution," Working Papers 150/11 (2011), http://eprints.lse.ac.uk/31741/1/WP150.pdf (accessed January 9, 2014) [used with permission] and "Deconstructing the British Industrial Revolution as a Conjuncture and

The "big questions" about path dependence raised at the beginning of the chapter deserve at least some tentative answers. France's economic difficulties during the Revolutionary decade certainly had some basis in the shift away from the socioeconomic structures of the society of orders. Privilege's persistence after 1789 and the general recovery of the economy in 1790–1791 are important indicators of the enduring importance of older approaches and of the resiliency of the French economy. In 1793–1794, the Revolutionary government eliminated the lingering vestiges of privilege amid a collapsing economy while at war against both domestic enemies and foreign armies. The drastic measures that created a command economy were a response rather than a cause of that economic breakdown. In fact, the economy suffered more from the end of wage and price controls in 1795 than it did from the onset of war and Revolutionary politics in 1792–1794. The economic performance of the Revolutionary decade demonstrates conclusively that France was not path dependent on old régime economic structures.[56]

Yet, a number of the policies pioneered by the Bourbons before 1789 were revived, at least temporarily, in the first two decades of the nineteenth century. Given the difficulties of dismantling the liberties of privilege and the privileges of liberty in 1789–1791 and beyond, do these resuscitations breathe new life into the possibility that the Revolutionary decade had only an ephemeral impact on France's economic pathway?

Similarity of tactics should not be conflated with path dependence. The legacy of the French Revolution fundamentally altered the approaches to economic development available to nineteenth-century French economic policymakers. The direction of state action in favor of liberty and the equality of individualism is incontrovertible. It would be equally mistaken

Paradigm for Global Economic History," Jeff Horn, Leonard N. Rosenband, and Merritt Roe Smith (eds.), *Reconceptualizing the Industrial Revolution* (Cambridge, MA: MIT Press, 2010), 21–46. In the debate between Allen and Joel Mokyr, the latter's emphasis on the existence and diffusion of mechanical knowledge, especially craft skills, is surely closer to the lived reality of the era. For a review of the arguments, see Morgan Kelly, Joel Mokyr, and Cormac Ó Gráda, "Precocious Albion: Human Capability and the British Industrial Revolution," (2011, revised 2012), http://www.stanford.edu/group/SITE/archive/SITE_2012/2012_segment_3/2012_Segment_3_papers/mokyr.pdf (accessed June 18, 2014). My findings also engage the important work of Kenneth Pomeranz in *The Great Divergence: China, Europe and the Making of the Modern World Economy* (Princeton University Press, 2000).

[56] On economic performance during the French Revolution, see Gérard Béaur and Philippe Minard (eds.), *Atlas de la Révolution française,* vol. 10, *Économie* (Éditions de l'École des Hautes Études en Sciences Sociales, 1997) and Guy Lemarchand, *L'Économie en France de 1770 à 1830: De la crise de l'Ancien Régime à la Révolution industrielle* (Armand Colin, 2008), 139–247.

to judge the long-term trend in British policy toward free trade by revitalization of the Corn Laws in 1815 and their persistence until 1846. The French Revolution was no blip on the radar screen. The examples explored in this chapter should not obscure the fact that nineteenth-century French economic policies exhibited more continuity with the early years of the Revolution than with the old régime. French political economy was influenced profoundly by the Revolution and its legacy, but was not path dependent during early industrialization.

Did the Revolution doom France to a second-class economic position? In *The Path Not Taken*, my answer to this important question was no. And so it remains. This book adds additional perspective to the arguments I advanced before. The search for a new institutional formula after 1789 was even more influenced by past practice than I had understood previously. French policymakers escaped these strictures several times. First in 1789–1791, again in 1793–1794, once more in 1800–1804, and conclusively after 1815, economic decision makers demonstrated their ability to depart from pre-1789 patterns. The state's shift in attitude toward development requires further emphasis. The loss of confidence so evident after 1815 can be attributed to the persistence of the threat from below, military defeat, and the relative decline of the colonies.[57] More positively, the state's self-imposed limitations can be viewed as an endorsement of the direction of "liberal" policymaking begun early in the eighteenth century. Starting this study in 1650 reinforces the conclusion that, over the long-term, France's economic pathway and political economy were no less effective in fostering economic development than the approaches followed by its competitors.

Policymakers experienced a fit of "beautiful madness" in their use of privilege as a tool of economic development. French management of economic relations with the Levant provides perhaps the best indication of privilege's effectiveness in encouraging economic growth. The creation of the free port of Marseille, along with the establishment of favored woolens producers in Languedoc required the thoroughgoing intervention of the state to achieve their full potential. State regulation and state inspection melded Marseille's

[57] The venerable or provisional nature of these works suggests that it is time to return to the economic history of the Restoration. Arthur Louis Dunham, *The Industrial Revolution in France 1815–1848* (New York: Exposition Press, 1955), Guillaume de Bertier de Sauvigny, *The Bourbon Restoration*, trans. Lynn M. Case (Philadelphia: University of Pennsylvania Press, 1966), 201–34, André Jardin and André-Jean Tudesq, *Restoration & Reaction 1815–1848*, trans. Elborg Forster (Cambridge University Press, 1983), 168–90, and Lemarchand, *L'Économie*, 249–96.

privileges of liberty and Languedoc's liberties of privilege to capture and retain a dominant position in the Levant. Many of these privileges survived the assaults of the Physiocrats and the upheavals of 1789–1791 only to disappear during the ordeals of the Year II. Recast as "exemptions," certain commercial and industrial privileges were reborn in the first decade of the nineteenth century and remained in place until the dawn of the railroad age. The durability and success of privilege in supporting French relations with the Levant are metaphors for the creative, sometimes paradoxical means and methods elaborated by early modern states to encourage economic development. France's eighteenth-century triumph in the Mediterranean can only be understood in light of this "beautiful madness."

Bibliography

This book draws on archival research for this and previous projects stretching back to 1990. In addition to the Bibliothèque nationale de France and the Archives Nationales located in Paris, I consulted departmental archives in the Aube, Bouches-du-Rhône (Aix-en-Provence and Marseille), Gironde, Loire, Seine-Maritime, and Somme. I also made use of the municipal archives and libraries of Amiens, Bordeaux, Paris, Rouen, Saint-Étienne, and Troyes, as well as specialized collections like the Archives de la Chambre de Commerce et industrie de Marseille-Provence and the archives of the Conservatoire National des Arts et Métiers in Paris. I was surprised and pleased to see how many pieces of information and primary sources, especially legal documents, could be found on Gallica (gallica.bnf.fr) or through Googlebooks (books.google.com). As a complement (never a replacement!) to archival research, these electronic repositories are enormously valuable. I could not have written this book in a reasonable amount of time without them. However, without deep familiarity with archival sources, I would neither have known what to look for nor understood what I had found.

LITERATURE CITED

Acemoglu, Daron, Simon Johnson, and James Robinson. "The Rise of Europe: Atlantic Trade, Institutional Change, and Economic Growth." *American Economic Review*, 95: 3 (2005), 546–79.

Allen, Douglas W. *The Institutional Revolution: Measurement & the Economic Emergence of the Modern World*. University of Chicago Press, 2012.

Allen, Robert C. *The British Industrial Revolution in Global Perspective*. Cambridge University Press, 2009.

Allinne, Jean-Pierre. "À propos des bris de machines textiles à Rouen pendant l'été 1789: Émeutes anciennes ou émeutes nouvelles?" *Annales de Normandie*, 31: 1 (1981), 37–58.

Andrew, Bradley B. "Unfair Trade, Mercantilism and Economic Development, Great Britain: 1660–1800." PhD dissertation, University of Connecticut, 2002.

Appleby, Joyce. *The Relentless Revolution: A History of Capitalism*. New York: W.W. Norton, 2010.

Archives Municipales de Bordeaux. *Livre des privileges*. Bordeaux: G. Gounouilou, 1878.

Ashton, Thomas S. *The Industrial Revolution 1760–1830*. Oxford University Press, 1948.

Austin, Gareth, and Kaoru Sugihara (eds.). *Labour-Intensive Industrialization in Global History*. New York: Routledge, 2013.

Babeau, Albert. *La Province sous l'Ancien Régime*. 2 vols. Firmin Didot, 1894.

Badré, Bertrand, and Philippe Colombet. *Entreprises en Révolution*. Jean-Claude Lattès, 1990.

Ballot, Charles. *L'Introduction du machinisme dans l'industrie française*. Claude Gevel (ed.). Geneva: Slatkine Reprints, 1978 [1923].

Bamford, Paul W. *Privilege and Profit: A Business Family in Eighteenth-Century France*. Philadelphia: University of Pennsylvania Press, 1988.

Bardet, Jean-Pierre. *Rouen aux XVIIe et XVIIIe siècles: Les mutations d'un espace social*. 2 vols. Société d'édition de l'enseignement supérieur, 1983.

Béaur, Gérard, and Philippe Minard (eds.). *Atlas de la Révolution française*. vol. 10. *Économie*. Éditions de l'École des Hautes Études en Sciences Sociales, 1997.

Becchia, Alain. *La draperie d'Elbeuf (des origines à 1870)*. Publications de l'Université de Rouen, 2000.

Beik, William. *Absolutism and Society in Seventeenth-century France: State Power and Provincial Aristocracy in Languedoc*. Cambridge University Press, 1985.

Bély, Lucien (ed.). *Dictionnaire de l'Ancien Régime: Royaume de France XVIe–XVIIIe siècle*. Quadrige/PUF, 2002 [1996].

Benbassa, Esther. *The Jews of France: A History from Antiquity to the Present*. Trans. M. D. DeBevoise. Princeton University Press, 1999 [1997].

Benedict, Philip. "The Huguenot Population of France, 1600–1685: The Demographic Fate and Customs of a Religious Minority." *Transactions of the American Philosophical Society*, 81: 5 (1991), 1–164.

Berg, Maxine. *Luxury & Pleasure in Eighteenth-Century Britain*. Oxford University Press, 2005.

Bergasse, Louis, and Gaston Rambert. *De 1599 à 1789*. vol. 4. Gaston Rambert (ed.), *Histoire du commerce de Marseille*. 7 vols. Plon, 1954.

Bergeron, Louis. *France Under Napoleon*. Trans. R. R. Palmer. Princeton University Press, 1981 [1972].

Bertaud, Jean-Paul. *Guerre et société en France: de Louis XIV à Napoléon Ier*. Armand Colin, 1998.

Bertier de Sauvigny, Guillaume de. *The Bourbon Restoration*. Trans. Lynn M. Case. Philadelphia: University of Pennsylvania Press, 1966.

Bicententaire de la fondation de la Chambre de Commerce de Rouen 1703–1903: Aperçu Historique. Rouen: Lecerf fils, 1908.

Birn, Raymond. "Religious Toleration and Freedom of Expression." In Dale Van Kley (ed.), *The French Idea of Freedom: The Old Regime and the Declaration of Rights of 1789*. Stanford University Press, 1994, 265–99.

Blanning, Tim C. W. *The French Revolution: Aristocrats versus Bourgeois?* Houndsmills: Macmillan, 1987.

Blaufarb, Rafe. *The Politics of Fiscal Privilege in Provence, 1530s–1830s*. Washington, DC: Catholic University of America Press, 2012.

Boislisle, Arthur Michel de, and Pierre de Brotonne (eds.). *Correspondance des contrôleurs généraux des finances avec les intendants des provinces*. 3 vols. Imprimerie Nationale, 1888, 1897.

Boissonnade, Pierre. "Colbert: son système et les entreprises industrielles d'état en Languedoc (1661–1683)." *Annales du Midi*, 14 (1902), 5–57.

Boissonnade, Prosper. *Colbert: le triomphe de l'étatisme, la fondation de la suprématie industrielle de la France, la dictature du travail: 1661–1683*. Marcel Rivière, 1932.

Bonnassieux, Pierre. *Examen des cahiers de 1789 au point de vue commercial et industriel*. Berger-Levrault, 1884.

Bonnassieux, Pierre. *Les grandes compagnies de commerce: Ètude pour server à l'histoire de la colonization*. Plon, 1892.

Bonnassieux, Pierre, and Eugène Lelong (eds.). *Conseil de Commerce et Bureau du Commerce 1700–1791: Inventaire analytique des process-verbaux*. Imprimerie nationale, 1900.

Bosher, John F. "Huguenot Merchants and the Protestant International in the Seventeenth Century." *The William and Mary Quarterly*, 52: 1 (1995), 77–102.

Bosher, John F. *The Canada Merchants 1713–1763*. Oxford: Clarendon Press, 1987.

Bosher, John F. *The Single Duty Project: A Study of the Movement for a French Customs Union in the Eighteenth Century*. London: Athlone Press, 1964.

Bossenga, Gail. "Capitalism and Corporations in Eighteenth-Century France." In Alain Plessis (ed.), *Naissance des libertés économiques: Liberté du travail et liberté d'entreprendre: le décret d'Allarde et la loi Le Chapelier, leurs conséquences, 1791-fin XIXe siècle*. Institut d'Histoire de l'Industrie – Ministère de l'Industrie, 1993, 13–31.

Bossenga, Gail. "Estates, Orders and Corps." In William Doyle (ed.), *The Oxford Handbook of the Ancien Régime*. Oxford University Press, 2012, 141–66.

Bossenga, Gail. "Protecting Merchants: Guilds and Commercial Capitalism in Eighteenth-Century France." *French Historical Studies*, 15: 4 (1988), 693–703.

Bossenga, Gail. *The Politics of Privilege: Old Regime and Revolution in Lille*. Cambridge University Press, 1991.

Boucher, Philip P. "French Proprietary Colonies in the Greater Caribbean." In Lou Roper and Bertrand Van Ruymbeke (eds.), *Constructing Early Modern Empires: Proprietary Ventures in the Atlantic World, 1500–1750*. Leiden: Brill, 2007, 163–88.

Boucher, Philip P. *Les Nouvelles Frances: France in America, 1500–1815 – An Imperial Perspective*. Providence, RI: The John Carter Brown Library, 1989.

Bouloiseau, Marc (ed.). *Cahiers de doléances du tiers État du bailliage de Rouen pour les États généraux de 1789*. 2 vols. Presses Universitaires de France, 1957, 1960.

Bourgeon, Jean-Louis. "Colbert et les Corporations." In Roland Mousnier (ed.), *Un Nouveau Colbert*. SEDES, 1983, 241–54.

Braudel, Fernand. *Civilization and Capitalism 15th–18th Century*. vol. 2. *The Wheels of Commerce*. Trans. Siân Reynolds. Berkeley: University of California Press, 1992 [1982, 1979].

Braure, Maurice. *Lille et la flandre wallonne au XVIIIe siècle*. Lille: Émile Raoust, 1932.

Brewer, John. *The Sinews of Power: War, Money and the English State, 1688–1783.* Cambridge, MA: Harvard University Press, 1990.

Brewer, John and Eckhart Hellmuth (eds.). *Rethinking Leviathan: The Eighteenth-Century State in Britain and Germany.* Oxford University Press, 1999.

Brewer, John and Roy Porter (eds.). *Consumption and the World of Goods.* London: Routledge, 1993.

Bueb, Renauld. "La théorie de l'enclave dans le droit féodale de l'Ancien Régime." In Paul Delasalle and André Ferrer (eds.), *Les enclaves territoriales aux Temps Modernes (XVIe-XVIIIe siècles): Actes du Colloque de Besançon.* Besançon: Presses Universitaires Franc-Comtoises, 2000, 9–22.

Bulut, Mehmet. "The Role of the Ottomans and Dutch in the Commercial Integration between the Levant and the Atlantic in the Seventeenth Century." *Journal of the Economic and Social History of the Orient,* 45: 2 (2002), 197–230.

Bush, Michael L. *Rich Noble, Poor Noble.* Manchester University Press, 1988.

Butel, Paul. "France, the Antilles, and Europe in the Seventeenth and Eighteenth Centuries: Renewals of Foreign Trade." In James D. Tracy (ed.), *The Rise of Merchant Empires: Long-distance Trade in the Early Modern World, 1350–1750.* Cambridge University Press, 1990, 153–72.

Butel, Paul. *Histoire des Antilles françaises XVIIe-XXe siècle.* Perrin, 2007 [2002].

Butel, Paul. *L'Ėconomie française au XVIIIe siècle.* SEDES, 1993.

Butel, Paul. *Les dynasties bordelaise de Colbert à Chaban.* Perrin, 1991.

Butel, Paul. *Les négociants bordelaise: L'Europe et les Iles au XVIIIe siècle.* Aubier, 1974.

Butel, Paul and Jean-Pierre Poussou. *La Vie quotidienne à Bordeaux au XVIIIe siècle.* Hachette, 1980.

Calonne, Albéric de. *Histoire de la ville d'Amiens.* 3 vols. Amiens: Piteux Frères, 1899–1906.

Campbell, Peter R. "Absolute Monarchy." In William Doyle (ed.), *The Oxford Handbook of the Ancien Régime.* Oxford University Press, 2012, 11–38.

Carpenter, Kenneth. *The Dissemination of* The Wealth of Nations *in French and in France: 1776–1843.* New York: Oak Knoll Press, 2002.

Carrière, Charles. *Négociants Marseillais au XVIIIe siècle: Contribution à l'étude des economies maritimes.* 2 vols. Marseille: Institut historique de Provence, 1973.

Carrière, Charles. *Richesse du Passé Marseillais: Le port mondiale au XVIIIe siècle.* Chambre de Commerce et d'Industrie de Marseille, 1979.

Castaldi, Carolina Giovanni Dosi and Evita Paraskevopoulou. "Path Dependence in Technologies and Organizations: A Concise Guide." Eindhoven Center for Innovation Studies: Working Paper 11.04 (2011). http://ideas.repec.org/p/dgr/tuecis/wpaper1104.html (accessed December 19, 2013).

Castel, Marguerite. "La formation topographique du quartier Saint-Seurin." *Revue historique de Bordeaux et du département de la Gironde,* 14: 3 (1921), 5–17.

Cavaignac, Jean. "Le compagnonnage dans les luttes ouvrières au XVIIIe siècle: L'exemple de Bordeaux." *Bibliothèque de l'Ėcole des chartes,* 126: 2 (1969 [1968]), 377–411.

Cazals, Rémy. *Les révolutions industrielles à Mazamet 1750–1900.* Toulouse: Privat, 1983.

Cazals, Remy, and Jean Valentin. *Carcassonne: ville industrielle au XVIIIième siècle*. Carcassonne: Service Educatif – Archives de l'Aude, 1984.

Chaplain, Jean-Michel. "Avoir ce qui manque aux autres: la manufacture de draps fins Van Robais, d'Abbeville au XVIIIe siècle face au milieu local." *Le Mouvement social*, 125 (1983), 13–24.

Chaplain, Jean-Michel. *La Chambre des tisseurs–Louviers: cité drapière 1680–1840*. Champ Vallon, 1984.

Chapman, Sara. *Private Ambition and Political Alliances: The Phélypeaux de Pontchartrain Family and Louis XIV's Government, 1650–1715*. University of Rochester Press, 2004.

Charles-Roux, François. *Les Èchelles de Syrie et de Palestine au XVIIIe siècle*. Paul Geuthner, 1928.

Charpenne, Pierre. *Histoire des réunions temporaires d'Avignon et du comtat Venaissin à la France*. 2 vols. Calmann Lévy, 1886.

Chartier, Roger Guy Chaussinand-Nogaret, Hubert Neveux, and Emmanuel Le Roy Ladurie. *La ville des temps modernes de la Renaissance aux Révolutions*. Seuil, 1998 [1980].

Chassagne, Serge. "La mobilité des ouvriers qualifiés de l'indiennage (1760–1860)." In Gérard Gayot and Philippe Minard (eds.), *Les ouvriers qualifiés de l'industrie (XVIe-XXe siècle). Formation, emploi, migrations: Actes du colloque de Roubaix, 20–22 1997*. Presses de l'Université Charles-de-Gaulle-Lille 3, 2001, 65–81.

Chassagne, Serge. *Le coton est ses patrons: France, 1760–1840*. Èditions de l'EHESS, 1991.

Chassagne, Serge. *Oberkampf: Un entrepreneur capitaliste au Siècle des Lumières*. Aubier, 1980.

Chaussinand-Nogaret, Guy. *The French Nobility in the Eighteenth Century: From Feudalism to Enlightenment*. Trans. William Doyle. Cambridge University Press, 1985 [1976].

Cheney, Paul. *Revolutionary Commerce: Globalization and the French Monarchy*. Cambridge, MA: Harvard University Press, 2010.

Church, William F. *Louis XIV in Historical Thought*. New York: W.W. Norton, 1976.

Clément, Pierre. *Histoire de Colbert et de son administration*. 2nd ed. Didier et Cie., 1874.

Clément, Pierre (ed.). *Lettres, instructions et mémoires de Colbert publiés d'après les ordres de l'empereur*. 10 vols. Imprimerie impériale, 1861–1873.

Cobban, Alfred. *The Social Interpretation of the French Revolution*. Cambridge University Press, 1965.

Coleman, Donald C. "Mercantilism Revisited." *The Historical Journal*, 23: 4 (1980), 773–91.

Collignon, Maurice. "Napoléon Ier dans l'Eure." *Bulletin de la Société d'études diverses de l'arrondissement de Louviers*, 12 (1909–1910), 1–249.

Collignon, Maurice. "Ternaux 1763–1833." *Bulletin de la Société d'études diverses de l'arrondissement de Louviers*, 7 (1903), 63–111.

Collins, James B. *The State in Early Modern France*. 2nd ed. Cambridge University Press, 2009.

Comité régional d'histoire de la Révolution française (Haute-Normandie). *La Révolution en Haute-Normandie 1789–1802*. Rouen: Editions du P'tit Normand, 1988.

Conchon, Anne. *Le Péage en France au XVIIIe siècle: Les privilèges à l'épreuve de la réforme*. Comité pour l'histoire économique et financière de la France, 2002.

Coornaert, Émile. *Les corporations en France avant 1789*. 5th ed. Gallimard, 1941.

Cordier, Louis. *Les Compagnies à charte et la politique colonial sous le ministère de Colbert*. Arthur Rousseau, 1906.

Crouzet, François. *Britain Ascendant: Comparative Studies in Franco-British Economic History*. Trans. Martin Thom. Cambridge University Press, 1990 [1985].

Crouzet, François. "La contrebande entre la France et les îles britanniques au XVIIIe siècle." In Gérard Béaur, Hubert Bonin, and Claire Lemercier (eds.), *Fraude, contrefaçon et contrebande de l'Antiquité à nos jours*. Geneva: Droz, 2006, 35–59.

Crouzet, François. "Les Origines du sous-développement économique du Sud-Ouest." *Annales du Midi*, 71 (1959): 3–21.

Crowley, John E. "Neo-mercantilism and the Wealth of Nations: British Commercial Policy after the American Revolution." *The Historical Journal*, 33: 2 (1990), 339–60.

Daire, Eugène and Hyppolite Dussard (eds.). *Oeuvres de Turgot*. Guillemin, 1844.

Daly, Gavin. *Inside Napoleonic France: State and Society in Rouen, 1800–1815*. Aldershot: Ashgate, 2001.

Dardel, Pierre. *Commerce, Industrie et Navigation à Rouen et au Havre au XVIIIème siècle: Rivalité croissante entre ces deux ports*. vol. 1. *La Conjoncture*. Rouen: Société libre d'émulation de la Seine-Maritime, 1966.

Daudin, Guillaume. *Commerce et prosperité: La France au XVIIIe siècle*. Presses de l'Université Paris-Sorbonne, 2005.

Daumalin, Xavier, Nicole Girard, and Olivier Raveux (eds.). *Du Savon à la puce: L'industrie marseillaise du XVIIe siècle à nos jours*. Marseille: Jeanne Laffitte, 2003.

Daunton, Martin J. *Progress and Poverty: An Economic and Social History of Britain 1700–1850*. Oxford University Press, 1995.

David, Paul A. *Path Dependence and the Quest for Historical Economics: One More Chorus of the Ballad of QWERTY*. University of Oxford: Discussion Papers in Economic and Social History 20 (November 1997). http://www.nuff.ox.ac.uk/economics/history/paper20/david3.pdf. (accessed December 19, 2013), 1–48.

Demeulenaere-Douyère, Christiane and David J. Sturdy (eds.). *L'Enquête du regent 1716–1718: Sciences, techniques et politique dans la France pré-industrielle*. Turnhout, Belgium: Brepols, 2008.

Demier, Francis. "L'impossible retour au régime des corporations dans la France de la Restauration, 1814–30." In Alain Plessis (ed.), *Naissance des libertés économiques: Liberté du travail et liberté d'entreprendre: le décret d'Allarde et la loi Le Chapelier, leurs conséquences, 1791-fin XIXe siècle*. Institut d'Histoire de l'Industrie – Ministère de l'Industrie, 1993, 117–42.

Derode, Victor. *Histoire de Lille et de la Flandre Wallonne*. 4 vols. Lille: Librairie de Vanackere, 1977 [1848–1877].

Deschamps, Léon. *Histoire de la question coloniale en France*. Plon, 1891.

Detcheverry, Arnaud. *Histoire des israélites de Bordeaux*. Bordeaux: Balarac jeune, 1850.

de Vries, Jan. *The Industrious Revolution: Consumer Behavior and the Household Economy, 1650 to the Present*. Cambridge University Press, 2008.

de Vries, Jan and Ad van der Woude. *The First Modern Economy: Success, Failure, and Perserverance of the Dutch Economy, 1500–1815*. Cambridge University Press, 1997.

Dewerpe, Alain and Yves Gaulupeau. *La fabrique des prolétaires: Les ouvriers de la manufacture d'Oberkampf à Jouy-en-Josas 1760–1815*. Presses de l'École normale supérieure, 1990.

Deyon, Pierre and Philippe Guignet. "The Royal Manufactures and Economic and Technological Progress in France before the Industrial Revolution." *Journal of European Economic History*, 9 (1980), 611–32.

Dincecco, Mark. "Fiscal Centralization, Limited Government, and Public Revenues in Europe, 1650–1913." *Journal of Economic History*, 69: 1 (2009), 48–103.

Dion, Marie-Pierre. *Emmanuel de Croÿ (1718–1784): Itinéraire intellectuel et réussite nobiliaire au siècle des Lumières*. Brussels: Editions de l'Université Bruxelles, 1987.

Doerflinger, Thomas M. "The Antilles Trade of the Old Regime: A Statistical Overview." *Journal of Interdisciplinary History*, 6: 30 (1976), 397–415.

Donaghay, Marie. "Calonne and the Anglo-French Commercial Treaty of 1786." *Journal of Modern History*, 50: 3 (1978), 1157–84.

Donaghay, Marie. "The Exchange of Products of the Soil and Industrial Goods in the Anglo-French Commercial Treaty of 1786." *The Journal of European Economic History*, 19: 2 (1990), 377–401.

Dromantin, Patrick Clarke de. *Les réfugiés jacobites dans la France du XVIIIe siècle*. Presses Universitaires de Bordeaux, 2005.

Dubuc, André (ed.). *Textile en Normandie: Études diverses*. Rouen: Société libre d'Émulation de la Seine-Maritime, 1975.

Ducaunnès-Duval, Ariste. *Inventaire sommaire des registres de la Jurade: 1520 à 1783*. vol. 3. Bordeaux: Nouvelle F. Pech, 1905.

Duhamel, Léopold. *Documents sur la Réunion d'Avignon et du Comtat-Venaissin à la France (1790–1791)*. Picard, 1891.

Dunham, Arthur Louis. *The Industrial Revolution in France 1815–1848*. New York: Exposition Press, 1955.

Duparc, Pierre. ed. *Recueil des instructions données aux ambassadeurs et ministres de France depuis les traités de Westphalie jusqu'à la Révolution française, Turquie*. vol. 29. Éditions du CNRS, 1969.

Durand, Georges (ed.). *Inventaire sommaire des Archives Départementales antérieures à 1790: Somme*. vol. 2. Amiens: Imprimerie picarde, 1888.

Dusevel, Hyacinthe. *Histoire de la ville d'Amiens, depuis les Gaulois jusqu'à nos jours*. 2nd ed. Amiens: Caron & Lambert, 1848.

Dutil, Léon. *L'État économique du Languedoc à la fin de l'ancien régime (1750–1789)*. Hachette, 1911.

Eager, John Macauley. *The Early History of Quarantine: Origin of Sanitary Measures directed against Yellow Fever*. Washington, DC: Government Printing Office, 1903.

Egret, Jean. *La Pre-Révolution Française (1787–1788)*. Presses Universitaires de France, 1978.

Epstein, Stephan R. *Freedom and Growth: The Rise of States and Markets in Europe, 1300–1750*. London: Routledge, 2000.

Farge, Arlette. *Fragile Lives: Violence, Power and Solidarity in Eighteenth-century Paris*. Trans. Carol Shelton. Cambridge University Press, 1993 [1986].

Farge, Arlette and Jacques Revel. *The Vanishing Children of Paris: Rumor and Politics before the French Revolution*. Trans. Claudia Miéville. Cambridge, MA: Harvard University Press, 1991 [1988].

Fitzsimmons, Michael P. *From Artisan to Worker: Guilds, the French State, and the Organization of Labor, 1776–1821*. Cambridge University Press, 2010.

Fitzsimmons, Michael P. *The Night the Old Regime Ended: August 4, 1789 and the French Revolution*. University Park: Pennsylvania State University Press, 2003.

Forrest, Alan. *Society and Politics in Revolutionary Bordeaux*. Oxford University Press, 1975.

Forster, Robert. *Merchants, Landlords, Magistrates: The Depont Family in Eighteenth-Century France*. Baltimore: Johns Hopkins University Press, 1980.

Forster, Robert. *The Nobility of Toulouse in the Eighteenth Century: A Social and Economic Study*. Baltimore: Johns Hopkins University Press, 1960.

Forster, Robert. "The Noble as Landlord in the Region of Toulouse at the End of the Old Regime." *Journal of Economic History*, 17: 2 (1957), 224–44.

Fox, Edward W. *History in Geographic Perspective: The Other France*. New York: W.W. Norton, 1971.

Gallinato, Bernard. *Les corporations à Bordeaux à la fin de l'ancien régime: Vie et mort d'un mode d'organisation du travail*. Lille: ANRT, 1988.

Garrioch, David. "The Protestants of Paris and the Old Regime." In Vesna Drapac and André Labelet (eds.), *French History and Civilization. Papers from the George Rudé Seminar*, 2 (2009), 16–24.

Gayot, Gérard. *Les draps de Sedan 1646–1870*. Éditions de l'École des Hautes Études en Sciences Sociales, 1998.

Gille, Bertrand. *Le Conseil général des manufactures (Inventaire analytique des procès-verbaux) 1810–1829*. S.E.V.P.E.N., 1961.

Gillispie, Charles Coulston. *Science and Polity in France: The End of the Old Regime*. Princeton University Press, 1980.

Goddard, Roger. "Small Boroughs and the Manorial Economy: Enterprise Zones or Urban Failures?" *Past & Present*, 210 (2011), 3–31.

Goubert, Pierre. *Louis XIV and Twenty Million Frenchmen*. Trans. Anne Carter. New York: Pantheon, 1970 [1966].

Goubert, Pierre. *The Ancien Régime: French Society, 1600–1750*. Trans. Steve Cox. New York: Harper & Row, 1973 [1969].

Grafe, Regina. *Distant Tyranny: Markets, Power, and Backwardness in Spain, 1650–1800*. Princeton University Press, 2011.

Grafe, Regina and Alejandra Irigoin. "A Stakeholder Empire: The Political Economy of Spanish Imperial Rule in America." *Economic History Review*, 65: 2 (2012), 609–51.

Grenier, Jean-Yves. *L'économie d'Ancien Régime: Un monde de l'échange et de l'incertitude.* Albin Michel, 1996.

Grenier, Jean-Yves. "Une économie d'indentification: Juste prix et ordres des marchandises dans l'Ancien Régime." In Alessandro Stanziani (ed.), *La qualité des produits en France (XVIIIe-XXe siècles)*. Paris: Belin, 2003, 25–53.

Griffin, Emma. *A Short History of the British Industrial Revolution.* New York: Palgrave, 2010.

Gross, Jean-Pierre. *Fair Shares for All: Jacobin Egalitarianism in Practice.* Cambridge University Press, 1997.

Grouchy, Emmanuel Henri de and Paul Cottin (eds.). *Journal inédit du duc de Croÿ, 1718–1784.* 4 vols. Flammarion, 1906–1907.

Gullickson, Gay. *Spinners and Weavers of Auffay: Rural Industry and the Sexual Division of Labor in a French Village, 1750–1850.* Cambridge University Press, 1986.

Haag, Eugène and Émile Haag. *La France protestante; ou, Vies des protestants français qui se sont fait un nom dans l'histoire depuis les premiers temps de la réformation jusqu'à la reconnaissance du principe de la liberté des cultes par l'Assemblée nationale; ouvrage précédé d'une notice historique sur le protestantisme en France, suivi de pièces justificatives, et rédigé sur des documents en grand partie inédits.* 10 vols. J. Cherbuliez, 1846–1859.

Hafter, Daryl M. *Women at Work in Preindustrial France.* University Park: Pennsylvania State University Press, 2007.

Hamon, Maurice. *Du Soleil à la Terre: Une histoire de Saint-Gobain.* JC Lattès, 1994.

Hamon, Maurice and Dominique Perrin. *Au coeur du XVIIIe siècle industriel: Condition ouvrière et tradition villageoise à Saint-Gobain.* Mesnil-sur-l'Estrée: Editions P.A.U., 1993.

Harris, John R. *Industrial Espionage and Technology Transfer: Britain and France in the Eighteenth Century.* Aldershot: Ashgate, 1998.

Harris, John R. "Michael Alcock and the Transfer of Birmingham Technology to France before the Revolution." *Journal of European Economic History*, 15 (1986), 7–57.

Haudrère, Philippe. *La Compagnie française des Indes au XVIIIe siècle (1719–1795).* thèse pour le Doctorat d'État. 4 vols. Librairie de l'Inde, 1989.

Hauser, Henri. "The Characteristic Features of French Economic History from the Middle of the Sixteenth to the Middle of the Eighteenth Century." *The Economic History Review*, 4: 3 (1933), 257–72.

Heckscher, Eli F. *Mercantilism.* rev. ed. 2 vols. E. F. Söderlund (ed.). London: Allen and Unwin, 1955.

Heimmermann, Daniel. "The Guilds of Bordeaux, les métiers libres and the sauvetats of Saint-Seurin and Saint-André." In Barry Rothaus (ed.), *Proceedings of the Western Society for French History: Selected Papers of the Annual Meeting*, 25. Boulder: University Press of Colorado, 1998, 24–35.

Heimmermann, Daniel. "Work and Corporate Life in Old Regime France: The Leather Artisans of Bordeaux (1740–1791)." PhD dissertation, Marquette University, 1994.

Heywood, Colin. *The Development of the French Economy, 1750–1914.* Cambridge University Press, 1992.

Hilaire, Yves-Marie (ed.). *Histoire de Roubaix.* Dunkerque: Les Editions des Beffrois, 1984.

Hilaire-Pérez, Liliane. "Invention and the State in 18th-Century France." *Technology and Culture,* 32: 4 (1991), 911–31.

Hilaire-Pérez, Liliane. *L'expérience de la mer: Les Européens et les espaces maritimes au XVIIIe siècle.* Seili Arslan, 1997.

Hilaire-Pérez, Liliane. *L'invention technique au siècle des Lumières.* Albin Michel, 2000.

Hirsch, Jean-Pierre. *Les deux rêves du commerce: Enterprise et institution dans la region lilloise (1780–1860).* Ėditions de l'EHESS, 1991.

Hirsch, Jean-Pierre and Philippe Minard. "'Laissez-faire nous et protégez-nous beaucoup' pour une histoire des pratiques institutionnelles dans l'industrie française (XVIIIe-XIXe siècle)." In Louis Bergeron and Patrice Bourdelais. (eds.), *La France n'est-elle pas douée pour l'industrie?* Belin, 1998, 135–58.

Hirschman, Albert O. *The Passions and the Interests: Political Arguments for Capitalism before Its Triumph.* Princeton University Press, 1977.

Hoffman, Philip T. *Growth in a Traditional Society: The French Countryside 1450–1815.* Princeton University Press, 1996.

Hoffman, Philip T. and Kathryn Norberg (eds.). *Fiscal Crises, Liberty and Representative Government 1450–1789.* Stanford University Press, 1994.

Hoffman, Philip T., Gilles Postel-Vinay, and Jean-Laurent Rosenthal. *Priceless Markets: The Political Economy of Credit in Paris, 1660–1870.* University of Chicago Press, 2000.

Hont, Istvan. *Jealousy of Trade: International Competition and the Nation-State in Historical Perspective.* Cambridge, MA: Belknap Press of Harvard University Press, 2005.

Horn, Jeff. "'A Beautiful Madness': Privilege, the Machine Question and Industrial Development in Normandy in 1789." *Past & Present,* 217 (2012), 149–85.

Horn, Jeff. "A Different Triangular Trade – from the Antilles to the Levant via Marseille." In Joelle Neulander and Robin Walz (eds.), *Proceedings of the Western Society for French History: Selected Papers of the 2012 Annual Meeting,* 40 (2014), 37–44.

Horn, Jeff. "Avoiding Revolution: The French Path to Industrialization." In Jeff Horn, Leonard N. Rosenband, and Merritt Roe Smith (eds.), *Reconceptualizing the Industrial Revolution.* Cambridge, MA: MIT Press, 2010, 87–106.

Horn, Jeff. "La police des ouvriers sous l'Empire: vers un ordre social européen?" In François Antoine, Jean-Pierre Jessenne, Hervé Leuwers, and Anne Jourdan (eds.), *L'Empire napoléonnien: une expérience européenne?* Armand Colin, 2014, 323–31.

Horn, Jeff. "Lasting Economic Structures: Successes, Failures, Legacies." In David Andress (ed.), *Oxford Handbook of the French Revolution*. Oxford University Press, 2015, 607–24.

Horn, Jeff. "Marseille et la question du mercantilisme: privilège, liberté et l'économie politique en France, 1650–1750." *Histoire, économie & société*, 2 (2011), 95–112.

Horn, Jeff. "Privileged Enclaves: Entrepreneurial Opportunities in Eighteenth-Century France." In Kathryn A. Edwards and Carol E. Harrison (eds.), *Proceedings of the Western Society for French History: Selected Papers of the 2004 Annual Meeting*, 32. Ann Arbor: Scholarly Publishing Office of the University of Michigan University Library, 2006, 29–45.

Horn, Jeff. *The Path Not Taken: French Industrialization in the Age of Revolution*. Cambridge, MA: MIT Press, 2006.

Howe, Anthony. *Free Trade and Liberal England 1846–1946*. Oxford: Clarendon Press, 1997.

Howe, Anthony. "Restoring Free Trade: the British Experience, 1776–1873." In Donald Winch and Patrick K. O'Brien (eds.), *The Political Economy of British Historical Experience, 1688–1914*. Oxford University Press for the British Academy, 2002, 193–214.

Hubscher, Ronald (ed.). *Histoire d'Amiens*. Privat, 1986.

Hufton, Olwen. "Attitudes Towards Authority in Eighteenth-Century Languedoc." *Social History*, 3: 3 (1978), 281–302.

Hume, David. *Writings on Economics*. Ed. and intro. Eugene Rotwein. New intro. Margaret Schabas. Piscataway, NJ: Transaction, 2007 [1955].

Hyman, Paula E. *The Jews of Modern France*. Berkeley: University of California Press, 1998.

Imbert, Jean. "Le 'décret' d'Allarde et ses suites immédiates." In Alain Plessis (ed.), *Naissance des libertés économiques: Liberté du travail et liberté d'entreprendre: le décret d'Allarde et la loi Le Chapelier, leurs conséquences, 1791-fin XIXe siècle*. Institut d'Histoire de l'Industrie – Ministère de l'Industrie, 1993, 103–10.

Inikori, Joseph E. *Africans and the Industrial Revolution in England: A Study of International Trade and Economic Development*. Cambridge University Press, 2002.

Isambert, François-André, Alphonse-Honoré Taillandier, and Decrusy (eds.). *Recueil général des anciennes lois françaises, depuis l'an 420 jusqu'à la révolution de 1789*. 29 vols. Berlin-Le-Prieur, 1821–1833.

Israel, Jonathan I. *Democratic Enlightenment: Philosophy, Revolution, and Human Rights 1750–1790*. Oxford University Press, 2011.

Israel, Jonathan I. *European Jewry in the Age of Mercantilism 1550–1750*. Oxford: Clarendon Press, 1985.

Jacob, Margaret C. *Scientific Culture and the Making of the Industrial West*. Oxford University Press, 1997.

Jardin, André, and André-Jean Tudesq. *Restoration & Reaction 1815–1848*. Trans. Elborg Forster. Cambridge University Press, 1983.

Johnson, Christopher H. *The Life & Death of Industrial Languedoc, 1700–1920*. Oxford University Press, 1995.

Journet, Jean-Louis and Daniel Dessert. "Le lobby Colbert: un royaume ou une affaire de famille?" *Annales, societies, civilisations*, 30: 6 (1975), 1303–36.

Kaplan, Steven L. *La fin des corporations*. Paris: Fayard, 2001.

Kaplan, Steven L. "Les corporations, les 'faux ouvriers' et le faubourg Saint-Antoine au XVIIIe siècle." *Annales. Histoire, sciences sociales*, 43: 2 (1988), 353–78.

Kaplan, Steven Laurence. *Provisioning Paris: Merchants and Millers in the Grain and Flour Trade during the Eighteenth Century*. Ithaca, NY: Cornell University Press, 1984.

Kaplan, Steven Laurence. "Social Classification and Representation in the Corporate World of Eighteenth-Century France: Turgot's 'Carnival.'" In Steven Laurence Kaplan and Cynthia J. Koepp (eds.), *Work in France: Representations, Meaning, Organization, and Practice*. Ithaca, NY: Cornell University Press, 1986, 176–228.

Kaplow, Jeffry. *Elbeuf during the Revolutionary Period: History and Social Structure*. Baltimore: Johns Hopkins University Press, 1964.

Kelly, Morgan, Joel Mokyr, and Cormac Ó Gráda. "Precocious Albion: Human Capability and the British Industrial Revolution" (2011, revised 2012) http://www.stanford.edu/group/SITE/archive/SITE_2012/2012_segment_3/2012_Segment_3_papers/mokyr.pdf (accessed June 18, 2014).

Keohane, Nannerl. *Philosophy and the State in France: The Renaissance to the Enlightenment*. Princeton University Press, 1980.

Kettering, Sharon. *Patrons, Brokers and Clients in Seventeenth-Century France*. Oxford University Press, 1986.

Krugman, Paul. "Increasing Returns and Economic Geography." *Journal of Political Economy*, 99: 3 (1991), 483–99.

Kwass, Michael. "Big Hair: A Wig History of Consumption in Eighteenth-Century France." *The American Historical Review*, 111: 3 (2006), 631–59.

Kwass, Michael. "Consumption and the World of Ideas: Consumer Revolution and the Moral Economy of the Marquis de Mirabeau." *Eighteenth-Century Studies*, 37: 2 (2004), 187–213.

Kwass, Michael. "Ordering the World of Goods: Consumer Revolution and the Classification of Objects in Eighteenth-Century France." *Representations*, 82: 1 (2003), 87–116.

Kwass, Michael. *Privilege and the Politics of Taxation in Eighteenth-Century France*. Cambridge University Press, 2000.

Kwass, Michael. "The Global Underground: Smuggling, Rebellion, and the Origins of the French Revolution." In Suzanne Desan, Lynn Hunt, and William Max Nelson (eds.), *The French Revolution in Global Perspective*. Ithaca, NY: Cornell University Press, 2013, 15–31.

Labouchère, Alfred. *Oberkampf (1738–1815)*. 3rd ed. Hachette, 1878.

La Comédie humaine de Honoré de Balzac. Trans. Katherine Prescott Wormeley. vol. 25. Boston: Roberts Brothers, 1896.

Landes, David S. *Revolution in Time: Clocks and the Making of the Modern World*. Cambridge, MA: Harvard University Press, 1983.

Landes, David S. *The Unbound Prometheus: Technological Change and Industrial Development in Western Europe from 1750 to the Present*. Cambridge University Press, 1969.

Landes, David S. *The Wealth and Poverty of Nations: Why Some Are So Rich and Some So Poor*. New York: W.W. Norton, 1999.

Landes, David S., Joel Mokyr, and William J. Baumol (eds.). *The Invention of Entrepreneurship from Ancient Mesopotamia to Modern Times*. Princeton University Press, 2010.

Langlois, Robert (vicomte d'Estaintot). *Recherches sur les hautes justices féodales existant en 1789 dans les limites du département de la Seine-Inférieure*. Rouen: A Lestringant, 1892.

Larsen, Robert M. "Adam Smith's Theory of Market Prices." In John Cunningham Wood (ed.), *Adam Smith: Critical Assessments*. 7 vols. London: Routledge, 1996 [1984], 479–90.

Le Bozec, Christine. *La Normandie au XVIIIe siècle: Croissance, Lumières et Révolution*. Rennes: Éditions de l'Ouest-France, 2002.

Lemarchand, Guy. *La fin du féodalisme dans le pays de Caux: Conjoncture économique et démographique et structure sociale dans une région de grande culture de la crise du XVIIe siècle à la stabilisation de la Révolution (1640–1795)*. ANRT, 1989.

Lemarchand, Guy. *L'Économie en France de 1770 à 1830: De la crise de l'Ancien Régime à la Révolution industrielle*. Armand Colin, 2008.

Lemarchand, Guy. "Le temporal et les revenues de l'abbaye de Fécamp pendant le XVIIe et le XVIIIe siècle." *Annales de Normandie*, 15: 2 (1965), 73–93.

Leuridan, Théodore. *Histoire de la fabrique de Roubaix*. Roubaix: V. Beghin, 1863.

Levasseur, Ėmile. *Histoire des classes ouvrières et de l'industrie en France avant 1789*. 2nd ed. 2 vols. Arthur Rousseau, 1901.

Lévi-Strauss, Monique. *The Cashmere Shawl*. New York: Abrams, 1988.

Lewis, Gwynne. *The Advent of Modern Capitalism in France 1770–1840: The Contribution of Pierre-François Tubeuf*. Oxford: Clarendon Press, 1993.

Lomüller, L.M. *Guillaume Ternaux 1763–1833: créateur de la première integration industrielle française*. Les Éditions de la Cabro d'Or, 1977.

Loth, Julien. *Histoire du Cardinal de la Rochefoucauld et du diocese de Rouen pendant la Révolution*. Ėvreux: Imprimerie de l'Eure, 1893.

Loubet, Louis. *Carpentras et le Comtat-Venaissin avant et après l'annexation: Etude historique*. Carpentras: Tourrette, 1891.

MacLeod, Christine. *Heroes of Invention: Technology, Liberalism and British Identity 1750–1914*. Cambridge University Press, 2007.

Maitte, Corine. "Labels, Brands, and Market Integration in the Modern Era." *Business and Economic History On-Line*, 7 (2009). http://www.thebhc.org/publications/BEHonline/2009/maitte.pdf. (accessed January 7, 2014).

Malvezin, Théophile. *Histoire des juifs à Bordeaux*. Bordeaux: Charles Lefebvre, 1875.

Mantoux, Paul. *The Industrial Revolution in the Eighteenth Century: An Outline of the Beginnings of the Modern Factory System in England*. rev. ed. New York: Harper & Row, 1961.

Margairaz, Dominique. *Foires et marches dans la France préindustrielle*. EHESS, 1988.

Marion, Marcel. *Dictionnaire des institutions de la France aux XVIIe et XVIIIe siècles*. New York: Burt Franklin, 1968 [1923].

Marzagalli, Silvia. "Commerce." In William Doyle (ed.), *The Oxford Handbook of the Ancien Régime*. Oxford University Press, 2012, 252–66.

Masson, Paul. *Histoire du commerce française dans le Levant aux XVIIe siècle.* Hachette, 1896.

Masters, Bruce. *The Origins of Western Economic Dominance in the Middle East: Mercantilism and the Islamic Economy in Aleppo, 1600–1750.* New York University Press, 1988.

Mathorez, Jules. *Les Étrangers en France sous l'Ancien Régime.* 2 vols. Champion, 1921.

Maupassant, Jean de. *Un grand armateur de Bordeaux: Abraham Gradis (1699?-1780).* Bordeaux: Feret et fils, 1917.

Mavidal, Jerôme and Émile Laurent (eds.). *Archives parlementaires, recueil complet des débats législatifs et politiques des Chambres françaises de 1800 à 1860, faisant suite à la réimpression de l'ancien "Moniteur" et comprenant un grand nombre de documents inédits.* 2nd series. 82 vols. Paul Dupont, 1862–1913.

Mayer, Arno J. "The Perils of Emancipation: Protestants and Jews." *Archives des sciences sociales des religions*, 90 (1995), 5–37.

Mazan, Joseph de. *Les Doctrines économiques de Colbert.* Arthur Rousseau, 1900.

McCloy, Shelby T. *French Inventions of the Eighteenth Century.* Lexington: University of Kentucky Press, 1952.

McCluskey, Philip. "Commerce before Crusade? France, the Ottoman Empire and the Barbary Pirates (1661–1669)." *French History*, 23: 1 (2009), 1–21.

McCollim, Gary B. *Louis XIV's Assault on Privilege: Nicolas Desmaretz and the Tax on Wealth.* University of Rochester Press, 2012.

Mendels, Franklin F. "Proto-industrialization: The First Phase of the Industrialization Process." *Journal of Economic History*, 32 (1972), 241–61.

Menkis, Richard. "The Gradis Family of Eighteenth-Century Bordeaux: A social and economic study." Doctoral dissertation, Brandeis University, 1988.

Menudo, José M. and José Mª O'kean. "A.-J.-R. Turgot and the Construction of an Economic Agent Called Entrepreneur." Universida Pablo de Olavide, Department of Economics Working papers series, 6: 25 (2006). http://www.upo.es/serv/bib/wps/econ0625.pdf (accessed July 29, 2013), 1–19.

Merrick, Jeffrey. "Conscience and Citizenship in Eighteenth-Century France." *Eighteenth-Century Studies*, 21: 1 (1987), 48–70.

Mettam, Roger. *Power and Faction in Louis XIV's France.* Oxford University Press, 1988.

Mettam, Roger. "Power, Status and Precedence: Rivalries among the Provincial Elites in Louis XIV's France." *Transactions of the Royal Historical Society.* 5th series. vol. 38 (1988), 43–62.

Miller, Judith A. *Mastering the Market: The State and the Grain Trade in Northern France, 1700–1860.* Cambridge University Press, 1999.

Minard, Philippe. "'France colbertiste versus 'Angleterre libérale'? Un myth du XVIIIe siècle." In Jean-Philippe Genet and François-Joseph Ruggiu (eds.), *Les idées passent-ils la Manche? Savoirs, representations, pratiques (France-Angleterre, Xe-XXe siècles).* Presses de l'Université Paris-Sorbonne, 2007, 197–209.

Minard, Philippe. *La fortune du colbertisme: Ėtat et industrie dans la France des Lumières.* Fayard, 1998.

Minard, Philippe. "Markets, Norms and Conventions in the Eighteenth Century." In Perry Gauci (ed.), *Regulating the British Economy, 166–1850*. Surrey: Ashgate, 2011, 177–94.

Minard, Philippe. "Réputation, norms et qualité dans l'industrie textile française au XVIIIe siècle." In Alessandro Stanziani (ed.), *La qualité des produits en France (XVIIIe-XXe siècles)*. Belin, 2003, 69–89.

Minovez, Jean-Michel. *La Puissance du Midi: Drapiers et draperies de Colbert à la Revolution*. Presses universitaires de Rennes, 2012.

Minovez, Jean-Michel. "Les Manufactures royales de draps fins du midi toulousain et leurs entrepreneurs au XVIIIe siècle." *Annales du Midi*, 112: 229 (2000), 21–40.

Minovez, Jean-Michel. "L'État et les draperies dans les Pyrénées centrales au milieu du XVIIIe siècle." *Annales du Midi*, 116: 246 (2004), 171–89.

Minovez, Jean-Michel. *L'industrie invisible: Les draperies du Midi XVIIe-XX siècles: Essai sur l'originalité d'une trajectoire*. CNRS, 2012.

Mokyr, Joel. *The Enlightened Economy: An Economic History of Britain 1700–1850*. New Haven, CT: Yale University Press, 2009.

Mokyr, Joel. *The Gifts of Athena: Historical Origins of the Knowledge Economy*. Princeton University Press, 2002.

Mokyr, Joel. *The Lever of Riches: Technological Creativity and Economic Progress*. Oxford University Press, 1990.

Montier, Armand. *Recherches sur le commerce et la fabrication dans le lieuvin aux XVIIe et XVIII siècles dites Rouens-Fleurets-Blancards d'après des documents inédits*. Pont Audamer: Ernest Dugas, 1874.

Moreau de Jonnès, Alexandre. *Statistique de l'industrie de la France*. Guillaumin, 1856.

Morieux, Renaud. *Une mer pour deux royaumes: La Manche, frontier franco-anglaise (XVIIe-XVIIIe siècles)*. Presses Universitaires de Rennes, 2008.

Mousnier, Roland E. *The Institutions of France under the Absolute Monarchy 1598–1789: Society and the State*. Trans. Brian Pearce. University of Chicago Press, 1979 [1974].

Muncipality of Bordeaux. *Bordeaux: Aperçu historique, sol, population, industrie, commerce, administration*. 3 vols. Bordeaux: Librairie Feret et fils, 1892.

North, Douglass C. *Institutions, Institutional Change and Economic Performance*. Cambridge University Press, 1990.

North, Douglass C. and Barry R. Weingast. "Constitutions and Commitment: The Evolution of Institutions Governing Public Choice in Seventeenth-Century England." *Journal of Economic History*, 49: 4 (1989), 803–32.

Nussbaum, Frederick L. "The Formation of the New East India Company of Calonne." *American Historical Review*, 38: 3 (1933), 475–97.

O'Brien, Patrick K. "Deconstructing the British Industrial Revolution as a Conjuncture and Paradigm for Global Economic History." In Jeff Horn, Leonard N. Rosenband, and Merritt Roe Smith (eds.), *Reconceptualizing the Industrial Revolution*. Cambridge, MA: MIT Press, 2010, 21–46.

O'Brien, Patrick K. "The Contributions of Warfare With Revolutionary and Napoleonic France to the Consolidation and Progress of the British Industrial Revolution." Working Papers 150/11 (2011). http://eprints.lse.ac.uk/31741/1/WP150.pdf (accessed January 9, 2014).

O'Brien, Patrick K. "The State and the Economy, 1688–1815." In Roderick Floud and Donald McCloskey (eds.), *The Economic History of Britain since 1700*. vol. 1. Cambridge University Press, 1994, 204–37.

Ogilvie, Sheilagh. *Institutions and European Trade: Merchant Guilds, 1000–1800*. Cambridge University Press, 2011.

Ogilivie, Sheilagh C., and Markus Cerman (eds.). *European Proto-industrialization*. Cambridge University Press, 1996.

Olive, Sophie, and Xavier Daugy (eds.). *Fonds Bonvallet: Sous-série 75 J Répertoire numérique détaillé*. (2003) http://www.somme.fr/oldpdf/application/1eb0797fd81496835d1630fdbd02ddaf.pdf (accessed July 15, 2013).

Ouin-Lacroix, Charles. *Histoire des anciennes Corporations d'Arts et Métiers et des Confréries Religieuses de la capital de la Normandie*. Rouen: Lecointe Frères, 1850.

Outhwaite, R. B. *Inflation in Tudor and Early Stuart England*. 2nd ed. London: Macmillan, 1982 [1970].

Pariset, François-Georges (ed.). *Bordeaux au XVIIIe siècle*. Bordeaux: Fédération historique du Sud-Ouest, 1968.

Parker, Harold T. *An Administrative Bureau during the Old Regime: The Bureau of Commerce and Its Relations to French Industry from May 1781 to November 1783*. Newark: University of Delaware Press, 1993.

Parthasarathi, Prasannan. *Why Europe Grew Rich and Asia Did Not: Global Economic Divergence, 1600–1850*. Cambridge University Press, 2011.

Passet, René. *L'Industrie dans la généralité de Bordeaux sous l'intendant Tourny*. Bordeaux: Éditions Bière, 1954.

Pfister-Langanay, Christian. *Ports, navires et négociants à Dunkerque (1662–1792)*. Société Dunkerquoise, 1985.

Pincus, Steve. "Rethinking Mercantilism: Political Economy, the British Empire, and the Atlantic World in the Seventeenth and Eighteenth Centuries." *The William and Mary Quarterly*, 69: 1 (2012), 3–34.

Pollard, Sidney. *Peaceful Conquest: The Industrialization of Europe 1760–1970*. Oxford University Press, 1981.

Pomeranz, Kenneth. *The Great Divergence: China, Europe, and the Making of the Modern World Economy*. Princeton University Press, 2000.

Porter, Roy. *The Creation of the Modern World: The Untold Story of the British Enlightenment*. New York: W.W. Norton, 2000.

Posener, Solomon V. "The Immediate Economic and Social Effects of the Emancipation of the Jews in France." *Jewish Social Studies*, 1: 3 (1939), 271–326.

Pourchasse, Pierrick. *Le Commerce du Nord: Les échanges commerciaux entre la France et l'Europe septentrionale au XVIIIe siècle*. Presses universitaires de Rennes, 2006.

Poussou, Jean-Pierre. "Recherches sur l'immigration anglo-irlandaise à Bordeaux au XVIIIième siècle." *Revue historique de Bordeaux et du departement de la Gironde*, 23 (1974), 163–80.

Prados de la Escosura, Leandro (ed.). *Exceptionalism and Industrialisation: Britain and its European Rivals, 1688–1815*. Cambridge University Press, 2004.

Pritchard, James. *In Search of Empire: The French in the Americas, 1670–1730*. Cambridge University Press, 2004.

Quilliet, Bernard. "Les fiefs parisiens et leurs seigneurs laïcs au XVIIIème siècle." *Histoire, économie et société*, 1: 4 (1982), 565–80.

Rambert, Gaston (ed.). *Histoire du commerce de Marseille*. 7 vols. Plon, 1954.

Ranum, Orest. *The Fronde: A French Revolution*. New York: W.W. Norton, 1993.

Rapp, Richard Tilden. *Industry and Economic Decline Seventeenth-Century Venice*. Cambridge, MA: Harvard University Press, 1976.

Rapport, Michael. *Nationality and Citizenship in Revolutionary France: The Treatment of Foreigners 1789–1799*. Oxford: Clarendon Press, 2000.

Raveux, Olivier. "Espaces et technologies dans la France méridionale d'Ancien Régime: l'exemple de l'indiennage marseillais (1648–1793)." *Annales du Midi*, 116: 246 (2004), 155–70.

Reddy, William M. *The Rise of Market Culture: The Textile Trade & French Society, 1750–1900*. Cambridge University Press, 1984.

Reddy, William M. "The Textile Trade and the Language of the Crowd at Rouen 1752–1871." *Past & Present*, 74 (1977), 62–89.

Rémond, André. *John Holker: Manufacturier et grand fonctionnaire en France au XVIIIième siècle 1719–1786*. Marcel Rivière, 1946.

Richard, Guy. *La noblesse d'affaires au XVIIIe siècle*. Armand Colin, 1974.

Ricommard, Jean. *La lieutenance générale de police à Troyes au XVIIIe siècle*. Hachette, 1934.

Riley, James C. *The Seven Years War and the Old Regime in France: The Economic and Financial Toll*. Princeton University Press, 1986.

Roberts, Lissa, Simon Schaffer, and Peter Dear (eds.). *The Mindful Hand: Inquiry and Invention from the Late Renaissance to Early Industrialization*. Amsterdam: Koninklijke Nederlandse Akademie van Weternschappen, 2007.

Root, Hilton L. *The Fountain of Privilege: Political Foundations of Markets in Old Regime France and England*. Berkeley: University of California Press, 1994.

Rosenband, Leonard N. *Papermaking in Eighteenth-Century France: Management, Labor and Revolution at the Montgolfier Mill, 1761–1805*. Baltimore: Johns Hopkins University Press, 2000.

Rosenthal, Jean-Laurent. "The Political Economy of Absolutism Reconsidered." In Robert H. Bates *et al.* (eds.), *Analytic Narratives*. Princeton University Press, 1988, 64–108.

Rosenthal, Jean-Laurent, and R. Bin Wong. *Before and Beyond Divergence: The Politics of Economic Change in China and Europe*. Cambridge, MA: Harvard University Press, 2011.

Rouff, Marcel. *Les mines de charbon en France au XVIIIe siècle 1744–1791*. F. Rieder, 1922.

Ruhlmann, Georges. *Les corporations, les manufactures et le travail libre à Abbeville au XVIIIe siècle*. Sirey, 1948.

Sabel, Charles F., and Jonathan Zeitlin. *World of Possibilities: Flexibility and Mass Production in Western Industrialization*. Cambridge University Press, 2002.

Sahlins, Peter. "Fictions of a Catholic France: The Naturalization of Foreigners, 1685–1787." *Representations*, 47 (1994), 85–110.

Sahlins, Peter. *Unnaturally French: Foreign Citizens: Foreign Citizens in the Old Regime and After*. Ithaca, NY: Cornell University Press, 2004.

Saint-Léger, Alexandre de. *La Flandre maritime et Dunkerque sous la domination française (1659–1789)*. Ch. Taillandier, 1900.

Salvador, Édouard. *L'Orient, Marseille et la Méditerranée, histoire des échelles du Levant et des colonies*. Amyot, 1854.

Sargent, Thomas J. and François R. Velde. "Macroeconomic Features of the French Revolution." *Journal of Political Economy*, 103: 3 (1995), 474–518.

Schechter, Ronald. *Obstinate Hebrews: Representations of Jews in France, 1715–1815*. Berkeley: University of California Press, 2003.

Schneider, Zoë. *The King's Bench: Bailiwick Magistrates and Local Governance in Normandy, 1670–1740*. University of Rochester Press, 2008.

Schui, Florian. *Early Debates about Industry: Voltaire and His Contemporaries*. Houndsmills: Palgrave, 2005.

Scott, Hamish M. (ed.). *The European Nobilities in the Seventeenth and Eighteenth Centuries*. vol. 1. *Western Europe*. New York: Longman, 1995.

Scoville, Warren C. *The Persecution of Huguenots and French Economic Development 1680–1720*. Berkeley: University of California Press, 1960.

Sewell, William H. Jr. "The Empire of Fashion and the Rise of Capitalism in Eighteenth-Century France." *Past & Present*, 206: 1 (2010), 81–120.

Sewell, William H. Jr. *Work & Revolution in France: The Language of Labor from the Old Regime to 1848*. Cambridge University Press, 1980.

Shapiro, Gilbert, and John Markoff. *Revolutionary Demands: A Content Analysis of the Cahiers de Doléances of 1789*. Stanford University Press, 1998.

Shennan, James H. *Philippe, Duke of Orléans: Regent of France 1715–1723*. London: Thames and Hudson, 1979.

Shovlin, John. *The Political Economy of Virtue: Luxury, Patriotism, and the Origins of the French Revolution*. Ithaca, NY: Cornell University Press, 2006.

Sibalis, Michael David. "Corporatism after the Corporations: The Debate on Restoring the Guilds under Napoleon I and the Restoration." *French Historical Studies*, 15: 4 (1988), 718–30.

Smedley-Weill, Anette (ed.). *Correspondance des Intendants avec le Contrôleur Général des Finances 1677–1689: Naissance d'une administration Sous-Série G7. Inventaire analytique*. 3 vols. Archives Nationales, 1989–1991.

Smith, Adam. *The Wealth of Nations*. Edwin Cannan (ed.). New York: The Modern Library, 2000.

Smith, David Kammerling. "'Au bien du commerce': Economic Discourse and Visions of Society in France." PhD dissertation, University of Pennsylvania, 1995.

Smith, David Kammerling. "The Nîmes Hosiery Guild and the Statutes Controversy of 1706–1712." *French Historical Studies*, 22: 4 (1999), 493–533.

Sonenscher, Michael. *Before the Deluge: Public Debt, Inequality, and the Intellectual Origins of the French Revolution*. Princeton University Press, 2007.

Sonenscher, Michael (ed.). *Emmanuel Joseph Sieyès: Political Writings including the Debate between Sieyès and Tom Paine in 1791*. Indianapolis: Hackett, 2003.

Sonenscher, Michael. "The Hosiery Industry of Nîmes and the Lower Languedoc in the Eighteenth Century." *Textile History*, 10 (1979), 142–60.

Sonenscher, Michael. *Work & Wages: Natural Law, Politics and the Eighteenth-Century French Trades*. Cambridge University Press, 1989.

Soublin, Léopold. *Le premier vote des Normands (1789)*. Fécamp: EMTN, 1981.

Stanziani, Alessandro (ed.). *La qualité des produits en France, XVIIIème-XXème siècles*. Belin, 2003.

Stanziani, Alessandro. *Rules of Exchange: French Capitalism in Comparative Perspective, Eighteenth to Early Twentieth Centuries*. Cambridge University Press, 2012.

Stark, Werner (ed.). *Jeremy Bentham's Economic Writings*. 3 vols. New York: Burt Franklin, 1952–1954.

Stern, Philip J. and Carl Wennerlind (eds.). *Mercantilism Reimagined: Political Economy in Early Modern Britain and Its Empire*. Oxford University Press, 2013.

Szajkowski, Zosa. *The Economic Status of the Jews in Alsace, Metz and Lorraine (1648–1789)*. New York: Editions Historiques Franco-Juives, 1954.

Szostak, Rick. *The Role of Transportation in the Industrial Revolution: A Comparison of England and France*. Montreal: McGill-Queen's University Press, 1991.

Takeda, Junko. *Between Crown and Commerce: Marseille and the Early Modern Mediterranean*. Baltimore: Johns Hopkins University Press, 2011.

Tarrade, Jean. *Le commerce colonial de la France à la fin de l'Ancien Régime: L'évolution du régime de "l'exclusif" de 1763 à 1789*. 2 vols. Presses Universitaires de France, 1972.

Temple, Nora. "The Control and Exploitation of French Towns during the Ancien Régime." In Raymond F. Kierstead (ed.), *State and Society in Seventeenth-Century France*. New York: New Viewpoints, 1975, 67–93.

Terjanian, Anoush Fraser. *Commerce and Its Discontents in Eighteenth-Century French Political Thought*. Cambridge University Press, 2013.

Thillay, Alain. *Le faubourg Saint Antoine et ses "faux ouvriers": La liberté du travail à Paris aux XVIIe et XVIIIe siècles*. Champ Vallon, 2002.

Thomson, James K. *Clermont-de-Lodève, 1633–1789: Fluctuations in the Prosperity of a Languedocian Cloth-making Town*. Cambridge University Press, 1982.

Tocqueville, Alexis de. *The Old Régime and the French Revolution*. Trans. Stuart Gilbert. Garden City, NY: Anchor Books, 1955.

Tollison, Robert D. and Robert Ekelund. *Mercantilism as a Rent Seeking Society*. College Station: Texas A&M University Press, 1982.

Trivellato, Francesca. *The Familiarity of Strangers: The Sephardic Diaspora, Livorno, and Cross-Cultural Trade in the Early Modern Period*. New Haven, CT: Yale University Press, 2009.

Truant, Cynthia M. *The Rites of Labor: Brotherhoods of Compagnonnage in Old and New Regime France*. Ithaca, NY: Cornell University Press, 1988.

Tsuda, Takumi (ed.). *Mémoires et lettres de Vincent de Gournay*. Tokyo: Kinokuniya Co., 1993.

Vanhaeck, Maurice. *Histoire de la sayetterie à Lille*. 2 vols. Lille: Lefebvre-Ducrocq, 1910.

Vardi, Liana. *The Land and the Loom: Peasants and Profit in Northern France, 1680–1800*. Durham, NC: Duke University Press, 1993.

Ventre, Madeleine. *L'imprimerie et la librairie en Languedoc au dernier siècle de l'Ancien régime 1700–1789*. Mouton, 1958.

Vernier, Jules-Joseph (ed.). *Cahiers de doléances du bailliage de Troyes (principal et secondaires) et du bailliage de Bar-sur-Seine pour les États généraux de 1789*. 3 vols. Troyes: Nouel, 1909–1911.

Veyrat, Maurice. *La haute justice des archevêques de Rouen, comtes de Louviers 1197–1790*. thèse de doctorat en droit. Rouen: Éditions Maugard, 1948.

Vidalenc, Jean. "Quelques remarques sur le rôle des Anglais dans la Révolution Industrielle en France particulièrement en Normandie, de 1750 à 1850." *Annales de Normandie*, 8: 2 (1958), 273–90.

Vries, Jan de. *The Industrious Revolution: Consumer Behavior and the Household Economy, 1650 to the Present*. Cambridge University Press, 2008.

Weber, Henry. *La Compagnie des Indes (1604–1875)*. Arthur Rousseau, 1904.

White, Eugene N. "Was There a Solution to the Ancien Régime's Financial Dilemma?" *Journal of Economic History*, 49: 3 (1989), 545–68.

Williams, Alan. *The Police of Paris 1718–1789*. Baton Rouge: Louisiana State University Press, 1979.

Wilson, Charles. "Cloth Production and International Competition in the Seventeenth Century." *The Economic History Review*, 13: 2 (1960), 209–21.

Winch, Donald. *Riches and Poverty: An Intellectual History of Political Economy in Britain, 1750–1834*. Cambridge University Press, 1996.

Wolf, John B. *Louis XIV*. New York: W. W. Norton, 1968.

Woloch, Isser. *Napoleon and His Collaborators: The Making of a Dictatorship*. New York: W.W. Norton, 2001.

Woronoff, Denis. *Histoire de l'industrie en France du XVIe siècle à nos jours*. Seuil, 1994.

Woronoff, Denis. *L'Industrie sidérurgique en France pendant la Révolution et l'Empire*. Éditions de l'École des hautes etudes en sciences sociales, 1984.

Wright, Robert E. "The Transition from Feudalism to Capitalism: the Role of Mercantilism." PhD dissertation, University of York [Canada], 2003.

Young, Arthur. *Travels in France during the years 1787, 1788 and 1789*. Ed. and intro. Jeffry Kaplow. Garden City, NY: Archor Books, 1969.

Zalio, Pierre-Paul. "Le 'savon de Marseille': Contribution à une sociologie économique des produits." In Alessandro Stanziani (ed.), *La qualité des produits en France (XVIIIe-XXe siècles)*. Belin, 2003, 93–122.

Zarb, Mireille. *Histoire d'une autonomie communale: Les privilèges de la ville de Marseille du Xe siècle à la Révolution*. A. et J. Picard, 1961.

Index